ZAGAT SURVEY

Back in 1979, we never imagined that an idea born during a wine-fueled dinner with friends would take us on an adventure that's lasted three decades – and counting.

The idea – that the collective opinions of avid consumers can be more accurate than the judgments of an individual critic – led to a hobby involving friends rating NYC restaurants. And that hobby grew into Zagat Survey, which today has over 350,000 participants worldwide weighing in on everything from airlines, bars, dining and golf to hotels, movies, shopping, tourist attractions and more.

By giving consumers a voice, we – and our surveyors – had unwittingly joined a revolution whose concepts (user-generated content, social networking) were largely unknown 30 years ago. However, those concepts caught fire with the rise of the Internet and have since transformed not only restaurant criticism but also virtually every aspect of the media, and we feel lucky to have been at the start of it all.

As we celebrate Zagat's 30th year, we'd like to thank everyone who has participated in our surveys. We've enjoyed hearing and sharing your frank opinions and look forward to doing so for many years to come. As we always say, our guides and online content are really "yours."

We'd also like to express our gratitude by supporting **Action Against Hunger,** an organization that works to meet the needs of the hungry in over 40 countries. To find out more, visit www.zagat.com/action.

Nina and Tim Zagat

ZAGAT®
CELEBRATING 30 YEARS

Hawaii
EAT | DRINK | STAY | PLAY

EDITOR
Donna Marino Wilkins

Published and distributed by
Zagat Survey, LLC
4 Columbus Circle
New York, NY 10019
T: 212.977.6000
E: hawaii@zagat.com
www.zagat.com

ACKNOWLEDGMENTS

We especially thank our local
consultant Lynn Cook. We also
thank Wanda Adams, Jenn
Barger, Lynn Britton, Linda
Burbank, Pam Davis, Lauryn
Galindo, Jason Genegabus,
Marylou Foley, Jeannette Foster,
Pualana Lemelle, Napua Leong,
Maile Meyer, James S. Pirga,
Stacy Pope, Sandra Ramani,
Paula Rath, Robert Seixas, Kapua
Sterling, Lilinoe Sterling and
Wayne Sterling, as well as the
following members of our staff:
Josh Rogers (associate editor),
Stacey Slate (assistant editor),
Brian Albert, Sean Beachell,
Maryanne Bertollo, Jane Chang,
Sandy Cheng, Reni Chin, Larry
Cohn, Bill Corsello, John Deiner,
Alison Flick, Jeff Freier, Shelley
Gallagher, Andrew Gelardi,
Michelle Golden, Roy Jacob,
Ashunta Joseph, Natalie Lebert,
Mike Liao, Allison Lynn, Dave
Makulec, Chris Miragliotta,
Andre Pilette, Kimberly Rosado,
Becky Ruthenburg, Aleksandra
Shander, Yoji Yamaguchi, Sharon
Yates, Anna Zappia
and Kyle Zolner.

Maps © 2009 GeoNova Publishing, Inc.

© 2009 Zagat Survey, LLC
ISBN-13: 978-1-60478-021-5
ISBN-10: 1-60478-021-5
Printed in the
United States of America

Contents

Ratings & Symbols

Zagat Top Spot	Name	Symbols		Cuisine	Zagat Ratings			
					FOOD	DECOR	SERVICE	COST

Area, Address & Contact	Ⓩ **Tim & Nina's** ◐ *Hawaiian*	▽ 23	9	19	$15

Waikiki | 1 Tiki Place (Kalakaua Ave.) | 212-977-6000 | www.zagat.com

Review, surveyor comments in quotes

The staff shows "plenty of aloha spirit" at this "local Hawaiian favorite" in Waikiki where the "umbrella-ed mai tais are strong", the pupus "plentiful" and the Diamond Head views "dazzling"; kamaaina are less crazy about the "tiki-tacky" decor with "enough torches and conch shells to start your own luau", but at least the price is right.

Ratings

Cover key aspects of each category (e.g. Food, Decor, Service for Dining; Appeal, Facilities, Service for Attractions). All are on the Zagat 0 to 30 scale:

0	–	9	poor to fair
10	–	15	fair to good
16	–	19	good to very good
20	–	25	very good to excellent
26	–	30	extraordinary to perfection
▽			low response	less reliable

Cost

Attractions: High-season adult admission: $0 (free); I ($10 and below); M ($11–$25); E ($26–$40); VE ($41 or more)

Dining: Our surveyors' benchmark estimate of the price of dinner with one drink and tip. For newcomers or write-ins listed without ratings, price is indicated as I ($25 and below); M ($26–$40); E ($41–$65); VE ($66 or more)

Golf: Non-member/non-guest price for 18 weekend holes in high season, i.e. the highest price; excludes extra cost of cart

Hotels: High-season standard double rack rate

All other costs are indicated as I (inexpensive); M (moderate); E (expensive); VE (very expensive); based on surveyor estimates.

Symbols

Ⓩ	highest ratings, popularity, importance
◐	dining: serves after 11 PM; shopping: usually open past 7 PM
Ⓢ Ⓜ	closed on Sunday; closed on Monday
⊟	no credit cards accepted

Also see Symbols keys in Golf and Hotels sections

About This Survey

Here are the results of our first survey of Hawaii's finest attractions, dining destinations, golf courses, hotels, nightspots and shops. Like all our guides, this one is based on the collective opinions of avid consumers – 4,149 all told.

WHO PARTICIPATED: Input from these enthusiasts forms the basis for the ratings and reviews in this guide (their comments are shown in quotation marks within the reviews). These surveyors are a diverse group: 48% are women, 52% men; 6% are in their 20s; 21%, 30s; 24%, 40s; 26%, 50s; and 23%, 60s or above. We sincerely thank these participants – this book is really "theirs."

HELPFUL LISTS: Our top lists and indexes can help you find exactly the right place for any occasion. See top lists for Oahu (pages 12–14), Maui (pages 74–75), Big Island (pages 106–107), Kauai (pages 128–129), Hawaii's Best Shopping (pages 158–159) and the 139 handy indexes starting on page 179.

OUR EDITORS: Special thanks goes to our Honolulu-based consultant, Lynn Cook, an arts and travel writer and columnist for island and national publications. We also thank our local Hawaii editors, Wanda Adams, food editor, *Honolulu Advertiser*; Jeanette Foster, editor, *Frommer's Hawaii 2009*; Jason Genegabus, nightlife editor, *Honolulu Star-Bulletin*; Molokai-based writer Napua Leong; Stacy Pope, author, *Honolulu & Oahu: Great Destinations Hawaii*; and Paula Rath, fashion editor, *Honolulu Advertiser*.

ABOUT ZAGAT: This marks our 30th year reporting on the shared experiences of consumers like you. What started in 1979 as a hobby has come a long way. Today we have over 350,000 surveyors and now cover airlines, bars, dining, entertaining, fast food, golf, hotels, movies, music, resorts, shopping, spas, theater and tourist attractions in over 100 countries.

INTERACTIVE: Up-to-the-minute news about restaurant openings plus menus, photos and more are free on **ZAGAT.com** and the award-winning **ZAGAT.mobi** (for web-enabled mobile devices).

VOTE AND COMMENT: We invite you to join any of our surveys at **ZAGAT.com**. There you can rate and review establishments year-round. In exchange for doing so, you'll receive a free copy of the resulting guide when published.

AVAILABILITY: Zagat guides are available in all major bookstores as well as on **ZAGAT.com**. You can also access our content when on the go via **ZAGAT.mobi** and **ZAGAT TO GO** (for smartphones).

FEEDBACK: There is always room for improvement, thus we invite your comments. Contact us at **hawaii@zagat.com**.

New York, NY
January 7, 2009

Nina and Tim Zagat

What's New

Hawaii gained some bragging rights after the historic election of Oahu born-and-raised Barack Obama to the U.S. presidency, calling one of the world's best known figures one of its own. The state hopes to capitalize on this exposure as the new leader begins his first term.

FEELING THE PINCH: The effects of a shaky global economy have reached the tourist-dependent 50th state. Among this Survey's respondents, 34% are eating out less because of worsening economic conditions; 36% are eating at less expensive places; 40% are more attentive to prices when ordering; and 42% say that higher gas prices mean they won't drive as far to dine. The upside of all this bad news is that travelers can now expect to receive more value-added offers, even at the very top hotels – e.g. free fourth or fifth nights, golf rounds, and food or spa credits – while kamaaina (resident) specials are part of the everyday mix for locals.

NATURAL BEAUTIES: Not surprisingly, beaches are one of the favorite aspects of the islands for 60% of respondents, who rank Kauai's **Ke'e Beach** No. 1 for Appeal. Some 57% of our surveyors say the natural landscape is what they love the most about Hawaii, and they vote the state's most dramatic natural attraction, the Big Island's **Hawaii Volcanoes National Park,** No. 1 for Appeal.

 WAIKIKI WINNERS: Oahu is cited by 87% of respondents as having the best dining, and 29% say Waikiki is the best neighborhood for restaurants. Half of our Survey's top 20 eateries are on Oahu, including the No. 1 for Food, the Hawaii Regional **Alan Wong's,** just outside of Waikiki. The average spent on a meal in Hawaii, $33.18, is on par with LA ($34.38), but considerably lower than NYC ($40.78).

KEEP IT LOCAL: Sixty-two percent of our surveyors are willing to spend more for sustainably raised ingredients, while 48% say it's either very important or extremely important that the food they eat is locally grown or raised. The islands' top-rated spots reflect this commitment. The top restaurants for Food – the Hawaii Regional **Alan Wong's** on Oahu and the Big Island's **Hualalai Grille,** as well as the French **Gerard's** on Maui and the Hawaii Regional **Roy's** on Kauai – all focus on farm-to-table fare using area produce and fresh-caught fish.

SERVICE STARS: Poor service is the greatest irritant for 77% of diners in our Survey. It's not surprising that two of the restaurants voted No. 1 for Service on their respective islands – the Big Island's **Pahu i'a** and Maui's **Ferraro's** – are located in Four Seasons resorts, known for stellar staffs (the Big Island **Four Seasons** was voted the Top Hotel in Hawaii). The No. 1 restaurants for Service on Kauai and Oahu are also located in upscale hotels: the Pacific Rim–seafooder **Tidepools** at the Grand Hyatt Kauai, and the French **La Mer** in Waikiki's Halekulani.

LINKS LOVERS: Golfers tip their visors to Maui's **Kapalua Plantation,** naming the site of the 2009 PGA Tour season opener Hawaii's Top Course. Meanwhile, duffers look forward to several re-openings in the coming year, including the Robert Trent Jones, Sr.

Mauna Kea course, and the reworking of two Jack Nicklaus runs at the **Lihue Kauai Lagoons.**

 PRIMPED PROPERTIES: Several hotels have completed or will soon finish major upgrades that bring fresh lodging, dining, spa, golf and retail options. Maui's **Ritz-Carlton Kapalua** reopened after a $180-million investment (and earned the No. 2 spot overall among Maui hotels in our Survey), debuting a fine-dining venue, **Banyan Tree,** as well as a spa. Waikiki's 1920s-era **Royal Hawaiian** (aka the 'Pink Palace') is to open its doors in early 2009 after a $110-million renovation that includes an Abhasa spa, new beachfront cabanas and the return of its famous Mai Tai Bar. On Kauai, the **Westin Princeville Ocean Resort Villas** opened in August, while the adjacent **Princeville Resort** is undergoing a face-lift and rebranding to a St. Regis for a 2009 reentry. On the Big Island, the long-shuttered **Mauna Kea Beach Hotel** is set to reemerge in the near future.

AFTER-DARK DOLLARS: Hawaii's night owls spend an average of $52.87 on an evening out, with 38% preferring a venue with live Hawaiian music, 34% choosing a cocktail lounge and 31% a neighborhood bar. Our Survey's Most Popular nightlife venue, the casual **Duke's Canoe Club** in Waikiki, as well as our No. 1 spot for Appeal, Waikiki's upscale lounge **House Without A Key,** feature local performers that appeal to tourists and residents. Honolulu partyers, however, are not pleased with a trend toward specialty cocktails (33% say it's an excuse to charge more) or bottle service (48% call it a rip-off).

NAME-BRAND BONANZA: A wave of retail has washed over Oahu, with expansions at several major complexes. **Ala Moana Center,** already the largest open-air mall in the country and filled with international designers, added a new wing and the state's first **Nordstrom's** department store. Not surprisingly, 45% of surveyors say Ala Moana is the best Oahu neighborhood for shopping, and nine of the Top 10 stores (ranked by Quality of merchandise) are found here. Meanwhile, Waikiki's **Royal Hawaiian Center** finished a significant refurb, adding apparel-maker **Marciano** and watch retailer **Tourneau,** among others, while debuting spiffed-up branches of **Bulgari, Fendi, Hermès, Juicy Couture** and **LeSportsac.** The Waikiki Beach Walk brought links of local labels including apparel retailer **Blue Ginger,** jeweler **Na Hoku** and **Mana Hawaii,** specializing in authentic, locally made gifts.

COMING UP: In 2009, the Hawaii Regional eatery **Merriman's** expands to Poipu, Kauai, and the new **Koa Kea Hotel,** a reconstruction of the former **Poipu Beach Hotel,** arrives there as well. In Waikiki, a branch of **Wolfgang's Steakhouse** and of popular Aloha wear retailer **Hilo Hattie** settle into the **Royal Hawaiian Center,** while singer Jimmy Buffet debuts an eatery at the Waikiki Beachcomber Hotel and **Trump International** opens a property near Beach Walk. Maui's newest resort, **Honua Kai Resort,** comes to Kaanapali in early 2009.

New York, NY
January 7, 2009

Donna Marino Wilkins

A Hawaii Primer

The six major Hawaiian islands present an incredible range of natural attractions, a blending of many Polynesian and Asian cultures and a diversity of restaurants and activities. Oahu – where Honolulu and Waikiki are located and where 75% of the population lives – is a wonderful jumping-off point for exploring the neighbor islands: the Big Island of Hawaii, Kauai, Lanai, Maui and Molokai.

WHEN TO VISIT: The 50th state is an all-season destination, with temperatures that rarely dip below 70 degrees even in the coldest months of December and January. But if you're looking for the best resort deals, aim for the shoulder seasons (spring and fall). Peak season for most resorts is during summer and school breaks, when lots of families visit. Of course, many couples choose to come right after they marry – honeymoons are a huge business. And there are several lively annual festivals that also draw their share of traffic, including Molokai's Ka Molokai Makahiki Festival in January; the Big Island's Merrie Monarch Festival and Maui's Celebration of the Arts, both in April; Oahu's Aloha Festivals in September; and Kauai's Coconut Festival in October. Foodies can check out Maui's Kapalua Wine & Food Festival or Oahu's Taste of Honolulu (both in June).

FROM HERE TO THERE: Since most island-hopping requires an interisland flight, getting around the state can be fairly expensive. The Hawaii Superferry offers three-hour trips between Oahu and Maui ($49-$59 per adult depending on the day), while various ferries make the 45–75-minute trip between Maui and Lanai, and the hour-and-a-half cruise between Maui and Molokai. While there's a Waikiki tourist trolley (passes are sold in one- to four-day increments starting at $27 per adult) and a public bus system on Oahu ($2 per ride), you'll need to rent a car on neighbor islands. Taxis are an option on all the islands, but most of the time you must call ahead for service.

LOCAL STYLE: Hawaii is a casual place – flip-flops, T-shirts and shorts work for most situations. The 'aloha spirit' is not just a phrase, it's a life attitude of friendly acceptance. You'll stick out as a tourist if you blow your car horn or otherwise seem rude and impatient. Say 'aloha' back when greeted; accept a lei (a floral wreath placed around your neck) with graciousness; take your shoes off at the door if entering someone's home.

WHAT TO DO: If you love water, you'll be in your element surrounded by the world's most beautiful beaches and fiercest surf. Longboarders come from across the globe to ride Oahu's North Shore waves, and simply watching these athletes is awe-inspiring. In fact, much of what draws people to the islands can be experienced at little cost, from beaches to parks to scenic drives. There's excellent snorkeling and scuba, as well as opportunities to canoe, kayak, windsurf and water-ski. Of course, if you're willing to spend, cosmopolitan Honolulu beckons with stores from the world's top designers, fine eateries and a vibrant nightlife. And all the islands have top-notch golf courses, spas and hiking options. But if you're mostly looking for R&R, the much-less-developed islands of Molokai and Lanai are the most laid-back options.

Glossary

The following is a brief glossary of Hawaiian and Japanese terms.

Ahi: yellowfin tuna
Aku: skipjack tuna
Bento: boxed meal, usually for lunch
Grinds: food
Hapuupuu: sea bass
Hauia: coconut pudding
Imu: underground oven
Kaiseki: elaborate Japanese tasting menu
Kajiki: Pacific blue marlin
Kalua pork: pork cooked in an underground oven
Kamaaina: longtime resident of Hawaii
Kau kau: food
Kiawe-grilled: grilled over aromatic wood
Kulolo: steamed pudding of coconut, brown sugar and taro
Lanai: terrace or patio
Laulau: pork, beef or fish steamed in ti leaves
Lilikoi: passion fruit
Loco Moco: a heap of white rice topped with a hamburger and a fried egg, smothered in gravy
Lomi salmon: salted salmon wiith onions and tomatoes
Luau: Hawaiian feast
Lumpia: Philippine egg roll
Mahalo: thanks, gratitude; to thank
Maju: sweet cake with black bean filling
Makai: in the direction of the sea
Malihini: newcomer, tourist
Malasada: Portuguese doughnut
Manapua: savory stuffed buns
Mauka: toward the mountains, upland
Ohana: family
Ohelo: berry eaten raw or cooked
Okazu-ya: Japanese deli
Ono: delicious
Opakapaka: pink snapper
Paniolo: Hawaiian cowboy
Pau hana: after work
Pipi kaula : beef jerky
Plate lunch: two scoops of rice and macaroni salad served with fried fish, beef or chicken
Poi: taro pounded in a liquid form
Poke: cubed raw fish with onions and seaweed served usually as an appetizer
Pupu: appetizer
Saimin: a thin broth with noodles, vegetables and fish, chicken or pork
Shave ice: snow cone
Taro: edible, starchy root, similar to potato
Teppanyaki: grilled at the table
Ti: leaf used in cooking, serving and decorating
Wikiwiki: fast
Yakiniku: cook your own

Top Statewide Ratings

For Nightlife and Shopping top lists, see pages 14 and 158.

Attractions

Most Popular

1. USS Arizona | *Oahu*
2. Hawaii Volcanoes | *Big Island*
3. Haleakala Nat'l Pk. | *Maui*
4. Diamond Head | *Oahu*
5. Hanauma Preserve | *Oahu*
6. Battleship Missouri | *Oahu*
7. Polynesian Cultural Ctr. | *Oahu*
8. Waikiki Beach | *Oahu*
9. Waimea Canyon Pk. | *Kauai*
10. Bishop Museum | *Oahu*

Top Appeal

29] Hawaii Volcanoes | *Big Island*
Kalalau Trail | *Kauai*
USS Arizona | *Oahu*
28] Haleakala Nat'l Pk. | *Maui*
Waimea Canyon Pk. | *Kauai*
Ke'e Beach | *Kauai*
Manele Bay | *Lanai*
Punalu'u Beach | *Big Island*
Lanikai Beach | *Oahu*
Waimea Bay Bch. | *Oahu*

Dining

Most Popular

1. Roy's | *multi.*
2. Alan Wong's | *Oahu*
3. Mama's Fish | *Maui*
4. Sansei | *multi.*
5. Hali'imaile General | *Maui*
6. Duke's Canoe | *multi.*
7. La Mer | *Oahu*
8. Merriman's | *multi.*
9. Beach House | *Kauai*
10. Spago | *Maui*

Top Food

28] Alan Wong's | *Oahu*
Sushi Sasabune | *Oahu*
Hualalai Grille | *Big Island*
Gerard's | *Maui*
27] La Mer | *Oahu*
Le Bistro | *Oahu*
Hali'imaile General | *Maui*
Merriman's | *multi.*
Mama's Fish | *Maui*
26] Spago | *Maui*

Golf

Top Courses

29] Kapalua/Plantation | *Maui*
28] Challenge/Manele | *Lanai*
Princeville/Prince | *Kauai*
27] Poipu Bay | *Kauai*
Experience/Koele | *Lanai*

26] Mauna Lani/N. | *Big Island*
Turtle Bay/Palmer | *Oahu*
Mauna Lani/S. | *Big Island*
Wailea Golf/Gold | *Maui*
Wailea Golf/Emerald | *Maui*

Hotels

Top Overall

28] Four Seasons Resort | *Big Island*
Four Seasons/Wailea | *Maui*
27] Four Seasons/Koele | *Lanai*
26] Halekulani | *Oahu*
Four Seasons/Manele | *Lanai*

Ritz-Carlton Kapalua | *Maui*
25] Hana-Maui | *Maui*
Fairmont Kea Lani | *Maui*
Kahala | *Oahu*
Grand Hyatt | *Kauai*

OAHU

Attractions

Most Popular

1. USS Arizona
2. Diamond Head
3. Hanauma Preserve
4. Battleship Missouri
5. Polynesian Cultural Ctr.

Top Appeal

29. USS Arizona
28. Lanikai Beach
    Waimea Bay Bch.
    Battleship Missouri
    Sunset Beach

Dining

Most Popular

1. Alan Wong's | *Hawaii Reg.*
2. Roy's | *Hawaii Reg.*
3. La Mer | *French*
4. Sansei | *Japanese/Pac. Rim*
5. Duke's Canoe Club | *American*
6. Orchids | *Pacific Rim*
7. Chef Mavro | *Fr./Hawaii Reg.*
8. 3660 on the Rise | *Pacific Rim*
9. Nobu Waikiki | *Japanese*
10. Hy's Steak | *Steak*
11. Sam Choy's | *Hawaii Reg.*
12. Assaggio | *Italian*
13. Michel's | *French*
14. Cheesecake Factory | *American*
15. Pineapple Room | *Hawaii Reg.*
16. Hoku's | *Pacific Rim*
17. Ruth's Chris | *Steak*
18. Zippy's | *American*
19. 12th Ave. Grill | *Amer.*
20. Longhi's | *Italian*

KEY NEWCOMERS

Our editors' take on the year's top arrivals. See page 202 for a full list.

Beachhouse | *Amer./Steak*

Downtown/HiSAM | *American*

'Elua | *French/Italian*

Fat Greek | *Greek*

Hakkei | *Japanese*

MAC 24/7 | *American*

Nobu Waikiki | *Japanese*

Stage | *American/Pan-Asian*

Sushi Doraku | *Japanese*

Tangö Cafe | *American*

Uncle's Fish Mkt. | *Seafood*

Wasabi & Nadaman | *Japanese*

Top Food Ratings

28. Alan Wong's | *Hawaii Reg.*
    Sushi Sasabune | *Japanese*
27. La Mer | *French*
    Le Bistro | *French*
26. Nobu Waikiki | *Japanese*
    Helena's Hawaiian | *Hawaiian*
    Hiroshi Eurasion | *Eurasian*
    Chef Mavro | *Fr./Hawaii Reg.*
    Sansei | *Japanese/Pac. Rim*
    Orchids | *Pacific Rim*

    Roy's | *Hawaii Reg.*
    Yohei Sushi | *Japanese*
25. Hoku's | *Pacific Rim*
    Akasaka | *Japanese*
    3660 on the Rise | *Pacific Rim*
    Pineapple Room | *Hawaii Reg.*
    Hakone | *Japanese*
    Ono Hawaiian* | *Hawaiian*
    Mekong Thai | *Thai*
    Michel's | *French*

* Indicates a tie with restaurant above

BY CUISINE

AMERICAN
25 Side Street Inn
23 town
  12th Ave. Grill
  Eggs 'n Things
  Prince Court

CHINESE
24 Kirin
23 Little Vill. Noodle Hse.
  Legend Seafood
  Pah Ke's
21 Mei Sum

FRENCH
27 La Mer
  Le Bistro
26 Chef Mavro
25 Michel's
24 Duc's Bistro

HAWAIIAN
26 Helena's Hawaiian
25 Ono Hawaiian
24 Young's Fish Mkt.
23 Highway Inn
21 Kaka'ako Kitchen

HAWAII REGIONAL
28 Alan Wong's
26 Chef Mavro
  Roy's
25 Pineapple Room
21 Ola

ITALIAN
24 Baci Bistro
  'Elua
23 Vino Italian Tapas
22 Arancino di Mare
  Sarento's Top of "I"

JAPANESE
28 Sushi Sasabune
26 Nobu Waikiki
  Sansei

  Yohei Sushi
25 Akasaka

MEDITERRANEAN
24 Olive Tree
22 Formaggio
19 Fat Greek

MEXICAN
19 Maui Tacos
18 Cholo's Homestyle
17 Wahoo's Fish Taco

PACIFIC RIM
26 Orchids
25 Hoku's
25 3660 on the Rise
24 Bali by the Sea
23 Chai's Island

SEAFOOD
23 Nico's at Pier 38
22 Nick's Fishmarket
20 Kincaid's
19 Jameson's
18 Uncle's Fish Mkt.

STEAKHOUSES
25 Morton's
  Ruth's Chris
  Hy's Steak
22 Kobe/Oku's
  d.k Steak

THAI
25 Mekong Thai
  Phuket Thai
22 Chiang Mai Thai
21 Keo's in Waikiki
  Singha Thai

VIETNAMESE
24 Bac Nam
  Duc's Bistro
23 Hale Vietnam

Top Decor Ratings

28 La Mer
  Orchids
27 Hau Tree
26 Bali by the Sea
  Michel's

  Hoku's
25 Ola
  Nobu Waikiki
  Beachhouse/Moana
24 Mariposa

Top Service Ratings

28 La Mer
27 Orchids
   Alan Wong's
26 Chef Mavro
   Michel's

25 Hoku's
   Bali by the Sea
   Hiroshi Eurasion
   Hy's Steak
   Morton's

Best Buys

In order of Bang for the Buck rating.

1. Matsumoto's Shave Ice
2. Ba-Le Sandwich
3. Goma Tei Ramen
4. Kua 'Aina Sandwich
5. Curry House CoCo
6. Eggs 'n Things
7. Bac Nam
8. Ezogiku
9. Maui Tacos
10. Tanioka's
11. L&L Drive-Inn
12. Young's Fish Mkt.
13. Original Pancake Hse.
14. Kozo Sushi
15. Nico's at Pier 38
16. Helena's Hawaiian
17. Highway Inn
18. I Love Country Cafe
19. Ono Hawaiian
20. Wahoo's Fish Taco

Golf

Top Courses

26 Turtle Bay/Palmer
25 Ko'olau
   Luana Hills
23 Ko Olina
22 Hawaii Prince

Top Value

23 Ko'olau
22 Kapolei
21 Luana Hills
20 Royal Kunia
   Hawaii Prince

Hotels

Top Overall

26 Halekulani
25 Kahala
24 JW Marriott
21 Hawaii Prince
   Moana Surfrider

   Hilton Hawaiian Vill.
20 Turtle Bay Resort
   Marriott Waikiki Beach
   Hyatt Regency Waikiki
18 Sheraton

Nightlife

Most Popular

1 Duke's Canoe Club
2 House Without/Key
3 Indigo
4 Yard House
5 Hula's Bar

Top Appeal

29 House Without/Key
27 Lewers Lounge
25 Twist at Hanohano
24 La Mariana Club
   Duke's Canoe Club

Oahu Attractions

Ala Moana Beach Park

| 22 | 18 | 12 | $0 |

Ala Moana | 1201 Ala Moana Blvd. (Piikoi St.) | Honolulu
Popular with "in-town locals" and "great for swimming", "early morning strolls", "all-day BBQs" and "watching paddling teams heading out to practice", this "alternative to Waikiki Beach" boasts "calm water" that's protected by a long artificial reef; facilities include lifeguards, picnic tables, tennis courts, bike paths and a snack bar, but "parking can be tricky" and it's hard to resist the call of the "huge Ala Moana shopping center across the street."

Aloha Stadium Swap Meet

| 22 | 16 | 16 | I |

Aiea | Aloha Stadium | 99-500 Salt Lake Blvd. (Kamehameha Hwy.) | 808-486-6704 | www.alohastadiumswapmeet.net
"You'll burn holes in your soles on the hot tarmac" as you "get all your gifts" at this "one-stop-souvenir-shopping spot" that's a 30-minute drive from Waikiki and offers "seemingly endless rows" of hawkers proffering "every trinket, knickknack and touristy item you can imagine" – plus a "variety of food vendors"; seasoned swappers swear that even though prices are a "fraction of the usual", it's still ok to "haggle."

Aloha Tower Marketplace

| 20 | 21 | 18 | $0 |

Downtown | 1 Aloha Tower Dr. (Fort St.) | Honolulu | 808-566-2337 | www.alohatower.com
"Take in a view of the city" and the cruise ships "entering the harbor" from the top of the "appealing historic monument" that's the centerpiece of this "crowded" bi-level mall where you can shop for "typical" tourist goods, dine at "passable restaurants" or listen to "live music" after dark at the on-site bars and clubs; but spoilsports dismiss it as a "used-to-be-happening" "tourist trap" and advise "you can see all there is from the road."

Atlantis Submarine

| 24 | 22 | 23 | E |

Waikiki | 1600 Kapiolani Blvd. (Kaheka St.) | Honolulu | 808-973-9840 | 800-548-6262 | www.atlantisadventures.com
"Non-snorkelers and non-scuba divers" who want to "get up close with Hawaii's amazing marine life" "without getting wet" are served by this fleet's submarines, offering views of "colorful fish" and "perhaps an endangered sea turtle"; dissenters deem the experience "hit-or-miss on what you'll see", but at least the crew is always "entertaining and knowledgeable"; P.S. though "wonderful for kids", they must be at least 32 inches tall.

Banzai Pipeline

| 27 | 14 | 11 | $0 |

Waimea | off Ehukai Beach Park (Ke Nui Rd.)
Head to this "breathtakingly beautiful" North Shore "hangout" in winter when "amazing" waves and "perfect tubes" bring out big-board "surfers working their magic" – "you have to see it to believe it"; there's "limited parking" (go early) and "virtually no facilities", but it's an "awesome" "sight to see"; P.S. "don't mess around", "if you're not a pro" "stay out of the water."

APPEAL | FACIL. | SERVICE | COST

Battleship Missouri Memorial
28 | 24 | 23 | I

Pearl Harbor | Battleship Row (off Kamehameha Hwy.) | 808-423-2263 | 877-644-4896 | www.ussmissouri.org

Expect "long lines" to get into this "real-deal" 58,000-ton battleship in Pearl Harbor where Japan formally surrendered to end World War II and a "moving memorial" now exists; history buffs recommend "specialized tours" led by "knowledgeable" guides, some of whom "served on the ship", making it an "emotional", "inspiring" "must-see."

Bishop Museum
25 | 25 | 22 | I

Kalihi | 1525 Bernice St. (bet. Kalihi St. & Kapalama Ave.) | Honolulu | 808-847-3511 | www.bishopmuseum.org

"Inventive displays" on subjects ranging from a "complete history of Oahu" to the "culture of Polynesia" plus an "impressive science center" are highlights of this "meticulously curated" museum 20 minutes from Waikiki that's the "absolute authority on all things Hawaiian"; hands-on activities and the "cool" volcano eruption exhibit are kid-pleasers, while "fascinating" artifacts, cultural demonstrations and more appeal to "true lovers of anthropology."

Chinatown
20 | 13 | 13 | $0

Chinatown | Bordered by Bethel & River Sts.; N. Beretania St. & N. Nimitz Hwy. | Honolulu | www.chinatownhi.com

"More diverse than the mainland Chinatowns", this "lively" district features a variety of Asian influences coming together in a "visual feast" of "shops pouring out onto sidewalks", "inexpensive lei stands" and "unusual food and curios"; the "recently renovated areas" (some say they still "need more work") are an "urban renaissance in the making", replete with "hipsters hitting the town for gallery hopping, live music and beer guzzling", while the older sections traffic in inexpensive produce, "fish heads and live frogs."

Contemporary Museum
22 | 25 | 24 | I

Makiki Heights | 2411 Makiki Heights Dr. (Mott-Smith Dr.) | Honolulu | 808-526-0232 | www.tcmhi.org
Chinatown | First Hawaiian Ctr. | 999 Bishop St. (bet. King & Merchant Sts.) | Honolulu | 808-526-1322 | www.tcmhi.org

"An excellent change of pace from other tourist attractions", this "off-the-beaten-path" boutique museum in Makiki Heights (with a smaller gallery in Chinatown's First Hawaiian Center) showcases cutting-edge international work as well as local art; even perusers who don't love the "exhibition of the moment" have trouble finding fault with its "friendly" staff, "intimate" setting in a "former mansion with breath-taking views" and a cafe that offers "tasty, healthy lunches."

Diamond Head Crater
26 | 16 | 14 | I

Kahala | Diamond Head Rd. (18th Ave.) | Honolulu | 808-587-0300

Sightseers who make the "somewhat strenuous" .7-mile hike up this "signature Hawaii" extinct volcano – past "cannons and bunkers" and up a slew of "steep, winding stairs" – are rewarded with a "glorious view" of Waikiki; "wear good walking shoes", "go early" to avoid heat and crowds and be aware that there are "no bathrooms or water along the way", so pack provisions (including a flashlight for navigating the "dark", "narrow" tunnel).

	APPEAL	FACIL.	SERVICE	COST

Fort DeRussy Park
21 | 20 | 16 | $0

Waikiki | Kalia Rd. (Ala Moana Blvd. to Saratoga Rd.) | Honolulu

"Much less crowded than the hotel beaches" and with "ample affordable parking" to boot, this "gorgeous" U.S. military–owned park is set along a "rough sand" stretch of Waikiki, making it a "peaceful oasis" amid the "hubbub of Honolulu"; its "amazing landscaping" with "shady lawn spaces" sets the stage for an exercise track, beach volleyball courts, BBQ grills and the Hawaii Army Museum, so "you'll run out of energy before you run out of things to do."

Germaine's Luau
22 | 21 | 21 | M

Kapolei | 91-119 Olai St. (Hanua St.) | 808-949-6626 | 800-367-5655 | www.germainesluau.com

Staged on a "private beach" with a "backyard feel" 45 minutes from Waikiki, this "laid-back" luau manages to "serve the masses pretty well" despite the fact that, given its size, there's always a wait for the "tasty" "food, beverages and your tour bus to go back home"; the requisite "kitschy" show is too "commercial" and "overrated" for some, while others revel in the "hokey" fun.

Haleiwa Beach
25 | 15 | 13 | $0

Haleiwa | Kamehameha Hwy. (Pahpahialua St.)

"Beloved by surfers" looking for waves in the winter and by canoe paddlers and families looking for shallow water in summer, this "beautiful", rugged stretch of the North Shore still remains off the beaten tourist track; "you'll find more locals" enjoying the nearby town amenities – surf shops with "friendly" vibes and laid-back eateries, including not-to-be-missed "shrimp trucks for lunch."

Hanauma Bay Nature Preserve
27 | 21 | 18 | I

Hanauma Bay | 100 Hanauma Bay Rd. (Kalanianaole Hwy./Rte. 72) | 808-396-4229 | www.hanaumabayhawaii.org

Voted the most popular water-based attraction on Oahu, this "always-crowded", "family-friendly" marine sanctuary set in a volcanic crater with "gorgeous views" is a "favorite place to snorkel"; the "vast array of sea life" and "tropical fish only a few feet from shore" makes it perfect for beginners who liken it to "swimming in an aquarium", just "go early for parking"; N.B. closed Tuesdays.

Hawaiian Waters Adventure Park
23 | 22 | 17 | E

Kapolei | 400 Farrington Hwy. (Kalaeloa Blvd.) | 808-674-9283 | www.hawaiianwaters.com

"Cool down" at this "superior-quality water park" (under new management since May 2008) in "almost-always-sunny" Kapolei, where the salt-free splashes, "excellent waterslides" and "new miniature golf facility" can be a "nice break" from the beach; if the food – "typical burgers, fries and hot dogs", as well as "local plate lunches" – comes at a "premium price", well, "you don't go here to eat."

Hawaii State Art Museum
▽ 22 | 22 | 21 | $0

Downtown | Capitol District Bldg. | 250 S. Hotel St. (Richards St.) | Honolulu | 808-586-0900 | www.state.hi.us/sfca

This seven-year-old free Downtown museum housed in an 1872 building has "lots of local talent on display", from changing exhibitions on fiber art to works exploring the islands' natural surroundings to an interactive educational gallery with hands-on activities; you can go for "an hour or so" in the morning and "be on the beach before lunch", unless you stay to enjoy chef Ed Kenney's "popular" on-site eatery, Downtown @ HiSAM; N.B. the gift shop offers Hawaiian-made crafts, jewelry and other items.

Honolulu Academy of Arts
26 | 26 | 23 | I

Ala Moana | 900 S. Beretania St. (Ward Ave.) | Honolulu | 808-532-8700 | www.honoluluacademy.org

When "you're sick and tired of beach and kitsch", join the "hip" crowd at this "overlooked cultural stop" in the Ala Moana area near Downtown where "serene gardens" and "unique open-air architecture" serve as the backdrop to a "sublime" collection of Asian, Western and Hawaiian art, plus "excellent movies and special events"; the "tasty" cafe food is "reasonably priced", the staffers "exceptionally nice" and its gift shop "fantastic"; N.B. tours of Doris Duke's Shangri-La estate depart from the Academy, just be sure to pre-book, since they "sell out in high season."

Honolulu Zoo
21 | 19 | 18 | I

Waikiki | 151 Kapahulu Ave. (Kalakaua Ave.) | Honolulu | 808-971-7171 | www.honoluluzoo.org

"If you have children", this "charming" Waikiki zoo near Kapiolani Park with "lovely grounds", a "pleasant" play area and an "unusual variety of animals" for such a "smallish" venue (including three new baby tigers) is "well worth a couple of hours"; it's "nowhere near the caliber" of some other city zoos and the parking can be "tight", but "special twilight tours" and free summer concerts are pluses.

Iolani Palace
26 | 24 | 23 | I

Downtown | 364 S. King St. (Richards St.) | Honolulu | 808-522-0832 | www.iolanipalace.org

"History is frozen in time" at this "gorgeous" Downtown venue – the "only royal palace in the U.S." – built by King Kalakaua in 1882; "enthusiastic, knowledgeable" docents fascinate visitors with the tale of "Hawaii's monarchy" and its "process to statehood" (there are also self-guided tour options), and on most Fridays the Royal Hawaiian Band performs free concerts on-site; N.B. children under five allowed only in basement galleries, which house the crown jewels, ancient regalia and historic photographs.

Kailua Beach Park
27 | 18 | 14 | $0

Kailua | end of Kailua Rd. (Alaia Rd.)

"Miles of sand" like "powdered sugar", remarkable turquoise water, a mellow vibe and facilities that include restrooms, showers and a lifeguard make this "in" beach in Kailua "great for families" and "activity-seekers" including kayakers, windsurfers, boogie boarders, joggers, dog walkers and surfers; "if the wind is blowing, the surf kicks up" and it can be too choppy for average swimmers, who should also beware of the occasional stinging jellyfish.

Kapiolani Park
23 | 17 | 13 | $0

Waikiki | 3840 Paki Ave. (Monsarrat Ave.) | Honolulu | 808-971-2504 | www.kapiolanipark.org

"Expansive fields and flowers" set the scene at this "historic" city park where "there's always something going on", including tennis matches, soccer games, kite flying, art fairs and the occasional "nighttime movie at the beach"; locals who gather for picnics and "excellent concerts" at the Waikiki Shell appreciate the "restroom facilities" and "lots of shade trees."

Kuhio Beach Park

▽ 23 | 18 | 14 | $0

Waikiki | 2552 Kalakaua Ave. (Kapahulu Ave.) | Honolulu
There's "tranquility in frenetic Waikiki" at this "crowded" but easygoing stretch of beach where boogie-boarders mingle with "lots of characters" like "musicians" and "chess players"; an outdoor movie screen, a strolling path and daily hula performances keep things interesting on land, while wetter entertainments include a small marine conservation zone, surfing lessons, outrigger canoe rides and seawalls that create bathtublike conditions; N.B. the facilities include showers and concession stands.

ⓩ Lanikai Beach

28 | 14 | 12 | $0

Kailua | Kailua Rd. (Kalanianaole Hwy.)
With "powdery white sand", "calm" water, "plenty of space" and an "awesome" view of the Mokulua Islands, this "breathtaking" piece of Lanikai waterfront is a popular swimming spot; its lack of facilities and "difficult-to-find" location "nestled in an exclusive residential community" ("parking is a challenge" and access available only via "public walkways between private homes") don't deter sunbathers who deem it near "perfection."

Makapu'u Beach

27 | 14 | 11 | $0

Waimanalo | 41-095 Kalanianaole Hwy. (Pacific Ocean)
On Oahu's easternmost point, this beach's "spectacular scenery" includes "amazing" mountains, startlingly blue water, offshore bird sanctuary islets and a cliff's-edge lighthouse; "be careful of the waves and undertow", since the dangerous "pounding shorebreak" here is "for advanced bodyboarders" and "experienced swimmers" only – on most days, you'll see red warning flags posted by roving lifeguards; N.B. showers are available.

Manoa Falls

26 | 14 | 12 | $0

Manoa | Paradise Park | Manoa Rd. (Pali Hwy.) | Honolulu | 800-464-2924
"Just 10 minutes from Waikiki", this "popular" rainforest respite is home to the "most accessible waterfall on Oahu", reached via a "fantastic" "short" hike through bamboo trees and "majestic" scenery; it's "spectacular after a heavy rainfall", but be sure to "wear good shoes" since the "trail is slippery" when wet; P.S. while the hike is free, there's a small fee for parking (and regulars advise "don't leave valuables in your vehicle").

Paradise Cove Luau

26 | 23 | 22 | E

Kapolei | 92-1089 Alii Nui Dr. (off Farrington Hwy.) | 808-842-5911 | www.paradisecovehawaii.com
"Go early" to wander the "lovely" grounds (the Kapolei "location alone is worth the trek from Waikiki") and enjoy the pre-show "demonstrations of ancient games" at this "crowded" luau that's laden with "cheesy but entertaining activities" for the whole family; the buffet is "plentiful", if "just ok", or you can opt for "pricier tickets" that come with "table service" and "upfront seating."

Polynesian Cultural Center

26 | 26 | 25 | E

Laie | 55-370 Kamehameha Hwy. (Laniloa St.) | 808-293-3333 |
800-367-7060 | www.polynesia.com

"Step back in time" at the seven "educational" villages where "traditional" Polynesian life is on display at this "extremely well-executed"
cultural center an hour's drive from Waikiki with a "Disney-meets-the-
South-Pacific" vibe – but "without the [themed] rides"; the "whole-
some family" attractions include boat tours, "wonderful" "interactive
demonstrations" by "charming" performers, "excellent Imax films"
and an "awesome" canoe pageant, so set aside a "full day to see it all."

Polynesian Cultural Center Ali'l Luau

23 | 23 | 22 | E

Laie | 55-370 Kamehameha Hwy. (Laniloa St.) | 808-293-3333 |
www.polynesia.com

The "amazing" Horizons Night Show is the highlight of this "campy"
luau that's a "good way to end your visit to the Polynesian Cultural
Center"; diners debate whether the food is "delicious" or "mediocre",
and advise that since it's a Mormon "church-sponsored event", "don't
even think to ask" about alcohol.

Punchbowl Crater

25 | 20 | 19 | $0

(aka National Memorial Cemetery of the Pacific)
Makiki Heights | 2177 Puowaina Dr. (Auwaiolimu St.) | Honolulu |
808-532-3720

"You'd think you'd not want to visit a cemetery on vacation", but you'd
be wrong say those who find this national resting place – inside a "long-
extinct volcano crater" in Makiki Heights with a "beautiful vista of
Diamond Head in the distance" – a "moving", "sobering" experience;
more than 48,000 WWII, Korea and Vietnam veterans are buried
alongside a "gorgeous" monument with "terrazzo maps" of Pacific
battles, and guides relay the history of the site and its 56 memorials.

Queen Emma Summer Palace

23 | 20 | 22 | I

Nuuanu | 2913 Pali Hwy. (Laimi St.) | Honolulu | 808-595-3167 |
www.daughtersofhawaii.org

This "breezy" Nuuanu "summer home of the beloved Queen Emma" in
the "cool Pali Pass" is an "interesting diversion" set amid "lush greenery" and filled with "authentic furnishings" that show how the "ill-
fated royal family" lived in the mid-1800s; "knowledgeable docents"
help flesh out the details, and there's also a "nice gift shop."

Sandy Beach

25 | 14 | 12 | $0

Hawaii Kai | Makai of Kalanianaole Hwy. | Honolulu

The "dangerous, neck-breaking surf" (not for schoolies or anyone un-
familiar with the shore break) at this "famous" Hawaii Kai "bodysurfing
beach" does little to deter the "good-looking local" crowd, since they
come for the "awesome" sunbathing and chance to gawk at the "latest
swimwear styles"; arrive early on weekends to score parking and a prime
spot on the sand, and then head to the east end to watch the action.

Sea Life Park

22 | 20 | 19 | E

Waimanalo | 41-202 Kalanianaole Hwy. (Makapuu Point) | 808-259-7933 |
866-365-7446 | www.sealifeparkhawaii.com

An aquatic park "with Hawaiian flair", this Waimanalo attraction
"might be smaller than you expect", yet still satisfies with "good hands-

on pools with turtles and rays" and opportunities to "feed sea lions", swim with dolphins and attend a penguin show; those who think it "needs a face-lift" hope the recent change in ownership will mean a "spruce-up."

Sunset Beach

28 | 14 | 12 | $0

Waimea | Kamehameha Hwy.

When the winter "surf's up", the "best-looking people in the world" are "packed like sardines" on the white sand at this long, "picturesque" beach that's the ultimate North Shore "must-stop for anyone interested in surfing" (you can watch "semi-pros" hang ten and get sandbagged on "killer" waves); summertime ushers in "smoother waters" and a slightly calmer scene, but the sunsets are "wonderful" year-round.

Turtle Bay

25 | 22 | 20 | $0

Kahuku | 57-091 Kamehameha Hwy. (Marconi Rd.) | 808-293-8811 | www.turtlebayresort.com

Even in winter when the North Shore can crank out body-crushing waves, a protective reef break keeps this "relaxing" cove's "cool waters" calm enough for good swimming and snorkeling; a large parking area, a "small" but "nice" white stretch of sand, frequent sightings of its namesake creature and plentiful amenities courtesy of the surrounding resort make this a prime "place to take the family."

☑ USS Arizona Memorial

29 | 26 | 25 | $0

Pearl Harbor | 1 Arizona Memorial Pl. (off Kamehameha Hwy.) | 808-422-0561 | www.nps.gov/usar

"No one should miss" this "elegant" memorial above the sunken *USS Arizona* in Pearl Harbor, an "unforgettable", "heartbreaking" "homage to the effects of war" that's ranked the state's Most Popular Attraction and the No. 1 for Appeal on Oahu; "arrive early" for the tour to avoid long lines, and prepare to spend some time watching the "poignant video" before taking a "motor launch trip to the final resting place" of more than 1,000 crewmen who lost their lives in the December 7th, 1941, attack.

Waikiki Aquarium

22 | 20 | 20 | I

Waikiki | 2777 Kalakaua Ave. (Kapahulu Ave.) | Honolulu | 808-923-9741 | www.waquarium.org

"Fauna of local waters" "seen nowhere else" are among the "finned and furry friends" at this "compact" aquarium in a "fabulous location" "right on Waikiki Beach"; though a small school of drylanders deem it "disappointing", most maintain that kids, at least, will be "enthralled" with the tidal pools, turtles, sharks and seals.

☑ Waikiki Beach

23 | 20 | 16 | $0

Waikiki | Kalakaua Ave. (bet. Hobron Ln. & Kapahulu Ave.) | Honolulu | 877-525-6248

"The world's most famous beach" is a "dynamic", "happening" destination (especially since all of the recent area renovations), where "every possible amenity is within walking distance" – from surf lessons and gear rentals to loads of restaurants to "helpful hawkers" to high-end designer luxury boutiques; even if it seems there are "more people than sand", the "breathtaking sunsets" against Diamond Head can make "you feel like you're in a postcard."

	APPEAL	FACIL.	SERVICE	COST

Waimanalo Bay Beach Park ▽ 24 | 12 | 7 | $0

Waimanalo | 41-741 Kalanianaole Hwy. (Huli St.) | 800-464-2924
Set "away from the big city" and behind a forest of whispering iron-wood trees in Waimanalo, this "family-friendly" white-sand beach draws in-the-know locals with its promise of water so blue "it rivals the Caribbean"; weekends are abuzz with "huge tents and parties", but weekdays are often "deserted" – unless school's out; N.B. stinging jellyfish are a sporadic problem.

☑ Waimea Bay Beach Park 28 | 17 | 14 | $0

Haleiwa | 61-031 Kamehameha Hwy. (Waimea Valley Rd.) | 808-233-7300
The granddaddy of North Shore beaches and arguably the most famous surfing site in the world, this "gorgeous" crescent of sand is the "place to be" in winter when the "surf kicks up" to 10 or 15 feet (on rare 30-ft. days a madhouse of onlookers gawks at "awesome" long-boarders scoring "perfect" rides); in summer, "you can try cliff diving" from the sea rock, as the waters are "calmer" and "safer" for schoolies and snorkelers; P.S. in either season, parking is "freakishly scarce after 9 AM", especially on weekends.

Oahu Dining

	FOOD	DECOR	SERVICE	COST

Aaron's Atop the Ala Moana *Continental* | 20 | 24 | 22 | $53

Ala Moana | Ala Moana Hotel | 410 Atkinson Dr. (Ala Moana Blvd.) | Honolulu | 808-955-4466 | www.tristarrestaurants.com

An "oldie but a goodie" say fans of this "romantic" Continental atop the "modest" Ala Moana Hotel, with the "best" "bird's-eye view" of the Honolulu skyline; although spoilsports snap that the "overpriced" fare is "uninspired", the "presentation is minimal" and the "hovering" service sometimes feels "pretentious", if you simply want "fabulous" vistas, "go for the early-bird/sunset special"; N.B. after 10 PM on Fridays and Saturdays it becomes a nightclub.

Akasaka ● *Japanese* | 25 | 13 | 21 | $40

Ala Moana | 1646B Kona St. (bet. Atkinson Dr. & Kaheka St.) | Honolulu | 808-942-4466

The "reasonably priced" "excellent nigiri sushi", "to-die-for butterfish" and other "tasty" Japanese "concoctions" keep "lots of regulars" returning to this "hard-to-find" Ala Moana "hole-in-the-wall", "tucked back behind a strip club" ("don't be put off by the location"); "late hours" and service "without pretentions" further ensure that it's "always busy."

Z Alan Wong's *Hawaii Reg.* | 28 | 22 | 27 | $67

McCully | McCully Ct. | 1857 S. King St., 3rd fl. (bet. Hauoli & Pumehana Sts.) | Honolulu | 808-949-2526 | www.alanwongs.com

"Your palate will thank you" gush gourmands of the "best restaurant" on the islands (voted No. 1 for Food in the state and Most Popular on Oahu), where the namesake chef turns out "ingenious" Hawaii Regional dishes "prepared to perfection" and "artfully presented" by a "superbly trained" staff; the "unusual setting in an inconspicuous business center" on McCully and the "understated decor" puts the "clear focus on food" – and it's "sensational", if expensive; P.S "reservations are a must."

Antonio's New York Pizzeria *Pizza* | 21 | 8 | 13 | $16

Kahala | 4210 Waialae Ave. (Hunakai St.) | Honolulu | 808-737-3333
NEW **Pearl City** | 719 Kamehameha Hwy. (Puu Poni St.) | 808-454-1233 M
www.antoniosnypizza.com

"Primarily for takeout", these Kahala and Pearl City pizzerias serve up "affordable", "thin-crust" varieties that fans find "tasty and filling"; but naysayers who argue that the subpar service and "dingy decor" make the "slightly-better-than-average" pies less enjoyable, stick to takeout.

Arancino di Mare *Italian* | 22 | 21 | 21 | $33

Waikiki | 255 Beachwalk (Kalakaua Ave.) | Honolulu | 808-923-5557
Waikiki | Waikiki Beach Marriott Resort & Spa | 2552 Kalakaua Ave. (bet. Ohua & Paoakalani Aves.) | Honolulu | 808-931-6273
www.arancino.net

A "casual yet festive" pair of Italians in the Waikiki Beach Marriott and on Beachwalk, this "surprisingly affordable" duo serves "creative" pastas, "excellent thin-crust pizzas" and "unique salads"; the service is generally "attentive" at both, but the ocean views and outdoor seating are only available in the hotel branch.

	FOOD	DECOR	SERVICE	COST

Assaggio *Italian* — 21 | 19 | 21 | $33

Ala Moana | Ala Moana Ctr. | 1450 Ala Moana Blvd. (bet. Atkinson Dr. & Piikoi St.) | Honolulu | 808-942-3446
Hawaii Kai | Koko Marina Shopping Ctr. | 7192 Kalanianaole Hwy. (Lunalili Home Rd.) | Honolulu | 808-396-0756
Kailua | 354 Uluniu St. (bet. Maluniu Ave. & Oneawa St.) | 808-261-2772
Kapolei | 777 Kamokila Blvd. (Uluohia St.) | 808-674-8801
Mililani | 95-1250 Meheula Pkwy. (Lanikuhana Ave.) | Honolulu | 808-623-5115
www.assaggiohi.com

"Consistently well-executed" Italian "classics" ("tableside Caesar salad", shrimp scampi, eggplant rollatini) and "generally attentive service" help make this Oahu mini-chain a "perennial favorite", especially among diners who dig the "generous portions"; even though a few find the fare "nothing special" and "not very authentic", they love the "convenient" Ala Moana Center outpost that's "an oasis in a busy shopping mall" as well as the views of Koko Marina at the Hawaii Kai branch.

Auntie Pasto's *Italian* — 17 | 14 | 17 | $23

Downtown | 1099 S. Beretania St. (Piikoi St.) | Honolulu | 808-523-8855
Waipahu | Kunia Shopping Ctr. | 94-663 Kupuohi St. (Lloyd Peterson Ln.) | 808-680-0005
www.auntiepastos.com

"There's always a line out the door" "during peak hours" at these "fun", "family-friendly" Italians in Downtown and Waipahu that turn out "large quantities" of "decent", "heavy-on-the-garlic" comfort fare; the "small", "loud" spaces are "not fancy" and the service is spotty, but it's "priced right", hence "popular with young people."

Baci Bistro *Italian* — 24 | 19 | 23 | $37

Kailua | 30 Aulike St. (bet. Kuulei Rd. & Uluniu St.) | 808-262-7555 | www.bacibistro.com

Expect "attention to detail" at this "romantic little Italian bistro" in Kailua where "interesting variations" emerge from the kitchen, "imaginative" offerings dot the wine list and "gardenlike decor" graces the "small but not cramped" space ("go early if you like quiet"); the "personal service from the owners" further makes it a "perennial favorite" in the area.

Bac Nam *Vietnamese* — 24 | 11 | 19 | $15

Downtown | 1117 S. King St. (bet. Pensacola & Piikoi Sts.) | Honolulu | 808-597-8201

"The quintessential dark horse" among "so many other good Vietnamese", this "unassuming" Downtown BYO "hole-in-the-wall" run by an "attentive" "husband-and-wife team" features "an exceptionally wide range" of "superb" dishes "from both the North and the South", plus top-notch standards like "heavenly spring rolls"; unfortunately, "as the word has spread", "the "tables have filled and service has slowed."

Ba-Le Sandwich Shop *Vietnamese* — 20 | 6 | 14 | $9

Aiea | Pearlridge Ctr. Downtown | 98-180 Kamehameha Hwy. (Lipoa Pl.) | 808-487-7280
Ala Moana | Ala Moana Ctr. | 1450 Ala Moana Blvd. (bet. Atkinson Dr. & Piikoi St.) | Honolulu | 808-944-4752

(continued)

Ba-Le Sandwich Shop

Chinatown | Kamehameha Shopping Ctr. | 1620 N. School St. (Makuahine St.) | Honolulu | 808-842-0013
Downtown | Fort Street Mall | 1154 Fort St. (Pauhuahi St.) | Honolulu | 808-521-4117 🗷
Hawaii Kai | Hawaii Kai Shopping Ctr. | 377 Keahole St. (Keahole Pl.) | Honolulu | 808-396-6556
Kahala | Kahala Mall | 4618 Kilauea Ave. (Pahoa Ave.) | Honolulu | 808-735-6889
Kailua | 345 Hahani St. (Hekili St.) | 808-261-2193
Manoa | UH Manoa | 2445 Campus Rd. (Maile Way) | Honolulu | 808-956-6462 🗷
Pearl City | Pearl City Shopping Ctr. | 850 Kamehameha Hwy. (bet. Kamehameha Hwy. & Waimano Rd.) | 808-456-1811
Ward | Ward Gateway Ctr. | 333 Ward Ave. (bet. Auahi & Halekauwila Sts.) | Honolulu | 808-591-0935
www.ba-le.com
Additional locations throughout Oahu

"Authentically wonderful" sandwiches and "awesome" ethnic cuisine, including "excellent" shrimp summer rolls, are "courteously" served at this "friendly" "fast-food" Vietnamese chain; the decor is strictly "no-frills", but the "bargain prices" and "quick counter service" make them "popular" "bangs for the buck."

🗷 Bali by the Sea 🗷 *Pacific Rim* | 24 | 26 | 25 | $66 |

Waikiki | Hilton Hawaiian Vill. | 2005 Kalia Rd. (Ala Moana Blvd.) | Honolulu | 808-941-2254 | www.hiltonhawaiianvillage.com
The "idyllic tropical setting" with an "amazing" ocean vista is the highlight of this "romantic" Pacific Rim restaurant in the Hilton Hawaiian Village, since it feels "like you're eating on the beach with no sand"; even if some feel the "pricey" island fare "isn't up to par" with the "gorgeous sunset view", there's a "deep and interesting wine list" and "bend-over-backwards service", making it a "special" spot for most.

NEW Beachhouse at | 21 | 25 | 20 | $50 |
the Moana *American/Steak*

Waikiki | Moana Surfrider | 2365 Kalakaua Ave. (Kaiulani Ave.) | Honolulu | 808-921-4600 | www.moana-surfrider.com
This "newly remodeled" space in Waikiki's Moana Surfrider has been reborn as a "pricey" New American steakhouse in an "elegant", "old Hawaii" setting with "spectacular ocean views" and an "open veranda"; fans label it a "wonderful splurge", but others are bothered by "slow" service.

Benihana *Japanese* | 18 | 17 | 19 | $42 |

Waikiki | Hilton Hawaiian Vill. | 2005 Kalia Rd. (Ala Moana Blvd.) | Honolulu | 808-955-5955 | www.benihana.com
The Honolulu branch of this "kitschy but reliable" national Japanese teppanyaki chain may be "tourist oriented" (it's in the Hilton Hawaiian Village) and "more expensive" than you'd expect, but the "kids love" the "knife-wielding" "showmanship" and socializers "get to meet new people sitting with" them at the communal table; but patrons who pooh-pooh "teflon" decor and "mediocre" food snap "are you kidding me – you'd fly to Hawaii and eat at a cookie-cutter?"

	FOOD	DECOR	SERVICE	COST

Big City Diner *American*   18 | 14 | 19 | $19

NEW **Aiea** | Pearlridge Ctr. E. | 98-211 Pali Momi St. (Haukapila St.) |
808-487-8188 ❂
Kailua | Foodland Mktpl. | 108 Hekili St. (Hamakua Dr.) | 808-263-8880
Kaimuki | 3565 Waialae Ave. (bet. 11th & 12th Aves.) | Honolulu |
808-738-8855
Waipahu | Waipio Shopping Ctr. | 94-800 Ukee St. (Oil Loop) | 808-678-8886
Ward | Ward Entertainment Ctr. | 1060 Auahi St. (bet. Kamakee St. &
Ward Ave) | Honolulu | 808-591-8891
www.bigcitydinerhawaii.com
"The 50th state's version of the '50s diner", this "friendly", "affordable"
mini-chain serves "monster portions" of American "favorites with an
Asian/Polynesian twist" (try the "kimchi fried rice") in a "child-friendly"
atmosphere draws lots of locals; but "disappointed" diners discover
"quantity over taste" and say it's "only popular" because the city's
"other diner options are so abysmal."

Brasserie Du Vin *French*   20 | 24 | 19 | $34

Chinatown | 1115 Bethel St. (bet. Hotel & Pauahi Sts.) | Honolulu |
808-545-1115 | www.brasserieduvin.com
Find "a piece of Paris in the heart of" Chinatown at this French brasse-
rie and wine bar across from the Hawaii Theatre with a "wonderful layout" that includes an "outdoor patio" with "outstanding ambiance";
"carefully selected music", a "tremendous", if "pricey", vino selection
and "small portions" perfect for a "light meal" win fans, but critics
contend that "inconsistency" plagues both food and service.

Bubba Gump Shrimp Co. ❂ *American/Seafood*   15 | 17 | 17 | $26

Ala Moana | Ala Moana Ctr. | 1450 Ala Moana Blvd. (bet. Atkinson Dr. &
Piikoi St.) | Honolulu | 808-949-4867 | www.bubbagump.com
Reviewers either love this "family"-friendly American chain with "dependable" seafood and "long lines" or call it a "touristy" choice that's
"fairly expensive" for "frozen deep-fried" fare ("stick to the bar"); it's
"definitely not a Hawaiian experience" (although the Kailua-Kona, Big
Island, outpost has "priceless water views"), but the staff exudes
"friendly" aloha spirit and fans of *Forrest Gump* dig decor "right out
of the movie."

NEW **Burgers on the Edge** *Burgers*   - | - | - | I

Kapahulu | Ave. Shops at Safeway | 890 Kapahulu Ave. (Olu St.) |
Honolulu | 808-737-8866 | www.burgersontheedge.com
From the owners of Formaggio Wine & Cheese Bar, this new fast-food
burger joint in Kapahulu's Safeway shopping center offers a choice of
ground chuck or Wagyu beef patties, topped with local produce, international extras (foie gras, anyone?) and an array of spicy and sweet
sauces; the casual, high-tech setting features a menu displayed on
flat-screen TVs.

Buzz's *Steak*   19 | 19 | 19 | $33

Lanikai | 413 Kawailoa Rd. (bet. Kawailoa & Popoia Rds.) | Kailua |
808-261-4661 ⊞
Pearl City | 98-751 Kuahao Pl. (Kaahumanu St.) | 808-487-6465
www.buzzssteakhouse.com
It's a taste of "good old Hawaii" at this "purely local" Lanikai steakhouse in a "funky" "beach bungalow" "across from Kailua Beach"

where the "mai tais are especially strong", the "service friendly" and "the salad bar killer"; but a portion of patrons "don't know what all the buzz is about" since the "food fails to live up to the prime location" – go for the "great bar scene" instead; N.B. a second affiliated outpost is in Pearl City.

Cafe Sistina *Italian*   21 | 22 | 18 | $34

Makiki | 1314 S. King St. (bet. Akoko & Keeaumoku Sts.) | Honolulu | 808-596-0061 | www.cafesistina.com

"Beautiful" "Sistine Chapel–inspired" murals "painted by the owner" set the scene at this "unassuming" Makiki eatery where the "extensive" pasta-heavy Northern Italian menu includes both "classic" and "madcap" creations; a "decent wine list" helps distract from the sometimes "slow" service.

California Beach Rock 'N Sushi *Japanese*   23 | 14 | 18 | $25

Ward | Ward Ctr. | 404 Ward Ave. (Halekauwila St.) | Honolulu | 808-597-8000

Penny-pinchers pining for "quality sushi and teriyaki" endure "long waits" to eat at this "affordable" Ward joint known for its "array of specialty rolls" and "insanely good early-bird special" (available before 6:30 PM); "personal" service adds to the allure, even if the decor in the "cramped" dining room "needs work."

California Pizza Kitchen *Pizza*   20 | 16 | 18 | $22

Aiea | Pearlridge Ctr. Downtown | 554 Pearlridge Ctr. (Rose Rd.) | 808-487-7741

Ala Moana | Ala Moana Ctr. | 1450 Ala Moana Blvd. (bet. Atkinson Dr. & Piikoi St.) | Honolulu | 808-941-7715

Kahala | Kahala Mall | 4211 Waialae Ave. (Kilauea Ave.) | Honolulu | 808-737-9446

Waikiki | 2284 Kalakaua Ave. (Seaside Ave.) | Honolulu | 808-924-2000
www.cpk.com

The "loud, hectic" Oahu outposts of this national chain are "always crowded" thanks to the family-friendly, "consistent" menu of "distinctive pizza and unusual salads", "upbeat surroundings" and service with "aloha spirit"; but those who balk at both the "cookie-cutter" experience ("no local twists") and pies that "taste like those you'd get out of your freezer" call it "shopping-center food."

Camellia, Restaurant *Korean*   20 | 9 | 13 | $23

Moiliili | 930 McCully St. (Algaroba St.) | Honolulu | 808-951-0511

Prepare to "eat till you drop" and "come out smelling like the inside of a chimney" at this "hole-in-the-wall" Moiliili all-you-can-eat Korean yakiniku buffet featuring an array of "perfectly seasoned" meats to BBQ at the table "on an open flame"; "constant service to check your grill" and affordable tabs make it a "local family favorite."

Chai's Island Bistro *Pacific Rim*   23 | 22 | 21 | $49

Downtown | Aloha Tower Mktpl. | 1 Aloha Tower Dr. (Ala Moana Blvd.) | Honolulu | 808-585-0011 | www.chaisislandbistro.com

At his Aloha Tower Marketplace eatery, chef Chai Chaowasaree turns out "inventive" Pacific Rim fare in a "tropical" setting that includes an outdoor dining garden, Thai artifacts, fresh orchids and a man-made waterfall; though nitpickers knock it as a "tourist magnet" with "ordinary", "overpriced" dishes, loyalists love the live "authentic" "contemporary Hawaiian entertainment" and "super-friendly hospitality."

Cheeseburger in Paradise *American*
17 | 18 | 17 | $21

Waikiki | 2500 Kalakaua Ave. (Kealohilani St.) | Honolulu | 808-923-3731 | www.cheeseburgerland.com

See review in Maui Dining Directory.

Cheesecake Factory *American*
21 | 19 | 19 | $28

Waikiki | Royal Hawaiian Ctr. | 2301 Kalakaua Ave. (Dukes Ln.) | Honolulu | 808-924-5001 | www.thecheesecakefactory.com

The Waikiki location of this national chain is "always packed" with fans of "gargantuan proportions" of "consistent" American fare (from "salads to burgers to sandwiches to pizza") plus "island specialties" and "phenomenal cheesecakes"; but critics cringe at servers who "wish they were someplace else", a dining room that "sounds like a train station" and "standardized" chow that's "not worth" the "hour-long waits."

☑ Chef Mavro Ⓜ *French/Hawaii Reg.*
26 | 23 | 26 | $90

Moiliili | 1969 S. King St. (McCully St.) | Honolulu | 808-944-4714 | www.chefmavro.com

Chef George Mavrothalassitis "elevates dining in paradise to a higher level" at his namesake Hawaii Regional–French where the "first-class" "tasting menus with paired wines" are "brilliantly prepared" and "outstandingly presented" by "informative" servers in a "subtly sophisticated" space; even if the McCully/Moiliili location is a little out of the way and the fare so "sinfully expensive" "you'll melt down a credit card", connoisseurs consider it a "must" experience.

Chiang Mai Thai *Thai*
22 | 17 | 19 | $24

Moiliili | 2239 S. King St. (Makahiki Way) | Honolulu | 808-941-1151

For "reliable" Thai fare in a "casual" setting, loyalists head to this Moiliili establishment with "warm service", "large portions" and "lots of options" including "great vegetarian dishes" (be careful if you order 'hot'"); the "cramped" interior space and "unreasonable corkage fee" are turnoffs, however.

Cholo's Homestyle Mexican *Mexican*
18 | 14 | 17 | $21

Haleiwa | North Shore Mktpl. | 66-250 Kamehameha Hwy. (bet. Amara Rd. & Kilioe Pl.) | 808-637-3059 | www.cholosmexican.com

This "touristy" Mexican eatery on Oahu's North Shore has a few things going for it: "excellent margaritas", a "fine tequila list" and a "festive" (read: "loud") atmosphere; but, unfortunately, the menu of "staples" ranges from *"muy excellente"* to *"ay caramba"* and some say the "surly" staff seems like it "would rather be surfing."

Chowder House *Seafood*
16 | 11 | 17 | $20

Ward | Ward Warehouse | 1050 Ala Moana Blvd. (bet. Kamakee St. & Ward Ave.) | Honolulu | 808-596-7944 •

Head to this unassuming, moderately priced Ward Warehouse seafooder for the "house specialty" "New England clam chowder in a bread bowl" that "comes pretty fast" even during "crowded lunch times"; though many say the rest of the fare is "ordinary" and the "old-fashioned" interior in "need of an update", regulars note that President-elect "Barack Obama ate here."

Ciao Mein *Chinese/Italian*
21 | 23 | 22 | $42

Waikiki | Hyatt Regency Waikiki Resort & Spa | 2424 Kalakaua Ave. (Uluniu St.) | Honolulu | 808-923-2426

"China meets Italy" at this Hyatt Regency Waikiki eatery where proponents praise the "unique" menu "combining the best of both worlds", the "nice setting" and the "excellent" service; but the "strange" "fusion doesn't work" for all diners, especially since "prices are quite a bit higher than at most Chinese restaurants."

Contemporary Café ⓜ *American*
19 | 22 | 17 | $19

Makiki Heights | Contemporary Museum, The | 2411 Makiki Heights Dr. (Mott-Smith Dr.) | Honolulu | 808-523-3362 | www.tcmhi.org

"Nestled" among "lovely" "gardens and modern art" at The Contemporary Museum in Makiki Heights, this lunch-only American cafe with oudoor seating has the "ambiance covered", especially considering the occasional "live music"; even if a few find the "limited" selection of moderately priced salads and sandwiches a "bit bland" and the service "hit-or-miss", it's a "fine" choice "if you're already at the museum."

Curry House CoCo Ichibanya *Japanese*
20 | 10 | 16 | $12

Aiea | Pearl Kai Shopping Ctr. | 98-199 Kamehameha Hwy. (Pali Momi St.) | 808-488-6659 ⊟

Ala Moana | Ala Moana Ctr. | 1450 Ala Moana Blvd. (bet. Atkinson Dr. & Piikoi St.) | Honolulu | 808-947-4889

McCully | McCully Shopping Ctr. | 1960 Kapiolani Blvd. (McCully St.) | Honolulu | 808-949-4590 ⊟

Moiliili | Puck's Alley Ctr. | 1009 University Ave. (bet. Coyne & King Sts.) | Honolulu | 808-947-2206 ▣⊟

For "inexpensive" Japanese-style "curry in a hurry", fans recommend this Japan-based mini-chain where the "addictive" house specialty, which comes with a "staggering" variety of toppings ("octopus and kimchi, anyone?"), "does not disappoint"; while some complain that the "seating is limited" and "service is rushed", it's still the "favorite" option of many for a "quick and simple counter lunch."

Da Spot *Middle Eastern*
▽ 20 | 7 | 18 | $13

Moiliili | 908 Pumehana St. (Waiola St.) | Honolulu | 808-941-1313

Loyalists line up at this "take-out" Middle Eastern "hole-in-the-wall" in McCully/Moiliili where the "shareable portions" of "tasty" "Mediterranean-influenced plate lunches" (try the signature "Egyptian chicken") are "made with love" by the "husband-and-wife" owners, and the "near-infinite variety of smoothies" draw lots of nearby UH students (there's also a kiosk at the University); still, the "scary appearance" means it's "not da spot" for finicky folks.

Diamond Head Grill *Eclectic*
22 | 19 | 20 | $44

Waikiki | W Honolulu | 2885 Kalakaua Ave. (Diamond Head Rd.) | Honolulu | 808-922-3734 | www.w-dhg.com

"Go early or you may be seated in the middle of the disco" at this "popular" and "swanky" Eclectic eatery in Waikiki's W that turns into "a nightclub after hours"; though the fare can be "imaginative" and the "view of Diamond Head" from the bar just as "beautiful" as the people who "seek to be seen" here, coin-counters caution it's all rather "pricey", especially given that some find "mediocre" service.

	FOOD	DECOR	SERVICE	COST

Dixie Grill *BBQ/Crab House* — 16 | 14 | 17 | $22

Aiea | 99-012 Kamehameha Hwy. (Honomanu St.) | 808-485-2722 | www.dixiegrill.com

This Aiea BBQ joint and "crab house" with a "honky-tonk atmosphere" serves up "finger-lickin'" Cajun and Southern favorites like Carolina smoked pulled pork, fried catfish and beer-battered fish 'n' chips; although critics say the fare is "underwhelming", service "spotty" and the theme "tired", "happy hour on the patio" almost makes up for it.

d.k Steak House *Steak* — 22 | 19 | 22 | $51

Waikiki | Waikiki Beach Marriott Resort & Spa | 2552 Kalakaua Ave., 3rd fl. (bet. Ohua & Paoakalani Aves.) | Honolulu | 808-931-6280 | www.dkrestaurants.com

The only place that serves in-house "dry-aged beef" in Hawaii, this "pricey", "clubby" steakhouse in the Waikiki Beach Marriott is known for "outstanding" meat, "a dizzying array of delicious sides" and a "fantastic wine list" proffered by a "knowledgeable" staff; though a few find the "bench seating hard", you can see a "spectacular sunset" when seated outside.

NEW Downtown @ the HiSAM Ⓢ *American* — - | - | - | M

Downtown | Hawaii State Art Museum | 250 S. Hotel St. (bet. Alakea & Richards Sts.) | Honolulu | 808-536-5900 | www.state.hi.us/sfca

Set on the first floor of the Hawaii State Art Museum, this casual Downtown sibling to town restaurant in Kaimuki offers New American lunches highlighting local, organic ingredients served in a cafeteria-like setting, including counter-service for takeout as well as alfresco dining; N.B. it closes at 2 PM except on First Fridays, when dinner is served until 8:30 PM.

Duc's Bistro Ⓢ *French/Vietnamese* — 24 | 20 | 23 | $45

Chinatown | 1188 Maunakea St. (bet. Beretania & Pauahi Sts.) | Honolulu | 808-531-6325 | www.ducsbistro.com

Owner "Duc Nguyen often welcomes his visitors" personally to this Vietnamese-French "sleeper" in Chinatown, where the "Asian fusion" menu "offers surprises along with classics", and the decor is that of "a Shanghai jazz joint in the '30s"; "live music" and "a nice wine list" make up for the "dicey" nabe, though penny-pinchers proclaim it "overpriced."

Ⓩ Duke's Canoe Club *American* — 19 | 23 | 20 | $33

Waikiki | Outrigger Waikiki | 2335 Kalakaua Ave. (bet. Dukes Ln. & Kaiulani Ave.) | Honolulu | 808-922-2268 | www.dukeswaikiki.com

It's all about "nostalgia" at the original Outrigger Waikiki Beach location of this "popular", "crowded" island institution named for "surfing legend" and Olympic champion swimmer Duke Kahanamoku; here and at the Kalapaki Beach location (which was voted Most Popular restaurant on Kauai), it's more about the "ultimate laid-back Hawaiian experience" with specialty drinks and "nightly music", than about the moderately priced "typical" American bar food.

E&O Trading Co. *SE Asian* — 20 | 24 | 20 | $36

Ward | Ward Ctr. | 1200 Ala Moana Blvd. (Ward Ave.) | Honolulu | 808-591-9555 | www.eotrading.com

The Ward outpost of this California-based chain offers "stylishly presented" Southeast Asian fare that's "heavy on small plates"; if the "service can seem a little stressed out" and the tabs "too expensive", few find fault with the "Far-East setting" that "hits the sweet spot between elegant and casual"; P.S. a "trendy crowd" hits happy hour.

Eggs 'n Things *American*

23 | 12 | 19 | $15

Waikiki | 1911B Kalakaua Ave. (McCully St.) | Honolulu | 808-949-0820 | www.eggsnthings.com

There's "always a line" outside this "quintessential" Waikiki breakfast spot where the "epic portions" of "hearty", "inexpensive" American fare include "giant omelets", pancakes "to die for" and "local favorites" like spam and eggs; while there's "no decor" and the staff is "harried", early-risers relish "starting the day" here.

NEW 'Elua *French/Italian*

24 | 22 | 24 | $61

Ala Moana | 1341 Kapiolani Blvd. (bet. Keeaumoku & Sheridan Sts.) | Honolulu | 808-955-3582 | www.eluarestaurant.com

Philippe Padovani and Donato Loperfido – "two executive chefs each with their own menu"– "alternate nights" in the kitchen at this Ala Moana-area French and Italian restaurant where "you can mix and match from either side" of the "ever-changing menu"; while diners praise the "innovative yet classic" cuisine, "superior service" and "elegant" interior, some claim the prices, coupled with "inconsistencies", mean "you can only justify it as a business expense."

Ezogiku ⊅ *Japanese/Noodle Shop*

19 | 8 | 15 | $12

Aiea | Waimalu Shopping Ctr. | 98-020 Kamehameha Hwy. (bet. Kaahumanu & Kaonohi Sts.) | 808-488-9850
Pearl City | 850 Kamehameha Hwy. (bet. Puu Momi St. & Waimano Home Rd.) | 808-455-2815
University | 1010 University Ave. (Beretania St.) | Honolulu | 808-942-3608
Waikiki | 2146 Kalakaua Ave. (Beachwalk) | Honolulu | 808-942-5363
NEW Waikiki | Royal Hawaiian Ctr. | 2201 Kalakaua Ave. (Dukes Ln.) | Honolulu | 808-447-7595
Waikiki | 2420 Koa Ave. (bet. Kaiulani & Uluniu Aves.) | Honolulu | 808-922-2473
www.ezogiku.com

Fans "come to rely on" this "hole-in-the-wall" Japanese noodle shop chain for "authentic, tasty" ramen, "melt-in-your-mouth" gyoza and more, including combos that "offer a lot of food for under $10"; the service is "quick", and together with the "filling" fare and "bargain" prices helps most overlook the "diner-style" digs.

NEW Fat Greek, The *Greek*

19 | 13 | 15 | $17

Kaimuki | 3040 Waialae Ave. (bet. 1st Ave. & St. Louis Dr.) | Honolulu | 808-734-0404

"Close to the campus" of UH-Manoa in Kaimuki, this "friendly" Greek "caters to the university crowd" with "big portions" of "flavorful" Hellenic eats at "reasonable prices"; while critics are cool to the counter service and "fast food–style" seating, others cite the "relaxing" outdoor garden and "BYOB-without-corkage" policy as pluses.

Fook Yuen ● *Chinese*

20 | 13 | 15 | $25

Moiliili | McCully Shopping Ctr. | 1960 Kapiolani Blvd. (bet. McCully & Pumehana Sts.) | Honolulu | 808-973-0168

"Make sure you pronounce the name right" at this "reasonably priced" Moiliili strip-mall Chinese, a "crustacean lovers' paradise" thanks to "bargain" live lobster prepared "in a variety of ways" on its "classic Cantonese" menu; while critics say the moniker "captures the attitude" of the "surly" staff, and the "unprepossessing" digs are "showing signs of wear", it remains a "local" "favorite" and popular "late-night" destination.

Formaggio Grill *Mediterranean* | 22 | 19 | 19 | $35

NEW **Kailua** | 305 Hahani St. (Kailua Rd.) | 808-263-2633

Formaggio Wine & Cheese Bar 🖫 *Mediterranean*

Kaimuki | Market City Shopping Ctr. | 2919 Kapiolani Blvd. (Harding Ave.) | Honolulu | 808-739-7719
www.formaggio808.com

A "hip and happening crowd" gravitates to this "sophisticated" bistro-wine bar duo serving "Italian-influenced" French-Med fare and an "extensive" (if "pricey") wine list; the Honolulu original is a "hidden treasure" in a "nondescript" strip mall, serving a "tapas-type" menu in a "dark", "intimate" space, while the newer Kailua sibling offers "family-style dining" in a "loud", "island-casual" setting that "gets really crowded on weekends."

Genki Sushi *Japanese* | 17 | 13 | 16 | $19

Ala Moana | Ala Moana Ctr. | 1450 Ala Moana Blvd. (bet. Atkinson Dr. & Piikoi St.) | Honolulu | 808-942-9102
NEW **Ward** | Ward Ctr. | 1200 Ala Moana Blvd. (Ward Ave.) | Honolulu | 808-591-5600
www.genkisushiusa.com

Expect "long lines" at this "cheap" and "casual" "sushi-go-round" chain, where you can "grab all you want" from the plates of "mid-quality" "standards" revolving around the "no-frills" room on a "never-ending conveyor belt"; it's basically "self-service", and some find the fare "not always fresh", but fans insist there are "more hits than misses", and deem it a "fine" option for a "low-cost night out."

Goma Tei Ramen *Japanese/Noodle Shop* | 21 | 18 | 19 | $14

Ward | Ward Ctr. | 1200 Ala Moana Blvd. (Piikoi St.) | Honolulu | 808-591-9188

"Hearty", "filling" noodles in "awesome" broth "rich with flavor" and "sesame accents" have the ramen chorus singing the praises of this Japanese noodle shop in Ward Centre, which also gets props for sides such as the "plump, tasty" gyoza; there's "nothing fancy" about the "small" space, but it's "clean and bright", the service is "friendly" and the beer's "cold" – just "go early" 'cause they "don't take reservations."

Green Door ⬧ *Malaysian/Singaporean* | 22 | 11 | 9 | $22

Kahala | 4614 Kilauea Ave. (bet. Makaiwa St. & Pahao Ave.) | Honolulu | 808-533-0606

"Bring your best behavior" to this "authentic Nonya" restaurant in Kahala presided over by owner Betty Pang, who "rules with an iron fist" yet maintains a "cultlike following" for her "unique" "sweet, salty, sour and spicy" Malaysian and Singaporean specialties; however, critics carp that the food is "overpriced" for a place with "ridiculously slow" "counter service."

Gyotaku *Japanese* | 19 | 14 | 18 | $23

Downtown | 1824 S. King St. (Artesian St.) | Honolulu | 808-949-4584

(continued)

Gyotaku

NEW **Niu Valley** | Niu Valley Shopping Ctr. | 5730 Kalanianaole Hwy. (Halemaumau St.) | Honolulu | 808-373-2731
Pearl City | 98-1226 Kaahumanu St. (Moanalua Rd.) | 808-487-0091
www.gyotakuhawaii.com

Families and larger groups gravitate to this "reasonably priced" Japanese trio with a "wide variety" of "dependable" "homestyle" dishes, including "outstanding" miso butterfish and "nattochos" ('nachos' of won ton crisps topped with ahi poke, fermented soybeans and avocado); critics are cool to the "dinerlike" setting and "slow" service, but loyal locals call it a "solid" "standby."

NEW Hakkei Ⓜ *Japanese*

▽ 25 | 22 | 23 | $44

Makiki | 1436 Young St. (bet. Kalakaua Ave. & Keeaumoku St.) | Honolulu | 808-944-6688 | www.hakkei-honolulu.com

You'll feel like you're at a *"ryokan* (inn) in Japan" at onetime *Iron Chef* winner Seiya Masahara's "tiny", "country-style" Makiki Japanese serving "authentic kaiseki-style" meals of "lovingly prepared small dishes", including courses featuring "comforting" oden (a stew with a variety of ingredients); you're "treated like a welcomed friend" in this "cute" spot "tucked away on Young Street", but insiders advise it's "better if you go with someone who speaks the language."

Hakone Ⓜ *Japanese*

25 | 21 | 24 | $52

Waikiki | Hawaii Prince Hotel Waikiki | 100 Holomoana St. (Ala Moana Blvd.) | Honolulu | 808-944-4494 | www.princeresortshawaii.com

"If Japanese cuisine is your thing", hightail it to these "first-class" eateries in the Maui and Waikiki Prince Hotels famed for their "sumptuous" buffets laying out an "amazing" array of sushi and "well-prepared" cooked items like tempura (they also offer à la carte selections); "it's not exactly cheap", but given the chance to "sample a wide range" of fare, most consider it a "good value"; N.B. hours vary by location, so call ahead.

Haleiwa Eats Thai *Thai*

▽ 26 | 21 | 24 | $20

Haleiwa | 66-079 Kamehameha Hwy. (Haleiwa Rd.) | 808-637-4247 | www.haleiwaeatsthai.com

This "down-to-earth" North Shore "secret" serves "reasonably priced", "scrumptious" Thai fare, including "first-rate" curried mandarin duck and "the best pineapple fried rice" to Haleiwa locals and others in-the-know; a "fast, friendly" staff, "bright and cheery" interior and lack of other Thai options in the area further contribute to the "mob scene" at peak hours.

Hale Vietnam *Vietnamese*

23 | 13 | 19 | $20

Kaimuki | 1140 12th Ave. (bet. Harding & Waialae Aves.) | Honolulu | 808-735-7581

"A venerable standard" with "no surprises", this Kaimuki Vietnamese offers "consistently delicious" and "efficiently" served "steaming pho", canh chua (sour soup), the "best" spring rolls and other "Southeast Asian comfort food" in an "informal" dining room with "no ambiance"; it may be "more expensive than most" of its counterparts, but it's also a "cut above" them, so it's "almost always crowded."

| | FOOD | DECOR | SERVICE | COST |

Hard Rock Cafe *American*   14 | 20 | 17 | $28

Waikiki | 1837 Kapiolani Blvd. (Kalakaua Ave.) | Honolulu | 808-955-7383 | www.hardrock.com

Even if it's a national chain, the Waikiki and Lahaina outposts "exude tropical cool" say their mostly tourist fans, who like the Oahu location's 'surf board wall of fame' and its "fantastic" "outdoor deck" that's especially "worth it" at sunset; there's the "typical" rock 'n' roll "memorabilia galore" at both, as well as merely "functional" American fare and "overpriced drinks", making critical kamaaina cry "what a cliche" – "it's not the least bit Hawaiian."

☑ Hau Tree Lanai *Pacific Rim*   21 | 27 | 22 | $47

Waikiki | New Otani Kaimana Beach Hotel | 2863 Kalakaua Ave. (Monsarrat Ave.) | Honolulu | 808-921-7066 | www.kaimana.com

"Million-dollar" ocean and sunset vistas from "beachside tables" shaded by a "grand old tree" keep diners coming back to this "subtly elegant" Waikiki hotel "hideaway" with a focus on "well-prepared" Pacific Rim seafood; it's especially popular for "family Sunday brunch", although skeptics say service can be "slow" and the "pricey" "food is never as good as the view."

Hee Hing *Chinese*   20 | 15 | 17 | $24

Kapahulu | 449 Kapahulu Ave. (bet. Date St. & Paki Ave.) | Honolulu | 808-735-5544 | www.heehinghawaii.com

"Always crowded with locals", this "reasonably priced" family-run mainstay in Kapahulu offers "tasty" dim sum and family-style Cantonese, including "imaginative" choices for both "conservative and adventurous" eaters; a smidgeon of surveyors knock the "typical Chinese"-eatery decor and worry that the eats have "taken a dive" in recent years.

☑ Helena's Hawaiian Food ⊅ *Hawaiian*   26 | 8 | 19 | $17

Kalihi | 1240 N. School St. (Houghtailing St.) | Honolulu | 808-845-8044

The late Helen Chock (a James Beard Award winner) may no longer be in the kitchen at her namesake, family-run Hawaiian "hole-in-the-wall", but "you can still feel her presence" inside the "bare-bones" Kalihi space she opened in 1946, where her grandson now mans the stoves; you can also still taste her touch in the "broke da mouth" fare, so loyalists say go "early to beat the crowds" angling for a plate of "luscious pipikaula ribs", kalua pig, laulau and "onolicious haupia"; N.B. it's BYO and cash-only.

Highway Inn *Diner*   23 | 9 | 19 | $16

Waipahu | 94-226 Leoku St. (bet. Farrington Hwy. & Waipahu St.) | 808-677-4345 | www.myhighwayinn.com

This "family-owned" Waipahu diner pleases island palates with Hawaiian specialties like "juicy" pipi kaula and beef stew, served up by a staff that "makes you feel at home"; with "great value" prices, who cares if the "decor isn't fancy" and it's "not the easiest to find"?

☑ Hiroshi Eurasion Tapas *Eurasian*   26 | 21 | 25 | $53

Restaurant Row | 500 Ala Moana Blvd. (Punchbowl St.) | Honolulu | 808-533-4476 | www.dkrestaurants.com

Chef Hiroshi Fukui's "delightfully creative tapas" featuring "local ingredients" are "small treasures of explosive taste" at this "casual-

	FOOD	DECOR	SERVICE	COST

upscale" Eurasion in Restaurant Row; though a few foes find the tabs "too expensive for the bite-sized portions", fans say "the only thing better" than the food is the wine list maintained by Chuck Furuya, "one of two master sommeliers in the state"; P.S. the quarterly "seasonal" "kaiseki dinners are a must."

Hoku's *Pacific Rim*

25 | 26 | 25 | $73

Kahala | Kahala Hotel & Resort | 5000 Kahala Ave. (Kealaolu Ave.) | Honolulu | 808-739-8780 | www.kahalaresort.com

In a "romantic" locale with "jaw-dropping" ocean views, this "insanely expensive" Pacific Rim "classic" at the Kahala Hotel is a favorite for the "freshest" seafood and an "outstanding Sunday brunch buffet"; its "impeccable", "unfailingly friendly" service also wins raves, though detractors deem the atmosphere "a little formal for Hawaii."

☒ Hula Grill Waikiki *Pacific Rim*

21 | 23 | 20 | $35

Waikiki | Outrigger Waikiki | 2335 Kalakaua Ave. (bet. Dukes Ln. & Kaiulani Ave.) | Honolulu | 808-923-4852 | www.hulagrillwaikiki.com

These "family-friendly" oceanside eateries in the Outrigger Waikiki and on Kaanapali Beach offer "fantastic views" and Pacific Rim fare showcasing "fresh seafood", "killer mai tais" and "surprisingly good" burgers, tacos and sandwiches; the Oahu location is "always a bit rowdy" with a Diamond Head backdrop and prime "people-watching", while the Maui spot boasts nightly hula.

Hy's Steak House *Steak*

25 | 22 | 25 | $62

Waikiki | Waikiki Park Heights Hotel | 2440 Kuhio Ave. (Uluniu Ave.) | Honolulu | 808-922-5555 | www.hyshawaii.com

Expect an "old-school" experience at this steakhouse in the Waikiki Park Heights Hotel where the "clubby" "library decor" is "more East Coast than Hawaii", the "waiters are in tuxedos" and the "incredible cuts of meat" are "cooked on a kiawe wood grill" and followed by "flambé desserts"; the majority lauds its "live entertainment" and "excellent service", though a few say those assets can't compensate for the "fairly expensive" tabs and "outdated" room with "no view."

Ichiriki Japanese Nabe Restaurant *Japanese*

24 | 22 | 21 | $33

Ala Moana | 510 Piikoi St. (bet. Hopaka & Kona Sts.) | Honolulu | 808-589-2299

"Diners cook at their table" using "fresh ingredients" "with a choice of broths" at this "tasteful", "authentic" "nabe-style Japanese" near Ala Moana where the "participatory preparation" makes it a "great place for small groups and couples"; enthusiasts appreciate the "good portions" and "reasonable prices", but others say the service can be "slow."

Ige's Restaurant & 19th Puka ☒ *American*

19 | 10 | 17 | $18

Aiea | 98-761 Oihana Pl. (Kaahumanu St.) | 808-486-3500 | www.igesrestaurant.com

This "laid-back" American "family restaurant" in Aiea serves up "large portions" of "plate lunch–style" shoyu pork and flap steak in an "unpretentious setting"; the "low prices" and "live bands" on "weekends" keep it "crowded", even if the "service is hit-or-miss."

	FOOD	DECOR	SERVICE	COST

I Love Country Cafe *American*

17 | 8 | 14 | $12

Ala Moana | 451 Piikoi St. (bet. Kona & Waimanu Sts.) | Honolulu | 808-596-8108

A "tantalizing variety" of "inexpensive" "local comfort food", "reasonably healthy plate lunches" and American standards are the draw at this Ala Moana purveyor of "generous portions" served "quickly"; the "fast-food"/"take-out" setting, however, wins few raves.

India Café *Indian*

19 | 11 | 17 | $21

Kapahulu | Kilohana Sq. | 1016 Kapahulu Ave. (bet. Kihei Pl. & Lincoln Ave.) | Honolulu | 808-737-4600 | www.indiacafehawaii.com

"A true hole-in-the-wall", this "impossible-to-find" eatery "tucked inside" Kapahulu's Kilohana Square sates with an "inexpensive" array of "southern-style Indian" eats heavy on the "dosai, a crêpelike bread"; though its food "has kick", the design-conscious say the space is "dull", while others lament that "service tends to be slow."

Indigo 🅂🅼 *Asian Fusion*

22 | 22 | 20 | $41

Chinatown | 1121 Nuuanu Ave. (Hotel St.) | Honolulu | 808-521-2900 | www.indigo-hawaii.com

Its "funky Chinatown location" draws a "hip, young crowd" that converges at this modern Asian fusion "hot spot" done up with "fountains, glowing lanterns, carved teak and incense"; the "unusual" tastes hit a high note in the "great pupus" and "terrific lunch buffet", though detractors say it's "better for drinks than for food" ("unique cocktails" fuel the happy-hour scene) and deem the service "inconsistent."

Island's Fine Burgers *Burgers*

18 | 17 | 17 | $18

Ala Moana | Ala Moana Ctr. | 1450 Ala Moana Blvd. (bet. Atkinson Dr. & Piikoi St.) | Honolulu | 808-943-6670 | www.islandsrestaurants.com

This "kid-friendly" Ala Moana Center branch of a West Coast chain metes out "delicious burgers, served island-style" with an "assortment of toppings" and accompanied by "huge piles of fries"; while service is "speedy", penny-pinching patrons point out that it's "expensive" for a "mall restaurant" with "mainland fare trying to masquerade as local grub."

Jameson's By The Sea *Seafood/Steak*

19 | 20 | 19 | $38

Haleiwa | 62-540 Kamehameha Hwy. (bet. Iwia Pl. & Mamao St.) | 808-637-4336 | www.jamesonshawaii.com

"Oh, the sunsets!" sigh surveyors sated by the "beautiful" ocean vistas at both halves of this "romantic", "reliable" longtime Haleiwa steak and seafooder, as well as its Kailua-Kona, Big Island, sibling; while some pooh-pooh the "expensive", "nothing-fancy" fare and "average" service, a majority doesn't mind "paying for the view."

Kaka'ako Kitchen *Hawaiian*

21 | 9 | 13 | $14

Ward | Ward Ctr. | 1200 Ala Moana Blvd. (Kamakee St.) | Honolulu | 808-594-3663

This "counter-service", "carry-out" (with limited terrace seating) "plate-lunch place on steroids" is a Ward Centre "standard bearer", serving "high-quality" Hawaiian "classics" plus some "fancier stuff, like a fish of the day"; even naysayers who claim the "quality and quantity have diminished" admit it's a "good value."

	FOOD	DECOR	SERVICE	COST

Keo's in Waikiki *Thai*
21 | 20 | 20 | $34

Waikiki | 2028 Kuhio Ave. (bet. Keoniana & Kuamoo Sts.) | Honolulu | 808-951-9355 | www.keosthaicuisine.com

A 25-year-old "island favorite", this Waikiki entry in Keo Sananikone's Siamese food empire pulls in crowds of locals and tourists for its signature "Evil Jungle Prince" entree and more standard standbys like "superb spring rolls" served by a "well-informed" staff; most surveyors are charmed by the "exotic", "tropical flower"–filled interior that resembles a "Thai antiques shop", yet a few longtimers feel it's "fallen slightly off its peak."

Kincaid's Fish, Chop & Steak House ● *Seafood/Steak*
20 | 19 | 20 | $37

Ward | Ward Warehouse | 1240 Ala Moana Blvd. (Ward Ave.) | Honolulu | 808-591-2005

"Overlooking Kewalo Basin", this "affordable" chain link in Ward Warehouse offers "consistently good", if "predictable", midpriced steaks and "fresh fish", followed by an "excellent dessert" selection; despite what some deem to be "dated decor" and sometimes "erratic service", it's popular for "business lunches" during the day and happy hour as night sets in.

Kirin Restaurant *Chinese*
24 | 16 | 19 | $35

Ala Moana | Ala Moana Ctr. | 1450 Ala Moana Blvd. (bet. Atkinson Dr. & Piikoi St.) | Honolulu | 808-946-1888

"Hong Kong–style dim sum" and "upscale Chinese" plates converge at this Ala Moana Center spot where enthusiasts find a menu of "excellent", "imaginative", "up-to-date" eats; a few detractors, however, can't see past the bill ("overpriced for the food and service") and the "uninviting", "palatial" interior.

Kobe Japanese Steak House & Sushi Bar *Japanese*
22 | 18 | 21 | $42

Waikiki | 1841 Ala Moana Blvd. (Kalia Rd.) | Honolulu | 808-941-4444 | www.honolulukobe.com

"Knife-tossing" toques "put on a show" at these "communal" teppan tables in Waikiki and Lahaina, Maui, that also boast "solid" sushi bars; the teppanyaki is "reliable" and kids "enjoy the action" (even if "some chefs are more entertaining than others"), but many say the "cavelike" quarters "need an update."

Kochi ● *Japanese*
∇ 18 | 15 | 17 | $23

Moiliili | 1936 S. King St. (bet. Artesian & McCully Sts.) | Honolulu | 808-941-2835

"Lounge meets restaurant" at this Moiliili Japanese where "local-style" dishes such as "misoyaki chicken" that "can't be beat" are "designed for sharing"; a "friendly" vibe and a "full bar" with "many TVs" are pluses, but some critics find the menu "strange" and feel the kitchen "hasn't found its stroke yet."

Kona Brewing Co. *American*
18 | 18 | 18 | $25

Hawaii Kai | Koko Marina Ctr. | 7192 Kalanianaole Hwy. (Lunalilo Home Rd.) | Honolulu | 808-394-5662 | www.konabrewingco.com
See review in Big Island Dining Directory.

Kozo Sushi *Japanese* | 17 | 9 | 15 | $13

Aiea | Pearlridge Ctr. Downtown | 98 Moanalua Rd. (Kamehameha Hwy.) | 808-483-6805
Kahala | Kahala Mall | 4211 Waialae Ave. (Hunakai St.) | Honolulu | 808-738-5696
Kapahulu | 625 Kapahulu Ave. (Mooheau St.) | Honolulu | 808-739-2785
Moiliili | 2334 S. King St. (bet. Hoawa Ln. & Isenberg St.) | Honolulu | 808-951-5696
NEW **Pearl City** | 1029 Makolu St. (Kuala Rd.) | 808-455-6805
www.kozosushihawaii.net

A popular spot for "party platters" or a "quick grab-and-go lunch", this "standard take-out" sushi chain offers the "usual choice" of raw fin fare that's "always fresh", even if some say it's "not top quality"; malcontents malign it as a maki "McDonald's", but the "fast-food" setting notwithstanding, it's one of the "best values around."

Kua 'Aina Sandwich *Burgers/Sandwiches* | 22 | 12 | 14 | $12

Haleiwa | 66-160 Kamehameha Hwy. (Haleiwa Rd.) | 808-637-6067
Ward | Ward Ctr. | 1200 Ala Moana Blvd. (Kamakee St.) | Honolulu | 808-591-9133

"Get your sandwich fix" at one of these "local Oahu favorites" (the tiny North Shore flagship is in Haleiwa) where "juicy" "oversized burgers" "cooked how you like them" and "topped high" with an "array" of ingredients plus "crispy" "shoestring fries" draw "thick crowds"; ignore the "attitude behind the counter" and the "somewhat faceless" look of the Ward Centre branch, and it'll be "worth the wait."

Kyoto Ohsho *Japanese* | 18 | 17 | 16 | $28

Ala Moana | Ala Moana Ctr. | 1450 Ala Moana Blvd. (bet. Atkinson Dr. & Piikoi St.) | Honolulu | 808-949-0040

The *teishoku* (meal sets) are "reasonably priced" at this contemporary Japanese on the top floor of Ala Moana Center that serves "satisfying" portions of "quality sashimi" and other "fresh, tasty" fare; but others find "nothing extraordinary", citing "mediocre" service and lackluster decor.

La Mer *French* | 27 | 28 | 28 | $96

Waikiki | Halekulani | 2199 Kalia Rd. (Lewers St.) | Honolulu | 808-923-2311 | www.halekulani.com

The No. 1 Decor and Service on Oahu are found at this "remarkable" New French "indulgence" in Waikiki's "famed Halekulani hotel", a "tasteful" room filled with "elegant Asian art", tables facing the "moonlit beach" and "exceptional" staffers who "treat you like royalty"; "world-class" chef Yves Garnier creates "flavors that will linger in your mind's eye forever", and while it's "frighteningly expensive", an "evening in paradise" "isn't supposed to be economical"; N.B. long-sleeve collared shirt or jacket required for gentlemen.

L&L Drive-Inn *BBQ/Hawaiian* | 16 | 6 | 12 | $10

Diamond Head | 3045 Monsarrat Ave. (bet. Kanaina & Leahi Aves.) | Honolulu | 808-735-1388
Downtown | 1111B Fort St. Mall (S. Hotel St.) | Honolulu | 808-521-8891
Kahala | 4618 Kilauea Ave. (Pahoa Ave.) | Honolulu | 808-732-4042
Mililani | 94-780 Meheula Pkwy. (Hokuahiahi St.) | 808-623-8886
Pearl Harbor | 427 Makalapa Dr. (Halawa Dr.) | 808-423-8885
Waikiki | 2280 Kuhio Ave. (bet. Nohonani St. & Seaside Ave.) | Honolulu | 808-924-7888

(continued)

L&L Drive-Inn

Ward | 1050 Ala Moana Blvd. (Ward Ave.) | Honolulu | 808-597-8878 ⊘
Ward | Ward Entertainment Ctr. | 310 Kamakee St. (bet. Auahi &
Queen Sts.) | Honolulu | 808-597-9088 ⊘
www.hawaiianbarbecue.com
Additional locations throughout Oahu

A "Hawaii institution", this "ubiquitous" statewide chain is "popular"
because its "traditional" plate lunches and local barbecue are "tasty",
"generously portioned" and cost "almost nothing"; "service varies
from location to location" and the decor generates almost "zero interest", but for "quick" takeout, you really "can't go wrong."

☑ Le Bistro   *French*

27 | 20 | 24 | $54

Niu Valley | Niu Valley Shopping Ctr. | 5730 Kalanianaole Hwy.
(Halemaumau St.) | Honolulu | 808-373-7990

Reaching "levels unheard of in a neighborhood restaurant", this "quaint"
bistro nearly "hidden in Niu Valley" Shopping Center is "always
crowded" with "locals" cooing over the "glorious" French fare; the
"sunny yellow" digs are just as "warm" as the "knowledgeable staff",
and though it's "a little pricey", "large portions justify" it.

Legend Seafood   *Chinese*

23 | 13 | 15 | $25

Chinatown | Chinese Cultural Plaza | 100 N. Beretania St. (Maunakea St.) |
Honolulu | 808-532-1868

"Decent dinner" is available, but dim sum for breakfast and lunch is
the real "claim to fame" of this "Hong Kong–style" Chinatown Chinese
where "carts laden with every type of delicious" dumpling imaginable
"zip around" to the delight of "bargain"-happy diners; "go early", especially on weekends, because the "bare-bones banquet hall" "gets
full" and "noisy."

Lei Lei's   *Pacific Rim*

▽ 22 | 20 | 22 | $32

Kahuku | Turtle Bay Resort | 57-091 Kamehameha Hwy. (Kuilima Dr.) |
808-293-2662

Set "on the golf course at Turtle Bay Resort", this all-day Kahuku grill
offers "tasty" Pacific Rim–accented seafood and steaks in a "casual",
"pleasant" atmosphere; "sit on the patio" for a "quick bite" with the
kids or join the "flirting" adults at the "entertaining" bar while indulg-
ing in mai tais that "will send you reeling."

Little Village Noodle House   *Chinese*

23 | 17 | 19 | $22

Chinatown | 1113 Smith St. (N. Hotel St.) | Honolulu | 808-545-3008 |
www.littlevillagehawaii.com

"A gem in the heart of Chinatown", this "comfortable" Chinese BYO
offers a "large menu" of "affordable" "family-style" dishes that exhibit
"more individuality" than others of its ilk (everyone "raves" about the
"wonderful honey walnut shrimp"); it's "always packed" and there's
often a "long wait" to get in, "but once you're seated", service is usually "quick" and "efficient."

Longhi's   *Italian*

20 | 20 | 20 | $45

Ala Moana | Ala Moana Ctr. | 1450 Ala Moana Blvd. (bet. Atkinson Dr. &
Piikoi St.) | Honolulu | 808-947-9899 | www.longhis.com
See review in Maui Dining Directory.

Lucy's Grill 'N Bar *Eclectic*

| 18 | 17 | 17 | $38 |

Kailua | 33 Aulike St. (bet. Kuulei Rd. & Uluniu St) | 808-230-8188 | www.lucysgrillnbar.com

A neighborhood restaurant with a "lively bar scene", this eclectic Kailua eatery offers "new tastes and presentations for classic favorites", like the popular "ahi tower", "smoky" "grilled Caesar salad" and "exceptional apple crisp"; fans love the "unique flavors", "local" touches and casual "beach bar" feel, but critics bemoan sketchy service and "loud music that can drown out conversations."

NEW MAC 24/7 ◐ *American*

| 19 | 20 | 17 | $24 |

Waikiki | Hilton Waikiki Prince Kuhio | 2500 Kuhio Ave. (Liliuokalani Ave.) | Honolulu | 808-921-5564 | www.mac247hawaii.com

Insiders "dare you" to order the "Viking-sized pancakes" at this "hip" take on a 24/7 diner in the Hilton Waikiki Prince Kuhio, where all of the "new-wave comfort food" (the name is an acronym for Modern American Cuisine) comes in "humongous" portions; though the tabs offer "value" for Oahu, the "service is hit-or-miss."

Makino Chaya *Japanese*

| 14 | 10 | 12 | $31 |

Aiea | Westridge Shopping Ctr. | 98-150 Kaonohi St. (Moanalua Loop) | 808-486-5100

Chinatown | Aloha Tower Mktpl. | 1 Aloha Tower Dr. (Fort St.) | Honolulu | 808-585-6360

Popular for its "huge" "seafood buffet", this Japanese duo in Aiea and Chinatown offers a "plentiful" "Asian smorgasbord" highlighted by sushi, sashimi, crab legs, lobster and steak in a "noisy" "cafeteria-style" setting; while fans find it "quite a bargain", detractors declare the service "poor" and complain that the emphasis is "quantity, not quality", contending it's "gone downhill since it first opened."

Mariposa *American*

| 22 | 24 | 23 | $43 |

Ala Moana | Neiman Marcus, Ala Moana Ctr. | 1450 Ala Moana Blvd. (bet. Atkinson Dr. & Piikoi St.) | Honolulu | 808-951-3420 | www.neimanmarcus.com

"Dreamy ocean views", especially from the "pretty" lanai, set the scene at this "airy, high-ceilinged" Neiman Marcus eatery in Ala Moana Center, where "chic shoppers" stop for "artfully presented" New American lunches that begin with "wonderful popovers"; the "attentive" staff "handles the bustling crowd with aplomb", and while it's "on the expensive side", it's "worthwhile"; P.S. it's "open for dinner" too.

Matsumoto's Shave Ice *Dessert*

| 24 | 11 | 17 | $6 |

Haleiwa | 66-087 Kamehameha Hwy. (bet. Haleiwa & Opaeula Rds.) | 808-637-4827 | www.matsumotoshaveice.com

You "can't go to the North Shore without stopping" at this "legendary" Haleiwa "mecca of shave ice" in a "general store", where the "fluffy" "mounds" are flavored from "a rainbow" of syrups, with the optional "surprise of sweetened azuki beans and ice cream" underneath; voted the Best Buy on Oahu, it often has "long lines", so "bring a book" and "know what you want" when you get to the counter.

Maui Tacos *Mexican*

| 19 | 9 | 15 | $12 |

Mililani | Mililani Shopping Ctr. | 95-221 Kipapa Dr. (Kuahelani Ave.) | 808-623-9405

(continued)

Maui Tacos

NEW Waikiki | Royal Hawaiian Ctr. | 2233 Kalakaua Ave.
(Royal Hawaiian Ave.) | Honolulu | 808-931-6111
www.mauitacos.com

See review in Maui Dining Directory.

Mediterraneo Ⓢ *Italian*   21 | 15 | 19 | $31

Makiki | 1279 S. King St. (bet. Akala Ln. & Akoko St.) | Honolulu |
808-593-1466

"Huge, hot plates of delicious pasta" and other "heavenly Italian food"
are the draws at this midpriced Makiki eatery; when not at the stove,
the "fetchingly eccentric" chef-owner "wanders through" the dining
room "greeting patrons", adding brio to the "modest setting."

Mei Sum Dim Sum *Chinese*   21 | 7 | 13 | $17

Chinatown | 65 N. Pauahi St. (bet. Maunakea & Smith Sts.) | Honolulu |
808-531-3268

"Inexpensive, delicious dim sum" "served from steaming rolling carts"
keeps this "no-frills" Chinatown Chinese "always crowded" at lunchtime (it's a "good stop for dinner before the theater" too); things move
"fast", so don't be surprised by "nasty looks" if you try to "linger" –
"they've got tables to turn!"

Mekong Thai I *Thai*   25 | 15 | 19 | $24

Moiliili | 1295 S. Beretania St. (bet. Keeaumoku & Piikoi Sts.) | Honolulu |
808-591-8842

Mekong Thai II *Thai*

Ala Moana | 1726 S. King St. (bet. Elsle & Pawaa Lns.) | Honolulu |
808-941-6184

"No-frills, just-satisfying", "scrumptious Thai" at "reasonable prices"
keeps regulars returning "again and again" to these "casual" Moiliili
and Ala Moana "standbys" "related to the famous" Keo's in Waikiki;
the "tiny" "Mekong I is BYOB" ("a real plus"), while the "King Street location is larger", but both employ "well-trained" staffers.

Mermaid Bar *American*   ▽ 21 | 17 | 16 | $21

Ala Moana | Neiman Marcus, Ala Moana Ctr. | 1450 Ala Moana Blvd.
(bet. Atkinson Dr. & Piikoi St.) | Honolulu | 808-951-3428

"Upscale" Ala Moana shoppers go "casual" at this lunchtime "respite"
in Neiman Marcus, serving "fresh salads, sandwiches" and larger
American plates; it's "not very spacious" and there's "no view", but if
you're just in need of "fast" sustenance, it's "less expensive" and "formal" than other nearby options.

Ⓩ Michel's *French*   25 | 26 | 26 | $76

Waikiki | Colony Surf Hotel | 2895 Kalakaua Ave. (Poni Moi Rd.) |
Honolulu | 808-923-6552 | www.michelshawaii.com

"Old-style" "sophistication" thrives at this "ritzy", "romantic" "on the
beach" at the Colony Surf Hotel, where a "guitarist serenades" while
the "impeccable", "tuxedoed" staff serves "superb" Classic French
fare, some with "tableside preparations"; everyone's "tempted" to
"dine early" to catch the "gorgeous sunset" from the terrace, but the
"fabulous" after-dark "lights of Waikiki" are equally "worth skipping
your next mortgage payment" for.

	FOOD	DECOR	SERVICE	COST

Morton's The Steakhouse *Steak*   25 | 22 | 25 | $70
Ala Moana | Ala Moana Ctr. | 1450 Ala Moana Blvd. (bet. Atkinson Dr. & Piikoi St.) | Honolulu | 808-949-1300 | www.mortons.com
Beef-seekers believe this mainland chophouse chain's "formula" of "big, robust" and "expensive" steaks coupled with "melt-in-your-mouth sides" and "exceptional service" is a "winner" in Ala Moana Center too; however, they don't agree on the "dark" "gentlemen's-clublike", "no-view" setting that seems "out of place in Honolulu."

Mr. Ojisan 🗷 *Japanese*   22 | 14 | 20 | $23
Kapahulu | Kilohana Sq. | 1018 Kapahulu Ave. (Kihei Pl.) | Honolulu | 808-735-4455 | www.mrojisan.com
Tucked away in Kilohana Square in Kapahulu, this "endearing" "neighborhood" izakaya is a "local gem" serving innovative Japanese small plates such as the "sizzling" *wafu* steak, as well as larger "traditional" dishes (try the "wonderful homemade ramen"); fans further praise the "friendly service", but a few find it "on the pricey side"; P.S. "reservations are recommended."

Nick's Fishmarket *Seafood*   22 | 20 | 23 | $59
Waikiki | Waikiki Gateway Hotel | 2070 Kalakaua Ave. (bet. Kuhio Ave. & Olohana St.) | Honolulu | 808-955-6333 | www.nicksfishmarket.com
A local "landmark", this seafooder in the Waikiki Gateway Hotel features "super-fresh" "local fish" and "excellent wines" served by an "old-school" staff "in tuxes" in a space that's a "throwback to the '70s"; still, some argue it's "not worth the cost" given a few critics say the "faded" room "feels like a tomb."

Nico's at Pier 38 🗷 *Seafood*   23 | 11 | 15 | $15
Iwilei | Pier 38 | 1133 N. Nimitz Hwy. (Alakawa St.) | Honolulu | 808-540-1377 | www.nicospier38.com
Just "steps from the fish auction", this "onolicious" "gourmet plate lunch" spot "crowded with friendly locals" in Iwilei's "harbor district" is known for seafood "so fresh it might swim off your plate", including the signature "furikake-crusted ahi"; the "takeaway paper plates" and alfresco seating with a view of the "working docks" aren't fancy, but there "aren't many tourists present" and the "bargain prices" for "breakfast, lunch and early dinner" make it "hard to get a table."

🆉 NEW Nobu Waikiki *Japanese*   26 | 25 | 25 | $80
Waikiki | Waikiki Parc Hotel | 2233 Helumoa Rd. (Lewers St.) | Honolulu | 808-237-6999 | www.noburestaurants.com
Sample "ambrosial" Japanese fusion in the Waikiki Parc Hotel at this "stylish" outpost of Nobu Matsuhisa's restaurant empire, where diners on "an all-out splurge" dig into "amazing" "edible art" and cry "wow!"; even though a few find the room "raucous" and the "innovative" menu too "complicated", the staff is "more than happy to recommend" one of the "mouthwatering" selections, including sushi, and suggest a "lovely pairing of sake" to boot.

Oceanarium *American/Seafood*   17 | 23 | 18 | $35
Waikiki | Pacific Beach Hotel | 2490 Kalakaua Ave. (Liliuokalani Ave.) | Honolulu | 808-921-6111 | www.pacificbeachhotel.com
Diners say "it's like eating inside a lagoon" at this seafood restaurant with a "gorgeous", "floor-to-ceiling aquarium" in Waikiki's Pacific

Beach Hotel, where a "mix of locals and tourists chow down on the treasures of the sea"; the "family-friendly" American buffet (including a "pasta station" and sushi) is a "real bargain" and the service is "decent", but a portion of patrons proclaim the scenery "definitely better" than the "mediocre" fare.

Ocean House *Pacific Rim/Seafood*   23 | 24 | 24 | $46

Waikiki | Outrigger Reef on the Beach | 2169 Kalia Rd. (Saratoga Rd.) | Honolulu | 808-923-2277 | www.outriggerreef-onthebeach.com

Set on a "gorgeous", "uncrowded section of Waikiki Beach", this open-air Pacific Rimmer at the Outrigger Reef hotel boasts "elegant, vintage Hawaii decor", the kind of "warm" service "you'd expect from a much more expensive restaurant" and lots of "fresh local fish"; P.S. it "books up fast", so "get there early" to enjoy the "wonderful sunset."

Okonomiyaki Chibo *Japanese*   ▽ 21 | 17 | 20 | $29

Waikiki | Royal Hawaiian Ctr. | 2201 Kalakaua Ave. (Lewers St.) | Honolulu | 808-922-9722

This local link of an Osaka-based Japanese chain housed in Waikiki's Royal Hawaiian Center showcases "genuine" *okonomiyaki* (savory pancakes) and "affordable" teppanyaki "for the common man", which are prepared in front of customers; fans applaud the "excellent" service, and while some find the space a bit "dark", purists say the "authentic" experience is "as close to being in Japan as you can get."

Ola *Hawaii Reg.*   21 | 25 | 19 | $41

Kahuku | Turtle Bay Resort | 57-091 Kamehameha Hwy. (Kuilima Dr.) | 808-293-0801 | www.olaislife.com

Set on a "beautiful" beach at the Turtle Bay Resort ("ask for a waterside table"), this "casual" yet "charming" North Shore Hawaii Regional earns accolades for its "superb view" and solid "eclectic menu" accompanied by "drinks done well"; even though a few fret over "uneven" service and claim the "pricey" fare "doesn't measure up to the location", at least you can "eat with your feet in the sand."

Olive Tree Café ⊄ *Greek*   24 | 10 | 13 | $18

Kahala | 4614 Kilauea Ave. (Pahoa Ave.) | Honolulu | 808-737-0303

"Be prepared to stand in line" with "jostling crowds" at this "laid-back" Kahala Greek cafe where you "order at the counter" from a menu of "perfectly seasoned dishes" like souvlaki, hummus, baba ghanoush, stuffed grape leaves and "outrageous falafel" plus "soul-warming pita bread"; reviewers love the "fresh flavors" and "reasonable prices", but because the "service is sometimes slow" and the tables "crowded", regulars recommend "ordering ahead."

Ono Hawaiian Foods ⊠⊄ *Hawaiian*   25 | 10 | 19 | $17

Kapahulu | 726 Kapahulu Ave. (Hunter St.) | Honolulu | 808-737-2275

An "institution" for "Hawaiian-style soul food", this Kapahulu "dive" "littered with autographed celebrity photos" is "where local residents and adventurous tourists" come for "gigantic portions" of "laulau, kalua pig, pipi kaula, lomi lomi salmon, chicken long rice, poi, haupia and poke" served on "classic cafeteria plastic dishware"; be warned that it's "a zoo at meal hours", so "go early or deal with the line."

	FOOD	DECOR	SERVICE	COST

☒ Orchids *Pacific Rim* | 26 | 28 | 27 | $65 |

Waikiki | Halekulani | 2199 Kalia Rd. (Lewers St.) | Honolulu | 808-923-2311 | www.halekulani.com

The Halekulani's "elegant" "oceanfront" Pacific Rim restaurant in Waikiki, appropriately decorated with the namesake flower, is "worth the splurge", especially for its "legendary Sunday brunch" (don't miss the "famous coconut cake") and "fabulous views of Diamond Head"; the "fantastic" service, "relaxing" vibe and "prix fixe lunch" also win praise, though many save dinner here for "special occasions only."

Original Pancake House, The *Diner* | 21 | 11 | 18 | $15 |

Ala Moana | 1221 Kapiolani Blvd. (Pensacola St.) | Honolulu | 808-596-8213
Kapalama | Waikamilo Shopping Plaza | 1414 Dillingham Blvd. (Waiakamilo Rd.) | Honolulu | 808-847-1496
www.originalpancakehouse.com

"Before starting on an activity-filled day", fuel up on "copious portions" of "oh-so-good pancakes", "fluffy omelets" and other "hearty breakfast" fare at one of the two Oahu locations of this coffee shop/diner national chain; "cheap" prices mean "lines are commonplace", especially on weekends, but the "friendly" servers set a "quick" pace.

Outback Steakhouse *Steak* | 16 | 15 | 17 | $32 |

Hawaii Kai | 6650 Kalanianaole Hwy. (Keahole St.) | Honolulu | 808-396-7576
Kapolei | 302 Kamokila Blvd. (bet. Kalaeloa Blvd. & Uluohia St.) | 808-674-1300
Waikiki | 1765 Ala Moana Blvd. (Hobron Ln.) | Honolulu | 808-951-6274
Waipahu | 94-810 Ukee St. (Oil Loop) | 808-671-7200
www.outback.com

"Homesick" mainlanders who frequent this chain find "pretty much the same" experience here, namely "large portions" of "reasonably priced" steaks and other "average food" in "laid-back" settings bedecked with "Aussie decor"; locals, however, are incredulous: why "come all the way to Hawaii" and not try as "many unique local places" as you can?

Pacific Place Tea Garden Café *Tearoom* | - | - | - | I |

Ala Moana | Ala Moana Ctr. | 1450 Ala Moana Blvd. (bet. Atkinson Dr. & Piikoi St.) | Honolulu | 808-944-2004 | www.pacific-place.com

"Not a real cafe" per se, this "casual", "oversized drink stand on the top floor" of Ala Moana Center is a place to explore an "excellent tea selection" in the midst of shopping; the sit-down service is by reservation-only, and though it does include light bites (like tasty macaroons), "it's definitely not enough to fill up" on.

Paesano *Italian* | 21 | 17 | 21 | $32 |

NEW **Aiea** | 98-1277 Kaahumanu St. (bet. Kamehameha Hwy. & Moanalua Rd.) | 808-485-8883
Manoa | Manoa Mktpl. | 2752 Woodlawn Dr. (Manoa Rd.) | Honolulu | 808-988-5923

These two "neighborhood" spots are "excellent values" for "simple", "plentiful" portions of Italian "red-sauce" classics; groups of friends appreciate the "deep wine lists" and "terrific service", but daters take issue with the Manoa location's "noise" and tables that are "too close together"; P.S. the newer Aiea branch has become a "go-to for lunch or dinner."

	FOOD	DECOR	SERVICE	COST

Pagoda Floating Restaurant *Eclectic* 16 | 17 | 17 | $31

Ala Moana | Pagoda Hotel | 1525 Rycroft St. (Keeaumoku St.) | Honolulu | 808-948-8356 | www.pagodahotel.com

Located in the somewhat "out-of-the-way" Pagoda Hotel in the Ala Moana area, this Eclectic breakfast and dinner buffet is "popular with local" families because not only can you "eat all you want" for a "reasonable price", but "kids love" the waterfalls, koi ponds ("stay for the feedings") and other "over-the-top" design elements that "surround" the dining room; so what if the food's merely "mediocre"?

Pah Ke's Chinese Restaurant *Chinese* 23 | 11 | 20 | $23

Kaneohe | 46-018 Kamehameha Hwy. (bet. Kahuhipa & Mehana Sts.) | 808-235-4505

"People from all over" Oahu come to this "friendly" Kaneohe "neighborhood gem" for its "extensive menu" of "reasonably priced", "family-style" "Chinese food with delicious twists" that border on the "innovative"; the "noisy room", on the other hand, is "old and tired."

NEW Panya Bistro *French/Japanese* 17 | 17 | 15 | $22

Ala Moana | Ala Moana Ctr. | 1450 Ala Moana Blvd. (bet. Atkinson Dr. & Piikoi St.) | Honolulu | 808-946-6388

Located in Ala Moana Center, this "small", "funky-art"-bedecked French-Japanese bakery/bistro proffers a "limited menu" of mid-shopping pick-me-ups like "filling noodle dishes", soups and sandwiches; but detractors "won't shell out for a meal" here because they think the "pricey-for-what-you-get" "menu sounds more interesting than it is", opting instead to grab some "fresh bread" and "yummy" pastries to go.

Pavilion Café ⑤Ⓜ *Mediterranean* ▽ 21 | 21 | 21 | $23

Ala Moana | Honolulu Academy of Arts | 900 S. Beretania St. (Beretania St.) | Honolulu | 808-532-8734 | www.honoluluacademy.org

The "lovely" environs in a "shaded courtyard" at the Honolulu Academy of Arts in the Ala Moana area near Downtown "relaxes" museum-goers at this "small" lunch-only cafe, while "reasonably priced" "fresh and consistently delicious" Mediterranean cuisine with Asian accents refreshes them; P.S. "reservations are a must" since this "popular" spot is often "hard to get into."

People's Café ⑤ *Hawaiian* ▽ 21 | 7 | 16 | $19

Downtown | 1300 Pali Hwy. (bet. S. Kukui St. & S. Vineyard Blvd.) | Honolulu | 808-536-5789

Fans applaud this casual Downtown "neighborhood" spot for its "authentic and tasty" Hawaiian eats (laulau, kalua pig, chicken long rice), "laid-back" service and cheap checks; they sit on their hands, however, for the "very downscale setting."

P.F. Chang's China Bistro *Chinese* 19 | 21 | 20 | $33

NEW Waikiki | Royal Hawaiian Ctr. | 2001 Kalakaua Ave. (Lewers St.) | Honolulu | 808-628-6760
Ward | Hokua Towers | 1288 Ala Moana Blvd. (bet. Auahi & Piikoi Sts.) | Honolulu | 808-596-4710
www.pfchangshawaii.com

"Even though it's a mainland chain" and its Chinese fare is "clearly not authentic", most critics "can't help but like" these Ward and Waikiki

	FOOD	DECOR	SERVICE	COST

outposts with "generous servings" of "reasonably priced" fare; since the "friendly" servers are "accommodating to groups", the "contemporary environs" always buzz with the "chatter of a lively crowd."

Phuket Thai *Thai*   25 | 18 | 20 | $24

McCully | McCully Shopping Ctr. | 1960 Kapiolani Blvd. (bet. McCully & Pumehana Sts.) | Honolulu | 808-942-8194
Mililani | Mililani Town Ctr. | 95-1249 Meheula Pkwy. (Lanikuhana Ave.) | Honolulu | 808-623-6228
NEW Ward | 401 Kamakee St. (Queen St.) | Honolulu | 808-591-8421
www.phuketthaihawaii.com

"Value"-hunters "can't believe how inexpensive" the "tasty Thai" is at these eateries where "accommodating" staffers customize items to the "desired degree of hotness" ("spicy" meals are best cooled down by the "amazing" sticky-rice ice cream); the McCully original is "small" but "pleasant" enough, the Mililani iteration is a bit bigger, while the "newish location near Ward" is "spacious" and "sleek."

Pineapple Room *Hawaii Reg.*   25 | 19 | 23 | $39

Ala Moana | Macy's, Ala Moana Ctr. | 1450 Ala Moana Blvd. (bet. Atkinson Dr. & Piikoi St.) | Honolulu | 808-945-6573 | www.alanwongs.com

You "can't go wrong" with this "innovative" Hawaii Regional "pleaser" via Alan Wong that's "embedded" in the Ala Moana Center Macy's, where you can enjoy the "expert" chef's "gustatory delights" at "half" the price of his namesake flagship; a "lovely wine list" helps to make the "cleanly elegant dining room" "fine for dinner", but "marathon shoppers" say it's "best for lunch."

Planet Hollywood *Californian*   12 | 18 | 14 | $29

Waikiki | ANA Kalakaua Ctr. | 2155 Kalakaua Ave. (Beachwalk) | Honolulu | 808-924-7877 | www.planethollywood.com

Film buffs find it's "worth going at least once" to see the "actual movie props" strewn around this "loud, crowded" "tourist trap" chain outpost in Waikiki; as far as the Californian fare goes, well, "don't experiment with anything fancy" and you should be "ok."

Plantation Café *American*   ▽ 17 | 15 | 16 | $30

Ala Moana | Ala Moana Hotel | 410 Atkinson Dr. (bet. Ala Moana & Kapiolani Blvds.) | Honolulu | 808-955-4811

Take your "shorts-and-jeans"-wearing family for a "quick", "relatively inexpensive" breakfast at this Ala Moana morning hotel buffet featuring a "variety" of American fare, "omelet and carving stations" and an "array of desserts"; it's "not exceptional", but you'll probably find "nothing to complain about" - except maybe the "stuck-in-the-'70s" "faux-island" decor.

Prince Court *American/Pacific Rim*   23 | 21 | 23 | $51

Waikiki | Hawaii Prince Hotel Waikiki | 100 Holomoana St. (Ala Moana Blvd.) | Honolulu | 808-944-4494 | www.hawaiiprincehotel.com

With branches in both the Maui Prince Hotel and the Hawaii Prince in Waikiki, these American–Pacific Rim eateries are most famous for their "international" "upscale buffets, with entreelike offerings", plus "crab legs, poke, sashimi, tempura, prime rib, made-to-order hand rolls and a wonderful dessert selection"; fans say the staff is "surpris-

	FOOD	DECOR	SERVICE	COST

ingly attentive for a buffet" and the "fabulous Sunday brunch" is definitely "worth the high price."

Rokkaku 🗷 Japanese — ▽ 24 | 24 | 23 | $57

Ala Moana | Ala Moana Ctr. | 1450 Ala Moana Blvd. (bet. Atkinson Dr. & Piikoi St.) | Honolulu | 808-946-3355

An "elegant" "oasis" in the Ala Moana Center, this "high-quality" Japanese is a popular stop for "tourists from Japan" thanks to its "subtly contemporary" takes on "authentic Kyoto-style" cuisine, including the "excellent" kamameshi, as well as the "spectacular" sake selection; the "stylish" decor and "attentive" service also win praise, but walletwatchers wail over the prices.

Romano's Macaroni Grill ⊅ Italian — 18 | 18 | 18 | $27

Ala Moana | Ala Moana Ctr. | 1450 Ala Moana Blvd. (bet. Atkinson Dr. & Piikoi St.) | Honolulu | 808-356-8300 | www.macaronigrill.com

"An all-time family favorite" that's "a great small group venue", the Ala Moana Center location of this midpriced nationwide chain serves "consistent" "Italian food for the masses" in a "casual setting"; supporters like the "crayons and draw-on tabletops" for kids, "operatic music" and "ample portions", but detractors say the "food is salty", the servers are "aggressively friendly" and the "wait can be torturous"; N.B. a second branch is scheduled to open in the Big Island's Waikoloa Beach Resort's King's Shops.

Round Table Pizza Pizza — 18 | 10 | 14 | $18

Kailua | 1020 Keolu Dr. (bet. Hele & Hui Sts.) | 808-261-4644
Waikiki | Ohana East Hotel | 150 Kaiulani Ave. (bet. Kalakaua & Kuhio Aves.) | Honolulu | 808-944-1199 ●
Waikiki | Hilton Hawaiian Vill. | 2005 Kalia Rd. (Ala Moana Blvd.) | Honolulu | 808-955-0137 ●
NEW Waikiki | Waikiki Beach Walk | 227 Lewers St. (bet. Helumoa Rd. & Kalakaua Ave.) | Honolulu | 808-923-2100 ●
www.roundtablepizza.com
See review in Maui Dining Directory.

🗷 Roy's Hawaii Reg. — 26 | 22 | 24 | $54

Hawaii Kai | 6600 Kalanianaole Hwy. (Keahole St.) | Honolulu | 808-396-7697
Kapolei | Ko Olina Resort & Marina | 92-1220 Aliinui Dr. (Kamoana Pl.) | 808-676-7697
NEW Waikiki | Waikiki Beach Walk | 226 Lewers St. (Helumoa Rd.) | Honolulu | 808-923-7697
www.roysrestaurant.com

They are "absolutely the best" gush groupies who vote chef Roy Yamaguchi's namesake Hawaii Regional eateries the state's Most Popular; it's a "bit of a drive" to the 20-year-old Hawaii Kai original, but the latest branch on Beach Walk boasts the same "outstanding" fare, and the Poipu outpost was voted No. 1 for Food on Kauai; "nothing compares" to his melting hot chocolate soufflé and most fans love the "lively" settings, but a "disappointed" handful complains of "rushed service" and "lost excitement."

Ruby Tuesday American — 15 | 15 | 15 | $22

Ala Moana | Ala Moana Ctr. | 1450 Ala Moana Blvd. (bet. Atkinson Dr. & Piikoi St.) | Honolulu | 808-943-2525

(continued)

(continued)

Ruby Tuesday

Mililani | Town Center Of Mililani | 95-1249 Meheula Pkwy. (bet. Lanikuhana Ave. & Makaimoimo St.) | 808-623-4949
Moanalua | Moanalua Ctr. | 930 Valkenburgh St. (Bougainville Dr.) | Honolulu | 808-422-8585
www.rubytuesday.com

"If you're looking for good burgers", a "fresh", "quality salad bar" and American standards, this "child-friendly" chain with three Oahu branches is a reliable choice; diners like the "friendly staff", "casual" feel and "local sports collectibles scattered throughout", but critics say "it's nothing special and expensive for what you get."

☑ Ruth's Chris Steak House *Steak*   `25` `22` `23` `$65`

Restaurant Row | 500 Ala Moana Blvd. (bet. Punchbowl & South Sts.) | Honolulu | 808-887-0800
NEW Waikiki | Waikiki Beach Walk | 226 Lewers St. (Helumoa Rd.) | Honolulu | 808-440-7910
www.ruthschris.com

To satisfy your "moo craving", head to an outpost of this "ultimate" beef chain where an "attentive" staff serves a "familiar menu in wonderful settings" "100% devoid of snotty high-end vibes"; sure, "there are far more unique places to eat" on the islands and the prices mean it's ultimately "meat for the expense-account crowd", but it may just serve "the best damn steak in Hawaii."

Sam Choy's Breakfast,   `20` `16` `19` `$32`
Lunch & Crab *Hawaii Reg.*

Iwilei | 580 N. Nimitz Hwy. (Iwilei Rd.) | Honolulu | 808-545-7979 | www.samchoy.com

"Off the beaten path" in a "funky" "warehouse" in Iwilei, chef Sam Choy's "casual" Hawaii Regional restaurant and brewery is a local "fixture" for "creative island-style comfort" food, including a variety of loco mocos, poke, "sophisticated fusion dishes" and "da bes crab legs"; hearty appetites love the "gigantic portions" and "fine" beer, but a "disappointed" minority finds "formulaic" fare and a staff that seems to "disappear for hours."

☑ Sansei *Japanese/Pacific Rim*   `26` `19` `21` `$44`

Waikiki | Waikiki Beach Marriott Resort & Spa | 2552 Kalakaua Ave. (bet. Ohua & Paoakalani Aves.) | Honolulu | 808-931-6286 | www.sanseihawaii.com

Fans call this contemporary Japanese chainlet a "favorite", contending "there aren't enough superlatives for the mouthwatering" "new wave sushi" and Pacific Rim fare; kudos go to the "inventive rolls", "excellent" sashimi, "plate-lickin' sauces" and several "early-bird and late-night specials", but detractors are less enthused about the "loud and chaotic atmosphere" and iffy service at some locales.

Sarento's Top of the "I" ● *Italian*   `22` `23` `22` `$57`

Waikiki | The Ilikai | 1777 Ala Moana Blvd. (Hobron Ln.) | Honolulu | 808-955-5559 | www.ilikaihotel.com

Commanding the top of The Ilikai hotel, this Italian eatery with a Maui sibling is known for its "priceless" "panoramic views" ("get a table on the ocean side"), "courteous and attentive service" and standards like

	FOOD	DECOR	SERVICE	COST

osso buco and "delicious pasta and seafood dishes" complemented by an "extensive wine list"; a small portion of critics, however, say the menu is "dated" and the food "not as good as it was years ago."

Sergio's *Italian/Mediterranean* | 17 | 19 | 19 | $50 |

NEW **Kapahulu** | 449 Kapahulu Ave. (Kanaina Ave.) | Honolulu | 808-737-4461
Waikiki | Hilton Hawaiian Vill. | 2005 Kalia Rd. (Ala Moana Blvd.) | Honolulu | 808-951-6900
www.sergioshonolulu.com

Supporters say this "informal" but "expensive" duo in Waikiki's Hilton Hawaiian Village and in Kapahulu features "creative and well-presented" Italian and Mediterranean dishes; but an equal number of critics claim that the "fare is inconsistent" and the "new owners and chef are not up to old standards", resulting in "high expectations with low deliveries."

Shirokiya *Japanese* | 20 | 9 | 12 | $13 |

Ala Moana | Ala Moana Ctr. | 1450 Ala Moana Blvd. (bet. Atkinson Dr. & Piikoi St.) | Honolulu | 808-973-9111 | www.shirokiya.com

Located on the "chaotic" upper level of Ala Moana Center's Shirokiya department store, this "inexpensive" Japanese "cafeteria" boasts "multiple food stands" that offer diners "endless options" including "fresh tempura, sushi" and "rotating weekend specials"; be prepared, however, for a "hectic" setting and "hard-to-find" seating.

Shokudo ● *Japanese* | 20 | 21 | 20 | $30 |

Ala Moana | Ala Moana Pacific Ctr. | 1585 Kapiolani Blvd. (Kaheka St.) | Honolulu | 808-941-3701 | www.shokudojapanese.com

"Great for a date or group of friends", this Ala Moana-area "contemporary Japanese" encourages "family-style" dining with an "eclectic" menu of "innovative fusion" dishes made "for sharing", including mochi cheese gratin and agedashi tofu; fans like the "late hours" and "hip" decor, but critics complain that the "warehouse" space is "noisy", the service can be "hit-or-miss" and the "prices are a bit high."

Shore Bird *American* | 19 | 21 | 18 | $29 |

Waikiki | Outrigger Reef on the Beach | 2169 Kalia Rd. (Saratoga Rd.) | Honolulu | 808-922-2887 | www.outriggerreef-onthebeach.com

"Be prepared to grill your own" mahi mahi at this American eatery in the Outrigger Reef hotel with an "amazing" location overlooking Waikiki Beach, "live music" and a "low-key" vibe; diners dig the "all-you-can-eat salad bar", the "generous cuts of meat and fish" and the "chefs who help you prepare it" on an outdoor barbecue, but party-poopers pout about "fighting the smoke" while playing cook; N.B. breakfast and lunch don't require manning the grill.

Side Street Inn ● *American* | 25 | 8 | 17 | $26 |

Ala Moana | 1225 Hopaka St. (Piikoi St.) | Honolulu | 808-591-0253

An ultimate "hole-in-the-wall" in an "alley near Ala Moana Center", this renowned "dingy" restaurant/bar "where the island's chefs go" is open late serving "simple, incredibly tasty" local-style American "comfort food"; loyalists rave over the "large" portions of "legendary" fried rice, pork chops, lilikoi ribs, "spicy edamame" and chicken katsu, but some say service can "decline as the bar gets busy", which happens most weekend nights.

Singha Thai Cuisine *Thai*
21 | 20 | 19 | $36

Waikiki | Canterbury Pl. | 1910 Ala Moana Blvd. (Kalakaua Ave.) | Honolulu | 808-941-2898 | www.singhathai.com

This Waikiki restaurant serves an "interesting", "East-meets-West" mix of local and "spicy" Thai cuisine in a setting that "takes you to Thailand", complete with "carvings everywhere" and "beautiful entertainment" provided by traditional dancers; diners like the "fresh", "top-quality ingredients" and menu "variety" (from "pad Thai" to "chocolate heart cake"), but some say the food comes with "a bit of sticker shock" for a somewhat "dated" eatery.

Sorabol ● *Korean*
22 | 13 | 16 | $26

Ala Moana | 805 Keeaumoku St. (Kapiolani Blvd.) | Honolulu | 808-947-3113

If you're craving "kimchi for breakfast", head to this 24-hour Ala Moana–area "icon" that's popular even in "the wee hours of the morning" for its "extensive menu" of "authentic Korean" and BBQ standards like kal bi and bulgogi with "all the trimmings", as well as some sushi; diners say "service is efficient", but "prices are a little high."

Spices Ⓜ *Pan-Asian*
20 | 16 | 18 | $24

Moiliili | 2671 S. King St. (University Ave.) | Honolulu | 808-949-2679

The "spicy" "mix of Laotian, Thai", Cambodian and Malaysian cuisine at this Southeast Asian in Moiliili yields "subtly balanced", "attractively presented" dishes, served in a "sunny-yellow" space by "attentive" staffers; but a handful warns of "small" portions and "problematic parking" on weekends.

NEW Stage Ⓢ *American/Pan-Asian*
- | - | - | E

Ala Moana | Honolulu Design Ctr. | 1250 Kapiolani Blvd. (Pensacola St.) | Honolulu | 808-237-5429 | www.stagerestauranthawaii.com

With an urban, edgy look, this Pan-Asian–New American newcomer on the second floor of the Honolulu Design Center (furnished with pieces from the sales floor) is already on its second head toque – sous-chef Ron de Guzman (formerly of the Pineapple Room) has taken the reins from Jon Matsubara; the creative menu highlights local ingredients – Kona lobster, Kahuku corn, Hirabara Farm greens – and a six-course tasting menu is paired with sake and wine; N.B. barflys at the adjoining Amuse can sample some of this fare.

Suntory, Restaurant *Japanese*
22 | 19 | 21 | $57

Waikiki | Royal Hawaiian Ctr. | 2201 Kalakaua Ave. (Lewers St.) | Honolulu | 808-922-5511 | www.suntory.co.jp

The "focus is on the food", not "gimmicks", at this Japanese located in Waikiki's Royal Hawaiian Center that purists say is "more like Japan than most in the islands", serving some of the "best teppanyaki", as well as sushi, nabemono and an eight-course chef's menu; while the "service is usually good", a few find it suffers when the "cramped room" gets "crowded."

NEW Sushi Doraku ● *Japanese*
- | - | - | M

Waikiki | Royal Hawaiian Ctr. | 2233 Kalakaua Ave. (Royal Hawaiian Ave.) | Honolulu | 808-922-3323 | www.sushidoraku.com

With one of the few sake sommeliers in the state, this new outpost of a South Beach, Florida-based chain owned by the son of the creator of Benihana has set up shop at the Royal Hawaiian Center, serving the namesake specialty, along with hot and cold appetizers, sashimi and robata-yaki skewers for lunch and dinner; it has a posh feel, with indoor/outdoor seating and pleasant Asian decor.

Sushi King *Japanese*

| 19 | 12 | 16 | $29 |

Moiliili | 2700 S. King St. (bet. University & Waialae Aves.) | Honolulu | 808-947-2836

"Always filled with locals", this Moiliili Japanese serves "big portions" of "reasonably priced" sushi and is especially popular for its "early-bird and late-night specials"; while the space can "accommodate large groups", critics complain that the "environment is bland", and the sometimes "rude" staff "rushes you through the meal."

☑ Sushi Sasabune ☒ *Japanese*

| 28 | 15 | 22 | $87 |

Makiki | 1419 S. King St. (bet. Keeaumoku & King Sts.) | Honolulu | 808-947-3800

Voted Oahu's No. 1 Japanese is this eatery located "on a nondescript street" in Makiki where "out-of-this-world sushi" is "carefully prepared by a master", aka Seiji Kumagawa, whose signature command to diners is 'trust me'; aficionados advise "sit at the bar" for the "omakase" meal and "do exactly as instructed or you'll be asked to leave", while critics gripe that for "all the hype" and the "sky-high prices", the "setting needs serious attention."

Sweet Basil Express ☒☞ *Thai*

| 19 | 16 | 19 | $23 |

Downtown | Nuuanu YMCA | 1441 Pali Hwy. (bet. Hwy. 1 & S. Vineyard Blvd.) | Honolulu | 808-545-5800

A casual Downtowner set in the lobby of the Nuuanu YMCA, "overlooking a golf course", this Thai eatery is popular among office workers for its "creative" "take-out" fare, "great service" and "nice decor"; the "excellent lunch buffet" and "wonderful wine selection" also garner praise, but a critical few find that the flavors "leave them wanting."

Tanaka of Tokyo *Japanese*

| 21 | 19 | 23 | $41 |

NEW **Ala Moana** | Ala Moana Ctr. | 1450 Ala Moana Blvd. (bet. Atkinson Dr. & Piikoi St.) | Honolulu | 808-945-3443
Waikiki | King's Vill. | 131 Kaiulani Ave. (Koa Ave.) | Honolulu | 808-922-4233
Waikiki | Waikiki Shopping Plaza | 2250 Kalakaua Ave. (bet. Royal Hawaiian & Seaside Aves.) | Honolulu | 808-922-4702
www.tanakaoftokyo.com

It's "all about the show" at this "authentic teppanyaki" trio where everything from steak to seafood "is cooked before your eyes" by "your personal tableside chef"; families find it a "total crowd-pleaser" and a "great place to take kids", but detractors dismiss it as "vastly overpriced" because "you're paying for the entertainment" and "a lot depends on your chef."

NEW Tangö Contemporary Cafe *American*

| - | - | - | M |

Downtown | Hokua Condominium | 1288 Ala Moana Blvd. (Auahi St.) | Honolulu | 808-593-7288 | www.tangocafehawaii.com

Inside Downtown Honolulu's Hokua condominium dwells this bright, white arrival decorated with a row of birch trees and sleek globe pendant lights suspended from the ceiling; the New American menu is surprisingly affordable, while dishes like shrimp tempura with pickled cucumbers and salmon gravlax take inspiration from both the island's bounty and chef Göran Streng's Swedish heritage.

Tanioka's *Japanese/Seafood*   24 | 8 | 17 | $14

Waipahu | 94-903 Farrington Hwy. (Moloalo St.) | 808-671-3779 | www.taniokas.com

"A constant favorite among residents for takeout" and catering, this "family-owned" seafood market in Waipahu is famous for a "variety of poke and fresh fish", as well as Japanese okazuya-style "grab-and-go" bento, laulau or kalua pig plate lunch and sushi that "never fail to tackle your hunger"; you'll have to "get there early to avoid long lines" at this "strip-mall" spot, but the "fast" service moves things along.

Tavola Tavola *Italian*   19 | 16 | 18 | $42

Diamond Head | 3106 Monsarrat Ave. (Kanaina Ave.) | Honolulu | 808-737-6600 | www.tavolatavola.net

An "upscale" but "low-key neighborhood restaurant" near Diamond Head, this fixture "on the tour group route" features an "interesting Italian menu" with an Asian "flair" ("the Japanese chef trained in Italy"); though fans call it "quaint" and "relaxing", critics claim it's "overpriced for the average" eats and the staff acts like it "doesn't care if you ever come back."

Therapy SportsGrill ● *American*   ▽ 17 | 15 | 17 | $21

Hawaii Kai | Koko Marina Ctr. | 7192 Kalanianaole Hwy. (Lunalilo Home Rd.) | Honolulu | 808-394-8200 | www.kokomarinacenter.com

With a Koko Marina Center location, this "unique" "waterside sports bar" features "sushi specialties" and traditional American fare, plus "basketball, darts, computer games and pool"; fans say it's a "good hangout" for drinks, but critics claim the "service is nonexistent" and the "black walls and conference table seating" are turnoffs.

Ⓩ 3660 on the Rise Ⓜ *Pacific Rim*   25 | 20 | 24 | $52

Kaimuki | 3660 Waialae Ave. (Wilhelmina Rise) | Honolulu | 808-737-1177 | www.3660.com

Chef Russell Siu's flagship Pacific Rim restaurant is known for "locally sourced", "artfully presented" dishes like the signature ahi katsu (sushi-grade tuna wrapped in nori and deep-fried) and "incredible desserts", served by a "pleasant" staff; a "place to be seen", it's "popular" with locals for "special occassions and parties" despite its "bland decor" and "unimpressive" location in a Kaimuki office building.

Tiki's Grill & Bar *Pacific Rim*   19 | 21 | 19 | $29

Waikiki | ResortQuest Waikiki Beach Hotel | 2570 Kalakaua Ave., 2nd fl. (Paoakalani Ave.) | Honolulu | 808-923-8454 | www.tikisgrill.com

Set in the ResortQuest Waikiki Beach Hotel, this "upbeat bar" and Pacific Rim restaurant "overlooking the bustling city" offers diners "a perfect view of the ocean" amid "tikis galore"; while loyalists enjoy the "live" "Hawaiian entertainment", "welcoming staff", "tropical drinks" and "ono pupu", others say it's "often way too busy" and more notable "for the location than the food."

Tony Roma's *BBQ*   19 | 14 | 17 | $31

Aiea | 98-150 Kaonohi St. (Haukapila St.) | 808-487-9911

Waikiki | 1972 Kalakaua Ave. (bet. Keoniana & Pau Sts.) | Honolulu | 808-942-2121

(continued)

Tony Roma's Express *BBQ*

Ala Moana | Ala Moana Ctr. | 1450 Ala Moana Blvd. (bet. Atkinson Dr. & Piikoi St.) | Honolulu | 808-951-9900
www.tonyromas.com

"A mainstay for ribs", the three Oahu locations of this national chain offer "consistent" "mainland-style BBQ" and "awesome onion loaves" in settings that range from "dark" to "bright and modern" at the newly remodeled Aiea outpost; surveyors say "service is fast", particularly at the Express Ala Moana food-court spot, but a critical contingent counters they're "overpriced" "tourist traps" "living on past glory."

town ⊠ *American/Italian* | 23 | 18 | 20 | $37 |

Kaimuki | 3435 Waialae Ave. (9th St.) | Honolulu | 808-735-5900 | www.townkaimuki.com

At this "industrial-chic", New American–Italian "neighborhood" spot in Kaimuki, "chef-owner Ed Kenney delivers beautifully nuanced dishes" "using local and organic ingredients" in "unexpected ways"; diners praise the daily menu changes and "hip", "unpretentious" vibe, but warn that the room "can be noisy" and service "spotty."

Tsukuneya Robata Grill ● *Japanese* | ▽ 20 | 19 | 18 | $35 |

University | 1442 University Ave. (Dole St.) | Honolulu | 808-943-0390 | www.tsukuneyarobatagrill.com

"Japanese food on a stick" – aka robatayaki – is served in a "cool" setting at this University spot that wins praise for its "irresistible" skewer fare, including "amazing" yakitori and "delicious" "homemade" tofu that's "perfect with sake"; the atmosphere is "laid-back", and insiders advise bringing "someone who speaks" *Nihongo* "to really appreciate it."

12th Ave. Grill ⊠ *American* | 23 | 18 | 22 | $37 |

Kaimuki | 1145C 12th Ave. (bet. Harding & Waialae Aves.) | Honolulu | 808-732-9469 | www.12thavegrill.com

"Hidden" in the suburb of Kaimuki, this "unpretentious" New American "neighborhood bistro" with a "friendly staff" and a "modern", though "cramped" and "noisy", dining room features "imaginative" "comfort food" with a "sophisticated" island twist; plan to "get there early", though, because the "inventive specials" showcasing local ingredients can "run out."

NEW Uncle's Fish Market *Seafood* | 18 | 14 | 13 | $21 |

Iwilei | 1135 N. Nimitz Hwy. (Pier 36) | Honolulu | 808-275-0063 | www.unclesfishmarket.com

Housed in a "loud" "rustic" warehouse "at the docks" in Iwilei, this "busy" seafooder with funky, cluttered decor offers everything from "mahi mahi to opah", with an "emphasis on freshness"; diners say the "efficient staff", "live entertainment" and "air-conditioning" are "bonuses", but detractors warn that "it's on the pricey side" for the location, contending it's "better for lunch than dinner."

Verbano Italiano *Italian* | 18 | 15 | 18 | $27 |

Waikiki | 1451 S. King St. (bet. Kaheka & Keeaumoku Sts.) | Honolulu | 808-941-9168
Waipahu | 3571 Waialae Ave. (9th Ave.) | 808-735-1777 ⊠

(continued)

(continued)

Verbano Pastaria *Italian*

NEW Aiea | Pearlridge Shopping Ctr. | 98-151 Pali Momi St.
(Kamehameha Hwy.) | 808-487-1118
www.verbanohawaii.com

This "casual" "family-oriented" trio of "reasonably priced" Oahu
Sicilians "caters to a local palate" ("don't expect authentic"), but each
one is nevertheless a "cozy", if "average" "standby"; fans like the
"awesome" bread and "variety of non-pasta dishes" served by an "efficient" staff, but others are confounded by settings that are too "dark"
and "crammed with tables."

Vietnam Café Pho Saigon *Vietnamese* ▽ 19 | 15 | 18 | $20

Chinatown | 52 N. Hotel St. (Smith St.) | Honolulu | 808-536-8462
Surveyors say "go for the pho" and the "fresh shrimp rolls" at this "basic,
authentic and cheap" Vietnamese restaurant in the heart of Chinatown,
where "the lines are a pain, but worth it" for the comforting hot noodle
soups and "charming ambiance."

Vino Italian Tapas & Wine Bar Ⓢ Ⓜ *Italian* 23 | 21 | 24 | $40

Restaurant Row | 500 Ala Moana Blvd. (South St.) | Honolulu |
808-524-8466 | www.dkrestaurants.com

At this "cozy", "casual" Restaurant Row wine bar, co-owner Chuck
Furuya, one of Hawaii's only master sommeliers, offers an "enticing",
"affordable" vino selection "by the taste or by the glass" to go with a
limited selection of "well-prepared" Italian tapas; although some say
the "food doesn't live up to the same standard" as the grape offerings,
the "knowledgeable" staff makes it a "place to relax."

Wahoo's Fish Taco *Mexican* 17 | 13 | 14 | $14

Ward | Ward Gateway Ctr. | 940 Auahi St. (Ward Ave.) | Honolulu |
808-591-1646 | www.wahooshawaii.com

This "California transplant" in Ward Gateway serves "fresh and tasty"
Mexican eats in a "vibrant" "fast-food" setting at "budget" prices; diners praise the "quick service" and favorites like the "tasty Wahoo
bowls" (chicken, fish or beef served over ahi rice and black beans) and
"terrific" "flame-broiled fish tacos", but some say the dishes "tend to
be over-seasoned" and the "menu confusing."

Wailana Coffee House ❶ *Diner* 17 | 11 | 17 | $17

Waikiki | 1860 Ala Moana Blvd. (Ena Rd.) | Honolulu | 808-955-1764
"Open 24 hours", this "old-time" American diner – "one of the last
great coffeehouses in Waikiki" – serves up "basic" "local favorites"
and "excellent breakfasts", including "all you can eat pancakes"; diners say the "bargain" prices and "huge portions" make it a "staple for
late-night revelers", but some caution against the "no-nonsense service", lack of decor and "lines in the morning."

NEW **Wasabi & Nadaman** *Japanese* ▽ 22 | 20 | 19 | $63

Kapahulu | 1006 Kapahulu Ave. (Kaimuki Ave.) | Honolulu | 808-735-2802
At this new Kapahulu outpost of a Japan-based international chain,
the "elegant", "artfully prepared" Japanese fare is "worthy of a fine
restaurant in Tokyo", but served in "larger American-size portions";
the "service is courteous and prompt", and the interior is "pleasant",
while the stark exterior, by contrast, strikes some as downright "ugly."

NEW Wild Ginger Asian *Pan-Asian* 17 | 15 | 20 | $22

Kaimuki | 3441 Waialae Ave. (bet. 8th & 9th Aves.) | Honolulu | 808-738-1168

A Kaimuki "neighborhood restaurant" with a "low-key vibe", this Pan-Asian eatery serves "casual, homestyle Thai-Malaysian-Chinese fusion" fare at "reasonable prices"; supporters like the "accommodating, friendly staff" and "reasonable prices", but others say the "dishes are hit-or-miss."

Willows, The ⊠ *American/Hawaiian* 18 | 23 | 18 | $36

Moiliili | 901 Hausten St. (King St.) | Honolulu | 808-952-9200 | www.willowshawaii.com

"You'll almost forget you're in Moiliili" at this "old-time" American (it's been operating since 1944) that's popular with "large groups" for "buffet dining" "under thatched roofs amid gardens" and "koi ponds" in a "charming" one-acre "oasis"; surveyors enjoy the "wide variety" of local Hawaiian favorites plus some Japanese dishes, although detractors say the "fairly pricey" spread "has gone downhill in recent years", and the "decor needs updating."

Yakiniku Seoul ⊭ *Korean* ▽ 22 | 14 | 17 | $32

McCully | 1521 S. King St. (bet. Kaheka St. & Kalakaua Ave.) | Honolulu | 808-944-0110

For a "homestyle, authentic Korean experience" that's "fun for small groups", reviewers head to this "all-you-can-eat Korean BBQ" eatery in McCully, where you can grill your own beef to pair with "an excellent array of kimchi"; while some say it's "expensive" and "you'll be thoroughly smoky" after the meal, most agree that it's "worth every penny" – although "lunch is a better value than dinner."

Yanagi Sushi ● *Japanese* 23 | 16 | 19 | $42

Kakaako | 762 Kapiolani Blvd. (bet. Clayton & Dreler Sts.) | Honolulu | 808-597-1525 | www.yanagisushi-hawaii.com

A "longtime standby for sushi" in Kakaako, this "traditional" Japanese is known for its "huge menu" of "high-quality" fin fare and "witty, friendly" chefs (regulars recommend dining at the sushi bar "for the best selection"); "service is quick", even if the "worn-around-the-edges" dining room is "often crowded."

Yohei Sushi ⊠ *Japanese* 26 | 16 | 21 | $37

Kapalama | 1111 Dillingham Blvd. (Kokea St.) | Honolulu | 808-841-3773

"Popular with both locals and Japan nationals", this "excellent" (and "expensive") sushi bar in an "industrial area" of Kapalama serves "traditional", "well-prepared" fin fare, as well as "meticulously presented" Japanese dishes; diners praise the "authentic flavors", but critics complain that it's in "the middle of nowhere" and the space is "small."

You Hungry? ⊠⊭ *Hawaiian* ▽ 18 | 6 | 16 | $11

Ala Moana | 1695 Kapiolani Blvd. (Atkinson Dr.) | Honolulu | 808-429-0070

"If you're looking for ono local fare", this "plate-lunch" "hole-in-the-wall" near Ala Moana Center offers "restaurant-quality" eats "at fast-food prices", including "mochiko chicken", "kalua pig and cabbage" and "fried poke"; but the verdict is mixed on service: some find the "counter staff friendly", others say "you better know what you want when you get to the front of the line."

	FOOD	DECOR	SERVICE	COST

Young's Fish Market ☒ *Hawaiian*   24 | 10 | 18 | $15

Kapalama | City Square Shopping Ctr. | 1286 Kalana St. (bet. Kohou St. & Waiakamilo Rd.) | Honolulu | 808-841-4885

This "unpretentious", "friendly", "family-run" Kapalama Hawaiian is known for the "best plate lunches" and "local favorites", including "laulau, kalua pig", "fresh poi", "tripe stew" and haupia (coconut pudding); the "nonexistent ambiance" means it's "mostly takeout" (they'll even ship laulau frozen to the mainland), but you can also "order at the counter" and eat at a "communal table" "talking story" (shooting the breeze) with kamaaina; N.B. early closing times make it best for lunch or late afternoon bites.

Zippy's *American*   16 | 11 | 15 | $14

Ala Moana | Ala Moana Ctr. | 1450 Ala Moana Blvd. (bet. Atkinson Dr. & Piikoi St.) | Honolulu | 808-973-0870

Hawaii Kai | Koko Marina Ctr. | 7192 Kalanianaole Hwy. (Lunalilo Home Rd.) | Honolulu | 808-396-6977 ◑

Kahala | 4134 Waialae Ave. (bet. Hunakai St. & 21st Ave.) | Honolulu | 808-733-3730 ◑

Kailua | 44 Oneawa St. (Uluniu St.) | 808-266-3780

Kaimuki | 3345 Waialae Ave. (7th Ave.) | Honolulu | 808-733-3722 ◑

Kalihi | 904 Mokauea St. (Akina St.) | Honolulu | 808-832-1755 ◑

Kaneohe | 45-270 William Henry Rd. (Kamehameha Hwy.) | 808-233-3343

Kapahulu | 601 Kapahulu Ave. (bet. Campbell Ave.& Hoolulu St.) | Honolulu | 808-733-3725 ◑

Mililani | Town Center Of Mililani | 95-1249 Meheula Pkwy. (bet. Lanikuhana Ave. & Makaimoimo St.) | 808-623-1110 ◑

Waipahu | 94-1082 Ka Uka Blvd. (bet. Puahi & Ukee Sts.) | 808-671-1865 ◑ www.zippys.com

Additional locations throughout Oahu

Even if it's "just fast food", it's "so much more" say fans of this "local-style", "plate-lunch" "institution" famous for a "varied" selection of American "favorites" including "addictive chili", saimin specials, sandwiches, bento boxes with Spam that are "ideal for trips to the beach" and "great" "apple and coconut napples"; patrons praise the "quick service", "consistency across locations" and "late hours", but critics cringe over "middling", "processed" food that's "pricey for the quality"; N.B. the first branch outside Oahu opened in Kahului, Maui, in 2008.

Oahu Golf

Symbols

Yardage, USGA Rating and Slope are listed after each address.

🏌 caddies/forecaddies   ⚬⇁ guests only
🛒 carts only   ⏱ restricted tee times (call ahead)

Ala Wai Golf Course
| 14 | 13 | 14 | 19 | $42 |

Waikiki | 404 Kapahulu Ave. | 808-733-7387 |
www.co.honolulu.hi.us/des/golf | 6208/5095; 69/64; 118/107

For a track touted as "the most played municipal in the U.S.", this "well-used course" on the edge of Waikiki is "in decent shape", with a "forgiving" layout that's "flat" and "short" but can also be "tricky" on its more "challenging holes"; it's "the furthest thing from a resort experience" and "play can be slow on weekends", but it's a "fun" "sandbagger's paradise" that's also "a bargain" – "where else can you play by the ocean for this little?"

Ewa Beach Golf Club
| 18 | 18 | 21 | 19 | $140 |

Ewa Beach | 91-050 Fort Weaver Rd. | 808-689-6565 |
www.ewabeachgc.com | 6711/4894; 72.5/69; 134/119

Though it "doesn't get much attention", this Robin Nelson design in Ewa Beach is a "challenging" links-style "treat" that's kept in "wonderful condition" – in fact, it's one of the first courses in the state to boast eco-conscious seashore paspalum grass; "terrific service" adds to the "fun", and while the earth-friendly O.B. "might not look intimidating", you may need a "wrist brace" to slash through it, so cognoscenti caution to keep the ball "out of the rough."

Hawaii Kai Golf Course, Championship 🛒
| 19 | 18 | 20 | 17 | $100 |

Hawaii Kai | 8902 Kalanianaole Hwy. | 808-395-2358 |
www.hawaiikaigolf.com | 6500/6192; 71.4/69.8; 123/120

"Take your camera" as well as your clubs to this William F. Bell layout, because the views of the Pacific and the Makapuu cliffs "can't be beat"; relatively short at 6,500 yards, "with a few strange holes due to housing", it's nonetheless "challenging enough for intermediate players" with "lots of roll on typically dry" but "well-maintained" fairways; N.B. players can sharpen their short game on Robert Trent Jones Sr.'s 18-hole par-3 executive course.

Hawaii Prince 🛒
| 22 | 22 | 21 | 20 | $140 |

Ewa Beach | 91-1200 Fort Weaver Rd. | 808-944-4567 |
www.princeresortshawaii.com
A/B | 7117/5275; 73.8/70.4; 137/120
B/C | 7255/5205; 74.8/69.5; 136/117
C/A | 7166/5300; 74.1/69.9; 137/118

A "beautifully kept course" and "outstanding facilities and staff" all help to make Hawaii Prince Hotel an "amazing place to stay", with three nine-hole routes "designed by Arnold Palmer" (and Ed Seay) that "offer a variety of challenging holes", including "several with water in play"; a few complain that they all "tend to have the same look" and crack that "a little more imagination" could have gone into the names – "come on, A, B and C?"

Kapolei 🏌

21	21	20	22	$150

Kapolei | 91-701 Farrington Hwy. | 808-674-2227 | www.kapoleigolf.com | 7001/5490; 74.3/71.8; 135/124

A "former stop on the LPGA tour", this "nice Ted Robinson setup" located 25 miles west of Waikiki is a "challenging and entertaining" option, with water on 12 of its holes and a waterfall on the 18th; a few critics find it "too expensive" (like "most Hawaiian courses"), but many insist the "well-maintained" layout, "totally renovated" club-house and "must-use" driving range and practice green all make it a "good value for visitors."

Ko'olau 🏌

25	21	21	23	$135

Kaneohe | 45-550 Kionaole Rd. | 808-247-7088 | www.koolaugolfclub.com | 7310/5102; 75.7/72.9; 152/129

"You rarely get a chance to play in a rainforest backed up to a mountain range", so "don't miss" this "magnificent" "favorite" that's so "brutal" – it has "one of the highest slope ratings in the U.S." – that "even skilled golfers" need to bring a "healthy supply of balls" to deal with the "many forced carries" "over ravines" and dense "jungle"; a convenient location and affordable rates (it was voted the Top Value course on Oahu) help make it a "must-play" for those who "want a challenge."

Ko Olina

23	23	23	19	$179

Kapolei | 92-1220 Aliinui Dr. | 808-676-5309 | www.koolinagolf.com | 6815/5359; 73.3/71.7; 133/114

"A wonderful gem on Oahu's West Shore", this "nicely kept" Ted Robinson design is "a treat" "for golfers on vacation", with a signature 18th featuring a man-made waterfall that strikes some as "gimmicky" but "cute"; there are "some challenging holes spread throughout" ("watch the wind"), but roundsmen reveal that if you "hit it straight, you can score", and since it's a "relaxing spot" "in paradise", it's always a "great course for consuming a few cocktails on."

Luana Hills 🏌

25	17	21	21	$125

Kailua | 770 Auloa Rd. | 808-262-2139 | www.luanahills.com | 6164/4654; 71/67.4; 134/129

"Like playing golf in *Jurassic Park*", this "beautiful" Pete Dye design nestled in a valley between Kailua and Waimanalo "tests how straight you can hit the ball" on a "thinking man's" layout that's "just as hard" as the nearby Ko'olau course but with "a bit more flash and finesse", so "leave your driver in the bag"; "the back nine is tougher than the front", so "ask the pro for playing tips" and then enjoy the type of "unique" "gem" that "everyone should experience."

Pearl Country Club 🏌

19	18	21	19	$110

Aiea | 98-535 Kaonohi St. | 808-487-3802 | www.pearlcc.com | 6787/5536; 72.7/71.5; 136/124

While "not as scenic as most Hawaiian courses", this track on the slopes of the Ko'olau mountains (about a 20-minute drive from Waikiki) is "well maintained" and "interesting", with "great views of Pearl Harbor"; home to the annual Pearl Open, it "challenges" players with "fast greens, tough fairways", "windy" conditions and "lots of hills" that keep roundsmen "on a slant on almost every hole"; P.S. "very good" service may help offset the "expense."

Royal Kunia 🏌

22 | 12 | 17 | 20 | $140

Waipahu | 94-1509 Anonui St. | 808-688-9222 | www.royalkuniacc.com | 7007/4945; 73.8/68.1; 135/110

Long known as the 'ghost course' of Hawaii, this "fun" Robin Nelson design – which was completed in 1994 but opened eight years later – was certainly worth the wait: it's a "well-designed and well-maintained", "wide-open" track with a nearly 600-yard 9th hole overlooking "all of Oahu's South Shore" and Diamond Head; while "the restaurant is very modest", the clubhouse has a "friendly" staff and you can't beat a "replay for half price."

ⓩ Turtle Bay, Arnold Palmer

26 | 22 | 22 | 20 | $195

Kahuku | 57-049 Kuilima Dr. | 808-293-8574 | www.turtlebayresort.com | 7218/4851; 74.4/64.3; 143/121

It may have "more wide-open fairways than you would expect at an LPGA" layout, but the top-rated course on Oahu, and the site of the 2009 SBS Open, is nonetheless a "long, tough", "classic" Arnold Palmer design that can "physically and mentally drain you", especially "if the wind is blowing"; "well worth the drive" to Oahu's North Shore, it's a "beautiful", "well-maintained" option – the signature 17th has a "scenic" oceanside finish – that can also be "a value if played at the afternoon rate."

Turtle Bay, George Fazio

18 | 20 | 19 | 19 | $160

Kahuku | 57-049 Kuilima Dr. | 808-293-8574 | www.turtlebayresort.com | 6535/5355; 71.2/70.2; 131/116

"A decent course for the money", George Fazio's only Hawaiian layout is "not the Palmer course" (some suggest it "pales in comparison") but it's nevertheless a "fun" option that's "not as expensive" as its big brother yet offers all the benefits of Oahu's North Shore – it's "pretty wild hearing the waves pound" on the three oceanside holes; plus, it has a "terrific back nine" that might give you an inkling of why the course was host of the very first Senior Skins Game.

Oahu Hotels

Symbols

- 🏃 children's programs
- ✗ exceptional restaurant
- ⓗ historic interest
- ⅋ kitchens
- 🖼 allows pets
- 👁 views
- ⌐ 18-hole golf course
- ⓢ notable spa facilities
- 🏊 swimming pool
- 🎾 tennis

Ala Moana Hotel 👁🏊 | 18 | 18 | 16 | 18 | $239 |

Ala Moana | 410 Atkinson Dr. | Honolulu | 808-955-4811 | fax 808-944-6839 | 800-367-6025 | www.alamoanahotelhonolulu.com | 1103 rooms, 51 suites
"Away from the crowds of Waikiki Beach", this renovated older tower appeals to those looking to be "close to everything but not in the middle of everything"; it's the "perfect location" for high-end shopping at the adjacent Ala Moana Center and just a "couple of blocks" from the beach, with "updated" accommodations that can be "quite nice" and a "pleasant" staff; P.S. "wonderful views" from some rooms are a bonus.

Embassy Suites Waikiki Beach Walk 👁🏊 | ∇ 23 | 22 | 20 | 22 | $549 |

Waikiki | 201 Beachwalk St. | Honolulu | 808-921-2345 | fax 808-931-3500 | 800-362-2779 | www.embassysuites.com | 369 suites
The newest all-suite hotel in Waikiki, this chain outpost at Beach Walk boasts plenty of "aloha" from the "beautiful music that surrounds you" to the "hula dancing at a nightly manager's reception"; "roomy" one- and two-bedroom units with separate living areas, flat-panel TVs, complimentary daily newspapers and coffeemakers are great for "families", as are the included breakfasts and a children's pool that's "large enough for many kids to play in"; P.S. there's no restaurant on-site, but "numerous choices", such as Roy's and Ruth's Chris, are right nearby.

ⓩ Halekulani 🏃✗👁ⓢ🏊 | 25 | 27 | 26 | 25 | $445 |

Waikiki | 2199 Kalia Rd. | Honolulu | 808-923-2311 | fax 808-926-8004 | 800-367-2343 | www.halekulani.com | 412 rooms, 43 suites
It's an "oasis of sanity" in the "midst of tourist action" applaud admirers who give this "amazing" place a "standing ovation", rating it the No. 1 hotel on Oahu; the warm staffers "somehow always know your name" and offer the "best service anywhere", the oceanside New French restaurant, La Mer, is "simply outstanding", the "gorgeous" pool is a "work of art" and sipping sunset cocktails while listening to Hawaiian music at House Without a Key is a "romantic way to end the day"; it's "still the best" in Waikiki, even if you have to trip over all the brides and grooms "having their pictures taken" in the lobby.

Hawaii Prince Hotel 👁ⓢ🏊 | 21 | 24 | 20 | 20 | $390 |

Waikiki | 100 Holomoana St. | Honolulu | 808-956-1111 | fax 808-946-0811 | 888-977-4623 | www.princeresortshawaii.com | 464 rooms, 57 suites
Dream big ("pretend it's your yacht" at the adjoining marina) or eat big (via the "abundant buffets") at this "well-run", "good-priced" "respite from the madness of Waikiki" near Ala Moana Center and a "short

walk to some very nice beaches"; the "friendly" staff "goes out of its way to satisfy", but while some appreciate the rooms for their "water views" and "zero noise", others carp that they're "starting to show their age" and "aren't what the Prince name" suggests.

Hilton Hawaiian Village ♔♧♨⑤≋ | 20 | 20 | 19 | 24 | $229

Waikiki | 2005 Kalia Rd. | Honolulu | 808-949-4321 | fax 808-951-5458 | 800-445-8667 | www.hilton.com | 3515 rooms, 345 suites

"Everything is at your fingertips" at this "extremely kid-friendly" "mega-resort" in a "wonderful location" "away from the noise and traffic" of the rest of Waikiki; it's best if you "like being in a crowd" because this "city unto itself" with "adorable penguins", myriad shopping and dining options, "awesome" renovated lagoons and pools, and the "best beachfront in Honolulu" attracts a lot of "families with kids"; although it may be "too big" for some, the great "variety" of rooms in six towers and the full-scale spa and medical wellness center allow for serenity.

Hyatt Regency Waikiki Resort & Spa ♔♨⑤≋ | 20 | 20 | 19 | 19 | $300

Waikiki | 2424 Kalakaua Ave. | Honolulu | 808-923-1234 | fax 808-926-3415 | 800-233-1234 | www.waikiki.hyatt.com | 1212 rooms, 18 suites

The zoo, aquarium and "one of the most scenic stretches of Waikiki" are a short walk from these two "well-maintained", if "ho-hum", high-rise towers with "excellent views" "in the center of the action"; while the "accommodating" staff (particularly on the club floor and pool-side) wins points, the "scores of shops on the first three levels" make some feel as if they're bunking "on top of a shopping mall."

Ilima Hotel ☜≋ | - | - | - | - | $188

Waikiki | 445 Nohonani St. | Honolulu | 808-923-1877 | fax 808-924-2617 | 800-801-9366 | www.ilima.com | 75 rooms, 24 suites

Fans of this affordable "little gem" "highly recommend it to friends" for its "ohana atmosphere", "cheerful" service and rooms with "plenty of space"; even if it's two blocks from Waikiki Beach and there's no restaurant on-site, it's a "great value" "not too far" from the action of the Kalakaua strip; N.B. the lobby is adorned with koa wood and paintings by local artist Ralph Kagehiro.

JW Marriott Ihilani Resort & Spa ♔✕♨▲⑤≋⚲ | 26 | 23 | 22 | 26 | $485

Kapolei | 92-1001 Olani St. | 808-679-0079 | fax 808-679-0080 | 800-626-4446 | www.ihilani.com | 351 rooms, 36 suites

"If you want "a wonderful place to forget about winter", this "beautiful" Kapolei resort with "doting service" about 30 minutes from Waikiki is "well worth the drive"; "play golf in the morning", hit the "relaxing spa" in the afternoon, "have a sunset dinner", then "sit under the moonlight at the lagoon" before heading back to your "spacious" room; it's "pure bliss" for all except those who don't want to be "away from" the action.

✪ Kahala Hotel & Resort, The ♔✕♧♨⑤≋ | 25 | 24 | 25 | 25 | $395

Kahala | 5000 Kahala Ave. | Honolulu | 808-739-8888 | fax 808-739-8800 | 800-367-2525 | www.kahalaresort.com | 312 rooms, 31 suites

A 15-minute drive from Waikiki in the "luxe residential area" of Kahala, this "quiet, unrushed" beachfront resort with "apartment-sized rooms" sporting "mahogany four-poster beds and 450-thread-count sheets" is "by far the favorite" Oahu lodging for many; maybe it's the "mesmerizing dolphin lagoon", the "excellent restaurants", the "glorious spa" with private suites or the staff that "treats you like royalty from check-in to check-out" that keep regulars returning, but even if you can't afford to stay here, stop in for the "decadent" Sunday brunch.

Marriott Waikiki Beach 🏨Ⓢﻬ | 21 | 21 | 18 | 21 | $425 |

Waikiki | 2552 Kalakaua Ave. | Honolulu | 808-922-6611 | fax 808-921-5255 | 800-367-5370 | www.marriottwaikiki.com | 1297 rooms, 13 suites

Flip-flop your way to the "beautiful beach across the street" from this "nicely located" twin-towered giant within "walking distance" of "plenty of dining options" and the "best Waikiki can offer"; the "attractive", "refurbished" rooms (the Kealohilani Tower just finished a $28-million redo) have balconies, WiFi access and 37-inch flat-screen TVs, the "staff is extremely friendly" and there's a spa, two freshwater pools and popular eateries d.k. Steak House and Sansei, so detractors look past the "mall-meets-paradise feel."

Moana Surfrider, A Westin Resort 🎎ⓗ🏨ﻬ | 21 | 23 | 19 | 22 | $450 |

Waikiki | 2365 Kalakaua Ave. | Honolulu | 808-922-3111 | fax 808-923-0308 | 800-325-3535 | www.moana-surfrider.com | 747 rooms, 46 suites

Order a mai tai, "sit under the banyan tree" and take in the "wonderful atmosphere" of this refurbished beachfront "resort treat" "in the heart of Waikiki" that was "rebranded a Westin" in mid-2007, but has been "the place to be seen since 1901"; expect "elegant", "old-fashioned Hawaiian ambiance", with an "attentive" staff and some of the area's top "people-watching", but be careful which of the "hit-or-miss" rooms you book; N.B. the oceanfront Beachouse serves surf 'n' turf overlooking the surf.

New Otani Kaimana Beach 🏨 | ∇ 16 | 20 | 22 | 14 | $180 |

Waikiki | 2863 Kalakaua Ave. | Honolulu | 808-923-1555 | fax 808-922-9404 | 800-356-8264 | www.kaimana.com | 102 rooms, 23 suites

Fans find a "quiet place on the edge of Waikiki" at this little spot with a "lovely location", "friendly staff" and fairly "standard rooms" that could use "some updating"; it may be "a bit off the beaten track at the foot of Diamond Head", but that means "amazing views" and a "local" feel.

Outrigger Reef on the Beach 🏨Ⓢﻬ | ∇ 16 | 20 | 15 | 15 | $289 |

Waikiki | 2169 Kalia Rd. | Honolulu | 808-923-3111 | fax 808-924-4957 | 800-688-7444 | www.outrigger.com | 195 rooms, 5 suites

Undergoing a "redo in a big way", this "beautiful" twin-towered oceanfronter near the Waikiki Beach Walk is "great for families", with a "premier" beach footsteps from the resort's refurbished lobby (and its collection of Polynesian canoe art); fans report the "new rooms are gorgeous and comfortable", while the über-connected praise the "free Internet and telephone calls to the mainland"; N.B. ongoing construction may outdate the above scores.

Outrigger Waikiki 🏨Ⓢﻬ | ∇ 19 | 19 | 17 | 20 | $369 |

Waikiki | 2335 Kalakaua Ave. | Honolulu | 808-923-0711 | fax 808-921-9798 | 800-688-7444 | www.outrigger.com | 494 rooms, 30 suites

Positioned "front and center on Waikiki Beach", Outrigger's "friendly" flagship has an "ideal" oceanfront location that offers "incredible" views of Diamond Head and the Pacific (even from "the cheapest city-view rooms"); thanks to the "wonderful" service, the penthouse-level Waikiki Plantation Spa and Duke's, its venerable beach bar, even the fussiest may overlook the "postage stamp–size pool."

Sheraton 🏃🏻 🏖️ 🏋️ 🌊 | 19 | 17 | 18 | 20 | $365 |

Waikiki | 2255 Kalakaua Ave. | Honolulu | 808-922-4422 | fax 808-923-8785 | 800-782-9488 | www.sheraton-waikiki.com | 1636 rooms, 128 suites
Guests at this "huge" Waikiki "Hawaii-meets-Vegas" high-rise are divided over whether it's a "bustling, fun place" or an "overcrowded, hectic" behemoth; devotees like the "renovated rooms", "gorgeous views", cool interactive surf simulator, shops that "entice you to max out your credit card" and "interesting" restaurants (including the new oceanfront RumFire), but others can't overlook the "convention mobs."

Turtle Bay Resort 🏃🏻 🏋️ ⬆️ 🕐 🌊 🔍 | 21 | 20 | 18 | 22 | $470 |

Kahuku | 57-091 Kamehameha Hwy. | 808-293-6000 | fax 808-293-9147 | 800-203-3650 | www.turtlebayresort.com | 375 rooms, 26 suites, 42 cottages
"Watch the sea turtles and surfers" from your balcony at this "North Shore hideaway" where the "spacious rooms" offer "spectacular views" and "the beach cottages are romantic"; with "an award-winning golf course", tennis, a "beautiful beach" and a variety of "tolerable" dining options, it pleases most; but others find this "windy" option "too far off the beaten path" with quarters that are "not the latest and greatest"; P.S. you "need your own transportation" since taxis to the airport or elsewhere will break the bank.

Waikiki Parc 🏋️ 🌊 | ▽ 19 | 20 | 18 | 16 | $280 |

Waikiki | 2233 Helumoa Rd. | Honolulu | 808-921-7272 | fax 808-923-1336 | 800-422-0450 | www.waikikiparc.com | 297 rooms
A "quaint" boutique-style sister to the Halekulani, this recently renovated boutique is great "if you're watching your budget", boasting "prompt" service and complimentary buffet breakfasts (from Japanese miso soup to pancakes) in a "convenient" Waikiki location; "ask for a room" with a "gorgeous view of the ocean" and be ready to walk to the beach; N.B. there's an outpost of Nobu restaurant on-site.

W Honolulu Diamond Head 🍽️ 🏋️ | 19 | 18 | 18 | 15 | $520 |

Waikiki | 2885 Kalakaua Ave. | Honolulu | 808-922-1700 | fax 808-923-2249 | 800-325-3535 | www.whotels.com | 50 rooms, 1 penthouse
Set "away from the hectic" part of Waikiki, this "swanky" spot with a "friendly staff" has a "peaceful" position near Diamond Head (the "rooms with views" of the crater are "stunning") as well as a "great restaurant"/nightclub "with a very local crowd" come weekends; but those who say it "falls short of expectations" are bothered by "small" quarters and the lack of a beachfront.

🆕 Wyland Waikiki 🏖️ 🕐 🌊 | - | - | - | - | $165 |

Waikiki | 400 Royal Hawaiian Ave. | Honolulu | 808-954-4000 | fax 808-954-4047 | 877-995-2638 | www.thewylandwaikikihotel.com | 315 rooms, 88 suites
The artwork of the namesake marine life conservationist distinguishes this recently remodeled Waikiki boutique hotel, which naturally features a 360-degree aquarium; other amenities include two swimming pools, a spa and rooms with pillow-top beds and high-def TVs.

Oahu Nightlife

Aaron's Atop the Ala Moana
21 | 21 | 20 | E

Ala Moana | Ala Moana Hotel | 410 Atkinson Dr. (Kapiolani Blvd.) | Honolulu | 808-955-4466 | www.tristarrestaurants.com
The "view is amazing" and the drinks "pretty" at this 36th-floor Waikiki restaurant lounge that features live musicians during the week and "sophisticated" after-hours parties on weekends; a good choice for a "romantic" evening – you feel like you're "dancing in the sky" – it also takes on "meat-market" vibes at various times.

Aku Bone
∇ 21 | 18 | 20 | E

Kakaako | 1201 Kona St. (Pensacola St.) | Honolulu | 808-589-2020
Named after the skeleton of a skipjack tuna, this "no-frills" Kakaako bar off Kapiolani Boulevard feels like it's "locals only", but "visitors are welcome" too; be sure to "arrive before the live Hawaiian music starts" around 8 PM (call for schedule), and "be prepared to get your hands dirty with the family-style eats."

Amuse
∇ 20 | 22 | 18 | E

Ala Moana | Honolulu Design Ctr. | 1250 Kapiolani Blvd. (Pensacola St.) | Honolulu | 808-956-1250 | www.honoluludesigncenter.com
Design divas are drawn to this "upscale", "self-serve–style wine bar" in the Honolulu Design Center, where patrons purchase ATM-like 'credit cards' to be used at electronic bottle carousels that dispense "one-ounce pours"; "if you want to try a dozen" different types, "you have endless options" (80 choices at any given time) as well as "great" pupus (from the adjacent Stage restaurant), but some say vino "dispensed like Slurpees" can be "dangerous" and "expensive"; N.B. on certain nights $25 gets you a $50 card.

Angles Waikiki ⌺
19 | 14 | 18 | M

Waikiki | 2256 Kuhio Ave., 2nd fl. (Seaside Ave.) | Honolulu | 808-926-9766 | www.angleswaikiki.com
Centrally located on Kuhio Avenue, the "friendliest gay bar in Waikiki" has a "charming owner and staff" and a "cute crowd" that lines up after midnight for dancing with DJ Kevin and "strong drinks made with cheap liquor"; "for a "total blast" enter the pool tournament or a 'best buns' contest, or just "hang out" on the "nice lanai."

Anna Bannana's
15 | 12 | 18 | M

Moiliili | 2440 S. Beretania St. (Kaialiu St.) | Honolulu | 808-946-5190
An "institution" among generations of college students, "local hippies" and bands of all genres, this "funky" Moiliili bar is a "total hole-in-the-wall" with "dirt going back as far as its history" and a live performance space upstairs with "interesting bands" that play almost every night; insiders say the shows "usually never run on time", and the tiny restrooms have seen better days.

Bar 35
22 | 21 | 19 | M

Chinatown | 35 N. Hotel St. (Smith St.) | Honolulu | 808-537-3535 | www.bar35hawaii.com
A favorite on Chinatown's redeveloped Hotel Street, this "hip lounge" with a "huge selection of beers" and "special" outdoor seating gets

packed with a "nouveau Downtown crowd" that munches on "great thin-crust pizza" during happy hour; just beware, when the $3 drinks deal is on, it gets crazy crowded and there "aren't enough bartenders."

Beach Bar, The
23 | 24 | 17 | E

Waikiki | Moana Surfrider | 2365 Kalakaua Ave. (Kaiulani Ave.) | Honolulu | 808-922-3111 | www.moanasurfrider.com

A "wonderful outdoor" lounge at the Moana Surfrider, this "usually crowded" Waikiki watering hole attracts barflys who "kick back" "under a huge banyan tree that once sheltered Mark Twain", soaking in the "great ocean views"; there's live entertainment and a limited dining menu, but the service doesn't do justice to the "relaxing" setting.

Brew Moon
20 | 19 | 19 | E

Ward | Ward Ctr. | 1200 Ala Moana Blvd. (Queen St.) | Honolulu | 808-593-0088 | www.brewmoon.com

DJs and live bands turn this "casual" Ward microbrewery into a night spot on weekends, attracting a "variety of crowds" keen on the "fabulous" housemade beers and "areas for dancing"; a "friendly", if sometimes "lackadaisical", staff can "fill a growler" for take-out liquid aloha, but don't expect much from the "predictable" American fare; P.S. a "lively" happy hour makes it a "favorite *pau hana* (after work)" choice.

Chiko's Tavern
- | - | - | M

McCully | 930 McCully St. (Alagaroba St.) | Honolulu | 808-949-5440

This "excellent" come-as-you-are McCully "neighborhood bar" caters to the "most fabulous", who kick back to karaoke, "live music" on Thursdays and hula nights that "guarantee a great time" for anyone who shows up – gay, straight, local or tourist.

Dave and Buster's
20 | 17 | 17 | E

Ward | Ward Entertainment Complex | 1030 Auahi St. (Kamakee St.) | Honolulu | 808-589-2215 | www.daveandbusters.com

"If you're looking for something unique to Hawaii", this Ward branch of the national "mega chain" "is not it", but it's nevertheless a "fun" indoor "hangout" that's "always crowded and hopping with families"; you "can't go wrong with the games" (video arcades, billiards, shuffleboard) or the "diverse drink menu", but you'll have to look past the "tasteless, fried" fare and service that "takes forever."

Don Ho's Island Grill
19 | 18 | 18 | E

Downtown | Aloha Tower Mktpl. | 1 Aloha Tower Dr. (Fort St.) | Honolulu | 808-528-0807 | www.donhos.net

"Romantic views" and "live Hawaiian music" make this restaurant at Aloha Tower Marketplace a destination that's a "good local spot, but fun for tourists also" and doubles as a nightclub-style venue on the weekends; "Tiny Bubbles" fans should get there ASAP – the owner lost the rights to use Don Ho's name and likeness after the singer passed away in 2007, so changes are on the horizon.

Dragon Upstairs, The
▽ 25 | 25 | 19 | M

Chinatown | above Hank's Café | 1038 Nuuanu Ave. (S. King St.) | Honolulu | 808-526-1411 | www.thedragonupstairs.com

A classy, "intimate" spot upstairs from Hank's Cafe, this Chinatown jazz club usually hosts an "older crowd" with a "more seasoned palate" that comes for a "nightcap and live music at the end of the night"; watch out for "expensive drinks" ("no specials"), and "get there early if you want a table."

☑ Duke's Canoe Club

24 | 23 | 20 | E

Waikiki | Outrigger Waikiki | 2335 Kalakaua Ave. (Kaiulani Ave.) | Honolulu | 808-922-2268 | www.dukeswaikiki.com

"Nostalgia" reigns at the original Outrigger Waikiki Beach location of this "crowded" island "institution", named for "surfing legend" and Olympic champion swimmer Duke Kahanamoku, and voted Oahu's Most Popular Nightlife venue; it's more about the "ultimate laid-back Hawaiian experience" with Diamond Head views, crowds of "locals, tourists and military", "nightly music" and specialty drinks, than about the moderately priced "typical" American bar food fare.

8 Fat Fat 8 Bar & Grille

20 | 16 | 21 | M

Makiki | 1327 S. Beretania St. (Keeaumoku St.) | Honolulu | 808-596-2779 While it "doesn't look like much from the outside", this affordable "local" watering hole is "perfect for casual dining, drinks and darts" (you'll find the "best crispy fried chicken" in Makiki); you "might meet anybody" given the laid-back, *Cheers*-style crowd, but the "noise" level makes it a challenge "to hold an intelligent conversation."

Gordon Biersch

21 | 19 | 18 | M

Downtown | Aloha Tower Mktpl. | 1 Aloha Tower Dr. (Fort St.) | Honolulu | 808-599-4877 | www.gordonbiersch.com

A "fantastic waterfront location" with indoor/outdoor seating that's perfect for "watching the boats come in", this Aloha Tower Marketplace brewpub offers "live music most nights", solid suds, "good pupus" and "pretty people-watching"; but the unimpressed yawn "s'ok, but you can find this anywhere."

Haleiwa Joe's Seafood Grill

∇ 24 | 20 | 19 | E

Haleiwa | 66-011 Kamehameha Hwy. (Lokoea Pl.) | 808-637-8005 | www.haleiwajoes.com

The bar of this North Shore eatery in Haleiwa is "tucked in the back" with "no view", but it's popular with "lots of locals" who love the "happy hour", and tourists who take the "adorable beach glasses with real sand on the bottom" home for souvenirs; interesting specialty cocktails and solid restaurant fare are further draws.

☑ House Without A Key

29 | 28 | 28 | VE

Waikiki | Halekulani | 2199 Kalia Rd. (Lewers St.) | Honolulu | 808-923-2311 | www.halekulani.com

Rated No. 1 for Appeal among Nightlife venues, this beachside "oasis of calm" in the Halekulani hotel is the place to "linger" outside over a "delicious" mai tai, soaking in the "unparalleled" Pacific views, "mellow" local bands and "lovely Hawaiian" hula dancers; with "relaxed" service and "gorgeous" sunsets, it's a "must-go for all first-time" visitors.

Hula's Bar & Lei Stand

23 | 20 | 23 | M

Waikiki | Waikiki Grand Hotel | 134 Kapahulu Ave. (bet. Kalakaua Ave. & Lemon Rd.) | Honolulu | 808-923-0669 | www.hulas.com

Located across Kapahulu Avenue from Kapiolani Park and the Honolulu Zoo, this gay "local hangout" in Waikiki is a "comfortable" spot to "enjoy cocktails, drag shows and hot dancing boys"; there's "plenty of room to roam around", a "welcoming" bar staff that's pure "eye candy" and an "open-air second story overlooking the park."

☒ Indigo
23 | 23 | 19 | E

Chinatown | 1121 Nuuanu Ave. (Hotel St.) | Honolulu | 808-521-2900 | www.indigo-hawaii.com
It's "always packed" at this "originator of the Downtown scene" in Chinatown, where the "exotic decor" is an appropriate backdrop for the long list of specialty martinis (lychee, Godiva, etc.) that dominates happy hours; the "innovative" dining gives way to "cool" late-night revelry that includes live music, dancing and "fun people-watching" – no wonder locals lament "can't we have a few secrets in this town?"

Kona Brewing Co.
23 | 21 | 20 | E

Hawaii Kai | Koko Marina | 7192 Kalanianaole Hwy. (Lunalilo Home Rd.) | Honolulu | 808-394-5662 | www.konabrewingco.com
The Big Island comes to Oahu via Kona Brewing's outpost in Hawaii Kai, where the "marina setting" is perfect for unwinding after snorkeling nearby Hanauma Bay; the "hip" crowd, "great pizza" and "occasional live music" are the reasons why some fans "always go."

La Mariana Sailing Club
24 | 22 | 20 | M

Sand Island | 50 Sand Island Access Rd. (Auiki St.) | Honolulu | 808-848-2800
"One of the few real tiki bars left in Hawaii", this "classic" Sand Island spot, whose longtime owner Annette Nahinu passed away in 2008, draws crowds of "colorful patrons" who love the "funky Polynesian decor" ("blowfish and glass balls hanging from the ceiling"), "chill staff" and "good entertainment"; ok, the menu definitely "isn't haute cuisine" and you "hear major air traffic overhead", but the overall atmosphere makes it "worth trekking to."

☒ Lewers Lounge
27 | 26 | 26 | VE

Waikiki | Halekulani | 2199 Kalia Rd. (Lewers St.) | Honolulu | 808-923-2311 | www.halekulani.com
Take a trip back to the turn-of-the-19th-century at this "classy" Waikiki lounge in the Halekulani Hotel, where "master mixologists" serve up "swanky" cocktails to "well-heeled tourists" and "Oahu's finest"; the "dark", "velvety atmosphere" includes "mellow live jazz" and lots of "old-school" charm, so it's just the spot for that "impressive date."

LuLu's Waikiki
▽ 21 | 19 | 19 | M

Waikiki | Park Shore Hotel | 2856 Kalakaua Ave. (Paki Ave.) | Honolulu | 808-926-5222 | www.luluswaikiki.com
Open 24 hours, this "casual" Waikiki sports bar and restaurant "overlooking the beach" in the Park Shore Hotel doubles as a "hangout" for "live music" that draws younger crowds at night; despite "mediocre" American fare and "rowdy" revelers when "big games" are on the multiple flat-screen TVs, the "drop-dead views" sell the place.

Mai Tai Bar
23 | 20 | 20 | M

Ala Moana | Ala Moana Ctr. | 1450 Ala Moana Blvd. (Piikoi St.) | Honolulu | 808-947-2900 | www.maitaibar.com
"Mingle with the singles" or "take a breather while shopping" at this "huge, open-air" Ala Moana Center bar with nightly live bands that are

"popular with young locals" who dig drinking beer "straight outta the pitcher"; the "packed" interior becomes "loud and crazy" with those "in search of digits", but if you go before 6 PM, you'll get a "bargain" drink and less chaos.

Mercury Bar
- | - | - | M

Downtown | 1154 Fort Street Mall (S. Beretania St.) | Honolulu | 808-537-3080

Find a "*Cheers* for hip people" at this "low-key, no-attitude" Downtown bar where proximity to Hawaii Pacific U means a college crowd and a "quirky, edgy vibe that's not for everyone"; still, most can appreciate the "interesting drinks", "cool regulars" and DJs and live music on weekends.

Moose McGillycuddy's
17 | 15 | 18 | M

Waikiki | 310 Lewers St. (Kalakaua Ave.) | Honolulu | 808-923-0751 | www.mooserestaurantgroup.com

Affectionately known as 'Moose's' by generations of UH-Manoa students, the Waikiki location of this sports pub chain (there are two others on Maui, as well as branches on the West Coast) is an "open-air college bar" "for the young looking to hook up"; DJs make "dancing fun" after dark, but unless "you're a frat boy on spring break" or want to "get drunk on a budget" and don't mind "intermittent" bartenders, "avoid it."

Murphy's Bar & Grill
21 | 20 | 22 | M

Downtown | 2 Merchant St. (Nuuanu Ave.) | Honolulu | 808-531-0422 | www.gomurphys.com

Downtown workers and UH football fans (it's practically the "home of the Warriors") flock to this veteran saloon for "the closest thing" to an "old-fashioned" Irish pub in town; "attentive" barkeeps, decor that's heavy on "odds-and-ends", live music and a "surprisingly" dependable menu of American fare (burgers, steaks, salads) make this a solid bet.

O'Toole's Irish Pub
- | - | - | M

Downtown | 902 Nuuanu Ave. (Marin Ln.) | Honolulu | 808-536-4138 | www.irishpubhawaii.com

If you crave live entertainment to go with that Black and Tan, head to this Downtown Irish pub where the music is "loud", the crowd "laid-back" and the space appropriately "dingy"; one of the holdouts against the city's nonsmoking ordinance, it makes ashtrays available to puffers (at their own risk).

Pearl Ultralounge
20 | 22 | 19 | E

Ala Moana | Ala Moana Ctr. | 1450 Ala Moana Blvd. (Ala Moana Park Dr.) | Honolulu | 808-944-8000 | www.pearlhawaii.com

Although it attracts a more mature crowd "than most nightclubs", this swanky Ala Moana lounge gets "pretty crowded" on Fridays with younger patrons who sip "fancy drinks" until 4 AM; "great bands", a dance floor with DJs spinning and "sophisticated" decor that's either "fabulous" or trying "too hard to be something from LA or New York" pull in the "chic" set.

Pipeline Cafe
▽ 16 | 15 | 18 | M

Kakaako | 805 Pohukaina St. (Koula St.) | Honolulu | 808-589-1999 | www.pipelinecafe.net

Despite a recent ownership change, this Kakaako performance venue is "one of the few" capable of hosting both "national music acts" for crowds up to 2,000, as well as "weekday happy hours" in the second-floor sports bar with "pool tables, dartboards" and "economical" food and drink; but even with an "efficient staff" and multiple bars, expect "long lines" for libations on concert nights.

RumFire

22	23	16	E

Waikiki | Sheraton Waikiki | 2255 Kalakaua Ave. (Seaside Ave.) | Honolulu | 808-922-4422 | www.rumfirewaikiki.com

The newest addition at the Sheraton Waikiki, this "dramatic", restaurant/lounge is "so close to the water" it feels "like you might get splashed" while sitting at the "outdoor fire pits" enjoying "unbeatable views", expensive cocktails and "the best rum selection" on Oahu; spoilsports, however, say the crowd veers toward "pretentious" after dark and the staff isn't up to the task.

Ryan's Grill

18	16	18	M

Ward | Ward Ctr. | 1200 Ala Moana Blvd. (Kamakee St.) | Honolulu | 808-591-9132 | www.ryansgrill.com

A "local institution" at Ward Centre, this "consistently good", "reasonably priced" mainstay provides a "popular" and "lively happy hour" with live bands on select nights; the "friendly staff" helps make it a "comfortable hangout" despite furnishings that "should have been updated years ago."

Sansei

22	19	20	E

Waikiki | Waikiki Beach Marriott Resort & Spa | 2252 Kalakaua Ave. (bet. Royal Hawaiian & Seaside Aves.) | Honolulu | 808-931-6286 | www.dkrestaurants.com

The "divine" dining at this Waikiki Beach Marriott Japanese gives way come dark to half-price sushi, "lots of drink specials" and "entertaining" Friday night karaoke where guests "dress like it's a nightclub" and belt out tunes from a small stage; the staff is "usually helpful" and the "terrace overlooking the beach" a plus, just watch out for a "short bar that easily gets crowded."

Señor Frog's

16	17	18	E

Waikiki | Royal Hawaiian Ctr. | 2201 Kalakaua Ave. (Lewers St.) | Honolulu | 808-440-0150 | www.senorfrogs.com

The Waikiki outpost of the Mexico-based restaurant/bar chain known for an 'anything goes' atmosphere is no less of a "meat market" at its Royal Hawaiian Center location thanks to a "sociable" staff that "whips up a spring break frenzy every night"; if you're looking for "lots of action" – karaoke, dancing, impromptu events – you'll think it's "cool", but it also helps if you're "under 35 and want to get wasted."

Shack, The

∇ 20	17	19	M

Hawaii Kai | Hawaii Kai Shopping Ctr. | 377 Keahole St. (Kalanianaole Hwy.) | Honolulu | 808-396-1919 | www.shackhawaiikai.com

Kailua | 1051 Keolu Dr. (Hele St.) | 808-261-1191 | www.shackwaikiki.com

Mililani | 95-221 Kipapa Dr. (Kuahelani Ave.) | 808-627-1561 | www.theshackmililani.com

NEW **Waikiki** | Waikiki Trade Ctr. | 2255 Kuhio Ave. (Seaside Ave.) | Honolulu | 808-921-2255 | www.shackwaikiki.com

Three locations outside Honolulu's urban core make this restaurant/ sports bar mini-chain a favorite among "locals from the 'burbs", while the new fourth branch, with a much different vibe in the Waikiki Trade Center, stays open until 4 AM and features "live music every weekend"; fans find "reasonable" happy hours, the "best burgers", "lots of TVs" and, at the Hawaii Kai outpost, a "great waterside" setting near Hanauma Bay.

thirtyninehotel

▽ 25 | 24 | 19 | M

Chinatown | 39 N. Hotel St. (Smith St.) | Honolulu | 808-599-2552 | www.thirtyninehotel.com
Credited with helping to launch Downtown's arts and entertainment rebirth, this "arty" four-year-old Chinatown lounge is an "urban oasis" with DJs spinning an "eclectic mix" of music, "late-night dance parties" and interesting "art installations"; with two bars (one on the rooftop) serving the "best fruit-infused drinks in town" and an always-changing happy-hour menu, this "super-cool" spot is "worth returning to repeatedly."

Tiki's Grill & Bar

21 | 20 | 20 | E

Waikiki | ResortQuest Waikiki Beach Hotel | 2570 Kalakaua Ave. (Kapahulu Ave.) | Honolulu | 808-923-8454 | www.tikisgrill.com
Those who "like tikis" will undoubtedly enjoy "grabbing a cocktail" at this oceanview indoor/outdoor restaurant bar that wraps around the dining room to the pool area on the second floor of the ResortQuest Waikiki Beach Hotel; locals suggest "bringing visitors here" for the "interesting pupus" and "good local bands" on weekends.

Twist at Hanohano

25 | 25 | 22 | E

Waikiki | Sheraton Waikiki | 2255 Kalakaua Ave., 30th fl. (Seaside Ave.) | Honolulu | 808-922-4422 | www.sheraton-waikiki.com
With "one of the most romantic" settings "overlooking Waikiki and Diamond Head", this "elegant" restaurant and lounge on the Sheraton's 30th floor is a "sophisticated" "sleeper" with an "attentive" staff and "fabulous", though "expensive", Eclectic-International fare focusing on locally sourced ingredients; after dark, there's "great" nightly music and dancing, and plenty of windows to take in the "spectacular" scene below.

Uncle Bo's

▽ 23 | 22 | 22 | M

Kapahulu | 559 Kapahulu Ave. (bet. Campbell Ave. & Herbert St.) | Honolulu | 808-735-8310 | www.unclebosrestaurant.com
A relative newcomer, this Kapahulu full-service restaurant with "incredibly delicious" pupus is a "welcoming" refuge come nighttime when the "relaxing vibe" and decor that's "anything but quaint" (lofted ceilings, chain curtains, a pink neon backlit bar) is "great for lounging"; "if you're lucky enough to score a seat", the "owners regularly stop to ask" how everything is.

Yard House, The

23 | 20 | 20 | E

Waikiki | Waikiki Beach Walk | 226 Lewers St. (Kalia Rd.) | Honolulu | 808-923-9273 | www.yardhouse.com
The Waikiki Beach Walk outpost of this national brewpub chain (founded by a former Hawaii resident) serves up a crowded "sports bar atmosphere" with "loud" classic rock and "beers of all kinds" (130 on tap); "great for big groups" and "people-watching", it draws flocks of young, "lively" revelers willing to withstand "long

waits" for what some nitpickers knock as "another chain experience to be found in any city."

Zanzabar

| 17 | 16 | 17 | E |

Waikiki | 2255 Kuhio Ave. (Seaside Ave.) | Honolulu | 808-924-3939 | www.zanzabarhawaii.com

Two dance floors, a VIP room and DJs who play "something for everyone" attract a strong twentysomething crowd of locals and military to this Waikiki club, especially on Thursdays and Fridays; even though "bored" cutting-edgers caution that the "dated decor" has "seen better days", others "spend the night dancing" (until 4 AM).

MAUI

Attractions

Most Popular

1. Haleakala Nat'l Pk.
2. Maui Ocean Ctr.
3. Old Lahaina Luau*
4. Black Rock Bch.
5. Hawaii Nature Ctr.

Top Appeal

28. Haleakala Nat'l Pk.
    Wailea Beach
    Old Lahaina Luau
27. Kapalua Bay Bch.
    Makena Beach

Dining

Most Popular

1. Mama's Fish | *Seafood*
2. Hali'imaile General | *Hawaii Reg.*
3. Roy's | *Hawaii Reg.*
4. Spago | *Californian/Pac. Rim*
5. Lahaina Grill | *American*
6. Hula Grill | *Pacific Rim*
7. Pacific'O | *Pacific Rim/Seafood*
8. Plantation House | *Med.*
9. Nick's Fishmkt. | *Seafood*
10. Sansei | *Japanese/Pac. Rim*
11. Kimo's | *American/Seafood*
12. Ferraro's | *Italian*
13. Aloha Mixed Plate | *Hawaiian*
14. Mala | *Hawaii Reg./Seafood*
15. Leilani's | *Seafood/Steak*
16. Gerard's | *French*
17. Pineapple Grill | *Pac. Rim*
18. I'O Restaurant | *Pan-Asian*
19. Chez Paul | *French*
20. Banyan Tree | *Eclectic*

Top Food Ratings

28. Gerard's | *French*
27. Hali'imaile Gen. | *Hawaii Reg.*
    Merriman's | *Hawaii Reg.*
    Mama's Fish | *Seafood*
26. Spago | *Californian/Pacific Rim*
    Chez Paul | *French*
    Sansei | *Japanese/Pac. Rim*
    Roy's | *Hawaii Reg.*
    Lahaina Grill | *American*
25. Pacific'O | *Pacific Rim/Seafood*

    Ferraro's | *Italian*
    Capische? | *Italian*
    Mala | *Hawaii Reg./Seafood*
    Hakona | *Steak*
    Ruth's Chris | *Steak*
    Waterfront Rest. | *Seafood*
    Nick's Fishmkt. | *Seafood*
24. Plantation House | *Med.*
    Son'z/Swan | *Seafood/Steak*
    T. Komoda | *Bakery*

BY CUISINE

AMERICAN (NEW)

26. Lahaina Grill
23. Prince Court
22. Joe's B&G

AMERICAN (TRAD.)

24. Gazebo
23. Kihei Caffe
22. Hana Ranch

HAWAIIAN

22. Da Kitchen
21. OnO B&G
    Aloha Mixed Plate

HAWAII REGIONAL

27. Hali'imaile General
    Merriman's
26. Roy's

---

* Indicates a tie with property above

ITALIAN

25 Ferraro's
    Capische?
20 Longhi's

JAPANESE

26 Sansei
25 Hakone
22 Kobe/Oku's

PACIFIC RIM

26 Spago
25 Pacific'O
23 Pineapple Grill

SEAFOOD

27 Mama's Fish
25 Pacific'O
    Mala

STEAKHOUSES

25 Ruth's Chris
24 Son'z/Swan Court
    DUO

Top Decor Ratings

28 Son'z/Swan Court
    Spago
27 Ferraro's
    Plantation House
26 Mama's Fish

    Humu's
    Sarento's/Beach
25 Banyan Tree
    Capische?
    Gerard's*

Top Service Ratings

27 Ferraro's
26 Gerard's
    Spago
25 Merriman's
    Son'z/Swan Court

    Chez Paul
    DUO
    Mama's Fish
    Lahaina Grill
24 Plantation House

Best Buys

In order of Bang for the Buck rating.

1. T. Komoda
2. Ba-Le Sandwich
3. Gazebo
4. Da Kitchen
5. Kihei Caffe
6. Maui Tacos
7. Aloha Mixed Plate
8. Cilantro Grill
9. Tasty Crust
10. L&L Drive-Inn
11. Kozo Sushi
12. Alexander's
13. Zippy's
14. Peggy Sue's

Golf

Top Courses

29 Kapalua/Plantation
26 Wailea/Gold
    Wailea/Emerald

25 Makena/North
    Kapalua/Bay

Hotels

Top Overall

28 Four Seasons Resort/Wailea
26 Ritz-Carlton Kapalua
25 Hana-Maui

    Fairmont Kea Lani
23 Grand Wailea Resort

Maui Attractions

Alexander & Baldwin Sugar Museum ▽ 20 | 19 | 19 | I
Puunene | 3957 Hansen Rd. (Mokulele Hwy.) | 808-871-8058 |
www.sugarmuseum.com

"You'll smell it miles before you see it" say sweet-toothed surveyors who sojourn to this museum "embedded in the heart of sugarcane country" that's a great place to "educate kids on the importance of" this crop to Hawaii's development; though some feel it's "not worth a special trip" to the remote Puunene location, those who are "fascinated" ask "who knew sugar could be so much fun?"

Atlantis Submarine 24 | 22 | 23 | E
Lahaina | 658 Front St. (bet. Dickenson & Prison Sts.) | 808-356-1800 |
888-349-7888 | www.atlantisadventures.com
See review in Oahu Attractions Directory.

Baldwin Home ▽ 21 | 18 | 19 | I
Lahaina | 120 Dickenson St. (Front St.) | 808-661-3262
"Learn about Maui's past" at this "wonderfully maintained" coral, stone and hand-hewn timber home in historic Lahaina that dates from 1835 and was once the residence of local physician the Rev. Dwight Baldwin; it "gives a good introduction to missionary life on the islands" as well as an "interesting" peek into the "history of this whaling town."

Black Rock Beach 26 | 18 | 15 | $0
Kaanapali | Kaanapali Bch.
You "can't beat the snorkeling" at this "naturally protected", "wide" beach steps from the Sheraton Maui in Kaanapali, where the "clear water" and "loads of fish, sea turtles and marine life" draw "wall-to-wall people" in flippers and masks; it's "fun for teens to jump off" the eponymous lava outcropping, and there's "easy access to food and shopping" nearby.

Drums of the Pacific Polynesian Spectacular 23 | 22 | 22 | E
Kaanapali | Hyatt Regency Maui | 200 Nohea Kai Dr. (Kaanapali Pkwy.) |
808-661-1234 | www.hyatt.com
"It feels like what it is – a huge resort's luau" that's "a little cheesy" but "full of the aloha spirit" with "enthusiastic performances" and audience participation ("be prepared to dance barefoot if it's your anniversary"); its "seating cattle call is a drag", the "food is just ok" and the tab "a bit expensive", but overall surveyors find this "fun-for-the-whole-family" Kaanapali Beach experience "better than anticipated."

Feast at Lele 27 | 25 | 25 | VE
Lahaina | 505 Front St. (Shaw St.) | 808-667-5353 |
www.feastatlele.com
"Not your typical luau", this "pricey", "five-star, five-course" production is "much more intimate" than most thanks to its "small" Lahaina "waterfront" venue and "private tables" with "spectacular service"; the "superb" food "from around the South Pacific" is "coupled with indigenous entertainment" and accompanied by "amazing lava flow drinks" from the "premium open bar"; it's "more Polynesian than Hawaiian", but it's "worth the splurge."

	APPEAL	FACIL.	SERVICE	COST

⚡ Haleakala National Park | 28 | 20 | 19 | I |

Makawao | Park Headquarters Visitor Ctr. | Hwy. 378 (off Hwy. 377) | 808-572-4400 | www.nps.gov/hale

The "winding ride up" and often "freezing" temperatures atop Maui's 10,023-ft. dormant volcano only add to the excitement say sojourners to this "jewel in the crown of Hawaii's parks", voted the island's Most Popular and top Attraction for Appeal; on clear mornings the "spectacular" sunrise is a "religious experience", and at any time of day the serene landscape will "take your breath away"; adventurers recommend hiking into the massive crater or biking from the top "down to the ocean."

Hawaii Nature Center/'Iao Valley | 24 | 17 | 14 | I |

Wailuku | 875 'Iao Valley Rd. (off Rte. 30) | 808-244-6500 | www.hawaiinaturecenter.org

The "easy hike" to 'Iao Needle (a 12,000-ft.-tall lava pinnacle) ascends through "lushly vegetated terrain" at this "mist-shrouded" "mystical" state park with a *Jurassic Park* feel in Central Maui; details of the "bloody battle" that took place here in 1790 are provided along the walkway – just be sure to bring your own provisions because, while the grounds are "steeped in history", they're lacking facilities "other than a restroom at the beginning of the trail."

Ho'okipa Beach | 26 | 13 | 8 | $0 |

Paia | Hwy. 36 (Stable Rd.)

Laid-back types "brave the wind" and "catch the local scene" of "teenagers and twentysomethings" "just hangin' out" at this "beautiful" Paia-area beach; "stand safely back and watch" as "awesome" windsurfers flip in the ocean's "huge" winter waves, especially during the world-class competitions held here; N.B. swimming is not recommended.

Kapalua Bay Beach | 27 | 21 | 16 | $0 |

Kapalua | bet. Bay Terr. & the Point (Lower Honoapiiliani Rd.) | 808-669-3448

"The water is so blue it looks like it's on a postcard" at this "dreamy" beach where the "gentle surf and beginner snorkeling" are just right for kids, and the "romantic" sunsets perfect for adults; set "in front of the Kapalua Resort", it's "not usually crowded", yet "parking is a problem."

Lahaina-Kaanapali Sugar Cane Train | 17 | 18 | 18 | I |

Kaanapali | 975 Limahana Pl. (Honoapiilani Hwy.) | 808-667-6851 | 800-499-2307 | www.sugarcanetrain.com

Surveyors are split over this slow, six-mile loop on a restored locomotive in Kaanapali: train buffs find it a "big adventure" for young kids and parents who "enjoy the commentary" by "singing conductors", while critics call the "meandering" route "through strip malls and golf courses" "a bit kitschy", "overpriced" and even "boring."

Makawao | 22 | 19 | 17 | $0 |

Makawao | Hwy. 365 (Makawao Ave.)

"One of the few old Hawaiian towns left", this "charming" community stretching "barely more than two blocks" harkens back to the heyday of "Upcountry Maui" ranches – and though today it's more "artsy-craftsy" than "cowboy", the streets still sport a "Western flair" (keep an eye out for "real paniolos"); with "upmarket shops", galleries and "reasonable restaurants", it makes a "wonderful" stop.

Makena Beach State Park

27 | 14 | 11 | $0

Makena | S. Makena Rd. (Wailea Alanui Rd.) | 808-879-4364

"Shockingly" large in both width and length, this park's "big beach" (also known as Oneloa Beach) is labeled "one of the most beautiful stretches of undeveloped white sand around" by locals who laud its "crystal-clear water" and "big, chunky waves" – not for kids or the "aquatically challenged"; "au naturel" types are drawn here, despite legal restrictions against nude sunbathing; N.B. facilities are limited.

Maui Ocean Center

26 | 25 | 22 | M

Maalaea | 192 Maalaea Rd. (Honoapiilani Hwy.) | 808-270-7000 | www.mauioceancenter.com

A "winner for all ages", this "fabulous" five-acre Maalaea aquarium features an "unbeatable variety of aquatic life" overseen by a "delightful cadre of staff and volunteers" who help you "identify the fish you've been snorkeling with"; "kids go ga-ga" over the "touch ponds", "cool coral reef exhibit" and "awesome walk-through tunnel filled with fish and sharks", while their folks favor the "excellent" "sit-down restaurant."

Maui Tropical Plantation

21 | 21 | 21 | M

Wailuku | 1670 Honoapiilani Hwy. (Wilikona Pl.) | 808-244-7643 | www.mauitropicalplantation.com

"Walk through the gardens" or pay for a tram ride tour at this 60-acre Wailuku working plantation where you'll learn "everything you've ever wanted to know about the flora and crops of Hawaii"; as for hands-on experience, you can "try coconut right off the trees" and "feed the ducks, geese and swans", though a few detractors deem it "touristy" and call the gift shop's "typical souvenirs" "a bit pricey."

⊠ Old Lahaina Luau

28 | 27 | 27 | E

Lahaina | 1251 Front St. (bet. Kapunakea & Keawe Sts.) | 808-661-9633 | 800-248-5828 | www.oldlahainaluau.com

Voted No. 1 luau in the state, this "most authentic" show – "no fire dancers" – boasts "professional" practicers of the "beautiful art of the hula", "talented musicians" and "educational" storytellers; add in "free-flowing mai tais, a feast to feed a king", "outstanding service" and a waterside setting, and consensus is this Lahaina attraction is "worth every penny."

Paia

23 | 18 | 19 | $0

Paia | along Hwy. 390 | www.paiamaui.com

"Once known for its congregation of hippies", this "funky" hamlet "on the drive to Hana" has recently become a "destination unto itself", with an "eclectic mix of chic boutiques, healthy restaurants and local artisans" in "quaint historic buildings"; though some decry its gentrification as "touristy", others insist it offers Maui's "best shopping", especially since the stores abut some serious shore, where "amazing" local wind and kite surfers "fly through the air."

Pools at O'heo

26 | 14 | 12 | $0

(aka Seven Sacred Pools)

Hana | O'heo Gulch | Hwy. 31, m.m. 42 | 808-572-4400

"Nothing says paradise more than playing around in waterfalls" amid "lush surroundings" say sojourners who've made the "long", "white-knuckle drive" to this "gorgeous destination" – "awe-inspiring" falls and pools ("neither sacred nor seven in number") that trail through the O'heo Gulch 10 miles from Hana; "call ahead to see if you can swim in the pools", since they close under flood watches.

Tedeschi Vineyards & Winery
(aka Maui's Winery)

22 | 21 | 21 | $0

Kula | Kula Hwy./Ulupalakua Ranch (Waipoli Rd.) | 808-878-6058

"Vineyards on the side of a volcano – who'da thought?" query quaffers who insist this "small-scale winery" with "unforgettable" "Upcountry vistas" and "free tours" run by an "enthusiastic" staff is "worth the long drive" to "remote South Maui"; if serious oenophiles find the "wines a little rough", most are happy to simply stroll the "pretty grounds" and try the complimentary tastes of "unusual" offerings, like a sparkling pineapple pour.

Wailea Beach

28 | 21 | 19 | $0

Wailea | Wailea Alanui Dr. (bet. Four Seasons Resort Maui & Grand Wailea Resort)

Sun-worshipers anoint this "magnificent" "sandy" stretch in a "ritzy", "absolutely beautiful area of South Maui" "one of the best beaches" on the island and beyond, especially given the "scenic beachwalk path" that fronts a slew of "luxurious" high-end resorts, shops and restaurants; the waters are relatively calm due to the location between two black lava points, though it can be "crowded" at various spots in high season.

Wailea Beach Marriott Honua-ula Luau

∇ 23 | 21 | 20 | E

Wailea | Wailea Beach Marriott | 3700 Wailea Alanui Dr. (Hale Alii Pl.) | 808-879-6160

The "well-done" show is the centerpiece at this Wailea luau that's "pretty good", with "plenty of mai tais" flowing alongside a spread of "adequate food"; pre-show activities include lei-making and Hawaiian games (audience participation is encouraged), and when it comes to the post-show, nothing beats its "marvelous sunsets."

Wainapanapa State Park

∇ 28 | 17 | 13 | $0

Hana | Wainapanapa Rd. (off Hana Hwy.) | 808-984-8109

The crown jewel of this 122-acre coastal park in Hana is its "awesome black sand beach" that's not for swimming, since the water can be "extremely rough"; "fabulous rock formations" – including a "stunning sea arch" and "small lava tube you can walk through" – are an added draw, plus there's native forest to hike in and anchialine pools (landlocked waters with subterranean connections to the ocean); N.B. there are cabins and a campground, but you must reserve months ahead.

Whalers Village Museum

19 | 20 | 18 | $0

Lahaina | Whalers Vill. | 2435 Kaanapali Pkwy. (Hwy. 30) | 808-661-5992 | www.whalersvillage.com

It's easy to overlook this "small, inconspicuous" free museum located on the third floor of the Whalers Village shopping center, yet those who do stop in get a "fascinating peek" into Lahaina's whaling past (e.g. photographs, 19th-century scrimshaw, ivory and bone utensils); a self-guided audio tour talks visitors through the "neat artifacts", though squeamish sorts should be warned that depictions of the "cutting of the blubber" can be "sickening", "even for the non-PETA crowd."

Maui Dining

AK's Café ⊠Ⓜ *American* ▽ 20 | 11 | 19 | $25
Wailuku | 1237 Lower Main St. (Kawaipuna Pl.) | 808-244-8774 | www.akscafe.com

An eclectic mix of "tasty", "reasonably priced" American fare makes this Wailuku eatery a weekday hot spot for lunch among area worker bees who like the "appealing" healthy choices and "friendly service"; but the "better-than-average" cooking is marred by the "unimpressive" storefront setting with "cramped", "uncomfortable" seating.

Alexander's Fish, Chicken & Ribs *American* 22 | 8 | 16 | $14
Kihei | 1913 S. Kihei Rd. (Keala Pl.) | 808-874-0788

"Unsurpassed", "decadently" crunchy fish 'n' chips "the Hawaiian way" drive seafood lovers to this "funky" Kihei fast-food shack that's low on decor but high on "budget"-priced American vittles (including "good ribs" and "deep-fried chicken"); given the foot traffic, the "fast" and "friendly" service is key; N.B. a new location is slated for the Queen Kaahumanu Center.

Aloha Mixed Plate *Hawaiian* 21 | 16 | 17 | $15
Lahaina | 1285 Front St. (Kapunakea St.) | 808-661-3322 | www.alohamixedplate.com

Seats and bellies "fill up" fast at this "true " Hawaiian "experience" in Lahaina combining an "authentic island" ambiance with the "best", "cheap" plate lunch around; the "ono grindz" and "million-dollar" ocean views from the "lovely beachfront deck" make up for the so-so service, and if "you're there at the right time, you'll hear music from the Old Lahaina Luau next door."

Anthony's Coffee Co. *Coffeehouse* ▽ 20 | 17 | 20 | $13
Paia | 90 Hana Hwy. (Kauiki St.) | 808-579-8340 | www.anthonyscoffee.com

Java junkies, the "'in' crowd" and tourists on their way to Hana "get their brew" at this "warm" and "lively" Paia coffeehouse that roasts its own beans and backs the "awesome" caffeine drinks with breakfast wraps, hot and cold lunch sandwiches, "amazing baked goods" and ice cream; the decor is "a bit overwhelming" considering all the "stuff" on the walls, but there's "great people-watching."

Aroma D'Italia *Italian* ▽ 18 | 18 | 19 | $31
Kihei | Kihei Town Ctr. | 1881 S. Kihei Rd. (Halelani Pl.) | 808-879-0133 | www.aromaditaliamaui.com

There's "not a palm tree in sight" at this Kihei address, where the portions of "tasty" Sicilian fare are "huge", the service "helpful" and the prices "reasonable"; even though it gets props for a seasonally changing wine selection, picky paesani who "have an Italian itch, scratch it elsewhere."

A Saigon Café *Vietnamese* 23 | 12 | 20 | $25
Wailuku | 1792 Main St. (Kaniela St.) | 808-243-9560

There's "no signage" outside this "inexpensive", "low-key" Wailuku eatery, but "who needs one when you're this good?" ask admirers who attest to the most "authentic", "tastiest Vietnamese on Maui", albeit in a rather "unpretentious" setting; the "exuberant staff" that treats

	FOOD	DECOR	SERVICE	COST

even newcomers "like regulars" makes it easy to "leave the beach" or "drive here from the other side of the island."

Asian Star *Vietnamese*

▽ 20 | 9 | 17 | $21

Wailuku | 1764 Wili Pa Loop (Imi Kala St.) | 808-244-1833

It may be seriously lacking in atmosphere, but this "no-frills" Central Maui Vietnamese in a Wailuku "light industrial park" scores points for "tasty" authentic fare at modest prices; those deterred by setting and service say it makes "great takeout."

Ba-Le Sandwich Shop *Vietnamese*

20 | 6 | 14 | $9

Kahului | Maui Mktpl. | 270 Dairy Rd. (Maui Marketplace Dr.) | 808-877-2400
Lahaina | Lahaina Cannery Mall | 1221 Honoapiilani Hwy. (Kaewe St.) | 808-661-5566
www.ba-le.com

See review in Oahu Dining Directory.

Banyan Tree 🄢Ⓜ *Eclectic*

24 | 25 | 24 | $69

Kapalua | Ritz-Carlton Kapalua | 1 Ritz-Carlton Dr. (Office Rd.) | 808-669-6200 | www.ritzcarlton.com

You'll find a "picture-perfect", open-air setting with "gorgeous" views of the Pacific and nearby Molokai at the "striking", and "pricey", signature restaurant of the newly renovated Ritz-Carlton Kapalua; the staff "treats you like an old friend" and the "innovative" International-Eclectic menu pulls from local sources, but it's the "wonderful" atmosphere that steals the show.

BJ's Chicago Pizzeria *Pizza*

19 | 16 | 16 | $21

Lahaina | 730 Front St. (bet. Dickenson St. & Lahainaluna Rd.) | 808-661-0700

Authorities "taste Chicago" in every bite of the "genuine" deep-dish delights delivered at this Lahaina pizzeria, where the "long waits" attest to the "fabulous" pies, "yummy" salads and worth-it desserts (white-chocolate-chip-mac-nut-cookie pies); "forget about decor or service" and focus on the "amazing" sunsets and "excellent" live music instead.

Bubba Gump Shrimp Co. *American/Seafood*

15 | 17 | 17 | $26

Lahaina | 889 Front St. (Papalaua St.) | 808-661-3111 | www.bubbagump.com

See review in Oahu Dining Directory.

Buzz's Wharf *Seafood/Steak*

19 | 18 | 19 | $36

Maalaea | Maalaea Bay Harbor (off Hwy. 30) | 808-244-5426 | www.buzzswharf.com

The "relaxing" water views and "excellent fresh" fish and steak at this "busy" Maalaea harborside seafooder has made it a "definite stopping place" for 40 years; though there are "wonderful shrimp dishes" and lots of "socializing", the service is "unexceptional."

Café Mambo *Eclectic*

▽ 23 | 21 | 20 | $21

Paia | 30 Baldwin Ave. (bet. Akoni & Kulia Pls.) | 808-579-8021 | www.cafemambomaui.com

The "ambitious" food delivers an "unexpected treat for the taste buds" at this "funky" Paia Eclectic, where the "reasonably priced" menu includes "delicious" breakfast burritos, "unique" salads, plate lunches, fajitas, burgers and paella; the "quirky" artwork, "surfer" crowd and once-a-week classic movie nights create a "festive" atmosphere.

	FOOD	DECOR	SERVICE	COST

Café O Lei Ⓜ *Seafood/Steak*
24 | 20 | 20 | $32

Kihei | Rainbow Mall | 2439 S. Kihei Rd. (bet. Keonekai St. & S. Kihei Rd.) | 808-891-1368 | www.cafeoleirestaurants.com

Admirers hail the "variety" and "quality" of offerings (e.g. "off-the-charts" seafood with a local twist, solid steaks, an "excellent" sushi bar) served at this "colorfully decorated", Kihei strip-mall spot where "friendly" staffers "hustle" to keep up with the flow (the "loud ambiance isn't for everyone"); though dinners are "reasonably priced", "budget-conscious" customers give a shout out to the "outstanding" lunch deals.

Capische? *Italian*
25 | 25 | 23 | $67

Wailea | Diamond Resort | 555 Kaukahi St. (Wailea Alanui Dr.) | 808-879-2224 | www.capische.com

A "refreshing surprise" awaits diners at this "expensive" hilltop Northern Italian in the Diamond Resort in Wailea, where the "exceptional" cuisine ("every plate is an experience") is complemented by a "fantastic" wine list; add in the "unbelievable sunset views" and "attentive", if sometimes "slow", service, and this becomes a "wonderfully" "romantic" choice.

Casanova *Italian*
20 | 15 | 18 | $32

Makawao | 1188 Makawao Ave. (Baldwin Ave.) | 808-572-0220 | www.casanovamaui.com

"Locals" favor this Upcountry Italian "mainstay" in Makawao for its "cozy", "family" atmosphere that "comes alive at night", sometimes with dancing and DJs; the "solid" menu of wood-oven-fired pizza, traditional pastas and mainstays such as eggplant parmigiana and osso buco is accompanied by a "reasonable" wine list, but a few naysayers deem it all just "ok in a pinch"; N.B. there's a deli and informal cafe attached.

Cascades Grille & Sushi Bar *Japanese/Pacific Rim*
23 | 25 | 23 | $51

Kaanapali | Hyatt Regency Maui | 200 Nohea Kai Dr. (Kaanapali Pkwy.) | 808-667-4727 | www.hyatt.com

"The sounds of the ocean", "tropical breezes" and "wonderful" water views help make for "memorable" meals at this "romantic" Pacific Rim restaurant in the Hyatt Regency Maui; the "well-versed" staff helps navigate the "delicious" choices, including "excellent" sushi, whether you're here for "afternoon drinks and apps" followed by a "gorgeous sunset" or for a "special night out."

Castaway Café *Continental*
22 | 20 | 24 | $29

Kaanapali | ResortQuest Maui Kaanapali Villas | 45 Kai Ala Dr. (Honoapiilani Hwy.) | 808-661-9091 | www.castawaycafe.com

A "secret breakfast spot for locals" that serves "large portions" of "great loco moco" at "reasonable prices", this "dependable" "hard-to-find" Continental with local flair at ResortQuest Kaanapali Villas rewards sojourners with "tables on the beach" and "lovely ocean views"; there are "dinner specials every night" ("Sunday babyback ribs" are a "favorite") and the "efficient" staff and setting are "kid-friendly", so even though it's "sure not gourmet", it's a "hidden gem" all the same.

Charley's Restaurant *American*

19 | 15 | 18 | $20

Paia | 142 Hana Hwy. (Alakapa Pl.) | 808-579-9453 | www.charleyspaia.com

The "low-key", "aging-hippie" vibe appeals to locals who "love" this Paia American that closed briefly last year after a fire, but is once again serving its beloved "industrial-size" breakfasts (e.g. "fabulous" mac-nut pancakes "like hubcaps on a Mack truck") and "awesome" sandwiches, as well as offering "good" live music and drinks; the "biker-bar facade" and "slack" service don't scare away insiders who swear it's a "popular" "Willie Nelson hangout."

Cheeseburger in Paradise *American*

17 | 18 | 17 | $21

Lahaina | 811 Front St. (Lahainaluna Rd.) | 808-661-4855 | www.cheeseburgerland.com

Enthusiasts say this burger chain with locations on Oahu and Maui can be a "fun" (if "overpriced") "tourist trap" since the "two-napkin burger", "awesome cocktails", "live music" and "tropical" "open-air" settings "aren't bad"; but those who can't get past the "cheesy decor", "non-stop souvenir sales", "hit-or-miss service" and constant Jimmy Buffet tunes snap "if this is cheesburger in paradise, then send me to hell."

Chez Paul *French*

26 | 21 | 25 | $62

Olowalu | 820B Olowalu Village Rd. (Honoapiilani Hwy.) | Lahaina | 808-661-3843 | www.chezpaul.net

"A rare breath of French air" on Maui, this "isolated" Olowalu destination "away from the crowds" offers "terrific" Provençal preparations backed by "well-trained" servers and a "charming" Gallic ambiance "perfect for celebrating"; thanks to "high standards" across the board, you're in for a "memorable", if "pricey", experience.

China Boat *Chinese*

16 | 11 | 15 | $23

Lahaina | 4474 Lower Honoapiilani Rd. (bet. Hua Nui & Omaikai Pls.) | 808-669-5089

China Bowl *Chinese*

Kaanapali | Fairway Shops | 2580 Kekaa Dr. (Kualapa Loop) | 808-661-0660 www.chinaboatandbowlmaui.com

The fare "arrives promptly" from the "relaxed" servers at this "old-fashioned" Chinese Maui duo in Lahaina and Kaanapali; though some find "well-prepared", "decent" dishes that are "not bad" "for takeout", those who discover "boring" fare and "run-down" digs dock elsewhere.

Cilantro Grill *Mexican*

22 | 14 | 18 | $16

Lahaina | Old Lahaina Ctr. | 170 Papalaua Ave. (bet. Front & Wainee Sts.) | 808-667-5444 | www.cilantrogrill.com

For "above-average" Mexican "fast food", amigos amble over to this "hard-to-find" BYOB Lahaina eatery, where the "fast", "friendly" staff delivers "large" portions of "delicious" standards at "budget prices"; the "casual" atmosphere with "just a couple of tables" means it's best suited for a "quick takeout to the beach."

CJ's Deli & Diner *American*

18 | 12 | 14 | $16

Kaanapali | Fairway Shops | 2580 Kekaa Dr. (Kualapa Loop) | 808-667-0968 | www.cjsmaui.com

"Large and filling" sandwiches (with meats from New York), "delicious" breakfast items like Hawaiian sweet bread French toast and other American comfort fare from this family-run Kaanapali eatery keep locals "going all day long"; the "casual" setting and service don't score points, but the "amazing" value means you can pack an "affordable" "picnic lunch for the road to Hana."

Colleen's at the Cannery *American*   - | - | - | M

Haiku | Haiku Cannery Mktpl. | 810 Haiku Rd. (Kokomo Rd.) | 808-575-9211 | www.colleensinhaiku.com

The comments are few but the praise is high for this casual, somewhat "rustic" New American at the Haiku Cannery Marketplace proffering a wide-ranging, all-day menu of "fresh", local, organic fare, from eggs Benedict to filet mignon; the "value" pricing for "huge portions" and the martini list make it all the more "worth the drive."

Da Kitchen *Hawaiian*   22 | 10 | 17 | $14

Kahului | 425 Koloa St. (Hana Hwy.) | 808-871-7782 ⑤
Kihei | Rainbow Mall | 2439 S. Kihei Rd. (bet. Alanui Ke Alii Rd. & Keonekai St.) | 808-875-7782
www.da-kitchen.com

"Go hungry" to better confront the "staggeringly" "huge", "coronary-in-the-making" portions at these "crowded" Hawaiians in Kihei and Kahului, "da best" when it comes to "good ol'" island cooking; the "cheap" eats, "friendly" service and "lots of favorites" (lomi lomi salmon, ahi poke, etc.) make them the "big kahunas of the mixed-plate joints."

Dollie's Pub & Café ❶ *American*   ▽ 16 | 8 | 15 | $19

Lahaina | 4310 L. Honoapiilani Rd. (bet. Hoohui Rd. & Kepola Pl.) | 808-669-0266

A "hole-in-the-wall" "watering hole" with "friendly" staffers and a "laid-back" attitude, this "inexpensive" Lahaina sports pub plys "game-watching" patrons with "basic" American bar food – burgers, pizza, sandwiches, beer; even if the decor is little more than a bunch of "large-screen TVs", it's "ok for a quick bite."

Dragon Dragon *Chinese*   ▽ 20 | 17 | 20 | $27

Kahului | Maui Mall | 70 E. Kaahumanu Ave. (Wharf St.) | 808-893-1628

If you "try the seafood platter" at this Kahului Chinese, you might have to "go home and sleep it off or walk the beach" say fans who find a good "value" at this "fast and efficient" mall-based eatery; although there's "nothing exquisite" here, with such little competition it may be Maui's "best Chinese by default."

🆕 DUO *Seafood/Steak*   24 | 25 | 25 | $74

Wailea | Four Seasons Resort Maui at Wailea | 3900 Wailea Alanui Dr. (Wailea Ike Dr.) | 808-874-8000 | www.fourseasons.com

Advocates "can't come up with enough adjectives to praise" this "first-class" Four Seasons Wailea steak-and-seafooder boasting a "lovely" poolside setting "overlooking the ocean" and dishes that "don't get any better" (the Kobe beef is "amazing"); "attentive" service means you'll "never want for anything", except, say some, lower tabs, since you may need to "inherit the old man's fortune" before venturing here.

🅩 Ferraro's *Italian*   25 | 27 | 27 | $64

Wailea | Four Seasons Resort Maui at Wailea | 3900 Wailea Alanui Dr. (Wailea Ike Dr.) | 808-874-8000 | www.fourseasons.com

The "absolutely outstanding" staff at this "magical" Italian "overlooking the ocean" in the Four Seasons Wailea earns this eatery the No. 1

rating for Service on Maui, since it helps deliver "one of the most memorable experiences you'll have on this island"; of course, the "unbelievable" sunsets and "creative" food "to die for" certainly help, so if you can "spend the big bucks" this is one "special night out."

Five Palms Beach Grill *Pacific Rim/Seafood* | 20 | 24 | 20 | $44 |

Kihei | 2960 S. Kihei Rd. (bet. Ala Koa St. & Kilohana Dr.) | 808-879-2607 | www.fivepalmsrestaurant.com

The "unmatched" location of this open-air, oceanfront Kihei Pacific Rim seafooder – with "gorgeous" sunsets, romantic tiki tourches and "nice breezes" – outscores a menu that some describe as "boring" and a staff that "wishes it were out on the waves"; for the best experience "keep expectations realistic", "demand the patio", and go "for breakfast" or "drinks and apps", then "call it quits."

NEW Flatbread Company *Pizza* | 23 | 17 | 19 | $24 |

Paia | 89 Hana Hwy. (Baldwin Ave.) | 808-579-8989 | www.flatbreadcompany.com

Pizza "with pizzazz" proclaim proponents of this Paia link in the New England–based chain that focuses on organic produce and free-range meats atop its "fantastic" wood-fired pies; the "welcoming" atmosphere and "funky", "arty" decor attract loads of youngsters – so be prepared for "crowds."

Gazebo, The *American* | 24 | 20 | 22 | $16 |

Napili | Napili Shores | 5315 Lower Honoapiilani Rd. (Hui Rd.) | 808-669-5621

"Memorable" macadamia-nut pancakes and other "amazing" American items have made this "casual", open-air breakfast-and-lunch cafe a Napili hilltop mainstay for three decades; its legions of fans brave "long lines" (the "to-die-for-views" help make "time fly by") to sit amid the "quintessential island" atmosphere; P.S. in season, you can "watch the whales play near the shore."

NEW Genki Sushi *Japanese* | 17 | 13 | 16 | $19 |

Lahaina | Lahaina Gateway Ctr. | 325 Keawe St. (Honoapiilani Hwy.) | 808-661-0333 | www.genkisushiusa.com

See review in Oahu Dining Directory.

Z Gerard's *French* | 28 | 25 | 26 | $68 |

Lahaina | The Plantation Inn | 174 Lahainaluna Rd. (Wainee St.) | 808-661-8939 | www.gerardsmaui.com

Voted No. 1 for Food on Maui, this *très chic* Lahaina classic is "hidden away" in a "charming" plantation-style inn, where "maestro" chef-owner Gerard Reversade's "masterfully executed" New French menu with contemporary island touches "blends fresh local fish and produce" in a "memorable way"; add in "stellar" wines, "outstanding" service and an "elegant", "tropical" setting – both inside and on the "lovely" veranda – and you've got a "delightful", if "expensive", experience.

Grandma's Coffeehouse *Coffeehouse* ∇ | 20 | 14 | 18 | $14 |

Kula | 153 Kula Hwy. (Waheldhi St.) | 800-375-7853 | www.grandmascoffee.com

"You really feel like you're home with grandma" at this "small" Kula "shack" that's a favorite coffeehouse for locals who pull in for "delicious" muffins, cinnamon rolls, savories and coffee that's "roasted freshly on-site"; its "casual" confines are enhanced by "wonderful" ocean and mountain views from the deck.

Hakone 🅈🅼 *Japanese* 25 | 21 | 24 | $52

Makena | Maui Prince Hotel | 5400 Makena Alanui Rd. (Hanoiki St.) | 808-874-1111
See review in Oahu Dining Directory.

🆉 Hali'imaile General Store *Hawaii Reg.* 27 | 22 | 24 | $49

Makawao | 900 Haliimaile Rd. (off Rte. 37) | 808-572-2666 | www.bevgannonrestaurants.com
Widely hailed as a "Maui treasure", this "magical", Upcountry eatery near the base of Haleakala impresses with "spectacular", "skillfully prepared" "locally sourced" Hawaii Regional fare under the guidance of chef-owner Bev Gannon; add in "professional" service and "quaint", plantation-style decor, and it's little wonder that "locals and visitors alike" insist it's been "worth the drive from anywhere" for more than 20 years.

Hana Ranch Restaurant *American/Burgers* 22 | 21 | 23 | $40

Hana | Hotel Hana-Maui | end of Hana Hwy. | 808-270-5280 | www.hotelhanamaui.com
Find "heaven" at the end of the long, "winding" Hana Highway at this "peaceful", ranch-style roadhouse serving "surprisingly fresh" American eats that hit a high note with the "incredible" burger; its "genuine" staff will "greet you like long-lost family", plus you get first-rate ocean views when dining outside.

Hard Rock Cafe *American* 14 | 20 | 17 | $28

Lahaina | 900 Front St. (Papalaua St.) | 808-667-7400 | www.hardrock.com
See review in Oahu Dining Directory.

🆉 Hula Grill *Pacific Rim* 21 | 23 | 20 | $35

Kaanapali | Whalers Vill. | 2435 Kaanapali Pkwy. (off Honoapiilani Hwy.) | 808-667-6636 | www.hulagrill.com
See review in Oahu Dining Directory.

Humu's *Pacific Rim* 22 | 26 | 22 | $62

Wailea | Grand Wailea Resort | 3850 Wailea Alanui Dr. (bet. Hoolei Cir. & Kaukahi St.) | 808-875-1234 | www.grandwailea.com
"One of most romantic" haunts in Hawaii, this thatched-roof, open-air Pacific Rim respite in the Grand Wailea Resort distinguishes itself with a "stunning" "tropical" setting (built over a saltwater pond stocked with fish) and swoon-worthy sunsets; diners are divided on the food, however, with fans calling it "excellent" and foes saying it "could be better" given the "too-pricey" tabs.

I'O Restaurant *Pan-Asian* 24 | 24 | 22 | $54

Lahaina | 505 Front St. (Shaw St.) | 808-661-8422 | www.iomaui.com
"Sublime" presentations lure fans to this "pricey", "romantic" beach-side Lahaina Pan-Asian (companion to the neighboring Pacific'O) that also boasts "spectacular" ocean and sunset views and "attentive" service; regulars recommend sitting outside "if you don't mind the music from the luau next door."

	FOOD	DECOR	SERVICE	COST

Isana, Restaurant _Korean_

| - | - | - | M |

Kihei | 515 S. Kihei Rd. (bet. Kaonoulu St. & Ohukai Rd.) | 808-874-5700 | www.isanarestaurant.net

A mix of "tasty" traditional Korean cookery, including "grill-at-your-table" BBQ and sushi plates, draws "laid-back" locals to this "comfort-able", "undiscovered" Kihei "gem"; prices fall in the "not-too-crazy" range, and "good sunset views" add to the allure.

Joe's Bar & Grill _American_

| 22 | 18 | 21 | $47 |

Wailea | 131 Wailea Ike Pl. (Wailea Ike Dr.) | 808-875-7767 | www.bevgannonrestaurants.com

Folks walk out "feeling good" after dinner at this "relaxed" New American (above the Wailea Tennis Club) where celeb chef Bev Gannon's "limited" menu of "hearty" comfort food "pleases"; its "friendly" staff includes "jovial" bartenders crafting "killer" cocktails, but just be sure to make a reservation, since it's "always packed."

Kihei Caffe ⊟ _American_

| 23 | 11 | 18 | $15 |

Kihei | 1945 S. Kihei Rd. (bet. Alahele & Keala Pls.) | 808-879-2230

"Grab a table outside and watch the surfers, hippies and tourists stroll by" at this "no-frills", counter-service American "shack" in Kihei that's an "excellent choice for budget eating", especially at breakfast when the "huge portions" of "luscious baked goods" and "artery-clogging" entrees mean "you may not need to eat again until dinner"; the only seats are outside, and they don't take credit cards, yet still, diehards "design their trips around a stop" here.

Kimo's ❶ _American/Seafood_

| 20 | 21 | 20 | $35 |

Lahaina | 845 Front St. (Lahainaluna Rd.) | 808-661-4811 | www.kimosmaui.com

"It's all about sitting on the waterfront patio" and "watching the sun-set" at this "longstanding Lahaina landmark" and "tourist fave" that "stays true to its roots" with "dependable" breakfasts and seafood-centric American lunches and dinners; the "outstanding" drinks, "friendly" staff and "reasonable" rates draw in both family groups and "romantic" duos; P.S. "don't leave without ordering the hula pie!"

Kobe Japanese Steak House & Oku's Sushi Bar _Japanese_

| 22 | 18 | 21 | $42 |

Lahaina | 136 Dickenson St, (Luakini St.) | 808-667-5555 | www.kobemaui.com

See review in Oahu Dining Directory.

Koho Grill & Bar _American_

| ▽ 18 | 14 | 18 | $27 |

Kahului | Queen Kaahumanu Ctr. | 275 W. Kaahumanu Ave. (S. Wakea Ave.) | 808-877-5588

A "relaxing", family-friendly Kahului mall "standby", this American fortifies shoppers throughout the day with "thick" burgers and a "va-riety" of other "well-priced", "basic" fare; it's "definitely a locals' place, and that's a compliment."

Kozo Sushi ⊠ _Japanese_

| 17 | 9 | 15 | $13 |

Wailuku | 52 N. Market St. (Main St.) | 808-243-5696 | www.kozosushihawaii.net

See review in Oahu Dining Directory.

	FOOD	DECOR	SERVICE	COST

Kula Lodge Restaurant *American* 20 | 22 | 20 | $31

Kula | 15200 Haleakala Hwy. (bet. Ainakula Rd. & Upper Kimo Dr.) |
808-878-1535 | www.kulalodge.com

A "fantastic place for breakfast" after a "sunrise over Haleakala", this
"rural" Kula kitchen's mountain views are equally "spectacular" over
lunch and dinner, and the American fare is just as "tasty" (bonus
points for "delicious" brick-oven pizzas); the "breezes are wonderful"
on the "nice deck", while the "lodgelike" interior is "warm and homey";
P.S. "don't forget" to check out the Curtis Wilson Cost Gallery's "local
artwork" "before you leave."

Lahaina Coolers ❷ *Eclectic* 18 | 17 | 19 | $29

Lahaina | 180 Dickenson St. (Walnee St.) | 808-661-7082 |
www.lahainacoolers.net

Everything from "enjoyable" breakfasts to "light lunches" to "late-
night eats" is available and "reasonably priced" at this "casual"
Eclectic "hangout" "a couple blocks off the main" drag in Lahaina;
the "cheery courtyard" is a "great spot" to meet friends, while
"sports fans" "have the most fun" at the bar where flat-screen TVs
broadcast the games.

Lahaina Fish Company *Pacific Rim/Seafood* 21 | 20 | 19 | $36

Lahaina | 831 Front St. (Lahainaluna Rd.) | 808-661-3472 |
www.lahainafishcompany.com

"Amazing ocean views" and "magical sunsets" (especially from the
"nice terrace") are the "selling points" of this "waterfront" Pacific
Rimmer in Lahaina, but the "fresh" seafood – much of which is "found
only in Hawaii" – holds its own; though some quarter-counters call it
"a bit pricey", fishing around usually yields some "good values."

Lahaina Grill *American* 26 | 23 | 25 | $63

Lahaina | 127 Lahainaluna Rd. (Front St.) | 808-667-5117 |
www.lahainagrill.com

"Deserving of its many accolades", this "exceptional" Lahaina New
American (formerly David Paul's Lahaina Grill) exhibits a "respect for
quality" in all areas, from the "expertly prepared" fare and "fantastic
wines" to the "impeccable service" and "sophisticated" decor, notable
for pressed-tin ceilings and "beautiful" artwork; no question, the "prices
are high", but this "delicious delight" is "well worth" the expense.

Lahaina Store Grille & 18 | 21 | 19 | $44
Oyster Bar *American/Hawaiian*

Lahaina | 744 Front St. (Dickenson St.) | 808-661-9090 |
www.lahainastoregrille.net

Everyone's "blown away" by the sunsets from the rooftop of this
Lahaina Hawaiian–New American whose "huge saloon-type" interior
boasts its own "fantastic views" of the "water across the street"; in
other respects, opinion on the expensive fare swings from "fails to delivers" to "acceptable", and service from "hit" to "miss."

L&L Drive-Inn *BBQ/Hawaiian* 16 | 6 | 12 | $10

Kahului | 270 Dairy Rd. (bet. Alamaha & Hukilike Sts.) | 808-873-0323
Kihei | 247 Piikea Ave. (Liloa Dr.) | 808-875-8898
Lahaina | Lahaina Cannery Mall | 1221 Honoapiilani Hwy. (Pilicana Pl.) |
808-661-9888 ⊅

(continued)

L&L Drive-Inn

Wailuku | 790 Eha St. (Hookahi St.) | 808-242-1380
www.hawaiianbarbecue.com
See review in Oahu Dining Directory.

Leilani's on the Beach *Seafood/Steak*

21 | 22 | 20 | $35

Kaanapali | Whalers Vill. | 2435 Kaanapali Pkwy. (Kekaa Dr.) | 808-661-4495 |
www.leilanis.com

"Reasonable prices", "well-prepared" fare, "friendly servers" and
"gorgeous views" are reasons why "everyone wants" to have "a nice
dinner" at this open-air seafood-and-steak spot on Lahaina's
Kaanapali Beach; a more "laid-back" scene is found at the sand-side
patio downstairs, plus there's "great people-watching" and lunch too.

Longhi's *Italian*

20 | 20 | 20 | $45

Lahaina | 888 Front St. (Papalaua St.) | 808-667-2288
Wailea | Shops at Wailea | 3750 Wailea Alanui Dr. (Wailea Ike Dr.) |
808-891-8883
www.longhis.com

This Italian chainlet, which originated on Maui, is a "favorite in Lahaina
and Wailea" (there's a branch in Oahu's Ala Moana Center as well),
where it's known for "celestial lobster omelets", "addictive pizza bread"
and "great pastas and seafood" served in "casual" dining spaces (with
a "sweeping view of the sea" from the Front Street location); but a
small portion of patrons say these spots may have been "cool" at one
time, but they are now "past their prime" with "overpriced", "inau-
thentic" fare that seems like "it's phoned in."

Ma'alaea Grill *Pacific Rim*

22 | 21 | 20 | $39

Maalaea | 300 Maalaea Rd. (Honoapiilani Hwy.) | 808-243-2206 |
www.cafeoleirestaurants.com

"Well-prepared" Pacific Rim fare including "onolicious whole fish"
served by "friendly" staffers draws fans to this relatively "out-of-the-
way", "reasonably priced" Maalaea address ("it's next door" to the
Maui Ocean Center); "wonderful" water views with "harbor breezes"
and live music conspire to create a "comfortable", "casual" ambiance.

Makawao Steak House *Steak*

22 | 19 | 22 | $43

Makawao | 3612 Baldwin Ave. (bet. Brewer Rd. & Makawao Ave.) |
808-572-8711

A "standard that hasn't slipped", this Makawao meat mecca has been
offering "solid pieces of beef, good sides", "old-fashioned salad-bar"
eats and "polite" service to Upcountry folks for over 30 years; the "homespun decor" is "not fancy", but the bills are "not expensive" compared to
other steakhouses; N.B. a separate room is devoted to afternoon tea.

Mala *Hawaii Reg./Seafood*

25 | 20 | 22 | $42

NEW **Wailea** | Wailea Beach Marriott | 3700 Wailea Alanui Dr.
(Wailea Ike Dr.) | 808-875-9394

Mala Ocean Tavern *Hawaii Reg./Seafood*

Lahaina | 1307 Front St. (Kapunakea St.) | 808-667-9394
www.malaoceantavern.com

Chef Mark Ellman's "delectable", "inventive" Hawaii Regional and
Mediterranean small and large plates, featuring "a wide variety of sea-

food", more than hold their own against this duo's "superb oceanfront locations" where "waves literally lap" at the "torch-lit" patios and a "competent" staff delivers the "delicious" fare; the "small" Lahaina original opens for lunch and dinner, the newer Southside outpost in the Wailea Beach Marriott offers a breakfast buffet as well as dinner, while meals at both come "at a premium."

☑ Mama's Fish House *Seafood*

27 | 26 | 25 | $60

Paia | 799 Poho Pl. (Hwy. 36) | 808-579-8488 | www.mamasfishhouse.com
"Never failing to enchant even the most jaded diner", this "simply amazing" "classic" converted beachhouse in Paia, voted the Most Popular restaurant on Maui, boasts a "magical", "drop-dead gorgeous" tropical beachside backdrop for "exceptional" seafood "caught daily, with credit given to the fisherman" on the menu; "impeccable service" is another element you'll "remember forever" – and it all comes at "giant prices" "you will never forget" either, no matter how many "killer mai tais" you down.

Mama's Ribs 'N Rotisserie *BBQ*

▽ 21 | 7 | 18 | $18

Napili | Napili Plaza | 5095 Napilihau St. (Honoapiilani Hwy.) | 808-665-6262
"Good portions" of "homecooked" "succulent ribs" and "wonderful" rotisserie chicken are what this Napili BBQ "hole-in-the-wall" is all about; though the "seating is basically in a parking lot", the staff could "put on a smile" more often, and the "limited menu" "gets sold out", it makes the "best takeout" on the island.

Marco's Grill & Deli *Italian*

17 | 15 | 18 | $29

Kahului | 444 Hana Hwy. (Dairy Rd.) | 808-877-4446
Jet-lagged travelers trot to this "solid" Italian eatery near Kahului Airport for a fix of "homestyle" cooking – salads, pastas, subs – served by a "friendly" staff; still, the "lousy view", "dinerlike setting" and overall "ordinariness to the extreme" make the "convenient" location for "late-night" fliers the best thing about it.

Matteo's *Italian*

19 | 17 | 18 | $41

Wailea | 100 Wailea Ike Dr. (Wailea Alanui Dr.) | 808-874-1234 | www.matteosmaui.com
"High-quality" victuals at a "reasonably priced" venue "with a view"? – "casual"-eats seekers "never heard of" such a thing in Wailea until this golf-course-adjacent Italian came along with its "gourmet pizzas", "delicious pastas" and "fresh salads"; sure, you have to "order at the counter, take a seat and await delivery" and some say the fare's pretty "typical", but most "recommend it"; N.B. the Waikiki location is closed for remodeling until February 2009.

Maui Brewing Co. ❶ *Eclectic/Pizza*

19 | 16 | 18 | $27

Kahana | Kahana Gateway Shopping Ctr. | 4405 Honoapiilani Hwy. (Hoohui Rd.) | 808-669-3474 | www.mauibrewingco.com
At this "welcoming" tavern in the Kahana Gateway Shopping Center, a "nice mix of locals and tourists" soak up "excellent microbrews" with Eclectic pub grub (ahi tar tar won tons, cuban sandwiches, bratwurst) plus an extensive array of pizza; though some report "relaxing lunches", most feel it's "better" after dark when it turns into more of a "nightclub"; N.B. the Decor score may not reflect a recent remodeling.

	FOOD	DECOR	SERVICE	COST

Maui Tacos *Mexican* | 19 | 9 | 15 | $12 |

Kahului | Queen Kaahumanu Ctr. | 275 W. Kaahumanu Ave. (S. Wakea Ave.) |
808-871-7726

Kihei | Kamaole Beach Ctr. | 2411 S. Kihei Rd. (Alanui Ke Alii Rd.) |
808-879-5005

Kihei | Piilani Village Shopping Ctr. | 247 Piikea Ave. (Liloa Dr.) |
808-875-9340

Lahaina | Lahaina Square Shopping Ctr. | 840 Wainee St. (Lahainaluna Rd.) |
808-661-8883

Napili | Napili Plaza | 5095 Napilihau St. (Honoapiilani Hwy.) |
808-665-0222
www.mauitacos.com

"Hawaiian flair" makes this "inexpensive" statewide Mexican chain
"really rock" exclaim the many who are "addicted" to its "fresh", "succulent fish tacos", "killer burritos" and "amazing salsa bar"; the
counter-serve stores are "not much to look at", so get it to go and take
it to the beach.

⚡NEW Merriman's *Hawaii Reg.* | 27 | 22 | 25 | $57 |

Kapalua | Kapalua Resort | 1 Bay Club Pl. (Bay Rd.) | 808-669-6400 |
www.merrimanshawaii.com
See review in Big Island Dining Directory.

Milagros Food Co. *Mexican* | ▽ 21 | 13 | 18 | $26 |

Paia | 3 Baldwin Ave. (Hana Hwy.) | 808-579-8755
Before or "after a grueling drive to Hana", get "lazy" in this "super-
casual corner" of Paia serving up "Maui-style Mexican food" notable
for "cool" concoctions, "hefty portions" and "reasonable prices";
it's "cramped" inside, so "sit outside, have a beer" or an "awesome
margarita" and "watch all the interesting people"; P.S. "excellent
breakfasts" served too.

Nick's Fishmarket *Seafood* | 25 | 25 | 23 | $66 |

Wailea | Fairmont Kea Lani | 4100 Wailea Alanui Dr. (Kaukahi St.) |
808-879-7224 | www.tristarrestaurants.com
Set on the "lush", "dreamy" grounds of Wailea's Fairmont Kea Lani,
this "first-class" endeavor beckons gourmets with its "superb", "elegantly presented" seafood backed by an "expansive" wine list, "in-
tense" service and "gorgeous" aquatic-themed decor; true, it's a
"pricey" investment, but the returns are undeniably "fabulous."

OnO Bar & Grill *American/Hawaiian* | 21 | 22 | 20 | $39 |

Kaanapali | Westin Maui Resort & Spa | 2365 Kaanapali Pkwy.
(Nohea Kai Dr.) | 808-667-2525 | www.westinmaui.com
"It's nice to have a place like this" say sun-worshipers at the Kaanapali
Resort's Westin Maui, who only have to go "poolside" in order to fill
up on American "comfort food" with an island twist, from "good
breakfast buffets" under thatched umbrellas to dinners with "sunset"
backdrops; however, dollar-watchers deem it all "overpriced for
what you get."

Outback Steakhouse *Steak* | 16 | 15 | 17 | $32 |

Kihei | 281 Piikea Ave. (Liloa Dr.) | 808-879-8400
Lahaina | 325 Keawe St. (Honoapiilani Hwy.) | 808-665-1822
www.outback.com
See review in Oahu Dining Directory.

Pacific'O Restaurant *Pacific Rim/Seafood*

25 | 25 | 23 | $56

Lahaina | 505 Front St. (Shaw St.) | 808-667-4341 |
www.pacificomaui.com

With "gorgeous outdoor seating", "breathtaking sunset views" and
live weekend jazz, this "festive" Lahaina beachsider is tailor-made for
"romance"; executive chef James McDonald's "fabulous", "innovative" Pacific Rim fare featuring New American accents and "freshly
caught local fish" "you've never heard of" (brought to table by "impeccable" servers) makes it a "memorable" "splurge."

Paia Fishmarket *Seafood*

24 | 12 | 15 | $21

Paia | 2A Baldwin Ave. (Hana Hwy.) | 808-579-8030 |
www.paiafishmarket.com

"Wow!" – the fish served in this Paia "shack" "wouldn't be fresher if
you caught it yourself", and it's available in so "many delicious"
permutations – "tasty sandwiches", "awesome burgers", "top-notch
quesadillas", etc. – no wonder it's often "standing room only"; if you
do "find a seat" after you "order at the counter", you'll be "sharing picnic tables" with your fellow "bargain"-hunters.

Peggy Sue's *Diner*

17 | 17 | 18 | $18

Kihei | Azeka Mauka Shopping Ctr. | 1279 S. Kihei Rd. (E. Lipoa St.) |
808-875-8944 | www.peggysues-maui.com

Take a "fun" stroll down "memory lane" at this "noisy" "'50s-style"
Kihei diner/coffee shop whipping up inexpensive burgers, fries,
malts, ice-cream floats and other "American teen" fare; the "crusty"
service "adds flavor" as do the "rockin' jukeboxes" stocked with
"oldies-but-goodies."

Penne Pasta Café *Italian*

20 | 11 | 16 | $22

Lahaina | 180 Dickenson St. (Front St.) | 808-661-6633 |
www.pennepastacafe.com

"One of Maui's few bargains" can be found on a "side street in Lahaina",
namely this cafe offering "quick, tasty", "simple" Italian pastas, pizzas
and sandwiches; "there's not much ambiance" (you "order at the
counter", "find a seat" and it's "dropped off at your table"), but it's
"great for families" or "takeout on a rainy evening."

Pineapple Grill *Pacific Rim*

23 | 23 | 23 | $53

Kapalua | Kapalua Resort | 200 Kapalua Dr. (Ridge Rd.) | 808-669-9600 |
www.pineapplekapalua.com

"Lush" golf-course views with the "Pacific in the distance" are "lovely"
preludes to the "artfully presented", "brilliant" Pacific Rim fare
ferried by "outstanding" servers at this mural-filled "keeper" in the
Kapalua Resort; it's a bit "expensive", but there are "cheaper alterna-
tives": "early-bird" prix fixes and "half-priced pupus" at the bar later
in the evenings.

Pioneer Inn Grill & Bar *American*

▽ 15 | 17 | 18 | $25

Lahaina | Best Western Pioneer Inn | 658 Wharf St. (Hotel St.) | 808-661-3636
"Conjuring up a time when the harbor was filled with whalers", this
"old-fashioned" American hotel eatery "next to the wharf" in Lahaina
is a "real treat" for bargain breakfasts "on the deck"; dinners in the
"dim" interior are strictly "standard", so "just go for a drink and soak
up the bar's atmosphere."

	FOOD	DECOR	SERVICE	COST

Pizza Paradiso *Italian*

∇ 20 | 10 | 19 | $19

Lahaina | Konokowai Mktpl. | 3350 Lower Honoapiilani Rd. (Honoapiilani Hwy.) | 808-667-2929 | www.pizzaparadiso.com
The "reasonable prices" on "delicious pizzas", pastas and "even gyros" make "family outings" to this "quick and friendly" Lahaina Italian that much more enjoyable; the setting surely isn't paradise, but you "don't go for the ambiance"; P.S. if it's too "crowded", get it to go.

Plantation House Restaurant *Mediterranean*

24 | 27 | 24 | $53

Kapalua | Plantation Golf Course | 2000 Plantation Club Dr. (Honoapiilani Hwy.) | 808-669-6299 | www.theplantationhouse.com
"Perched above the 18th fairway of the beautiful Plantation Course" in the Kapalua Resort sits this "heavenly" Mediterranean displaying "unbelievable" "views of the ocean", nearby islands and "spectacular sunsets" from "big windows" open to the "breeze"; the setting's partnered with equally "awesome", "fresh and fantastic" fare utilizing local ingredients, which the "outstanding" staffers serve "anytime of day" for "pricey but well-worth-it" tabs.

Polli's Mexican Restaurant *Mexican*

∇ 21 | 12 | 21 | $23

Makawao | 1202 Makawao Ave. (Baldwin Ave.) | 808-572-7808
"If you're near Makawao" and need a "Mexican fix", find it at this "little" Upcountry "hangout" known for "great chips and salsa" followed by "fresh" entrees brought "promptly" by "friendly servers"; frozen margaritas make for "fun happy hours" and negate complaints that the "decor could use some help."

Prince Court *American/Pacific Rim*

23 | 21 | 23 | $51

Makena | Maui Prince Hotel | 5400 Makena Alanui (Kaukahi St.) | 808-875-5888
See review in Oahu Dining Directory.

NEW RB Black Angus Steakhouse *Steak*

– | – | – | M

Kahana | Kahana Gateway Shopping Ctr. | 4465 Honoapiilani Hwy. (bet. Hoohui & Kahana Nui Rds.) | 808-669-8889 | www.rbsteakhouse.com
The steakhouse goes casual with this family-friendly entry in Kahana's Gateway Shopping Center whose understated look incorporates dark-wood details and tablecloths topped with butcher paper; prices are similarly modest, with a lineup that prominently features an array of Angus beef cuts, alongside chophouse staples like lobster and shrimp cocktail.

Round Table Pizza *Pizza*

18 | 10 | 14 | $18

NEW Kaanapali | Fairway Shops | 2580 Kekaa Dr. (Honoapiilani Hwy.) | 808-662-0777
Kihei | 207 Piikea Ave. (Liloa Dr.) | 808-874-8485
www.roundtablepizza.com
This "cool" mainland pizza chain transplant with outposts on Maui and Oahu is recognized for pies that come "loaded with toppings" and have interesting names (e.g. Guinevere's Garden and Maui Zaui), but connoisseurs are split on quality, with some finding "delish" creations for when you're homesick and others comparing it to the "frozen" variety; "fun arcade games" and flat-screen TVs provide amusement but don't earn the decor many points.

	FOOD	DECOR	SERVICE	COST

Ⓩ Roy's *Hawaii Reg.* | 26 | 22 | 24 | $54 |

Kahana | Kahana Gateway Shopping Ctr. | 4405 Honoapiilani Hwy.
(Hoohui Rd.) | 808-669-6999
Kihei | 303 Piikea Ave. (bet. Liloa Dr. & Piilani Hwy.) | 808-891-1120
www.roysrestaurants.com
See review in Oahu Dining Directory.

Ruby's *Diner* | 17 | 15 | 17 | $19 |

Kahului | Queen Kaahumanu Ctr. | 275 W. Kaahumanu Ave. (S. Wakea Ave.) |
808-248-7829 | www.rubys.com
"Relax and recharge" at the Queen Kaahumanu Center's "kitschy",
"kid-friendly" 1940s-style diner, where "attentive" servers swing by
with "large portions" of "dependably" good burgers, shakes and the
like from a "broad" American menu; it's a "value", so you'll have extra
cash for shopping.

Ⓩ Ruth's Chris Steak House *Steak* | 25 | 22 | 23 | $65 |

Lahaina | Lahaina Ctr. | 900 Front St. (Papalaua St.) | 808-661-8815
Wailea | Shops at Wailea | 3750 Wailea Alanui Dr. (Wailea Ike Dr.) |
808-874-8880
www.ruthschris.com
See review in Oahu Dining Directory.

Saeng's Thai Cuisine *Thai* | 20 | 16 | 19 | $24 |

Wailuku | 2119 W. Vineyard St. (Church St.) | 808-244-1567
A "respite from the tourists", this "off-the-beaten-path" Wailuku
"charmer" with a waterfall in the dining room turns out a mostly "fine"
Thai menu, from noodles and curry dishes to "great vegetarian fare";
even though the "pleasant" service and "low prices" help, "frustrated"
diners discover "uneven" food that veers from "excellent" to "mediocre."

NEW Sammy's Beach Bar & Grill *American* | – | – | – | M |

Kahului | Kahului Airport | 1 Kahului Airport Rd. (Keolani Pl.) |
808-877-5858
Former Van Halen frontman and Maui resident Sammy Hagar is behind this new beach-themed eatery in the center concourse of the
Kahului Airport; set against a backdrop of surf and rock memorabilia,
it serves well-priced American fare featuring Hawaiian and Mexican
twists (think ahi tuna burgers and margaritas), with 100% of the prof-
its set to be donated to children's charities.

Ⓩ Sansei *Japanese/Pacific Rim* | 26 | 19 | 21 | $44 |

Kapalua | Kapalua Resort | 600 Office Rd. (Lower Honoapiilani Rd.) |
808-669-6286
Kihei | Kihei Town Ctr. | 1881 S. Kihei Rd. (Waimahainai St.) |
808-879-0004
www.sanseihawaii.com
See review in Oahu Dining Directory.

Sarento's on the Beach *Mediterranean* | 23 | 26 | 24 | $58 |

Kihei | 2980 S. Kihei Rd. (Kilohana Dr.) | 808-875-7555
The "gorgeous" beach setting and "spectacular" sunset views "can't
be beat" from the vantage point of this Kihei Mediterranean, run by
the same owners as Waikiki's Sarento's Top of the "I"; "excellent" service and "stellar" food "easily compare to anything you'd experience
in NYC", but it adds up to a "high-cost" outing.

MAUI DINING

	FOOD	DECOR	SERVICE	COST

Sea House Restaurant *Pacific Rim* — 22 | 22 | 23 | $41

Napili | Napili Kai Beach Resort | 5900 Lower Honoapiilani Rd. (Honoapiilani Hwy.) | 808-669-1500

Still a "solid" performer after 30 years, this Pacific Rim stalwart (a "hidden treasure" situated on a "quiet" beach in Napili) is counted on for its "unique preparations" and "scrumptious" meals backed by a "friendly" staff; the decor may be a bit "tired", but the "absolutely magnificent" bay views continue to enthrall, while thrifty sorts suggest the early-bird specials that "keep the tab down."

SeaWatch *Seafood* — 22 | 24 | 23 | $47

Wailea | Golden Emerald Golf Course | 100 Wailea Golf Club Dr. (Makena Alanui Dr.) | 808-875-8080

"What more can you ask for?" wonder fans who fall for the "lovely sight" of sunsets, Molikini Island and Haleakala Crater from this Wailea seafooder overlooking a golf course; rounding out the experience is the "helpful" service, "fine wine" and "upscale and creative" food, though some guests deem the latter "not as inspiring" as the ambiance.

☑ Son'z at Swan Court *Seafood/Steak* — 24 | 28 | 25 | $65

Kaanapali | Hyatt Regency Maui | 200 Nohea Kai Dr. (Kaanapali Pkwy.) | 808-667-4506

Voted the No. 1 for Decor on Maui, this "high-end" Hyatt seafooder-steakhouse boasts an "impressive" open-air design with a "fabulous", "romantic" view that syncs up with the "superb" food, service and "wonderful wine selection"; "don't hesitate", "just go" and book a "table by the pond" for a VIP vista of the "priceless sunsets", waterfalls and "swimming swans."

☑ Spago *Californian/Pacific Rim* — 26 | 28 | 26 | $79

Wailea | Four Seasons Resort Maui at Wailea | 3900 Wailea Alanui Dr. (Wailea Ike Dr.) | 808-879-2999

Wolfgang Puck, Maui and the Four Seasons are the "ultimate combination" say adoring worshipers of the celebrity chef's "spectacular" Wailea spin-off of his "LA classic"; here, guests are dazzled by the consistently "fantastic" Californian–Pacific Rim cuisine, "top-notch" service, "stunning" Pacific views and "gorgeous" contemporary rooms with exotic murals and custom glasswork; it all comes with a "hefty" price tag, but it's a "sure bet."

Stella Blues *American* — 19 | 15 | 20 | $27

Kihei | Azeka Mauka Shopping Ctr. | 1279 S. Kihei Rd. (bet. E. Lipoa St. & Piikea Ave.) | 808-874-3779 | www.stellablues.com

"Feed your inner flower child" at this Kihei shopping-center American serving a variety of "tasty", "upscale" comfort food (including "several vegan and vegetarian" items) in a room tricked out in Grateful Dead memorabilia; thanks to "reasonable" prices and "large portions", (tie) dyed-in-the-wool types call it the "best place to take the family", while others rave it's a local "tradition in an unlikely setting."

NEW Taqueria Cruz ☒☄ *Mexican* — - | - | - | I

Kihei | 2395 S. Kihei Rd. (Alanui Ke Alii Rd.) | 808-875-2910

A tiny newcomer in the back of Dolphin Plaza, this inexpensive Kihei taqueria with a walk-up counter and outdoor tables serves authentic

Mexican fare, specializing in tacos with meat, fish, pork and vegetable fillings using corn tortillas made fresh daily; expect favorites such as burritos, quesadillas, rice, beans and salsa on the menu as well.

Tasty Crust ⊅ *American/Hawaiian* | 19 | 6 | 15 | $12 |

Wailuku | 1770 Mill St. (Kaniela St.) | 808-244-0845

The "ultimate local's place" and a quintessential "greasy" spoon with "peeling Formica countertops and vinyl seats", this "never-gets-old" Wailuku breakfast specialist has been purveying "excellent" pancakes, "opakaka and eggs", "cornbread" and other "home-cooked" American and Hawaiian standards since the 1940s; insiders caution "wear flip-flops and shorts" or risk looking "out of place" – and "don't peek in the kitchen."

Thai Cuisine 🗷 *Thai* | ∇ 23 | 17 | 22 | $24 |

Kihei | Kukui Mall | 1819 S. Kihei Rd. (Uilani St.) | 808-875-0839

The curries are fit "for the gods" rave enthusiasts of this Kihei Siamese, a "local favorite" for its "solicitous" service and "wonderfully prepared" Thai fare; the decor may be "typical" and the "strip-mall" location "lame", but few care when the fixin's are "so fresh and so good."

Tiki Terrace *Hawaii Reg.* | ∇ 19 | 21 | 18 | $28 |

Kaanapali | Kaanapali Beach Hotel | 2525 Kaanapali Pkwy. (Kekaa Dr.) | 808-667-0124 | www.kbhmaui.com

You really "feel like you're in paradise" at this "open-air" Kaanapali Beach Hotel restaurant serving "inexpensive" Hawaii Regional fare for breakfast and dinner, along with "great views overlooking the beach"; the nightly "throwback hula/music shows" are a "bonus" that make it even more "charming."

T. Komoda Store & Bakery 🗷⊅ *Bakery* | 24 | 7 | 18 | $9 |

Makawao | 3674 Baldwin Ave. (Makawao Ave.) | 808-572-7261

"From the outside", this "funky, authentic", circa-1916 Makawao bakery "looks like a place to store farm equipment", but inside fans feast on "killer" cream puffs, "out-of-this-world" stick doughnuts, "piping hot butter bread" and the "best custard anywhere" in a showroom filled with inexpensive, "wonderful" delicacies that make this our Survey's Best Buy on Maui; not surprisingly, you should come "in the morning" – usually by 11 AM – before the goods are gone.

Tokyo Tei *Japanese* | ∇ 21 | 12 | 20 | $33 |

Wailuku | 1063 Lower Main St. (Kane St.) | 808-242-9630 | www.tokyoteimaui.com

Even the "the most finicky palates" are pleased by all the "exciting options" at this "friendly" Wailuku Japanese, an "oldie but goodie" (circa 1935) revered by "locals", who especially "love the shrimp tempura and chicken hekka" (sukiyaki); the unassuming space is "always crowded", so "make sure you get reservations."

Tommy Bahama's Tropical Café *Asian Fusion/Caribbean* | 20 | 23 | 20 | $44 |

Wailea | Shops at Wailea | 3750 Wailea Alanui Dr. (Wailea Ike Dr.) | 808-875-9983 | www.tommybahama.com

See review in Big Island Dining Directory.

	FOOD	DECOR	SERVICE	COST

Waterfront Restaurant *Seafood*

25 | **21** | **24** | **$54**

Maalaea | 50 Hauoli St. (Maalaea Rd.) | 808-244-9028 |
www.waterfrontrestaurant.net

The seafood "doesn't get any fresher" and the preparations couldn't
be "tastier" than at this "relaxing", "off-the-beaten-path", family-run
"fresh fish house" in Maalaea, also lauded for its "fabulous" tableside
Caesar salads, "incredible wine list" and "first-rate" service; to augment
what's sure to be a "memorable" meal, "go early" for an outside seat
and enjoy the "to-die-for" sunsets and water views.

NEW Zippy's ❍ *American*

16 | **11** | **15** | **$14**

Kahului | 15 Hookele St. (S. Puunene Ave.) | 808-856-7599 | www.zippys.com
See review in Oahu Dining Directory.

Maui Golf

Dunes at Maui Lani 🛺
| 23 | 19 | 21 | 22 | $99 |

Kahului | 1333 Maui Lani Pkwy. | 808-873-7911 |
www.dunesatmauilani.com | 6841/4768; 74.1/70.4; 141/120

A wee bit of "Ireland comes to Hawaii" at this "superb" "local course" in Kahului, a "gorgeous" linkslike layout designed by Robin Nelson and set on a "dune several hundred feet high" with "a lot of elevation changes" that "require some shot-making", especially "later in the day" when it gets "very windy"; in short, it's an "out-of-the-way gem" that's "perfect for a last-minute round before heading to nearby Maui airport."

Kaanapali Golf Resort, Kaanapali Kai 🛺
| 20 | 19 | 21 | 19 | $195 |

Kaanapali | 2290 Kaanapali Pkwy. | 808-661-3691 |
866-454-4653 | www.kaanapali-golf.com | 6388/4522; 70.7/66.2; 135/112

Proponents swear Royal Kaanapali's "underrated" sibling (redesigned by Robin Nelson in 2005) is "not the ugly stepsister it's made out to be", offering "phenomenal" greens, "spectacular" views and a back side that "has more character" according to some; while the "spectacular" scenery can be "distracting" and the "wind is a problem", the "wide-open" Maui track is "friendlier" than its big brother, and you "can't beat the location or the service."

Kaanapali Golf Resort, Royal Kaanapali 🛺
| 22 | 20 | 22 | 19 | $235 |

Kaanapali | 2290 Kaanapali Pkwy. | 808-661-3691 |
866-454-4653 | www.kaanapali-golf.com | 6700/5016; 74.2/70.1; 131/123

Duffers may deem this the "tougher of the two Kaanapali courses", but this track is still "manageable for the average golfer" thanks to some "terrific downhill par 4s that allow you to bomb your driver"; still, "bring your wind game, good legs" and "a boatload of money" ("it is Maui", after all) and be sure to take in the "breathtaking" "views of the mountains and ocean", as well as the steam-powered Sugar Cane Train, which chugs by with "added island flavor."

Kahili 🛺
| ∇ 24 | 20 | 24 | 25 | $125 |

Wailuku | 2500 Honoapiilani Hwy. | 808-242-4653 | www.kahiligolf.com | 6554/4948; 72.3/71.4; 135/126

Fans are glad this privately owned golf club in Kahili is open to public play, for the Robin Nelson/Rodney Wright design built "on the side" of the West Maui Mountains is "top-notch", with "no houses" to impede the "panoramic views" of "both sides" of the island; while the track an be "very playable", it features "lots of volcanic rock" and "challenging" island trade winds that can make it a "real test."

Kapalua, Bay ⛳

| 25 | 25 | 25 | 20 | $215 |

Kapalua | 300 Kapalua Dr. | 808-669-8044 | 877-527-2582 |
www.kapaluamaui.com | 6600/5124; 72.1/69.6; 136/121

"Dolphins, whales and turtles, oh my!" – the "ocean holes are stunning" on Plantation's "li'l sister", a track that many call the "friendliest course" on "the north end of Maui", with "great new greens" installed just in time for 2008's inaugural Kapalua LPGA Classic; the "excellent layout" is "well maintained" and a "good test" for "players of all skills", while "wonderful" service adds to an "enjoyable" experience that's well "worth the price of admission."

∃ Kapalua, Plantation ⛳

| 29 | 27 | 26 | 22 | $295 |

Kapalua | 2000 Plantation Club Dr. | 808-669-8044 | 877-527-2582 |
www.kapaluamaui.com | 7263/5627; 74.9/73.2; 138/129

"As beautiful and breathtaking as they come" and the top-rated Course in Hawaii is "a beast no matter how you play", "a model for wind power" that's "as tough as it looks on TV" during the PGA's Mercedes-Benz Championship; what's more, the staff is "helpful and attentive" and the "facilities, especially the restaurant, measure up to the golf", if not "the famous 18th" hole, the longest on the Tour; P.S. it's "expensive", but all agree it's "worth every penny."

Makena, North ⛳

| 25 | 20 | 23 | 21 | $210 |

Makena | 5415 Makena Alanui | 808-879-3344 | 800-321-6284 |
www.makenagolf.com | 6914/5303; 73.6/70.5; 138/120

An "out-of-the-way gem" just south of the airport, this "Maui favorite" is "worth the drive" thanks to a "tough" "but fair" RTJ Jr. resort design (his firm is overseeing the renovation of the South course) featuring "gorgeous views of the ocean" and Molokini Island, "plenty of volcanic rock" and "some of the best greens around, fast with little grain"; what's more, you can expect "first-rate service" – "mahalo!" – and a clubhouse that's "wonderful for drinks afterward."

Wailea Golf Club, Blue ⛳

| 23 | 23 | 24 | 21 | $155 |

Wailea | 120 Kaukahi St. | 808-875-7450 | 888-328-6284 |
www.waileagolf.com | 6765/5208; 72.2/69.3; 129/117

"Hit the driver and let it fly" at this "extremely playable" course that may be the oldest of the three Wailea tracks but is also "the cheapest", while still being "kept in excellent condition" and offering "amazing views" of "lush greenery, the blue Pacific and jagged lava rocks"; "friendly" service adds to the experience, and while it's "windy", the "wide-open" fairways "will keep your ball in play", so "do this one the first day you get to Maui" – "you'll have a blast."

Wailea Golf Club, Emerald ⛳

| 26 | 26 | 25 | 23 | $180 |

Wailea | 100 Wailea Golf Club Dr. | 808-875-7450 | 888-328-6284 |
www.waileagolf.com | 6825/5256; 72.6/69.5; 128/114

It's "an expensive jewel", but "the view is worth the money alone" at this RTJ Jr. resort course that's "always a pleasure" – some "would play here a thousand times" – thanks to its "immaculate" conditions and "female-friendly" layout; while there are "not a lot of forced carries", "tough rough" can make it "penal if you're off the fairway", so "expect

	COURSE	FACIL.	SERVICE	VALUE	COST

a slow round" – in fact, "bring your camera" to snap photos of the "whales frolicking off the coast."

Wailea Golf Club, Gold 🏌

26	26	25	22	$180

Wailea | 100 Wailea Golf Club Dr. | 808-875-7450 | 888-328-6284 | www.waileagolf.com | 7078/5442; 73.4/70.1; 137/119

"If you play one round on Maui, this has to be it" say swingers who insist this "challenging" RTJ Jr. design is "definitely the best of the bunch" in Wailea, so "play where the Champions Skins Game was held" in 2008; while the cart paths aren't lined with gold, the course itself is so "beautifully landscaped, you'll think you're in a botanical garden" as you also enjoy "fabulous" ocean views, "excellent conditions" and "exemplary service" and facilities.

Maui Hotels

Symbols

👪 children's programs	👀 views
✗ exceptional restaurant	⌐ 18-hole golf course
Ⓗ historic interest	Ⓢ notable spa facilities
☞ kitchens	♒ swimming pool
🐾 allows pets	✎ tennis

Diamond Hawaii
Resort & Spa ☞ 👀 Ⓢ ♒

-	-	-	-	$320

Wailea | 555 Kaukahi St. | 808-874-0500 | fax 808-874-8778 |
800-800-0720 | www.diamondresort.com | 72 suites
This "Japanese-flavored" resort park "on a secluded hillside" may be
"about two miles from the beach" at Wailea, but pluses include "beautiful gardens", a "don't-miss" koi pond and a "wonderful" spa at which
to "wind down"; although the "large, condominium-style" suites with
kitchenettes all have "top-notch" craftsmanship and some kind of
ocean view, they're also looking "a little worn"; be ready for some
"sticker shock" at the restaurants too, which "need a few more items
under $30" on the menu.

Fairmont Kea Lani 👪 ☞ 🐾 👀 Ⓢ ♒

ROOMS	SERVICE	DINING	FACIL.	COST
27	25	23	26	$525

Wailea | 4100 Wailea Alanui Dr. | 808-875-4100 | fax 808-875-1200 |
800-441-1414 | www.fairmont.com | 413 suites, 37 villas
"Elegantly appointed all-suite" lodgings with a "vibrant Hawaiian ambiance" and "enormous baths" are the highlights of this "fabulous"
"Moroccan-inspired" Wailea resort where "aloha greets you at every
turn", the staff provides "superb personalized service" and "the views
from high floors are hypnotizing"; with "really nice pools and its own
beach", it's "great for families" yet also has a "very adult feel";
P.S. fans say Nick's Fishmarket is a "big winner" for on-site dining.

**⑦ Four Seasons Resort Maui
at Wailea** 👪 ✗ 👀 Ⓢ ♒ ✎

ROOMS	SERVICE	DINING	FACIL.	COST
28	28	27	28	$495

Wailea | 3900 Wailea Alanui Dr. | 808-874-8000 | fax 808-874-2244 |
800-334-6284 | www.fourseasons.com | 328 rooms, 52 suites
The vibe is "LA in Hawaii" at this "beautiful" Wailea oasis that was voted
Maui's Top Hotel, where the recently upgraded rooms are "spacious and
luxurious", the "outstanding food" (at restaurants including Spago) is
paired with "amazing sunset/ocean views" and the "seamless service"
is exemplified by an "amazing concierge staff"; relaxation-seekers
sigh "ah, the spa", while sun-worshipers choose between a "perfect
stretch of beach" or "pristine" pools where guests are pampered with
"Evian face spritzes" and may see "a celebrity in the next cabana."

Grand Wailea Resort 👪 👀 Ⓢ ♒ ✎

ROOMS	SERVICE	DINING	FACIL.	COST
24	22	21	27	$780

Wailea | 3850 Wailea Alanui Dr. | 808-875-1234 | fax 808-879-4077 |
800-888-6100 | www.grandwailea.com | 728 rooms, 52 suites
When you enter this "gorgeous" Hawaiian "Disneyland" in Wailea,
with an "awesome beach", "winding paths through lush gardens",

"eye-catching sculptures", the "planet's best spa" and a "magnificent" water park, you'll find it's "perfect for the whole family" (tip: "if you don't have kids, avoid school-break periods" when it's "filled to the brim"); although a handful say this property "seems to be slipping of late" and needs "more focus on service" and food, others "come here for the best pool" on the islands, not the "overpriced dining."

Hana-Maui, Hotel 🏃🛁⑤🌊🔍 | 27 | 26 | 23 | 25 | $495

Hana | 5031 Hana Hwy. | 808-248-8211 | fax 808-248-7202 | 800-321-4262 | www.hotelhanamaui.com | 47 cottages, 22 suites, 1 house
For a "breathtaking look into old Hawaii", this "secluded" Maui member of Small Luxury Hotels of the World is "super-luxurious yet simple at the same time"; the "adventurous" drive to get there along the winding Hana Highway is "almost as spectacular as watching the waves" from your lanai or "riding bareback on the beautiful beach", and the "friendly" staff "goes out of its way" to "pamper" you; the "romantic", "remote" setting, "excellent" spa and "serene" rooms ("stay in the plantation-style cottages") further impress, so "the only drawback" is the "limited" dining.

Ho'oilo House 🛁🌊 | – | – | – | – | $345

Lahaina | 138 Awaiku St. | 808-667-6669 | fax 808-661-7857 | www.hooilohouse.com | 6 rooms
With most of its decor and furnishings from Bali, this romantic bed-and-breakfast in the West Maui Mountains 10 minutes south of Lahaina is a "unique" retreat that's the perfect spot "for honeymooners" since "you feel like you have it to yourself"; each room boasts high-end touches like black lava stone walls, outdoor showers and private lanais, and there's an on-site pool, in-room massages and beautiful ocean views.

Hyatt Regency 🏃🛁⑤🌊🔍 | 22 | 23 | 21 | 25 | $535

Kaanapali | 200 Nohea Kai Dr. | 808-661-1234 | fax 808-667-4498 | 800-233-1234 | www.maui.hyatt.com | 774 rooms, 32 suites
"You feel transported the minute you drive up" to this "stunning" hotel on Kaanapali Beach, starting with the "breathtaking lobby" and its "gorgeous water elements and resident penguins"; though there's "not much beachfront", the "lush gardens", "first-class spa" and "fabulous" pool (with its "waterfalls, grotto bar and waterslide") more than compensate, and while some praise the "attractive" rooms, quibblers say the "baths need updating."

Kaanapali Alii 🏃🍽🛁🌊🔍 | ▽ 25 | 20 | – | 20 | $425

Kaanapali | 50 Nohea Kai Dr. | 808-667-1400 | fax 808-661-1025 | 800-642-6284 | www.classicresorts.com | 264 condos
Families cheer this "well-located", "beautiful" condo resort on Kaanapali Beach that's "an easy walk" from the shops and restaurants at Whalers Village, and boasts "vibrant", individually decorated one- and two-bedroom units with fully equipped kitchens, lanais and "spacious" living areas; everything is "well maintained", but there's no restaurant on-site.

Kaanapali Beach Hotel 🏃🛁⑤🌊 | 17 | 22 | 16 | 22 | $209

Kaanapali | 2525 Kaanapali Pkwy. | 808-661-0011 | fax 808-667-5978 | 800-262-8450 | www.kbhmaui.com | 419 rooms, 13 suites
"Let the breezes carry your stress away" at this "charming", "family-friendly hotel" in the "heart of Kaanapali" that's "Hawaiian all the

way" from the "extraordinary" staff to the "beautiful grounds" and "wide sandy beach"; it may not be the "most plush hotel" around – it's "on the older side" with "simple" rooms and a "somewhat small" pool – but it's a "reasonably" priced option in a "wonderful location."

Kapalua Villas ♯♯⌂♨⌂♨⚓ ▽ 23 | 21 | 19 | 23 | $299

Kapalua | 500 Office Rd. | 808-665-5400 | fax 808-669-5234 | 800-545-0018 | www.kapaluavillas.com | 230 villas

The "spacious" rooms at this "upscale" Kapalua condo on the bay are "great for families who want seclusion and couples who need a romantic getaway", since there's "everything you'd want to do" yet it's "away from the bustle of nearby tourist areas"; the upgraded villas are "beautifully decorated" and some feature "unbelievable ocean views", plus there are "wonderful restaurants within a 15-minute drive" and guests have signing privileges at the newly reopened Ritz-Carlton.

Lahaina Inn ♨ - | - | - | - | $150

Lahaina | 127 Lahainaluna Rd. | 808-661-0577 | fax 808-667-9480 | 800-669-3444 | www.lahainainn.com | 12 rooms

Even if it's "more like a motel", this "historic", "restored" lodging built in the early 1900s "in the center" of Lahaina wins fans who appreciate a "location" that's especially good for the quirky, annual "Halloween festivities" as well as for shopping, nightlife and dining along Front Street; rooms have period furnishings and lanais with rocking chairs, but there are no TVs.

Maui Prince Hotel ♯♯♨⌂♨⚓ 19 | 21 | 20 | 20 | $380

Makena | 5400 Makena Alanui Rd. | 808-874-1111 | fax 808-879-8763 | 888-977-4623 | www.princeresortshawaii.com | 291 rooms, 19 suites

"Plenty of sea turtles" share the "awesome beach" at this "quiet", "uncrowded" Makena resort with a "warm staff" that "works for those looking for total seclusion" (or a bargain, as veterans insist it's a "great value"); but critics find the property "a little long in the tooth", with "simple" rooms that "could use updating"; N.B. the South golf course is closed for renovations.

Napili Kai Beach Club ♯♯Ⓢ♨ ▽ 18 | 22 | 21 | 22 | $320

Napili | 5900 Lower Honoapiilani Hwy. | 808-669-6271 | fax 808-669-5740 | 800-367-5030 | www.napilikai.com | 163 condos

Condo-sseurs love this full-service, oceanfront Hawaiian-style lodging in Napili with "fabulous water views", four pools, two putting greens, a spa, shuffleboard and a work-out room; "spacious" units with fully equipped kitchens and a "lagoonlike beach" that's "outstanding for swimming and snorkeling" make it "perfect" for "families with small kids", although critics caution some accommodations "need improvement."

Old Wailuku Inn ⓗ - | - | - | - | $150

Wailuku | 2199 Kahookele St. | 808-244-5897 | fax 808-242-9600 | 800-305-4899 | www.oldwailukuinn.com | 10 rooms

A secluded 1924 Wailuku home restored into a bed-and-breakfast, this off-the-beaten-path spot has a 1920s Hawaii theme; high-ceilinged rooms have ohia-wood floors, clawfoot tubs and down-soft beds covered in Hawaiian quilts, while a separate, modern three-room building is decorated with fabrics by local designer Sig Zane; a full gourmet breakfast is served on the outdoor lanai.

	ROOMS	SERVICE	DINING	FACIL.	COST

Ritz-Carlton
Kapalua 👫✕🏨⬆️⑤⛱️🔍

| 25 | 27 | 25 | 26 | $719 |

Kapalua | 1 Ritz-Carlton Dr. | 808-669-6200 | fax 808-665-0026 | 800-262-8440 | www.ritzcarlton.com | 331 rooms, 132 suites

A "spectacular" $180-million refurb has enthusiasts buzzing about this "huge, lush" Kapalua "golf paradise" that "you won't want to leave"; besides its "two amazing courses", devotees cite the "beautiful" rooms (with dark-wood floors, private lanais and "fantastic views"), the "superb" food at its six restaurants (including the Asian-inspired Banyan Tree) and the "exceptional" service; yes, it's "too windy to be perfect" and the beach is "small, rough and fairly distant", but fans focus on the "well-appointed" spa and "wonderful pool" instead.

Sheraton Maui
Resort & Spa 🏨⑤⛱️🔍

| 22 | 23 | 19 | 24 | $500 |

Kaanapali | 2605 Kaanapali Pkwy. | 808-661-0031 | fax 808-661-0458 | 800-325-3535 | www.sheraton.com | 464 rooms, 46 suites

They've got "the best spot" on Kaanapali Beach say fans of this "comfortable" chainster with a "superb location" at Black Rock where you "can snorkel from the beach", enjoy "awesome sunsets" from a "quiet" stretch of sand and be "within walking distance" of many restaurants at Whalers Village; though some say the "small" rooms are strictly "standard", a staff that's "willing to help with anything" makes up for it; N.B. a new spa opened in 2008.

Wailea Marriott 🏨⑤⛱️

| 21 | 20 | 17 | 20 | $525 |

Wailea | 3700 Wailea Alanui Dr. | 808-879-1922 | 888-236-2427 | www.marriott.com | 498 rooms, 48 suites

Soak up the "lovely Hawaiian atmosphere" while floating in the newly restored "serene infinity pool with a view of the ocean and whales breaching" at this "beautiful" Wailea spot that completed a major renovation post-Survey; although some say the property's beachfront is "too rocky, with rough waves", it makes for "exceptional" vistas from the redesigned restaurants and public spaces, as well as from upgraded rooms boasting new Revive bedding; the redo also included the addition of a Mandara spa and an enhanced fitness facility.

Westin Maui
Resort & Spa 👫🏨⬆️⑤⛱️

| 22 | 22 | 19 | 25 | $545 |

Kaanapali | 2365 Kaanapali Pkwy. | 808-667-2525 | fax 808-661-5764 | 800-937-8461 | www.westinmaui.com | 731 rooms, 27 suites

A "fantastic lobby with waterfalls and pools" greets visitors to this "lush Kaanapali resort" where the "impressive scenery", "friendly service", "fabulous spa" and "awesome swimming pools" are the highlights; but it can be so "crowded with conventions that remind you of the business you left at home" that it "lacks traditional Hawaiian charm", and further disappointment is found in the "mediocre" dining; P.S. critics caution "keep your hands on your wallet" given the extra resort fees.

BIG ISLAND

Attractions

Most Popular

1. Hawaii Volcanoes Pk.
2. Akaka Falls
3. Atlantis Sub
4. Hapuna Beach
5. Punalu'u Beach

Top Appeal

- 29 Hawaii Volcanoes Pk.
- 28 Punalu'u Beach
- 27 Hapuna Beach
   Hawaii Tropical Gdn.
   Kealakekua Bay

Dining

Most Popular

1. Merriman's | *Hawaii Reg.*
2. Hualalai Grille | *Hawaii Reg.*
3. CanoeHouse | *Pacific Rim*
4. Roy's | *Hawaii Reg.*
5. Pahu i'a | *Hawaii Reg./Seafood*
6. Café Pesto | *Eclectic*
7. Brown's Beach Hse. | *Seafood*
8. Kona Brewing Co. | *American*
9. Jameson's | *Seafood/Steak*
10. Huggos | *Pacific Rim/Seafood*
11. Bamboo | *Pacific Rim*
12. Kilauea Lodge | *Eclectic*
13. Sansei | *Japanese/Pac. Rim*
14. Hilo Bay Café | *Pacific Rim*
15. Kenichi | *Asian Fusion/Japanese*
16. La Bourgogne | *French*
17. Merriman's Market | *Med.*
18. Ruth's Chris* | *Steak*
19. Tommy Bahama* | *Asian/Carib*
20. Beach Tree | *Cal./Italian*

Top Food Ratings

- 28 Hualalai Grille | *Hawaii Reg.*
- 27 Merriman's | *Hawaii Reg.*
- 26 Pahu i'a | *Hawaii Reg./Seafood*
   Sansei | *Japanese/Pac. Rim*
   Roy's | *Hawaii Reg.*
- 25 Hilo Bay Café | *Pacific Rim*
   La Bourgogne* | *French*
   Ruth's Chris | *Steak*
   Brown's Beach Hse. | *Seafood*
- 24 Kenichi | *Asian Fusion/Japanese*

   Ke'ei Café | *Eclectic*
   CanoeHouse | *Pacific Rim*
- 23 Beach Tree | *Cal./Italian*
   Bamboo | *Pacific Rim*
   Café Pesto | *Eclectic*
   Daniel's | *Hawaii Reg.*
   Kilauea Lodge | *Eclectic*
- 22 Donatoni's | *Italian*
   Teshima Rest. | *Japanese*
- 21 Jackie Rey's | *Eclectic*

BY CUISINE

AMERICAN (TRAD.)

- 21 Big Island Grill
   Manago Hotel
- 19 Café 100

ECLECTIC

- 24 Ke'ei Café
- 23 Café Pesto
   Kilauea Lodge

HAWAIIAN

- 21 Manago Hotel
- 19 Café 100
- 15 Blane's

HAWAII REGIONAL

- 28 Hualalai Grille
- 27 Merriman's
- 26 Pahu i'a

---

* Indicates a tie with restaurant above

JAPANESE

26	Sansei Seafood
22	Teshima Rest.
21	Imari

PACIFIC RIM

25	Hilo Bay Café
24	CanoeHouse
23	Bamboo

SEAFOOD

26	Pahu i'a
	Sansei Seafood
25	Brown's Beach Hse.

Top Decor Ratings

28	Pahu i'a		24	Beach Tree B&G
27	CanoeHouse		23	Kilauea Lodge
	Brown's Beach Hse.			Coast Grille
	Hualalai Grille			Tommy Bahama's
25	Donatoni's			Don The Beachcomber

Top Service Ratings

27	Pahu i'a		24	CanoeHouse
	Hualalai Grille			Roy's
25	Merriman's		23	Brown's Beach Hse.
	Beach Tree B&G		22	Bamboo
	La Bourgogne			Donatoni's

Best Buys

In order of Bang for the Buck rating.

1. Café 100
2. Ba-Le Sandwich
3. Blane's Drive-In
4. Maui Tacos
5. L&L Drive-Inn
6. Manago Hotel
7. Ken's/Pancakes
8. Teshima Rest.
9. Big Island Grill
10. Kona Brewing Co.
11. Pancho & Lefty's
12. Hilo Bay Café
13. Café Pesto
14. Bamboo
15. Bubba Gump
16. Quinn's
17. Jackie Rey's
18. Harbor House
19. Merriman's Mkt. Café
20. Jameson's

Golf

Top Courses

26	Mauna Lani/North		24	Mauna Kea/Hapuna
	Mauna Lani/South		23	Waikoloa Bch./Bch.
	Hualalai			

Hotels

Top Overall

28	Four Seasons Resort			Kona Village Resort
24	Mauna Lani Resort		23	Hapuna Beach Prince
	Fairmont Orchid			

Big Island Attractions

Akaka Falls State Park
26 | 15 | 11 | $0

Honomu | end of Akaka Falls Rd. (off Mamalahoa Hwy.) | 808-974-6200 | www.state.hi.us/dlnr

"Worth the drive" from nearby Hilo, this free-of-charge "picturesque" slice of "Old Hawaii" features views of the "spectacular" 442-ft. Akaka Falls and smaller-but-charming Kahuna Falls, both of which are an "easy hike" along a 0.4-mile "self-guided" paved path that is "ridiculously romantic", looping through tropical jungle and bamboo forest; just "take your umbrella" in case of rain, and know that "there are no services except for bathrooms."

Anaeho'omalu Beach
∇ 23 | 20 | 16 | $0

Waikoloa | south of Waikoloa Beach Marriott

This "picture-perfect" Waikoloa beach is a "peaceful" spot for snorkeling, swimming, lounging beneath shady coconut and kiawe groves, watching the "sun set" or exploring the tidepools and the ancient petroglyphs; you'll see "local canoe paddlers" and you can even float "with sea turtles" if you're lucky enough to spot some, plus there's plenty of accessible amenities thanks to nearby resort hotels.

Atlantis Submarine
24 | 22 | 23 | E

Kailua-Kona | 75-5669 Alii Dr. (Hualalai Rd.) | 800-548-6262 | 800-548-6262 | www.atlantisadventures.com

See review in Oahu Attractions Directory.

Hapuna Beach State Recreation Area
27 | 18 | 15 | $0

Kohala Coast | Hwy. 19, m.m. 69 | Kamuela | 808-974-6200 | www.hawaiistateparks.org

An easily accessible and "truly magnificent" Kohala Coast beach, this "long" stretch of "talcum-soft sand" (rare on the Big Island) boasts water that's "blue, blue, blue", a congenial atmosphere, restrooms, picnic tables and a lifeguard; just be warned that summer's sweet swimming conditions give way to sometimes-"dangerous" surf and "lots of undertow" in winter; P.S. "bring a beach umbrella."

Hawaii Tropical Botanical Garden
27 | 22 | 20 | I

Papaikou | 27-717 Old Mamalahoa Hwy. (Old Onomea Rd.) | 808-964-5233 | www.htbg.com

"Bring the camera" to snap the "gorgeous blooms" at this "over-the-top" botanical garden in Papaikou, a "natural wonder" with an "immense collection of indigenous and introduced species" just eight miles north of Hilo; a "stunning, steep walk" weaves through its "tropical jungle valley" and past a "private waterfall" to the ocean where "sea turtles cavort in tidal pools"; as for the trip back up, staffers "will come get you in a golf cart" for a fee, if you ask in advance.

☒ Hawaii Volcanoes National Park
29 | 22 | 21 | I

Hawaii National Park | Crater Rim Dr. (off Hwy. 11) | 808-985-6000 | www.nps.gov/havo

"One of the best national parks ever" (and voted the state's top Attraction for Appeal and the Most Popular on the Big Island), this "awe-inspiring" active volcano that's a "long drive from anywhere" (30 miles

SW of Hilo) is the "closest thing to being there for the birth of the planet"; whether you get "up close" with the flowing, "glowing lava" on a ranger-led tour at night, motor along Crater Rim Drive or hike through the "very-cool" Thurston Lava Tube during the day, "no trip to Hawaii is complete without a visit"; N.B. there's an on-site full-service restaurant and snack bar, as well as a visitor center that shows a 25-minute film about Kilauea caldera once every hour.

Hilton Waikoloa Village Luau   21 | 21 | 19 | E

Waikoloa | Hilton Waikoloa Vill. | 69-425 Waikoloa Beach Dr.
(Queen Kaahumanu Way) | 808-886-1234 | www.hiltonwaikoloavillage.com
"What a show!" enthuse fans of this "authentic", if "expensive", luau where fire dancers and hula performers "give it their all"; surveyors are split on the food, however ("delicious" vs. "mediocre"), and some don't like "being herded to the buffet line" and having to "flag someone down" for drinks; P.S. it may be "worth the price just to tour" the "extravagant" grounds of the Hilton Waikoloa on your way in.

Kaloko-Honokohau National Historical Park   ▽ 27 | 20 | 21 | I

Honokohau | Hwy. 19, 3 miles north of Kailua-Kona | Kailua-Kona |
808-326-9057 | www.nps.gov/kaho
Real Hawaii comes to life on the West Coast of the Big Island at this 1,160-acre national park, an "amazing archeological and historical" former settlement that has "recently been improved", making it "more accessible, with more services"; old aquaculture ponds, petroglyphs, house platforms and a temple site are situated in a landscape rich in dry, black lava, so expect "hot" temperatures.

Kealakekua Bay   27 | 10 | 8 | $0

Kailua-Kona | bottom of Napoopoo Rd.
"Snorkel or kayak" across the "clear, deep water" (with visibility reaching 100 feet) to the memorial that marks the spot where Captain Cook was killed in 1779, and you'll get a glimpse of "some of the nicest coral you can see without scuba diving" say saltwater sports who insist this bay, a marine life conservation district, "should be on everyone's short-list for a Big Island trip"; there's "limited parking" (it can also be reached by boat tour from Kailua-Kona) and "no facilities" on-site.

Kona Village Resort Luau   ▽ 25 | 25 | 26 | E

Kailua-Kona | Kona Village Resort | Queen Kaahumanu Hwy. | 808-325-5555 |
www.konavillage.com
"Renowned for its private, oceanfront, tropical setting", this "authentic luau" at the Kona Village Resort offers two different shows – a "total Hawaiian experience" with songs about the island's history and cowboys, and one that spans the South Pacific with Maori, Samoan and Tahitian entertainment; either way, revelers report it's "informative" and "family-friendly", with "impressive" food ("the best roast pig I've ever had").

☑ Punalu'u Beach Park (Black Sand Beach)   28 | 14 | 10 | $0

Pahala | 96-876 Government Rd. (Hwy. 11) | 808-961-8311 |
www.hawaii-county.com
The enticing combo of "caviarlike black sand" and "deep blue water" has locals anointing this "must-see", "magnificent" beach between

APPEAL FACIL. SERVICE COST

the towns of Naalehu and Pahala "one of Hawaii's wonders", despite its "out-of-the-way" locale and "rough" surf; views of coconut groves and the often snow-capped Mauna Loa round out the picture, and as for the frequent sightings of "nesting turtles", remember to "respect the law" and keep your distance.

Royal Kona Resort Luau

∇ 26 | 23 | 24 | M

Kailua-Kona | Royal Kona Resort | 75-5852 Alii Dr. (bet. Hualalai Rd. & Lunapule Rd.) | 808-329-3111

Its waterside location is the draw of this "reasonably priced" "Polynesian luau" set inside the Royal Kona Resort's Coconut Grove; entertainment includes songs and dances from throughout the South Pacific, while the buffet focuses on "good local" fare like "delicious roasted pig", paired with "all-you-can-drink" mai tais and other beverages.

	FOOD	DECOR	SERVICE	COST

Big Island Dining

Ba-Le Sandwich Shop *Vietnamese* | 20 | 6 | 14 | $9 |

Kailua-Kona | Kona Coast Shopping Ctr. | 74-5588 Palani Rd. (Kopiko St.) |
808-327-1212 | www.ba-le.com
See review in Oahu Dining Directory.

Bamboo Ⓜ *Pacific Rim* | 23 | 21 | 22 | $35 |

Hawi | Hwy. 270 (Hwy. 250) | 808-889-5555 |
www.bamboorestaurant.info
Nestled in the "tropical setting" of Hawi, on the northern tip of the Big
Island, this "off-the-beaten-track" "oasis" with an "old Hawaii atmosphere" is prized as much for its "delicious" "fusion-style" Pacific Rim
cuisine as its "vintage tiki bar" serving "killer" mai tais; the live music,
including a "local slack key guitarist", and the "warm" staff create a
"pervading sense of aloha."

Bangkok House Thai *Thai*   ▽ | 22 | 17 | 21 | $30 |

Kailua-Kona | King Kamehameha Mall | 75-5626 Kuakini Hwy.
(bet. Kona Bay Dr. & Palani Rd.) | 808-329-7764
Tucked away in a tiny Kailua-Kona mall, this "dependable" Thai bistro
offers "affordable", "authentic" fare (try the "sweet sticky rice with
mango ice cream – sooo ono"); though the "casual" surroundings are
"nothing fancy", the service is a "cut above" at this "reliable" spot.

Beach Tree Bar & Grill *Californian/Italian* | 23 | 24 | 25 | $51 |

Kaupulehu-Kona | Four Seasons Resort Hualalai | 72-100 Kaupulehu Dr.
(Kumukehu St.) | 808-325-8000 | www.fourseasons.com
The "relaxing", "beachside" setting (put your "toes in the sand")
nearly overwhelms the Cal-Italian fare at this outdoor eatery in the
"glorious" Four Seasons Hualalai, but the "delicious" dishes served by
a "wonderful" staff hold their own ("don't miss the Italian buffet
dinners"); it may be "pricey" for what it is, but you "can't beat" the
"gorgeous views"; N.B. a renovation post-Survey may outdate some of
the above scores.

Big Island Grill Ⓢ *American* | 21 | 14 | 19 | $24 |

Kailua-Kona | 75-5702 Kuakini Hwy. (bet. Hanama Pl. & Henry St.) |
808-326-1153
"Bring your appetite" to this coffee shop in Kailua-Kona, where the
"cheap" and "reliable" local-style American eats come in "huge portions" ("order the plate-sized pancakes with mac nuts and papaya" or
"the best loco moco"); just don't go "if you're in a rush" or want atmosphere since the "friendly" service is "slow" and there's "not much decor to speak of."

Blane's Drive Inn *Hawaiian* | 15 | 8 | 15 | $9 |

Hilo | 217 Wainuenue Ave. (bet. Kinoole & Ululani Sts.) |
808-969-9494
The verdict is mixed on this "always busy" Hilo drive-in: proponents
praise the "cheap", onolicious, local plate lunches "piled high with
meat and starch" along with "quick service" from a staff that "cares",
but foes fret over the "extremely greasy" fare that's "not the best"
Hawaiian food in the area.

	FOOD	DECOR	SERVICE	COST

Brown's Beach House *Seafood* — 25 | 27 | 23 | $64

Kohala Coast | Fairmont Orchid | 1 N. Kaniku Dr. (S. Kaniku Dr.) | Kamuela | 808-885-2000 | www.fairmont.com/orchid

For a "truly romantic" experience, book this oceanfront seafooder in the Kohala Coast's Fairmont Orchid "prior to sunset" and watch the outdoor "tiki torch-lighting ceremony" under "swaying palms"; "sumptuous" food, "attentive" service and "live entertainment" (hula dancer and musician) guarantee a "most memorable" meal.

Bubba Gump Shrimp Co. *American/Seafood* — 15 | 17 | 17 | $26

Kailua-Kona | 75-5776 Alii Dr. (Hualalai Rd.) | 808-331-8442 | www.bubbagump.com

See review in Oahu Dining Directory.

Café 100 ☒ *American/Hawaiian* — 19 | 8 | 16 | $9

Hilo | 969 Kilauea Ave. (Maile St.) | 808-935-8683

"Flavorful", "artery-clogging" Hawaiian and American "comfort" fare comes in "huge", "fattening", "affordable" portions at the purported "birthplace of the loco moco" (over-easy eggs and a hamburger patty on top of rice, doused with gravy); the "down-home" service attracts plenty of Hilo locals, but, with only a few picnic tables, our Survey's Best Buy on the Big Island is best left to takeout.

Café Pesto *Eclectic* — 23 | 16 | 21 | $31

Hilo | Historic S. Hata Bldg. | 308 Kamehameha Ave. (bet. Haili & Mamo Sts.) | 808-969-6640

Kawaihae Harbor | Kawaihae Harbor Ctr. | Hwy. 270 (Kohala Mountain Rd.) | Kamuela | 808-882-1071

www.cafepesto.com

Expect a mix of Italian fare and "sophisticated" island flavors at this "kid-friendly" Eclectic duo of "off-the-beaten-path" eateries where the specialties include wood-fired pizzas "par excellence", fresh-caught fish and Asian-inspired pastas; "attentive" service reigns over both the Hilo location, set in a "historic building", and the Kawaihae Harbor haunt, which is "near the ocean" (yet with "no view").

CanoeHouse *Pacific Rim* — 24 | 27 | 24 | $69

Kohala Coast | Mauna Lani Resort | 68-1400 Mauna Lani Dr. (Mauna Lani Ter.) | Kamuela | 808-885-6622 | www.maunalani.com

"It's what you come to Hawaii for" sigh sojourners who sup at this "beautiful" open-air Pacific Rim eatery at the Kohala Coast's Mauna Lani Resort, where "sweeping" ocean views make it "outrageously perfect" for "romantic moments" or just for "watching the sun set over the waves"; the "inventive" fare is "beautifully presented" by a "young, cheerful" staff, even if it is "pricey."

Coast Grille *Pacific Rim* — 20 | 23 | 21 | $57

Kohala Coast | Hapuna Beach Prince Hotel | 62-100 Kaunaoa Dr. (Old Puako Rd.) | Kamuela | 808-880-3023 | www.princeresortshawaii.com

Perched above the ocean on an "open-air" terrace with "killer" sunset views and "gently wafting breezes", this Pacific Rim spot at the Hapuna Beach Prince Hotel on the Kohala Coast is all about the "beautiful" water vista; however, spoilsports snap over "high-priced", "unspectacular" fare and service that's "not polished."

	FOOD	DECOR	SERVICE	COST

Daniel's Restaurant *Hawaii Reg./Pan-Asian* `23` `20` `20` `$50`

Waimea | 65-1259 Kawaihae Rd. (Lindsey Rd.) | 808-887-2200 |
www.danielthiebaut.com

Located in a "charming", century-old "former plantation store", this
"highly recommended" Waimea eatery is "the place for foodies" who
applaud French chef Daniel Thiebaut's "fantastic" Hawaii Regional
menu with Pan-Asian undertones that incorporates lots of Big Island
local ingredients; antique furnishings and "bright" Sig Zane fabrics
"add flavor", but a minority maintains the service is "lacking" and the
"prices a little high" unless you go for the "bargain Sunday brunch."

Donatoni's *Italian* `22` `25` `22` `$59`

Kohala Coast | Hilton Waikoloa Vill. | 425 Waikoloa Beach Dr.
(Queen Kaahumanu Hwy.) | Kamuela | 808-886-1234 |
www.hiltonwaikoloavillage.com

"So romantic it's almost an aphrodisiac" swoon lovebirds smitten by
this Italian in the Hilton Waikola Village where you can arrive "in style"
via a boat ride, sit "at the water's edge for sunset" and gaze at "beautiful" tiki torches come twilight; the "homestyle" fare is "expensive",
and some say they "wouldn't go out of their way for it", but the "fine"
service and setting may make you want to propose.

Don The Beachcomber Ⓜ *Pacific Rim* `19` `23` `18` `$40`

Kailua-Kona | Royal Kona Resort | 75-5852 Alii Dr. (bet. Hualalai &
Lunapule Rds.) | 808-329-3111

The "dazzling" "seaside setting" and retro-tiki decor win fans at this
Pacific Rim eatery in the Royal Kona Resort, where the "amazing sunsets" and "sweeping shoreline views" (see "spinner dolphins jumping") clearly outrate what some call "ordinary" fare and lackluster
service; luckily, the "variety of umbrella drinks", including 10 types of
mai tais, means you might not care after a while.

Hale Samoa *French/Pacific Rim* ▽ `26` `29` `29` `$61`

Kailua-Kona | Kona Village Resort | Queen Kaahumanu Hwy. (Melelina St.) |
808-325-5555 | www.konavillage.com

"If the gang from *Gilligan's Island* opened a four-star restaurant, this
would be it" exclaim fans of this "adult version" of a "tropical" "beach
party", complete with "superb" service, "gourmet" French–Pacific Rim
fare and "excellent" wines; situated in the sand on the ocean's edge at
the Kona Village Resort in North Kona, it's the "epitome of romantic."

Harbor House *American* `19` `17` `19` `$34`

Kailua-Kona | Honokohau Harbor | 74-425 Kealakehe Pkwy.
(Queen Kaahumanu Hwy.) | 808-326-4166

"Regulars outnumber the newbies" at this "open-air, yachty" bar and
grill located just outside Kailua-Kona in Honokohau Harbor, where the
"inexpensive" American "comfort" eats include "good" burgers,
"fresh-off-the-boat" fish and "lots of fried food"; "servers with a little
sass" deliver 16-oz "schooners" of the "coldest beer on the island" in
front of "great views of fishing boats."

Hilo Bay Café *Pacific Rim* `25` `19` `22` `$34`

Hilo | 315 Makaala St. (bet. Hawaii Belt Rd. & Holomua St.) | 808-935-4939
"Fine dining comes to Hilo" with this "hidden gem" that may be the
area's "best-kept" culinary secret, proffering "innovative", "upscale"

European–Pacific Rim plates that are "worthy of a New York hot spot"; "don't be turned off by the location" in a strip mall, since "inside, the decor is classy", the service "friendly" and the prices "palatable."

☑ Hualalai Grille by Alan Wong *Hawaii Reg.*

28 | 27 | 27 | $72

Kaupulehu-Kona | Four Seasons Resort Hualalai | 100 Kaupulehu Dr. (Queen Kaahumanu Hwy.) | 808-325-8525 | www.hualalairesort.com

"Absolute perfection!" gush gourmands about this "incredibly elegant" dinner-only open-air restaurant overlooking the golf course at the Four Seasons in North Kona, where an "outstanding" staff serves "endlessly creative" Hawaii Regional selections that earn it the No. 1 ranking for Food on the Big Island; it's an "exquisite" experience "from start to finish" – though you'll need "a high credit-card limit" to foot the bill; N.B. chef Alan Wong ceded the kitchen to James Ebreo post-Survey.

Huggos *Pacific Rim/Seafood*

19 | 21 | 19 | $40

Kailua-Kona | 75-5828 Kahakai Rd. (Alii Dr.) | 808-329-1493 | www.huggos.com

This "casual" Kailua-Kona "institution" has been dishing out "dependable", "well-prepared" seafood and Pacific Rim cuisine for nearly 40 years in its "campy", "touristy" oceanfront digs; the staff is "well informed", and if it seems a bit "pricey", well, "you're paying for the view", which is "outstanding."

Imari *Japanese*

21 | 22 | 22 | $62

Kohala Coast | Hilton Waikoloa Vill. | 425 Waikoloa Beach Dr. (Queen Kaahumanu Hwy.) | Kamuela | 808-886-1234 | www.hiltonwaikoloavillage.com

A "serene" "oasis" in Kohala Coast's Hilton Waikola Village – complete with "koi pond", a stand-alone teahouse for private dining and a "romantic" room graced with Imari porcelain – this "traditional" Japanese "has it all", from sukiyaki to sushi to teppanyaki, and everything's "well prepared and attractively presented"; the staff is "attentive", but wags warn that a meal can be so "expensive" that a "significant credit line" plus a "couple of beers before the bill" arrives are warranted.

Jackie Rey's Ohana Grill *Eclectic*

21 | 15 | 21 | $34

Kailua-Kona | Pottery Terr. | 75-5995 Kuakini Hwy. (Walua Rd.) | 808-327-0209 | www.jackiereys.com

A "hidden treasure" in a Kailua-Kona office park, this eatery "caters to locals" with "innovative" Eclectic entrees that range from "great" seafood to "just plain good" hamburgers, served by a "fast", "personable" staff; "reasonable prices" and an "amazing wine list" help make up for what it lacks in atmosphere.

Jameson's By The Sea *Seafood/Steak*

19 | 20 | 19 | $38

Kailua-Kona | 77-6452 Alii Dr. | 808-329-3195 | www.jamesonshawaii.com
See review in Oahu Dining Directory.

Kamuela Provision Company *Pacific Rim*

21 | 22 | 20 | $54

Kohala Coast | Hilton Waikoloa Vill. | 425 Waikoloa Beach Dr. (Queen Kaahumanu Hwy.) | Kamuela | 808-886-1234 | www.hiltonwaikoloavillage.com

A "spectacular" sunset view is the reason romantics call this Pacific Rim steak-and-seafooder in the Kohala Coast's Hilton Waikoloa "worth the visit"; so "sit outside" on the "beautiful", torch-lit oceanside patio – the "tropical", "traditional-wood" indoor decor rates a "nothing special", as does the food – and expect what some call "high (even for Hawaii) prices."

Kawaihae Harbor Grill & Seafood Bar *Pacific Rim/Seafood*

20 | 15 | 18 | $37

Kawaihae Harbor | Kawaihae Harbor Ctr. | Hwy. 270 (Kohala Mountain Rd.) | Kamuela | 808-882-1368

"A genuine Hawaiian slice of life", this "funky" "hidden gem" in a "hundred-year-old building" across from the "working" Kawaihae Harbor keeps with the seafood theme by setting out a "fine selection of fish" and Pacific Rim specialties; an "efficient staff" enhances a vibe that's entirely "laid-back" – except, say some, for the "pricey" tabs.

Ke'ei Café *Eclectic*

24 | 21 | 17 | $42

Honaunau | 79-7511 Mamalahoa Hwy. (Hokukano Rd.) | 808-328-8451

Once located in an "old gas station" but now inhabiting newer, "fancier digs" (done up with "lovely screens and island art") in Honaunau, this "always packed" Eclectic proffers "fresh", "simple" fare at "reasonable" prices; if service in the "noisy" dining room can be "slow", regulars retort that they go here to "enjoy themselves and take their time."

NEW Kenichi Pacific M *Asian Fusion/Japanese*

24 | 19 | 21 | $45

Keauhou | Keauhou Shopping Ctr. | 78-6831 Alii Dr. (Kamehameha III Rd.) | Kailua-Kona | 808-322-6400
Kohala Coast | Shops at Mauna Lani | 68-1330 Mauna Lani Dr. (Kaniku Dr.) | Kamuela | 808-881-1515 ⊠
www.kenichirestaurants.com

"Spectacular sushi" wins over the masses at this "pricey" Keauhou Japanese (and its newer spin-off at The Shops at Mauna Lani on the Kohala Coast) whose "fabulously creative" menu also includes "artfully prepared" Asian fusion dishes like seared ono with mashed yams; add in a "courteous" staff and "modern" feel, and the only negative, note regulars, is that there's "no view."

Ken's House of Pancakes ❶ *American/Diner*

19 | 10 | 19 | $15

Hilo | 1730 Kamehameha Ave. (Kanoelehua Ave.) | 808-935-8711
This Hilo "institution" (the only 24-hour eatery on the Big Island) features a "massive menu" of American diner grub, like "excellent", "thick, thick" pancakes, three-inch-high omelets and other "homestyle" fare delivered by a "fast", "friendly" staff; the "huge portions" make it a "super value for your buck."

Kiawe Kitchen *Mediterranean/Pacific Rim*

▽ 23 | 14 | 19 | $25

Volcano | 19-4005 Haunani Rd. (bet. Hawaii Belt & Old Volcano Rds.) | 808-967-7711

A "snug" "refuge" hidden at 4,000 feet in the town of Volcano, this eatery surprises with "beautiful", "crisp" wood-fired pizzas (the salmon–goat cheese pie is "not to be missed"), the "best lamb sandwiches on home-baked baguette" and other Mediterranean–Pacific Rim fare; its "casual ambiance" is matched by inexpensive prices and "friendly" service.

Kilauea Lodge Restaurant *Eclectic*

23 | 23 | 22 | $45

Volcano | Kilauea Lodge | 19-3948 Old Volcano Rd. (bet. Kalanikoa St. & Post Office Ln.) | 808-967-7366 | www.kilauealodge.com

Nestled in the "cozy mountain" setting of Volcano, this "rustic" former YMCA lodge tempts high-altitude visitors with an "exotic" "daily changing" menu of "delicious" Eclectic cuisine with European-influenced specials (heavy on meat and game); an "always friendly" staff and a "lovely fireplace" help make this "expensive" experience "worth every cent."

Kona Brewing Co. *American*

18 | 18 | 18 | $25

Kailua-Kona | 75-5629 Kuakini Hwy. (Palani Rd.) | 808-329-2739 | www.konabrewingco.com

"Fantastic" "beers are the specialty" at the Big Island and Oahu pub spin-offs of the Kona-based microbrewery ("sample as many suds as you can" via "great flights"), but there's also "delicious pizzas", sandwiches and other "competently prepared" "mainland comfort food" served to the sounds of "occasional live music"; the patio at the Big Island spot is an "oasis in the middle of warehouses", while the outdoor seating at Hawaii Kai boasts "enjoyable marina" views.

Kona Mix Plate ⊠ *Hawaiian*

▽ 21 | 11 | 17 | $13

Kailua-Kona | Kopiko Plaza | 75-5660 Ololi Rd. (Palani Rd.) | 808-329-8104 | www.konamixplate.biz

"Locals and tourists alike" breeze into this "convenient" Kailua-Kona "hole-in-the-wall" for "quick, tasty" lunches and dinners featuring a "wide variety" of Hawaiian fare (sample up to three at once with the "solid mix plate" option); those turned off by "linoleum, folding chairs and metal tables" pick up the "cheap, cheap, cheap" eats at the counter and vamoose.

Kuhio Grille *Hawaiian*

▽ 21 | 13 | 18 | $17

Hilo | Prince Kuhio Plaza | 111 E. Puainako St. (off Hawaii Belt Rd.) | 808-959-2336

Plan to "hike around a volcano" to "burn off" the "huge portions" of "homestyle" Hawaiian cuisine doled out at this all-day Hilo haunt, "home of the one-pound laulau", an "awesome" specialty of meat steamed in taro leaves; locals keep it perpetually "popular", proving once again that "plain decor" is no match for "friendly, fast service" and true value.

La Bourgogne ⊠Ⓜ *French*

25 | 19 | 25 | $57

Kailua-Kona | 77-6400 Nalani St. (Kuakini Hwy.) | 808-329-6711

"Step out of Hawaii and into France" at this "elegant" Kailua-Kona dinner destination where the chef-owners "greet, cook and serve" "outstanding", "classic" Gallic dishes whose "expensive" tabs are offset by a "vast, value-packed wine list"; "don't skip dessert" ("a real treat"), but do "make reservations", because tables in the "quaint" cottage-style digs "sell out quickly."

L&L Drive-Inn *BBQ/Hawaiian*

16 | 6 | 12 | $10

Hilo | Waiakea Shopping Ctr. | 315 Makaala St. (Kanoelehua St.) | 808-935-3888

Hilo | 348 Kinoole St. (Mamo St.) | 808-834-0888

Kailua-Kona | Lanihau Shopping Ctr. | 75-5595 Palani Rd. (bet. Kuakini Hwy. & Queen Kaahumanu Hwy.) | 808-331-8886

(continued)

L&L Drive-Inn
Kailua-Kona | Keauhou Shopping Ctr. | 76-6831 Alii Dr. (Kamehameha III Rd.) | 808-322-9888
Kamuela | Parker Ranch Shopping Ctr. | 67-1185 Mamalahoa Hwy. (off Waikola Rd.) | 808-885-8880
Keaau | 16-586 Old Volcano Rd. (bet. Keaau-Pahoa Rd. & Pili Mua St.) | 808-982-6668
NEW **Pahoa** | 427 Pahoa Rd. (Old Cemetery Dr.) | 808-965-9533
www.hawaiianbarbecue.com
See review in Oahu Dining Directory.

Manago Hotel Ⓜ *American/Hawaiian*   21 | 13 | 21 | $17
Captain Cook | 82-6155 Mamalahoa Hwy. (Kinue Rd.) | 808-323-2642 | www.managohotel.com
"Dine in a different era" at this all-day Captain Cook hotel canteen, which looks pretty much like it did in 1929 (kind of "plain"); while its "claim to fame" is the "delicious pork chops", "everything else" on the American-Hawaiian "chalkboard menu" is "yummy" – and offered at "throw-back" prices to boot.

Maui Tacos *Mexican*   19 | 9 | 15 | $12
Hilo | Prince Kuhio Plaza | 111 E. Puainako St. (off Hawaii Belt Rd.) | 808-959-0359 | www.mauitacos.com
See review in Maui Dining Directory.

Z Merriman's *Hawaii Reg.*   27 | 22 | 25 | $57
Waimea | Opelo Plaza | 65-1227 Opelo Rd. (bet. Kawaihae Rd. & Pomaikai Pl.) | 808-885-6822 | www.merrimanshawaii.com
A "pilgrimage" "must" for admirers of both Hawaii Regional and farm-to-table cuisine, the "classy" original Waimea eatery via chef Peter Merriman was voted the Most Popular restaurant on the Big Island, and serves "lovingly prepared", "innovative" dishes using "fresh local ingredients" in a "cozy" setting (the Maui location is oceanside); even if some reviewers say the "smallish portions" and a "menu that hasn't changed much" over the years are downsides, most love it; N.B. the first Kauai branch opens in Poipu in 2009.

Merriman's Market Café Ⓩ *Mediterranean*   20 | 17 | 18 | $36
Waikoloa | Kings' Shops | 250 Waikoloa Beach Dr. (off Hwy. 19) | 808-886-1700
From top toque Peter Merriman comes this Kohala Coast "casual", "outdoor" bistro in Waikoloa's Kings' Shops, where the "dependable" Mediterranean fare is "half the price" of the chef's Hawaii Regional Waimea outpost; but critics cry it's "not even in the same class" as its sibling, citing "ordinary"; "basic" fare and "subpar" service that's a "huge disappointment."

Miyo's *Japanese*   ∇ 22 | 15 | 16 | $21
Hilo | Waiakea Villas Hotel | 400 Hualani St. (Mililani St.) | 808-935-2273
This "family-run" "darling" of diners in Hilo serves "country-style" Japanese fare featuring "local produce" in a "relaxed", "homey" setting with "wonderful views" of the lagoon ponds and the Wailoa River; the staff is "sweet" and "attentive", although some say it's "a little disorganized" at times.

	FOOD	DECOR	SERVICE	COST

Nihon Restaurant 🅜 *Japanese* ▽ 19 | 15 | 19 | $25

Hilo | 123 Lihiwai St. (Banyan Dr.) | 808-969-1133
"Say hello to old Hilo" at this veteran eatery where "first-class views" of the bay and Mauna Kea are a backdrop to "traditional" Japanese fare and sushi ("sit at the bar and let the chef present his best"); if the "decor is uninspired", at least the "service is friendly" and the "price is right."

Norio's Japanese Restaurant & Sushi Bar 🅜 *Japanese* ▽ 27 | 23 | 25 | $55

Kohala Coast | Fairmont Orchid | 1 N. Kaniku Dr. (S. Kaniku Dr.) | Kamuela | 808-887-7320 | www.fairmont.com/orchid
"Pricey but authentic" Japanese attracts fans to this "secluded spot" tucked away inside the Kohala Coast's Fairmont Orchid hotel, where "fantastic" sushi highlights an "imaginative" menu, complemented by what some call the island's "best selection" of sake; the service is "impeccable", and while a few critics liken the decor to a "coffee shop", most are too smitten by the "beautiful" outdoor views to notice.

Nori's Saimin & Snacks *Hawaiian/Pacific Rim* ▽ 20 | 9 | 16 | $14

Hilo | Kukuau Plaza | 688 Kinoole St. (Hualalai St.) | 808-935-9133
"Hawaiian down-home cooking" including "soul-warming saimin", "delicious ramen" and Pacific Rim seafood are what "those in-the-know highly recommend" at this Hilo "hole-in-the-wall" that's "hard to find"; the "service is spotty", but can be overlooked for such "cheap" eats, especially when you're "late-night snacking."

Orchid Thai 🅜 *Thai* ▽ 24 | 20 | 21 | $27

Kailua-Kona | 77-5563 Kaiwi St. (Palani Rd.) | 808-327-9437
Don't let the fact that this BYO is located in a Kailua-Kona strip mall deter you if you're famished – the interior's "pretty" enough and the Thai fare is "awesome"; the "bargain" prices and "family-friendly" vibe are further pluses.

Outback Steakhouse *Steak* 16 | 15 | 17 | $32

Kailua-Kona | Coconut Grove Mktpl. | 75-5809 Alii Dr. (Hualalai Rd.) | 808-326-2555 | www.outback.com
See review in Oahu Dining Directory.

🄰 Pahu i'a *Hawaii Reg./Seafood* 26 | 28 | 27 | $82

Kaupulehu-Kona | Four Seasons Resort Hualalai | 72-100 Kaupulehu Dr. (Kumukehu St.) | 808-325-8000 | www.fourseasons.com
"Ocean surf, sensual trade winds", "moonlight" and "stars" form the backdrop for "idyllic" "open-air" dinners at this "luxurious" Hawaii Regional seafooder in North Kona's Four Seasons Hualalai, voted No. 1 for Decor and Service on the Big Island; the "shockingly expensive", "innovative cuisine" is "all it should be": "exquisitely prepared", paired with a "superb wine list" and brought to table by servers who "nearly read your mind"; P.S. the à la carte and buffet breakfasts are an "outstanding" way to "begin the day."

Pancho & Lefty's Cantina & Restaurante *Mexican* 15 | 16 | 17 | $23

Kailua-Kona | 75-5719 Alii Dr. (Sarona Rd.) | 808-326-2171
Since it's been around a while, some locals get "nostalgic" about this midpriced Kailua-Kona cantina boasting a "convenient" location,

FOOD | DECOR | SERVICE | COST

"good people-watching" and "nice ocean views" from the patio; however, Mexican connoisseurs say the eats are too "bland" to be memorable; N.B. breakfast is served too.

Paniolo Country Inn Eclectic
▽ 16 | 14 | 18 | $21

Kamuela | 65-1214 Lindsey Rd. (Mamalahoa Hwy.) | 808-885-4377

For a "quick, tasty alternative to higher priced restaurants", this "Hawaiian-style", somewhat "divey" Eclectic diner in Kamuela is "handy", especially if you have the "kids" in tow; it's *the* place for breakfast for locals", especially on weekends, so don't be surprised if you "have to wait."

Peaberry & Galette French
▽ 21 | 15 | 20 | $15

Keauhou | Keauhou Shopping Ctr. | 78-6740 Makolea St. (Kamehameha III Rd.) | Kailua-Kona | 808-322-6020 | www.peaberryandgalette.com

"Incredible" "sweet and savory" crêpes are "the draw" at this counter-serve "mini-cafe" in Keauhou Shopping Center, but the sandwiches and snacks on the French-accented menu are "tasty" too; since it's "across from the movie theater", it's also a "comfortable" "place for a pre- or post-film espresso."

Quinn's Almost by the Sea Seafood
18 | 12 | 17 | $26

Kailua-Kona | 75-5655 Palani Rd. (Kuakini Hwy.) | 808-329-3822

A "local's favorite" in the heart of Kailua-Kona, this seafooder with "the best" fish 'n' chips in town may be "nondescript from the outside", but it has a surprisingly "delightful" courtyard garden that's reminiscent of "old Hawaii" within; "large portions", "fast" service and "drinks poured with a generous hand" combine to make this "reasonable fall-back" a "good value."

☑ Roy's Hawaii Reg.
26 | 22 | 24 | $54

Kohala Coast | 250 Waikoloa Beach Dr. (Hwy. 19) | 808-886-4321 | www.roysrestaurant.com

See review in Oahu Dining Directory.

☑ Ruth's Chris Steak House Steak
25 | 22 | 23 | $65

Kohala Coast | Shops at Mauna Lani | 68-1330 Mauna Lani Dr. (Queen Kaahumanu Hwy.) | Kamuela | 808-887-0800 | www.ruthschris.com

See review in Oahu Dining Directory.

☑NEW Sansei Seafood Japanese/Pacific Rim
26 | 19 | 21 | $44

Kohala Coast | Waikoloa Beach Resort | 201 Waikoloa Beach Dr. (Queen Kaahumanu Hwy.) | 808-886-6286 | www.dkrestaurants.com

See review in Oahu Dining Directory.

Seaside Restaurant Ⓜ Seafood
▽ 23 | 12 | 18 | $35

Hilo | 1790 Kalanianaole Ave. (Keaukaha Rd.) | 808-935-8825 | www.seasiderestaurant.com

The fish is so fresh here, it "practically jumps out of the pond into your dish", literally, since this "cozy", "family-style" restaurant overlooking picturesque views of the adjacent fish ponds and Mauna Kea in the distance" raises its own mullet and moi; "friendly" and "generous portions" at "reasonable" prices help make this a "Hilo favorite."

	FOOD	DECOR	SERVICE	COST

Teshima Restaurant ⌿ *Japanese* — 22 | 11 | 20 | $22

Kealakekua | 79-7251 Mamalahoa Hwy. (bet. Kuakini Hwy. & St. Paul's Rd.) | 808-322-9140

Keeping it "real" since 1941, this cash-only Kealakekua "landmark" serves *teishoku* (set meals) of "Hawaiian Japanese" "comfort food" that are "nothing fancy" but "consistently" "onolicious" and an "excellent value"; it's a "step back in time" when you enter the "old-fashioned" space, where 101-year-old matriarch Shizuko Teshima "personally greets customers" and the "friendly" family provides "superb" service.

Thai Thai *Thai* — ▽ 24 | 16 | 20 | $29

Volcano | 19-4084 Old Volcano Rd. (Havani Rd.) | 808-967-7969

Our reviewers are mixed when it comes to this "nondescript" Thai eatery in Volcano: some claim "unexpected excellence" ("they grow their own herbs") that makes it "worth the drive", while others scoff at "unremarkable" fare that's priced "steeply" for "what you get"; all agree "reservations are a must", especially on weekends.

Tommy Bahama's — 20 | 23 | 20 | $44
Tropical Café *Asian Fusion/Caribbean*

Kohala Coast | Shops at Mauna Lani | 68-1330 Mauna Lani Dr. (Kaniku Dr.) | Kamuela | 808-881-8686 | www.tommybahama.com

This "trendy" tropical clothing store chain, with Big Island and Maui branches, offers a Caribbean and Asian fusion menu to mixed reviews, ranging from "surprisingly good" to a "major disappointment"; it's a "nice retreat for tropical drinks", but the "faux" setting and "highly variable" service can make it seem "overpriced."

U-Top-It *Hawaiian* — ▽ 23 | 12 | 18 | $16

Kailua-Kona | Coconut Grove Mktpl. | 75-5809 Alii Dr. (Hualalai Rd.) | 808-329-0092

A "storefront" eatery in the center of Kailua-Kona, this inexpensive spot offers "cheap", "onolicious" crêpes "with a local twist" – you pick from a variety of "tasty" toppings to accompany Hawaiian taro pancakes; it's an "awesome", if "crowded", choice for breakfast (try the "best loco moco" and "eggs cooked to perfection"), and it also offers good "value" lunches.

Volcano Golf & Country Club — ▽ 15 | 14 | 18 | $27
Restaurant *American*
(aka Pele's Restaurant)

Volcano | Volcano Golf & Country Club | Pii Mauna Dr. (Hwy. 11) | 808-967-8228 | www.volcanogolfshop.com

If you're touring Hawaii Volcanoes National Park, this golf-course eatery is a "quiet" way to start the day with "local comfort-food" breakfasts away from the "crowds" (it serves lunch too); the "average" American fare with Hawaiian touches is "nothing memorable, but satisfying", and affordable, nonetheless.

Big Island Golf

Symbols

Yardage, USGA Rating and Slope are listed after each address.

🏌 caddies/forecaddies   o⊸ guests only
🛺 carts only   🕐 restricted tee times (call ahead)

Big Island Country Club

| 20 | 11 | 18 | 22 | $169 |

Kailua-Kona | 71-1420 Mamalahoa Hwy. | 808-325-5044 |
7125/4837; 76.3/67.5; 140/114

"One of the best-kept secrets on the island", this inland Pete and Perry Dye design comes "recommended" by locals as a "narrow, challenging" course with something "for all levels of play", including "risk-reward holes" and a "memorable island green on the 17th"; nestled near Kailua-Kona in a "beautiful" setting with views of Mauna Kea, it's "an excellent value", especially if you use one of the local coupons, which are "found almost everywhere."

Hualalai o⊸

| 26 | 28 | 27 | 19 | $250 |

Kaupulehu-Kona | 100 Kaupulehu Dr. | 808-325-8480 |
www.hualalairesort.com | 7117/5374; 73.7/70.2; 139/117

"Tested by the Champions Tour every January", this "impeccable" Jack Nicklaus design on the Big Island's Kohala Coast is "open and fair for the average player", although insiders advise keeping the pellets in play, for the lava hazards "will shred the balls"; the service is among the "best anywhere" ("they even clean your spikes before you get on the course"), and staying at the affiliated Four Seasons Resort is like being "in paradise."

Mauna Kea, Hapuna 🛺

| 24 | 24 | 23 | 20 | $165 |

Kohala Coast | 62-100 Kaunaoa Dr. | 808-880-3000 |
www.princeresortshawaii.com | 6895/5067; 73.3/64.4; 136/117

A snow-capped volcano "provides a spectacular backdrop" for this "wonderful" Kohala Coast layout that's one of "the best links-style target courses in Hawaii" thanks to a Palmer/Seay design that "requires a straight ball"; some say the "views were better before the onslaught of new houses", but it's still a "breathtaking" option, especially now that the Mauna Kea course is closed for renovations; P.S. "nice facilities" and a "helpful staff" add appeal.

🅩 Mauna Lani, Francis H. I'i Brown North

| 26 | 24 | 24 | 22 | $260 |

Kohala Coast | 68-1310 Mauna Lani Dr. | 808-885-6655 |
www.maunalani.com | 6913/5307; 74/70.6; 135/120

A "gorgeous" setting featuring "green fairways between black lava rock" "adds to the experience" at the top-rated course on the Big Island that's considered "tougher" than its South sibling, especially when "you hit your ball into a lava outcropping - consider it a donation to the golf gods"; it's "not to be missed", but some suggest there are "too many houses on the course", while others insist it's "pricey if you're not a resort guest" receiving deeply discounted rates.

	COURSE	FACIL.	SERVICE	VALUE	COST

Mauna Lani, Francis H. I'i Brown South

26 | 25 | 25 | 21 | $260

Kohala Coast | 68-1310 Mauna Lani Dr. | 808-885-6655 | www.maunalani.com | 6938/5128; 72.8/69.6; 133/117

"Possibly the most beautiful course on the face of the earth", this "amazing" Big Island resort track features "lava outcroppings surrounding the fairways", so "pray to Pele if you're not straight off the tee" and "don't even think about searching for a ball" on the "treacherous" O.B.; all in all, it's "not to be missed", especially if you book a "twilight time", which will "get you to the 15th" ("a tee shot over the ocean") "at sunset – it doesn't get better than that."

Waikoloa Beach Resort, Beach 🏡

23 | 22 | 22 | 18 | $195

Kohala Coast | 1020 Keana Pl. | 808-886-6060 | www.waikoloabeachresort.com | 6566/5122; 71.6/70; 134/118

The course name may be a bit "misleading since there are very few holes on the ocean", but this "well-maintained" resort track – "one of the better on the Big Island" – still offers some "stunning" visuals, including "lava outcroppings" and two holes that head "into an amphitheater", making this RTJ Jr. design a little "like playing racquetball on a golf course"; those intent on "spectacular" seaside vistas will find them on the "beautiful 12th", a par-5 double dogleg.

Waikoloa Beach Resort, Kings' 🏡

23 | 23 | 22 | 19 | $195

Kohala Coast | 600 Waikoloa Beach Dr. | 808-886-7888 | 877-924-5656 | www.waikoloabeachresort.com | 7074/5459; 73.4/72.2; 135/120

"The more challenging of the two Waikoloa courses", this "well-kept" Weiskopf/Morrish design has "tighter fairways than the Beach", along with "soft greens" and "strong winds" that can nevertheless "help" on the homeward trip since the breeze is "at your back"; it's "loaded with tourists" who can contribute to "slow play", but mongoose sightings "make it even more interesting" and the "friendly staff" is "ready to help you with all of your needs."

Waikoloa Village ⊙

22 | 20 | 22 | 24 | $80

Kohala Coast | 68-1792 Melia St. | 808-883-9621 | www.waikoloa.org/golf | 6791/5501; 73.9/71.7; 130/120

Located in the foothills of Mauna Kea, this Big Island "value" can be "a challenge" thanks to "windy conditions" that have earned it "the nickname 'Waiko-blowa'" and a final hole that causes "first-timers [to] regularly go for a swim" in the "huge lake running in front of the green"; otherwise, this RTJ Jr. design is "friendly to higher handicaps", so even if the pace is "slow at times because so many choose to play here", most agree "it's well worth the wait."

Big Island Hotels

Symbols

children's programs
exceptional restaurant
historic interest
kitchens
allows pets

views
18-hole golf course
notable spa facilities
swimming pool
tennis

Fairmont Orchid

| 25 | 24 | 23 | 26 | $579 |

Kohala Coast | 1 N. Kaniku Dr. | Kamuela | 808-885-2000 | fax 808-885-5778 | 00-257-7544 | www.fairmont.com | 486 rooms, 54 suites

"Gorgeous rooms and perfectly manicured grounds", a "private beach with sea turtles" and the "not-to-be-missed spa without walls" are enough to sell this Kohala Coast resort as a "favorite"; even if a few say the food could be better" and the "beach is a little shrimpy", the super-friendly staff" that "meets every need" makes up for that.

Four Seasons Resort Hualalai

| 29 | 29 | 27 | 29 | $775 |

Kaupulehu-Kona | 72-100 Kaupulehu Dr. | 808-325-8000 | fax 808-325-8200 | 888-340-5662 | www.fourseasons.com | 12 rooms, 30 suites, 1 villa

You may "cry when you check out" of this "indescribably beautiful" ohala Coast "paradise in paradise", and not just because of the "jaw-dropping cost" – rated the No. 1 resort in Hawaii (and in the entire .S.), it boasts "almost perfect" rooms (some with "sexy outdoor lava ock showers"), service that's "unrivaled yet unobtrusive" and a setting at's "never overly crowded"; it's also rated No. 1 for Facilities on Hawaii even the "over-the-top spa", "magnificent Jack Nicklaus golf course", vely lagoons and a "variety of dining", including Hualalai Grille.

Mapuna Beach Prince Hotel

| 23 | 22 | 20 | 25 | $415 |

Kohala Coast | 62-100 Kaunaoa Dr. | Kamuela | 808-880-1111 | fax 808-880-3200 | 866-774-6236 | www.princeresortshawaii.com | 14 rooms, 36 suites

ne of the "best beaches on the island", combined with access to an excellent" Arnold Palmer/Ed Seay-designed golf course, makes this quiet" Kohala Coast lodging a sometimes "overlooked gem"; some of e otherwise "ordinary" rooms have "fantastic" ocean views, but a w faultfinders feel it "fails in the dining department"; N.B. its sister sort, the Mauan Kea, is closed for renovations.

Hilton Waikoloa Village

| 21 | 21 | 20 | 26 | $299 |

Kohala Coast | 69-425 Waikoloa Beach Dr. | Kamuela | 808-886-1234 | fax 808-886-2900 | 800-445-8667 | www.hilton.com | 1155 rooms, 7 suites, 28 cabanas

"Walt Disney would approve" of this "large, large, large" Kohala oast "kid paradise" where you can "take a tram or boat to your room" or "hoof it" to burn calories (wags dub it the "Walk-a-lot-a"); "beauti-ful grounds with a Zen theme", waterslides that slosh into "a gazil-lion pools", a "top-notch spa" and a "cool" "dolphin encounter" program give it "lots of wow factor", so even if naysayers deem the rooms "nothing special" and gripe there's "not much of a beach", fans still liken it to the "greatest show on earth"; N.B. suites are undergoing renovation.

Inn at Volcano 🐕🏨🏊

| - | - | - | - | $159 |

Volcano | Wright Rd. | 808-967-7786 | fax 808-967-8660 | 800-937-7786 | www.volcano-hawaii.com | 4 rooms, 2 suites

A "rustic" spot "right on the rim" at Volcanoes National Park, this inn offers views from the main building "unlike any you've ever seen" given the quite active crater nearby; although the accommodations in-clude flat-screen TVs, Jacuzzi tubs, continental breakfast and after-noon tea, "you don't stay here for the rooms", but for the "convenience of the location."

Kilauea Lodge

| ▽ 18 | 21 | 23 | 18 | $160 |

Volcano | 19-3948 Old Volcano Hwy. | 808-967-7366 | fax 808-967-7367 | www.kilauealodge.com | 12 rooms, 2 houses

This "charming mountain lodge nestled in a tropical garden" near Volcanoes National Park gets "raves" for its Eclectic restaurant where you can "always find plenty of local folks dining and celebrating" (it of-fers "tasty breakfasts" as well); the rooms, "scattered in several build-ings", are "variable", but the "serene" atmosphere is "welcoming after a day of crater trekking."

Kona Village Resort 🏃🏨🏊🐠

| 25 | 25 | 21 | 26 | $660 |

Kailua-Kona | Queen Kaahumana Hwy. | 808-325-5555 | fax 808-325-5124 | 800-367-5290 | www.konavillage.com | 125 bungalows

Escapists looking to "drop off the face of the planet" "love" the "luxu-rious" bungalows "nestled in the tropical garden or on the beach" at "one of the last authentic Hawaii hideaways", this all-inclusive Kona veteran with a "no-TV, no-radio, no-telephone" rule ("go elsewhere for nightlife"); loyalists rhapsodize over the "excellent" food, the "wonderful" staff and the "first-class entertainment, from the luau to the cowboys", but a few critics cry for a "makeover"; N.B. rates in-clude three daily meals.

Mauna Lani Resort 🏃✕🐕🏨↥⑤🏊🐠

| 24 | 24 | 23 | 26 | $445 |

Kohala Coast | 68-1400 Mauna Lani Dr. | Kamuela | 808-885-6622 | fax 808-885-1484 | 800-367-2323 | www.maunalani.com | 328 rooms, 10 suites, 5 bungalows

It "always feels like home" at this "fabulous" Kohala Coast resort, "an oasis in nature" sporting some of the "best snorkeling spots", a "beau-tiful beach", "excellent golf" courses on reclaimed lava beds (one voted the Top Course on the Big Island) and "lots of sealife", includ-ing turtles, cavorting in ancient fishponds; quibblers insist that the "grande dame" is "in need of a face-lift", but devotees shrug it off given the "considerate service", "gracious dining" and "unbelievable" rooms; N.B. the Mauna Lani Spa offers some treatments in open-air thatched-roof huts.

BIG ISLAND HOTELS

	ROOMS	SERVICE	DINING	FACIL.	COST
Waikoloa Beach Marriott 🏨⑤🏖	21	20	18	21	$239

Kohala Coast | 69-275 Waikoloa Beach Dr. | Kamuela | 808-886-6789 |
fax 808-886-3601 | 888-236-2427 | www.waikoloabeachmarriott.com |
508 rooms, 20 cabanas, 17 suites

"Gorgeous, serene and peaceful" wax nostalgics over this "elegant"
Kohala Coast resort on 15 oceanfront acres that recently completed a
$50-million renovation (possibly outdating some of the above scores);
it manages to be both "romantic and child-friendly", with three "spectacularly beautiful pools" (the "kids' pool is a winner"), a new Mandara
spa, a redesigned restaurant and "plenty of space to spread out";
rooms, now equipped with WiFi, feature "modern" Polynesian/Asian
decor with shoji screens and soft lighting, the chain's new 'Revive' bed
with designer duvets and flat-screen TVs.

	ROOMS	SERVICE	DINING	FACIL.	COST
Waimea Plantation Cottages ⑪🛏⑤🏖	-	-	-	-	$220

Waimea | 9400 Kaumualii Hwy. | 808-338-1625 | fax 808-338-2338 |
800-992-4632 | www.waimeaplantation.com | 57 cottages

If you want to "see what old Hawaii was about", "get away from the
tourists" and head to these "sweet", "secluded" plantation cottages in
Waimea built by a sugar company in the early 1900s for its employees;
individual "spacious" units, some oceanfront, offer fully equipped
kitchens, "giant lanais" with rocking chairs, barbecues and DVD players.

40,000 places to eat, drink, stay & play – free at ZAGAT.com

KAUAI

Attractions

Most Popular

1. Waimea Canyon Pk.
2. Hanalei Bay Bch.
3. Poipu Beach
4. Ke'e Beach
5. Grand Hyatt Luau

Top Appeal

29. Kalalau Trail
28. Waimea Canyon Pk.
    Ke'e Beach
27. Hanalei Bay Bch.
26. Wailua Falls

Dining

Most Popular

1. Beach House | *Pacific Rim*
2. Roy's | *Hawaii Reg.*
3. Tidepools | *Pacific Rim/Seafood*
4. Hamura Saimin | *Noodle Shop*
5. Keoki's Paradise | *Pacific Rim*
6. Gaylord's | *Pacific Rim*
7. Hanalei Dolphin | *Seafood*
8. Duke's Canoe Club | *American*
9. Brennecke's | *American/Seafood*
10. Postcards Café | *Eclectic*
11. Brick Oven Pizza | *Italian/Pizza*
12. Kintaro | *Japanese*
13. Bar Acuda | *Med.*
14. Plantation Gardens | *Pacific Rim*
15. Dondero's | *Italian*
16. Cafe Portofino | *Italian*
17. Bubba Burgers | *Burgers*
18. Casa di Amici | *Eclectic/Italian*
19. Hukilau Lanai | *Hawaiian Reg.*
20. Shrimp Station | *Seafood*

Top Food Ratings

26. Roy's | *Hawaii Reg.*
25. Koloa Fish | *Hawaiian/Seafood*
    Beach House | *Pacific Rim*
    Kintaro | *Japanese*
24. Blossoming Lotus | *Vegan*
    Hamura Saimin | *Noodle Shop*
    Shrimp Station | *Seafood*
    Tidepools | *Pacific Rim/Seafood*
    Postcards Café | *Eclectic*
    Brick Oven Pizza | *Italian/Pizza*

23. Kalaheo Café | *Coffeehouse*
    Plantation Gardens* | *Pac. Rim*
    Duane's Ono Burger | *Burgers*
    Bar Acuda | *Med.*
    Casa di Amici | *Eclectic/Italian*
    Pomodoro | *Italian*
    Dondero's | *Italian*
22. Scotty's BBQ | *BBQ*
    Hanapepe Café | *Bakery/Veg.*
    Hanalei Dolphin | *Seafood*

BY CUISINE

AMERICAN

21. Hanalei Gourmet
19. Duke's Canoe Club
18. TomKat's Grille

HAWAIIAN

20. Dani's∇
19. Ono Family Rest.
15. Oki Diner

ECLECTIC

24. Postcards Café
23. Casa di Amici
21. Hanalei Gourmet

ITALIAN

24. Brick Oven Pizza
23. Casa di Amici
    Pomodoro

---

* Indicates a tie with restaurant above

PACIFIC RIM

25 Beach House
24 Tidepools
23 Plantation Gardens

SEAFOOD

25 Koloa Fish Market
24 Shrimp Station
   Tidepools

STEAKHOUSES

19 Poipu Beach Broiler
17 Bull Shed
   CJ's Steak/Seafood

Top Decor Ratings

28 Tidepools
27 Beach House
   Plantation Gardens
26 Dondero's
25 Gaylord's

23 Keoki's Paradise
   Duke's Canoe Club
22 Roy's
   Cafe Portofino
21 Postcards Café

Top Service Ratings

25 Tidepools
24 Dondero's
   Roy's
   Beach House
23 Postcards Café

   Pomodoro
   Gaylord's
   Blossoming Lotus
21 Casa di Amici
   Plantation Gardens

Best Buys

In order of Bang for the Buck rating.

1. Hamura Saimin
2. Bubba Burgers
3. Duane's Ono Burger
4. Tropical Taco
5. L&L Drive-Inn
6. Koloa Fish Market
7. Kalaheo Café
8. Shrimp Station
9. Brick Oven Pizza
10. Eggbert's

11. Oki Diner
12. Hanapepe Café
13. Scotty's BBQ
14. Ono Family Rest.
15. Genki Sushi
16. TomKat's Grille
17. Hanalei Gourmet
18. Waimea Brewing Co.
19. Blossoming Lotus
20. Duke's Canoe Club

Golf

Top Courses

28 Princeville/Prince
27 Poipu Bay
26 Kauai Lagoons

21 Puakea
19 Kiahuna

Kauai Attractions

	APPEAL	FACIL.	SERVICE	COST

Allerton Garden
| | - | - | - | M |

Koloa | 4425 Lawai Rd. (Poipu Rd.) | 808-742-2623 | www.ntbg.org
Set on Kauai's South Shore along the banks of the Lawai stream, this member of the National Tropical Botanical Garden network features towering rainforests, golden bambo, bronze mermaids, fruit trees and fountains; the visitor center for both this venue and neighboring McBryde is on a beautiful scenic overlook just outside the gardens, and all guided tours require a 15-minute tram ride into the valley.

Fern Grotto
| | 22 | 18 | 18 | M |

Wailua | Wailua Marina State Park | off Hwy. 56, south of Wailua River | 808-821-6892 | www.smithskauai.com
A "family favorite for generations", this "busy" tour starts with a "slow, smooth ride" up the Wailua River to the accompaniment of "hokey" "ukulele strumming", followed by a walk through a "lush tropical forest" ("don't forget bug spray") to a "damp", "romantic" grotto; visitors can no longer enter the caves, but instead observe from a viewing platform – which may be one reason foes "can't believe people still go."

Grand Hyatt Kauai Luau
| | 23 | 25 | 24 | E |

Poipu | Grand Hyatt Kauai | 1571 Poipu Rd. (Ala Kinoiki Rd.) | Koloa | 808-742-1234 | www.kauai.hyatt.com
"Enjoy your vacation in royal style" at this "first-class" if "corporate" luau in Poipu's Grand Hyatt that's "great for children of all ages" with "wonderful food" ("pig prepared to perfection"), "ample drinks" and "excellent service"; choose your spot wisely, since the "spectacular" show is "hard to see from many of the seats" in the "enclosed courtyard" setting, especially if you're "stuck in the back."

Haena Beach Park Tunnels
| | ∇ 25 | 10 | 6 | $0 |

Hanalei | near end of Kuhio Hwy. | 808-274-3444
"Look for the red surfboard on the side of the road" and you'll find "one of the most beautiful beaches in the world", this "must-see" stretch of white sand and calm waters in Hanalei, protected by a reef so large it's rumored to be visible from space; there's "great snorkeling" despite the North Shore's often strong ocean currents, but amenities are limited, so "use the facilites in town before getting there."

Hanalei Bay Beach Park
| | 27 | 16 | 13 | $0 |

Hanalei | end of Weke Rd. (off Kuhio Hwy.)
Enjoy "360 degrees of tropical beauty" at this "idyllic" slice of "Hawaii like it used to be", with a long crescent of "soft white sand", a vintage pier and the Hanalei River's waterfalls, all set against the backdrop of "simply stunning" peaks; the summer's glassy, calm water (perfect for families) gives way to powerful waves in winter, making it not safe for swimming or snorkeling; P.S. "parking is rough during the high season."

☒ Kalalau Trail
| | 29 | 10 | 7 | $0 |

Hanalei | Haena State Park | northwest end of Kuhio Hwy. | www.kalalautrail.com
Starting out in Haena State Park, this "excellent" hike with "superb views" is voted the top Attraction for Appeal on Kauai; it comes in two

sizes: a perfect-for-daytrippers two-mile stretch to Hanakapiai Beach (risky for swimming) that includes some of the trail's most "spectacular" scenery, or the full 11-mile trek that's "strenuous", "often muddy" and "not for the fainthearted"; permits, camping equipment, proper hiking gear and "lots of water" are a must for long-distance adventurers.

Kauai Coffee Visitor Center

| 22 | 21 | 21 | I |

Kalaheo | 870 Halewili Rd. (Hwy. 50) | 808-335-3237 | www.kauaicoffee.com

If "beach bumming's got you slugged out", then take a "quick break" and "get a major buzz sipping free samples" at this Kalaheo coffee plantation where there's "no pressure to buy" from the "warm and friendly" staff at the "cute gift store"; "learn about the growing and harvesting process" on the self-guided tour – just know that while caffeine-hounds call it "lovely", a few deem it too "commercial."

Kauai Museum

| ∇ 23 | 21 | 22 | I |

Lihue | 4428 Rice St. (Haleko Rd.) | 808-245-6931 |
www.kauaimuseum.org

"Small but interesting" is how culture buffs describe this "snapshot of Hawaiian heritage" lodged in two "lovely old" buildings in Downtown Lihue; its trove of photographs, art, textiles and artifacts paint a picture of the area's history and "local lore", making it a "worthwhile" stop, especially on days when there are special presentations, workshops and family events; N.B the gift shop sells locally made and traditional goods.

☑ Ke'e Beach Park

| 28 | 12 | 9 | $0 |

Hanalei | Haena State Park | end of Rte. 560 (Aawa Rd.)

Its "end-of-the-road mystique", "stunning sunsets", "amazing snorkeling" and shallow water that's "great for kids" explain why "you need to get there early" to park at this "long, sandy" North Shore strip, voted the state's No. 1 beach for Appeal; though the challenging Kalalau Trail starts here and continues up the jagged coastline, some of the most "spectacular views" of Na Pali can be had right from your towel on the sand.

Kilauea Point National Wildlife Refuge

| 26 | 19 | 18 | I |

Kilauea | Kilauea Lighthouse Rd. | 808-828-0168 | www.fws.gov

A "rare variety" of winged creatures – including the state bird, the "protected and endangered" Nene – are cared for by a "knowedgeable, helpful" staff at this "picture-perfect" Kilauea sanctuary perched on a narrow lava peninsula on the "northernmost point of Hawaii"; interpretive panels line the short .2-mile walk, while the 1912 lighthouse boasts "amazing" views of the "sea crashing on the cliffs below" – and the promise of whale, dolphin and seal sightings; N.B. an on-site visitor center and book store offer more information about local fauna.

Kilohana Plantation

| ∇ 23 | 24 | 23 | $0 |

Lihue | 3-2087 Kaumualii Hwy./Rte. 50 (Nuhou St.) | 808-245-5608 |
www.kilohanakauai.com

A "stunning array" of "interesting little shops" is nestled inside this "well-preserved", if "touristy", 1936 mansion where transportation around the grounds includes "fun" "horse-drawn carriage" rides and a tour aboard a vintage narrow-gauge train; visitors are also invited to "see the plants" and "feed the animals" of the still-working farm, drop by the

	APPEAL	FACIL.	SERVICE	COST

new rum distillery plant and dine at the on-site Gaylord's restaurant for a chance to "eat lunch like you're a manager of a sugar plantation."

Lumahai Beach ▽ 28 | 9 | 6 | $0

Hanalei | Hwy. 560, west of Hanalei

Don't even think about swimming at this "hard-to-find" "beautiful and secluded" Hanalei area beach that's best known for its appearance in the movie *South Pacific,* since its "deadly waves" make it almost always unsafe for watersports; instead, spend the day strolling, "collecting shells" and relaxing on the sand soaking in "lovely views"; N.B. no facilities.

Lydgate Beach Park ▽ 22 | 21 | 15 | $0

Koloa | Hwy. 56, mouth of the Waimea River | www.kauai-hawaii.com

A favorite of locals and "a must for traveling families" with children, this semi-busy "sleeper" with "excellent protected" waters in the Koloa area is "basically a big saltwater swimming pool" and fish haven that offers "safe snorkeling" (even for beginners) within its lava rock barrier; there's a lifeguard (a rarity on Kauai) and a community-built public playground just across the way.

McBryde Garden - | - | - | M

Koloa | 4425 Lawai Rd. (Poipu Rd.) | 808-742-2623 | www.ntbg.org

Tucked between cliffs and the Lawa'i Valley, this nonprofit-run National Tropical Botanical Garden outpost shelters the largest collection of native Hawaiian plants in the world – many endangered or extinct in the wild – alongside exotics and the 'canoe plants' that Polynesian explorers brought with them for food, medicine and building; self-guided or Sundays-only guided tours require a 15-minute tram ride, departing hourly from the Southshore Visitors Center.

Opaeka'a Falls 25 | 13 | 11 | $0

Kapaa | Kuamoo Rd., 1½ miles past m.m. 6

Viewed from an overlook area "right off the highway" on the eastern side of Kauai, this 150-ft. cascade (no longer accessible by foot trail) is a "jewel" "when it has been raining", but less-thrilling during drier weather, so some surveyors suggest it "may not be worth the drive in summer"; still, the parking lot itself can be entertaining, with "chickens running loose" and "street vendors selling coconuts."

Poipu Beach Park 25 | 19 | 14 | $0

Poipu | 2250 Kuai Rd. (Hoone Rd.) | Koloa | 808-245-3971

A "lovely spot" for "enjoying the ocean and sun on the South Shore", this "crowded", "sandy" beach hugs a "small, protected" bay that makes for "fantastic snorkeling"; with a "good playground, bathrooms, lifeguards" and "plenty of tables for picnicking", it's "outstanding" for families, plus there are "several restaurants in the area" and "abundant" parking; P.S. "if you're lucky, you'll see a monk seal sunning on the beach."

Polihale State Park ▽ 28 | 12 | 9 | $0

Lihue | end of Rte. 50 | 808-274-3448 | www.hawaiistateparks.org

A "beautiful place, if you dare drive there", this "tricky-to-find", "sacred spot for Hawaiians" can only be reached by navigating a four-wheel-drive vehicle over an "extremely bumpy dirt road", at the end of which persistent adventurers are rewarded with a "near-deserted", "wide, empty beach", "views of the Na Pali cliffs" and "amazing sunsets"; currents are strong and there's "not a lifeguard to be found for miles", so swimming is not recommended.

Smith's Tropical Paradise

▽ 21 | 23 | 21 | M

Kapaa | 174 Wailua Rd. (Kuamoo Rd.) | 808-821-6895 | www.smithskauai.com

Budding horticulturists "love" to stroll the rambling paths through the "beautifully maintained gardens", tropical fruit orchards and bamboo forest on this 30-acre Kapaa property; sure, it's "not nearly as educational as the National Tropical Botanical Gardens", but it's "not nearly as expensive", either, plus there's a decent evening luau.

Wailua Falls

26 | 14 | 12 | $0

Kapaa | Wailua River State Park | end of Rte. 583

Made famous in the opening credits of *Fantasy Island,* these "mesmerizing" double falls in the Wailua River State Park are easily viewable "directly from the road", though die-hard falls-chasers recommend embarking on the "amazing hike" down a steep, slippery trail for a closer look and a photo op; the water's force varies from "rushing" to "just trickling" based on recent rainfall, but the "beautiful" "drive up the canyon" is "pleasant" regardless.

☑ Waimea Canyon State Park

28 | 17 | 14 | $0

Waimea | Waimea Canyon Dr. (off Hwy. 50) | 808-274-3444 | www.hawaiistateparks.org

The "temperatures are cool and the views are breathtaking" at the Most Popular Attraction on Kauai – the mile-wide "Grand Canyon of the Pacific" that's "bound on its northern flank by the stunning Na Pali Coast" and is full of "well-marked trails" and "incredible scenery" you might "not expect"; the "white-knuckle drive up" is "long and winding", however, and once there, the vistas may be "obscured by rain and clouds"; N.B. take a helicopter tour for a bird's-eye perspective.

Kauai Dining

Bar Acuda ⓜ *Mediterranean*   23 | 21 | 20 | $47

Hanalei | Hanalei Town Ctr. | 5-5161 Kuhio Hwy. (Aku Rd.) | 808-826-7081 | www.restaurantbaracuda.com

"Inventive" small plates featuring "fresh, local" flavors make this "casual-chic" Hanalei Town Center Mediterranean "tapas-and-wine" destination "worth the drive from anywhere on the island"; insiders recommend "reserving a space at the bar" where "the service is better", while critics warn that "prices are outrageously high" for the "small serving sizes."

Barefoot Burgers *Burgers*   ∇ 18 | 15 | 15 | $15

Waimea | 9643 Kaumualii Hwy. (Makeke Rd.) | 808-338-2082

"Burgers and beer by the beach, oh boy!" exclaim acolytes of this "casual, convenient" Waimea joint where the "melt-in-your-mouth" beef is locally raised and finished off with toppings from the islands; though there's "not much atmosphere", that may change with its imminent relocation to Eleele.

☒ Beach House *Pacific Rim*   25 | 27 | 24 | $54

Poipu | 5022 Lawai Rd. (Hoona Rd.) | Koloa | 808-742-1424 | www.the-beach-house.com

"Sunset is the toughest reservation to snag" at this Pacific Rim "gem" on Poipu Beach, voted the island's Most Popular, where the "drop-dead" "panoramic" "ocean views" are "so romantic you can barely remember the fare", even though the "creative" "seafood with an island" flair is "spectacularly presented" and served; while locals find it "pricey" and "too touristy" at twilight, others are happy to "splurge" here.

Blossoming Lotus *Vegan*   24 | 20 | 23 | $34

Kapaa | 4504 Kukui St. (Kuhio Hwy.) | 808-822-7678 | www.blossominglotus.com

Even carnivores coo over this recently renovated "unforgettable" vegan cafe and juice bar in Kapaa serving "creative cuisine" that "shows off a wealth of produce" with "excellent flavors" and "beautiful presentations"; its "unusual brunch offerings" and nightly "live music" add to the experience, though a handful of hearty eaters hunger "for a Big Mac" after dinner here.

Brennecke's *American/Seafood*   18 | 17 | 19 | $32

Poipu | 2100 Hoone Rd. (Poipu Rd.) | Koloa | 808-742-7588 | www.brenneckes.com

Surfers, locals and tourists congregate in the "open-air" dining room at this "throwback" "from the '70s", an American seafooder situated "across the street from Poipu Beach" that's an "old favorite" for its "fantastic views", "strong mai tais" and "generous portions"; if the dinner fare strikes some as "basic" and "overpriced", regulars retort it's "best for lunch" and the "location can't be beat."

Brick Oven Pizza *Italian/Pizza*   24 | 15 | 21 | $20

Kalaheo | 2-2555 Kaumualii Hwy. (Hokua Rd.) | 808-332-8561

Located in upcountry Kalaheo, this "typical" "family-style", "friendly" Italian with "awesome pizza" and "tasty" salads is "always crowded" with tourists and locals; decor that includes "license plates from around the U.S." doesn't impress, but the pie is "about as good as you'll do on Kauai", so expect "long waits" and a yearning to "come back."

Bubba Burgers *Burgers*

| 21 | 14 | 17 | $13 |

Hanalei | 5-5161 Kuhio Hwy. (Aku Rd.) | 808-826-7839
Kapaa | 4-1421 Kuhio Hwy. (Lehua St.) | 808-823-0069
www.bubbaburger.com

There's "always a line" at these "inexpensive", "quality roadside burger stands" in Kapaa and Hanalei boasting "satisfying", "saucy" (if "small") "old-fashioned burgers" plus "incredible chili fries" and onion rings "cooked to order, but at a fast-food pace"; sure, it's "gotten a little touristy", but the "quite funny" staff still "has a blast."

Bull Shed, The *Steak*

| 17 | 13 | 17 | $36 |

Kapaa | 4-796 Kuhio Hwy. (Kamoa Rd.) | 808-822-3791 |
www.bullshedrestaurant.com

This oceanside "back-to-the-'70s" steakhouse in Kapaa has been a "local favorite for over four decades" for its "big portions" of prime rib and rack of lamb; though critics call the fare "mediocre" and the "groovy" decor "dated", an "overpowering crowd" still lines up at opening time (reservations for groups of six or more only).

Cafe Portofino *Italian*

| 21 | 22 | 20 | $46 |

Kalapaki Beach | Kauai Marriott Resort & Beach Club | 3481 Hoolaulea Way (Westin Rd.) | Lihue | 808-245-2121

This Northern Italian in the Kauai Marriott serves "consistent" "classics" ("osso buco", "lasagna") in a "romantic", "Portofino-like setting" complete with a harpist; a "beautiful beach view from the covered outdoor seating area" helps make up for prices that are "a little expensive" and "service" that's sometimes "brusque."

Caffe Coco Ⓜ *Health Food/Pacific Rim*

| ▽ 23 | 17 | 19 | $23 |

Kapaa | 4-369 Kuhio Hwy. (Wailua Homesteads) | 808-822-7990

"Don't be fooled by the location just off the highway or the simple outdoor tables" at this "über-relaxed" BYO Pacific Rim health-food "hideaway" in Kapaa because you'll find an "inventive mix of locally grown food" within; most don't mind service that's "so mellow you may feel neglected", since there's live "local bands" to listen to while waiting; P.S. "be prepared for a few mosquitoes."

Casablanca at Kiahuna *African/Mediterranean*

| 19 | 16 | 18 | $34 |

Poipu | Kiahuna Swim & Tennis Club | 2290 Poipu Rd. (Kiahuna Dr.) |
Koloa | 808-742-2929 | www.casablancakauai.com

"Alfresco dining" in an "oddball" setting – "buried inside" an "airy", "bougainvillea-framed" poolside tent at the Kiahuna Swim & Tennis Club near Poipu – describes this Mediterranean with a menu of "enjoyable" North African–tinged eats that include "something for everyone" (including "wonderful salads" and "tapas for happy hour"); on the downside, "service can be very slow."

Casa di Amici *Eclectic/Italian*

| 23 | 18 | 21 | $44 |

Poipu | 2301 Nalo Rd. (Hoone Rd.) | Koloa | 808-742-1555

"Shoehorned" into a Poipu residential neighborhood (ergo, "parking is limited"), this "comfortable" Eclectic–Italian "blends island and

European" flavors on its "good value menu"; fans say the "wine list is great" and the staff "gracious", and if the interior "decor needs updating", at least there's a "romantic" deck "draped in vines and flowers."

CJ's Steak & Seafood Seafood/Steak

17 | 14 | 18 | $40

Princeville | Princeville Shopping Ctr. | 5-4280 Kuhio Hwy. (Ka Haku Rd.) | 808-826-6211

Located in the Princeville Shopping Center, this "old-fashioned" "surf 'n' turf" steakhouse is a "no-frills" "local favorite" for its prime rib, "fresh fish" and "extensive salad bar" that's "included with the entrees"; "reasonable prices" and "efficient" service help make up for an experience some call "typical" and atmosphere-free "unless you're on the porch – and even then, the view is of the parking lot."

Dani's Restaurant ⊠ Hawaiian

∇ 20 | 7 | 18 | $13

Lihue | 4201 Rice St. (bet. Hardy & Hoolako Sts.) | 808-245-4991

A "no-pretenses" "breakfast-and-lunch only" eatery that offers a "simple slice of Kauai life", this Lihue coffeehouse attracts locals eager for its "traditional" Hawaiian morning munchies like taro pancakes ("where else can you get laulau for breakfast?") at "reasonable prices"; given that it's "not quite a secret", it gets "noisy" and "a bit crowded."

Dondero's Italian

23 | 26 | 24 | $62

Poipu | Grand Hyatt | 1571 Poipu Rd. (Alnako St.) | Koloa | 808-742-1234

An "elegant" setting (inlaid marble floors, Italianate murals) and a "well-trained", "superior" staff make the "excellent Northern Italian fare" taste that much better at this "pricey" Poipu restaurant in the Grand Hyatt; for the most "romantic experience", "sit outside" with a "beautiful" "view of the ocean and stars."

Duane's Ono Burger Burgers

23 | 7 | 15 | $12

Anahola | 4-4350 Kuhio Hwy. (Aliomanu Rd.) | 808-822-9181

The long lines are a "testimony to the quality" at this "cheap", "strictly local" Anahola burger "hut" that's been making "first-rate", "cooked-to-order" patties since 1975; as a result, few care if the counter "service is poor" and there are "lots of chickens and cats" "begging for your food" at the "outdoor cement tables"; N.B. it closes at 6 PM daily.

⊠ Duke's Canoe Club American

19 | 23 | 20 | $33

Kalapaki Beach | Kauai Marriott Resort & Beach Club | 3610 Rice St. (Hoolaulea Way) | Lihue | 808-246-9599 | www.dukeskauai.com

See review in Oahu Dining Directory.

Eggbert's American

18 | 13 | 17 | $17

Kapaa | Coconut Mktpl. | 4-484 Kuhio Hwy. (Papaloa Rd.) | 808-822-3787

This "homespun" American "open-air diner" is popular for its "huge variety" of "satisfying" breakfast fare (it also serves lunch) like macadamia-and-banana pancakes, Portuguese sausage omelets and eggs Benedict, all served at a "reasonable price" in "casual" Kapaa digs; while some longtime patrons lament it "used to be better when it was in Lihue", diehards declare it's "still a favorite."

Garden Island Barbecue ⊠ BBQ/Chinese

∇ 19 | 9 | 18 | $19

Lihue | 4252 Rice St. (Kalena St.) | 808-245-8868

"Always jammed", this "casual" Chinese in Lihue lures "lots of locals" with "giant" plates of BBQ and a lengthy lineup of "fresh"-tasting Sino standards; there's "no decor" to speak of, but the "food comes out quick" and prices are "reasonable" too – little wonder families have long considered it a "take-out favorite."

Gaylord's *Pacific Rim*
22 | 25 | 23 | $50

Lihue | Kilohana Plantation | 3-2087 Kaumualii Hwy. (Nuhou St.) | 808-245-9593 | www.gaylordskauai.com

Occupying a "peaceful" corner of the "gorgeous" Kilohana Plantation in Lihue, this "romantic" enclave feels utterly "away from it all", thanks to pampering "white-tablecloth" service and a wraparound porch enhanced by "gentle breezes" and "pastoral views"; diners divide on the "well-presented" Pacific Rim fare ("wonderful" vs. "adequate"), though most agree it's "pricey", especially at dinner; N.B. there's also a luau on the grounds on Tuesdays and Fridays.

Genki Sushi *Japanese*
17 | 13 | 16 | $19

Lihue | Kukui Grove Shopping Ctr. | 3-2600 Kaumualii Hwy. (Nawiliwili Rd.) | 808-632-2450 | www.genkisushiusa.com

See review in Oahu Dining Directory.

Hamura Saimin Stand ⌿ *Noodle Shop*
24 | 6 | 15 | $11

Lihue | 2956 Kress St. (Rice St.) | 808-245-3271

A "Kauai classic" since 1952, this "bargain" Lihue shop, voted Kauai's Best Buy, is where loads of "locals and tourists" go for "steaming hot" bowls of saimin (an island specialty made with "homestyle" noodles and "savory" broth), "delicious" yakitori and "heavenly" lilikoi-chiffon pie; service is "efficient", while "old-fashioned counter seating" and strictly "no-frills" decor add to its "funky" charm.

Hanalei Dolphin Restaurant *Seafood*
22 | 19 | 20 | $39

Hanalei | Hanalei Dolphin Ctr. | 5-5016 Kuhio Hwy. (Hanalei Bridge) | 808-826-6113 | www.hanaleidolphin.com

This "casual" seafooder "right on the Hanalei river" promises "no surprises" – just "ample portions" of "fresh, local" fish served with a "wonderful" family-style salad; "reasonable prices" ensure it's often "busy", but regulars report the usually "attentive" staff gets "overwhelmed" when the "crowds" hit; N.B. the adjacent market sells a variety of raw and cooked selections for takeout.

Hanalei Gourmet *American/Eclectic*
21 | 14 | 18 | $27

Hanalei | 5-5161 Kuhio Hwy. (Aku Rd.) | 808-826-2524 | www.hanaleigourmet.com

"Ideal for lunch", or a "perfect post-beach" snack, this "cute, little" American-Eclectic in Hanalei charms customers with "excellent" sandwiches, salads and burgers served up in a converted schoolhouse decorated with old chalkboards and desk-style chairs; fans say the "outdoor tables" and "live music" add "lots of local flavor", even if others insist that "so-so service" ultimately hampers the experience.

Hanama'ulu *Japanese/Tearoom*
▽ 20 | 16 | 18 | $28

Hanamaulu | 1-4291 Kuhio Hwy./Rte. 56 (Hanamaulu Rd.) | 808-245-2511

An "old-style" Hanamaulu Japanese modeled after an "authentic" "teahouse", this eatery features a dining space with tatami mats that opens up onto a koi pond and garden; the ginger-fried chicken and shrimp are the "must-have" picks among the moderately priced selections, though some diners point out that the "subpar" sushi and "unimpressive" service are among the disappointments.

Hanapepe Café ⓩ *Bakery/Vegetarian* | 22 | 17 | 21 | $24 |

Hanapepe | 3830 Hanapepe Rd. (Kona Rd.) | 808-335-5011

A "charming" spot housed in a "quaint" "plantation-style" building amid the art galleries on Hanapepe's main street, this "tiny" cafe and bakery offers a "limited, but tasty" lineup of mostly vegetarian vittles capped by "homemade" desserts; on Friday nights – the only evening it's open for dinner – they host "local musicians", but be sure to "make reservations" as "it books up fast"; N.B. closed Saturdays and Sundays.

House of Noodles *Noodle Shop* | ▽ 22 | 14 | 20 | $21 |

Kapaa | 4-1330 Kuhio Hwy. (bet. Inid & Kauwila Sts.) | 808-822-2708

A "varied and delicious" assortment of noodle dishes – from saimin to chow fun – are on offer at this "casual" Kapaa eatery also serving salads and sandwiches; though it's "easily overlooked" due to its strip-mall locale, wallet-watchers appreciate its "affordable" tabs and overall "family"-friendly vibe.

Hukilau Lanai Ⓜ *Hawaii Reg.* | ▽ 25 | 21 | 24 | $39 |

Kapaa | Kauai Coast Resort | 520 Aleka Loop (Kuhio Hwy.) | 808-822-0600

"Local ingredients" and "inventive" techniques come together at this "classy" respite in the Kauai Coast Resort in Kapaa, where feasts of "fresh island fish" and other Hawaii Regional dishes are served on a lanai overlooking the "beautiful gardens"; service is generally "top-notch", and while tabs aren't cheap, early-bird specials and deals on wine help minimize the damage.

JJ's Broiler *American* | 17 | 16 | 17 | $30 |

Nawiliwili | Anchor Cove | 3416 Rice St. (Lala Rd.) | 808-246-4422

A "friendly" bi-level American overlooking Nawiliwili Harbor in Anchor Cove, this casual eatery is favored for "quick" meals of "tasty" burgers and other well-priced eats; though it also offers a more "upscale" dinner, insiders insist it's "better for lunch" or "umbrella drinks" and "cold beer" imbibed in the "laid-back" bar area surrounded by flat-screen TVs.

Kalaheo Café & Coffee *Coffeehouse* | 23 | 16 | 19 | $19 |

Kalaheo | 2-2560 Kaumualii Hwy. (Silva Tract Rd.) | 808-332-5858 | www.kalaheo.com

"Popular with locals", this "order-at-the-counter" Kalaheo cafe earns kudos for its "outstanding coffee", "satisfying" breakfasts and lunches and "fresh" baked goods ("make sure you get the cinnamon knuckles" – a "warm pastry that is out of this world"); dinner is offered Wednesdays–Saturdays, and features full table service plus "innovative" plates like Asian skirt steak from chef-owner John Ferguson.

Kalapaki Beach Hut *Burgers/Sandwiches* | ▽ 22 | 13 | 18 | $15 |

Kalapaki Beach | 3474 Rice St. (Nawiliwili Rd.) | Lihue | 808-246-6330

Customers in "flip-flops and sarongs" fill up this "lowbrow" Kalapaki beachside burger and sandwich shack that boasts an open-air space made for "lounging"; there's "limited" fast food–style service, but a "cool" second-story deck overlooking the harbor and bay is a nice touch.

Kalypso Island Bar & Grill *Seafood*   16 | 15 | 16 | $30
(fka Zelo's Beach House)

Hanalei | 5-5156 Kuhio Hwy. (Aku Rd.) | 808-826-9700

Formerly Zelo's Beach House, this "fun" and "casual island seafooder" in Hanalei features "a large variety" of dining options and "generous portions"; fans say it's "most famous for its happy hour" and "bar scene" ("good for groups"), but critics complain that the "overpriced and mediocre food" has declined in "quality" "since it changed ownership."

Kauai Hula Girl *Pacific Rim*   ▽ 19 | 16 | 19 | $27

Kapaa | Coconut Mktpl. | 484 Kuhio Hwy. (Kapuna Rd.) |
808-822-4422

"Cheesy, but lovable" sums up this tropical-themed eatery in Kapaa's Coconut Marketplace attracting loads of "tourists" for hula dancing and live ukulele several nights a week; the "surprisingly good" Pacific Rim menu includes seafood combos and babyback ribs plus plenty of fruity drinks, all at moderate prices.

Kauai Pasta *Italian*   ▽ 21 | 13 | 18 | $26

Kapaa | 4-939 Kuhio Hwy. (Ala Rd.) | 808-822-7447
NEW Lihue | 3142 Kuhio Hwy. (Kali Rd.) | 808-245-2227

"Pasta lovers" sing the praises of this "popular" Italian duo in Kapaa and Lihue dishing out "filling" bowls of fettuccine and "unpretentious" fare like big salads, eggplant parmigiana and pesto chicken; "reasonable prices" make them a "good bet" for the area, overcoming "uninspiring" environs and occasionally "slow" service.

Keoki's Paradise *Pacific Rim*   20 | 23 | 20 | $35

Poipu | Poipu Shopping Vill. | 2360 Kiahuna Plantation Dr. (Poipu Rd.) |
Koloa | 808-742-7534 | www.keokisparadise.com

Like a "Hawaiian TGI Friday's", this "touristy" "haunt" in Poipu Shopping Village pulls in plenty of "families" for "reliable" Pacific Rim dishes (think "macadamia-crusted everything") and "bar-type" snacks backed by tropical drinks; service can be "spotty", and "you'll either love or hate" the "over-the-top Polynesian theme park" decor.

Kintaro, Restaurant 🗷 *Japanese*   25 | 19 | 21 | $37

Kapaa | 4-370 Kuhio Hwy. (Kapaa Byp.) | 808-822-3341

"A favorite for celebrations", this "noisy" Japanese in Kapaa is "popular" with "families and kids" thanks to its "fairly priced" cuisine including an "amazing selection" of "quality" sushi and teppanyaki items cooked up "in front of you" by "entertaining" chefs; since it gets "swamped" at peak hours, "arrive early" or prepare to "wait."

🗷 Koloa Fish Market ⴕ *Hawaiian/Seafood*   25 | 8 | 18 | $15

Koloa | 5482 Koloa Rd. (Kaumualii Hwy.) | 808-742-6199

"Eat like a local" at this "excellent value", "takeout-only" Koloa market, voted the top seafooder on Kauai, where the dishes include "awesome poke", daily fish specials and "to-die-for" plate lunches that make "excellent grab-and-go" Hawaiian meals "for the beach"; they don't take credit cards and there's "zero atmosphere", but acolytes aver the "decor does not matter here."

Kukui's Restaurant & Bar *Pacific Rim*

▽ 19 | 22 | 20 | $31

Kalapaki Beach | Kauai Marriott Resort & Beach Club | 3610 Rice St. (Hoolaulea Way) | Lihue | 808-245-5050 | www.marriott.com

A "family-friendly" vibe and "typical" "Marriott-brand consistency" mark this "casual" Kalapaki Beach hotel restaurant purveying "fresh" Pacific Rim fare in a "beautiful poolside setting"; the buffets (for breakfast daily and dinner on Friday and Saturday nights) draw accolades, and penny-pinchers are pleased the "happy-hour specials help defray the cost."

L&L Drive-Inn *BBQ/Hawaiian*

16 | 6 | 12 | $10

Kapaa | 4-733 Kuhio Hwy. (Pouli Rd.) | 808-821-8880
Lihue | 3-2600 Kaumualii Hwy. (bet. Nani St. & Puhi Rd.) | 808-246-3688
www.hawaiianbarbecue.com

See review in Oahu Dining Directory.

Lemongrass Grill *Pan-Asian/Seafood*

17 | 16 | 17 | $37

Kapaa | 4-885 Kuhio Hwy. (Kapaa Byp.) | 808-821-2888

Expect the "right amount of spicy" in the midpriced specialties at this Kapaa Asian seafooder where the experiences range from "very good" to "nothing special"; seating is available in the two-story, pagoda-esque building's "pleasant" interior, which is enlived by fresh orchids and Pacific Rim artwork, or outside on a "noisy" patio that's "separated from a busy road only by some shrubs."

Lighthouse Bistro *Pacific Rim*

21 | 18 | 20 | $35

Kilauea | Kong Lung Sq. | 2484 Keneke St. (Kilauea Rd.) | 808-828-0480 | www.lighthousebistro.com

Pacific Rim meets European fusion at this "lovely", "open-air", plantation-style respite where the menu includes "large portions" of "always fresh fish" and an all-you-can-eat pasta bar that's a "great deal", plus there's an "excellent wine list"; even most who feel it's merely "reliable" admit the location is convenient for a bite "after visiting the local lighthouse" in Kilauea.

Lihue Barbecue Inn Ⓢ *American/Pan-Asian*

▽ 20 | 12 | 20 | $19

Lihue | 2982 Kress St. (Rice St.) | 808-245-2921

Don't let the name fool you, this "family-owned" Lihue mainstay since 1940 goes beyond BBQ to serve a "widely varied menu" of "cheap, solid" American and Asian eats that "include an appetizer, coffee or tea" and "wonderful" homemade pie at dinnertime; with a "coffee-shop atmosphere", a "friendly" staff and "no pretensions", it draws a "mostly local clientele."

NEW Market Street Diner *Diner*

- | - | - | I

Lihue | 3501 Rice St. (Nawiliwili Rd.) | 808-246-1100

This "friendly" family-owned diner in Lihue slings "generous portions" of inexpensive eats like omelets and meatloaf; while the digs are nothing "fancy", it suits most for an easy meal "before or after a movie."

Naupaka Terrace *Pacific Rim*

▽ 19 | 20 | 19 | $36

Lihue | Hilton Kauai Beach Resort | 4331 Kauai Beach Dr. (Kuhio Hwy.) | 808-245-1955 | www.hilton.com

Set in the Hilton Kauai Beach Resort in Lihue, this "reasonably priced", "kid-friendly" canteen features "good, not great" Pacific Rim fare, includ-

FOOD DECOR SERVICE COST

ing a breakfast spread with "fresh fruits and juices, muffins and eggs" and a prime rib and seafood buffet on Friday and Saturday eves; service isn't always "up to par", but luckily the "beautiful pool views" distract.

Norberto's El Café 🗷 *Mexican*

– | – | – | M

Kapaa | 4-1373 Kuhio Hwy. (bet. Kukui & Niu Sts.) | 808-822-3362
Homestyle "authentic hippie Mexican" eats are on the menu at this dinner-only Kapaa spot that's been around for 30 years "because they do it right" (no lard); "try the taro leaf enchiladas" and "fantastic tostadas" recommend regulars, who relish the "large portions", cozy booths and walls decorated with south-of-the-border hats and photos of Tijuana.

Oki Diner ◑ *Bakery/Hawaiian*

15 | 8 | 15 | $15

Lihue | 4479 Rice St. (Haleko Rd.) | 808-245-5899
"Delicious pancakes and smooth coffee" are the stars at this Lihue "hole-in-the-wall" where chef Dominic Benzon (formerly of Nick's Fish Market in Waikiki) has debuted a new menu with plenty of "real Hawaiian" "local flavor and color"; even though the "service isn't good when it's busy", reviewers say "you can't go wrong" given the "large portions", solid bakery items and "reasonable prices"; P.S. "sit outside and try the loco moco with fried rice" for breakfast.

Ono Family Restaurant *American/Hawaiian*

19 | 8 | 16 | $18

Kapaa | 4-1292 Kuhio Hwy. (Inia St.) | 808-822-1710
This "funky" breakfast/lunch Kapaa "dive" that closed briefly after a fire in 2007 is "again a favorite among locals" who like the "updated" decor with local artwork and lots of flowers, the "best" "stacks of pancakes with Portuguese sausage" covered in "yummy homemade syrup" and the "authentic Hawaiian" "grindz" with "real local flavor"; tourists "stop here at least once per trip", and locals say it's "worth the wait."

NEW Pacific Island

∇ 24 | 19 | 21 | $46

Bistro *Pacific Rim/Pan-Asian*

Kapaa | Kauai Village Shopping Ctr. | 4831 Kuhio Hwy. (Wana Rd.) | 808-822-0092 | www.kauaibistro.com
"Watch surfers in training" from this new Kapaa "strip-mall" spot serving a "tempting", "inventive menu" of "well-cooked and generous" Pan-Asian and Pacific Rim specialties like "hot and sour soup", "ahi and eggs" and "outstanding sea bass"; fans say "service is good" and it's all "fairly priced", but critics claim the "quality sometimes wavers."

Plantation Gardens *Pacific Rim*

23 | 27 | 21 | $50

Poipu | Outrigger Kiahuna Plantation | 2253 Poipu Rd.
(Kiahuna Plantation Dr.) | Koloa | 808-742-2216 | www.pgrestaurant.com
For a "quiet, romantic dinner", surveyors seek out this "transporting" venue set on a historic Poipu plantation surrounded by "breathtaking" gardens; service is "warm", but while the "creative" Pacific Rim fare "never disappoints", some say it's not as "memorable" as the setting; P.S. don't miss their selection of "fine cocktails" crafted from fresh juices.

Poipu Beach Broiler *American/Steak*

19 | 18 | 18 | $35

Poipu | 1941 Poipu Rd. (bet. Ala Kinoiki & Kipuka St.) | Koloa | 808-742-6433 | www.pbbroiler.com
Hang ten at this "open-air" surf-themed Poipu steakhouse that "overlooks the beach" and is filled with memorabilia - i.e. long boards, vin-

tage photos, a pair of Duke Kahanamoku's swimshorts autographed by family members; while finicky folks find the American fare "just above-average" and the "easy going" service on the "slow" side, "if you want a burger after swimming", it's a "convenient" choice.

Polynesia Café ⊞ *Eclectic* | 18 | 12 | 14 | $24 |

Hanalei | Ching Young Vill. | 5-5190 Kuhio Hwy. (bet. Aku Rd. & Malolo St.) | 808-826-1999 | www.polynesiacafe.com

An "Eclectic", "reasonably priced" menu of "imaginative and tasty" fare, including "lots of local fish, delicious BBQ pork" and "tantalizing baked goods", draws "locals and tourists" to this "popular North Shore hangout"; the "ultracasual setting" and "takeout"-friendly counter service fit the "gourmet-food-on-paper-plates" approach, but even fans gripe that "parking is a pain" and there's only "seating outside the shopping center."

Pomodoro *Italian* | 23 | 16 | 23 | $35 |

Poipu | Rainbow Plaza | Kaumualii Hwy./Rte. 50 | Koloa | 808-332-5945

Loyalists "love" this "mom-and-pop" Italian tucked into a Poipu strip-mall that dishes out "hearty" specialties with an "authentic" "New York" bent; plain-Jane decor may be "uninspiring", but the "accommodating" staff ensures you're always "comfortable."

Postcards Café *Eclectic* | 24 | 21 | 23 | $46 |

Hanalei | 5-5075A Kuhio Hwy. (Aku Rd.) | 808-826-1191 | www.postcardscafe.com

A "charming" "converted" plantation-style cottage in Hanalei that's, fittingly, "postcard"-pretty, is an appropiate setting for the "imaginative", "fabulously presented" Eclectic seafood and vegetarian dishes delivered at this "North Shore delight"; most find it "worth a detour" "off the beaten track", but a handful deem the daring fare rather "expensive" and a little too "faux hippie-chic", preferring it for a "cozy" breakfast instead.

⊠ Roy's *Hawaii Reg.* | 26 | 22 | 24 | $54 |

Poipu | Poipu Shopping Vill. | 2360 Kiahuna Plantation Dr. (Poipu Rd.) | Koloa | 808-742-5000 | www.roysrestaurant.com

See review in Oahu Dining Directory.

Saffron Ⓜ *Mediterranean* | ▽ 20 | 14 | 18 | $33 |

Princeville | Pali Ke Kua | 5300 Ka Haku Rd. (Liholiho Rd.) | 808-826-6225 | www.saffron-hawaii.com

A "tremendous chef who creates a diverse Mediterranean menu" that veers from contemporary Spain to Italy to Greece is a "romantic" choice in Princeville; the "good use of local resources" result in stand-out "paella and pizza" and an "excellent lunch buffet", but the dining space doesn't live up to the rest.

Scotty's Beachside BBQ *BBQ* | 22 | 17 | 19 | $24 |

Kapaa | 4-1546 Kuhio Hwy. (bet. Kou & Lehua Sts.) | 808-823-8480 | www.scottysbbq.com

Enjoy "great BBQ right on the beach" at this "group-friendly" Kapaa spot, where the "smoky flavors" and wide "variety of meats, sauces and sides" are a little bit Texas, a little Kansas City and altogether "incredibly tasty"; some fans recommend sitting "by the large roll-top window for the best views" of the sand and sea, while others praise the "funny staff", "good value" and "relaxing" vibe.

Shells *Seafood/Steak*

∇ 20 | 23 | 21 | $46

Poipu | Sheraton | 2440 Hoonani Rd. (Kapili Rd.) | Koloa | 808-742-1661 | www.sheraton.com

"Standard" hotel fare is the name of the game at this surf 'n' turfer in the Poipu Sheraton that takes an adventurous turn on Saturday nights when it hosts an "excellent" Japanese buffet, rolling out plates of wok-fried snapper, barbecued eel and Hokkaido-style prime rib; prices are moderate, and its understated look gets a boost from "great" shoreline views.

Shrimp Station *Seafood*

24 | 8 | 16 | $16

Waimea | 9652 Kaumualii Hwy. (bet. Makeke & Pokole Rds.) | 808-338-1242 | www.shrimpstation.com

It "isn't much to look at" but this "awesome" little "walk-up" shrimp stand with a couple of outdoor picnic tables that "fill up fast" is a "must" for an inexpensive "lunch on your way back from Waimea Canyon" "as long as they don't run out" before you arrive; the offerings are "fresh out of the sea and onto your plate" – whether fried with coconut, garlic-laden, Cajun spiced or stuffed in tacos – and are perfect for toting "to the beach" to "eat with your fingers" "off of paper plates."

Tidepools *Pacific Rim/Seafood*

24 | 28 | 25 | $57

Poipu | Grand Hyatt | 1571 Poipu Rd. (bet. Ainako St. & Keleka Rd.) | Koloa | 808-742-1234 | www.hyatt.com

Sit among "thatched tikis" "surrounded by water with koi and swans" at this "romantic" Poipu eatery in the Grand Hyatt, where you can "gaze at the stars" as you dine on "interesting" Pacific Rim seafood dishes; the "service and atmosphere" make it "unforgettable" (it was voted No. 1 for Decor and Service on Kauai), but high expectations lead to some picky patrons being slightly "underwhelmed."

TomKat's Grille *American*

18 | 15 | 17 | $22

Koloa | Old Koloa Town | 5402 Koloa Rd. (Maluhia Rd.) | 808-742-8887

A "remarkable value" in Koloa, this "small and crowded" American "family place" with "great roasted chicken", burgers and "kalua pork" boasts a "casual garden setting" "in a courtyard with trees", "lots of locals" and "cats wandering around"; service is "friendly" but "slow", so those who find the fare too "greasy" and the "friendly" service too "slow", "skip the food" and "go for cheap drinks at happy hour."

Tropical Taco ⊠⌷ *Mexican*

21 | 12 | 15 | $13

Hanalei | Halele'a Bldg. | 5-5088 Kuhio Hwy. (Aku Rd.) | 808-827-8226 | www.tropicaltaco.com

It's "an island tradition" to grab some "huge, messy" "fish tacos and burritos" from Roger Kennedy at this inexpensive eatery in "the little town of Hanalei" that used to operate "out of a trailer" (it's still "parked out in the lot") and now has a "casual" space with a porch from which you can "watch the parade of life passing by"; those who "pine for" the "fresh" Mexican treats "all year" say it's "absolutely essential Kauai eating", complemented by "hospitable" service.

	FOOD	DECOR	SERVICE	COST

Wahoo Seafood
Grill & Bar *Pacific Rim/Seafood*

∇ 19 | 18 | 20 | $30

Kapaa | 4-733 Kuhio Hwy. (Aleka Loop) | 808-822-7833 |
www.wahooogrill.com

"Owned by a local fishing company", this "creative" Kapaa seafooder with "beautifully presented" Pacific Rim–oriented fin fare, including mahi mahi stuffed with macadamia-nut-crusted crabmeat, and a "view of the surfers" wins some admirers who "tell friends"; but spoilsports snap "it pretends to be much better than it is", citing "overpriced", "nondescript" eats.

NEW Waimea Brewing
Company *Eclectic/Pub Food*

19 | 17 | 19 | $28

Waimea | Waimea Plantation Cottages | 9400 Kaumualii Hwy.
(Menehune Rd.) | 808-338-9733

With an "out-of-the-way" location in the Waimea Plantation Cottages, this "westernmost brewpub" gets "crowded with locals and tourists alike" who enjoy the "nice setting" – hardwood floors, rattan furniture and petrogylph designs – and the "homemade beers on tap"; though the Eclectic "pub grub" offers "no surprises", it's "decent" given "there aren't a lot of choices" in the area.

Kauai Golf

Symbols

Yardage, USGA Rating and Slope are listed after each address.

🏌️ caddies/forecaddies   🔑 guests only
🛺 carts only   🕐 restricted tee times (call ahead)

Kauai Lagoons, Kiele/Maile 🛺

| 26 | 23 | 24 | 22 | $150 |

Lihue | 3351 Hoolaulea Way | 808-241-6000 | 800-634-6400 |
www.kauailagoonsgolf.com | 6758/5230; 72.4/69.3; 129/115

Located minutes from Lihue Airport, this Kauai "must-play" is "partly
closed for reconstruction", offering a still-"challenging" placeholder
that combines the Kiele front nine with the Mokihana (now Maile)
back nine; the redo "seems to be taking forever", however, and until it
fully reopens as a 27-hole spread in 2009, the lack of the Kiele back
nine – with its "gut-check" of a par-3 13th, featuring a shot "right over
the ocean to a spot of green" with harbor views – may "make the
experience less attractive."

Kiahuna

| 19 | 17 | 19 | 20 | $99 |

Poipu | 2545 Kiahuna Plantation Dr. | 808-742-9595 | www.kiahunagolf.com |
6925/4887; 73.5/64.4; 134/114

A "less expensive alternative to nearby Poipu Bay", this RTJ Jr. design
in Poipu Beach is "not too difficult unless it's really windy", and offers
"paspalum greens" that are "fast and true" as well as Kauai's only set
of junior tees; the staff is "eager to help" at this "hidden gem", but
some cronies complain that because it lacks a "resort component", it
"often gets short shrift, which it shouldn't"; P.S. "come early for a
great breakfast" at Joe's on the Green.

Poipu Bay 🛺

| 27 | 26 | 26 | 22 | $200 |

Poipu | 2250 Ainako St. | 808-742-8711 | 800-858-6300 |
www.poipubaygolf.com | 7123/5372; 73.9/70.4; 134/122

"Stunning beauty" and a "challenging" layout provide an "awesome
experience" for "average players to low handicappers" at this RTJ Jr.
design on the cliffs of Kauai; although the "gorgeous views" "can be
distracting" ("humpbacks breeching off the 17th tee") and the wind
makes it "physically exhausting", it's still "great fun" to play at this
former host of the PGA Grand Slam of Golf; P.S. a "top-drawer" restaurant and "outstanding service" seal the deal.

▣ Princeville, Prince

| 28 | 27 | 25 | 22 | $200 |

Princeville | Hwy. 56 S. | 808-826-5001 | 800-826-1105 |
www.princeville.com | 7309/5346; 75.7/71.4; 140/124

For "golf at its finest", this "beautiful yet brutal" RTJ Jr. design on the
North Shore, Kauai's top-rated course, offers a "challenging" experience, with "tight fairways and jungle roughs on many holes" ("after
the first two, you wonder if you're going to survive the day"); nevertheless, "the extraordinary view makes up for the difficult terrain", and
the service and clubhouse spa are "excellent" too; N.B. its 27-hole sister, Makai, is being renovated and should reopen in late summer 2009.

	COURSE	FACIL.	SERVICE	VALUE	COST

Puakea ⚐

	21	13	21	25	$135

Lihue | 4150 Nuhou St. | 808-245-8756 | 866-773-5554 |
www.puakeagolf.com | 6954/5225; 73.3/69.3; 135/113

At this "gorgeous" Robin Nelson track tucked away near Lihue Airport, "you'll be rewarded" with a layout that promises "great vacation value", roaming through "tropical terrain" (it's where *Jurassic Park* was filmed) and featuring "beautiful design and top-notch maintenance"; in 2003, AOL founder Steve Case put up the funding to finish what "was only 10 holes for years", and the result is an 18-hole layout that's "challenging for any skill."

Wailua Golf Course

	▽ 20	16	20	26	$44

Kapaa | 3-5350 Kuhio Hwy. | 808-241-6666 | www.kauai.gov/golf |
6991/5974; 73.3/73.4; 129/119

Redesigned and expanded by Toyo Shirai in 1962, this muni is "the best $44 you'll spend in a long time" thanks to a "spectacular back nine" and a front that "lets you play almost at beach level" ("unlike other Kauai courses") to take in the "fabulous views"; still, while it's kept "in excellent shape" and offers the chance to "meet local golfers", the "facilities are basic" and its "great-value" pricing can lead to "heavy play and frustrating delays"; P.S. "cash only."

Kauai Hotels

Symbols

🎎 children's programs	🔭 views
✗ exceptional restaurant	丄 18-hole golf course
ⓗ historic interest	Ⓢ notable spa facilities
ℰ kitchens	≋ swimming pool
🐾 allows pets	✎ tennis

ⓩ Grand Hyatt 🎎ℰ🔭Ⓢ≋✎ — | 24 | 24 | 23 | 28 | $550 |

Poipu | 1571 Poipu Rd. | Koloa | 808-742-1234 | fax 808-742-1557 |
800-233-1234 | www.grandhyattkauai.com | 565 rooms, 37 suites

"Bring your walking shoes" to this sprawling Poipu "hideaway" that's
the "definition of casual elegance" with its "gorgeous grounds"
(awash in "more flowers than a funeral"), "vibrant Hawaiiana-style
rooms" and "accommodating" staff that's "well trained in 'aloha'"; it
offers lots of "family-friendly" "free activities, from lei making to parrot
talks", and is "rightly known" for its "amazing pools", but some say it
may be best to "avoid in summer if you're kid-free."

Hanalei Bay Resort 🎎ℰ🔭≋✎ — | 20 | 21 | 18 | 22 | $215 |

Princeville | 5380 Honoiki Rd. | 808-826-6522 | fax 808-826-6680 |
800-827-4427 | www.hanaleibayresort.com | 30 rooms, 15 suites

"The real star is the beach" at this "affordable", "cozy" option on
Kauai's North Shore, a "good all-around family hotel" that also manages to have a "romantic Bali Hai atmosphere"; though rooms (some
are time-shares) are merely "fine", they're undergoing renovation,
and compensations include a "great outdoor bar" and some of the
"best views anywhere."

Hilton Kauai Beach Resort 🎎🔭Ⓢ≋ — | ∇ 21 | 19 | 14 | 20 | $329 |

Lihue | 4331 Kauai Beach Dr. | 808-245-1955 | fax 808-246-9085 |
888-243-9178 | www.hilton.com | 343 rooms, 7 suites

Fans find "bang for the buck" at this 25-acre "family fun" resort in a
"nice location near Lihue" where the "pretty grounds", "beautiful"
open-air spa (a "mandatory visit") and recently refurbished "contemporary" (if "small") rooms win over fans; but sourpusses snap it's "not
up to standards" given the unimpressive dining, spotty service and
"beach" location where "swimming is not recommended."

Kauai Marriott Resort & Beach Club 🎎🔭Ⓢ≋ — | 21 | 22 | 20 | 24 | $390 |

Kalapaki Beach | 3610 Rice St. | Lihue | 808-245-5050 | fax 808-245-5049 |
800-220-2925 | www.marriott.com | 345 rooms, 11 suites

"Ask for an ocean view, it's worth it" say fans of this recently renovated
"laid-back", "friendly" "beachfront" resort near Lihue with vacation
ownership villas, a "Vegas-type" lobby, "one of the biggest pools
you've ever seen", a "secluded bay beach", "two golf courses" and a
"variety of daily activities"; though some say the "best rooms are dom-
inated by time-shares", "hey - it's still paradise."

	ROOMS	SERVICE	DINING	FACIL.	COST

Sheraton Kauai
Resort 🏨 🍴 🏋 💲 🏊 🎾

| 20 | 22 | 17 | 23 | $420 |

Poipu | 2440 Hoonani Rd., Poipu Bch. | Koloa | 808-742-1661 |
fax 808-742-9777 | 888-488-3535 | www.sheraton-kauai.com |
386 rooms, 8 suites

"Pay more" and "upgrade to the oceanfront rooms" with "lanais to die
for" ("it's so worth it") at this "intimate" resort on Poipu Beach offering "all the amenities you would want without being overly touristy";
admirers laud a staff that's "friendly, courteous and helpful" and the
"nightly entertainment with complimentary mai tais", though others
gripe that the "food's not great" ("stay here and eat elsewhere").

NEW Westin Princeville Ocean
Resort Villas 🐕 🏋 ⬆ 🏊

| - | - | - | - | $800 |

Princeville | 3838 Wyllie Rd. | 808-827-8700 | fax 808-827-8701 |
800-601-8699 | www.starwoodhotels.com | 346 villas

Marking Starwood's third partial vacation ownership resort in Hawaii,
this new North Shore oceanfront property (sister to the under-
renovation Princeville Resort) is perched 200 feet above Anini Beach
and features studios, one- and two-bedroom villas set in seven build-
ings; accommodations boast Westin Heavenly beds, whirlpool tubs,
LCD flat-screen TVs, Bose Wave radios and WiFi access, while the
grounds include four pools, a two-story clubhouse, a restaurant and
a general store.

LANAI & MOLOKAI

Lanai & Molokai Attractions

Garden of the Gods
23 | 12 | 11 | $0

Lanai City | 8 miles north of Hwy. 440 | Lanai

The "eerie", Marslike topography of the rock spires in this "beautifully maintained" garden (also known as Keahiakawelo) is an "amazing display of nature" in a "remote, hot, dusty" locale seven miles north of Lanai City; if the rutted dirt entrance road (four-wheel-drive required) puts visitors at risk of "brain damage from the jostling", the payoff is that once there, "you'll most likely have the place to yourself."

⚡ Manele Bay
28 | 22 | 20 | $0

Manele | Hwy. 440 | Lanai City | Lanai

Voted the top Attraction for Appeal on Lanai, and easily one of its most accessible waterfronts, this bay that's part of the Manele-Hulopoe Marine Life Conservation District is "what paradise was meant to be", complete with dolphin sightings, "delightful swimming", "amazing sunsets" and "some of the best snorkeling"; too bad facilities and service are lacking, "unless you're staying at the [Four Seasons] hotel" nearby.

Molokai Mule Ride
∇ 25 | 18 | 21 | M

Kalaupapa | 100 Kalae Hwy., Rte. 470 (Kolea Ave.) | Molokai | 808-567-6088 | 800-567-7550 | www.muleride.com

"Adventurous" vacationers trade their beach towels for pack mules to make this "exhilarating" "once-in-a-lifetime" trek down 1,700 feet of the "highest sea cliffs in the world" to the "breathtaking" Kalaupapa peninsula and its notorious former leprosy (Hansen's Disease) settlement; neither the "interesting" village tour "led by former patients of the colony" nor the "harrowing" ride to get there are for the faint of heart – all in all, the experience "will leave you mesmerized."

Molokai Museum & Cultural Ctr.
- | - | - | I

(aka R.W. Meyer Sugar Mill)

Kualapuu | Hwy. 470 (Hwy. 460) | Molokai | 808-567-6436

A "treasure trove" of Molokai memorabilia, this quaint museum with a "friendly" staff explores the history and impact of the sugar cane industry using photos, artifacts and personal stories, set alongside rotating exhibits and a well-stocked gift gallery; its highlight is the 1870s-era R.W. Meyer Sugar Mill, a fully restored and functioning operation that's on the National Register of Historic Places.

Purdy's Natural Macadamia Nut Farm
∇ 22 | 18 | 21 | I

Hoolehua | Lihi Pali Ave. | Molokai | 808-567-6601

Expect all-things-macadamia at this working farm and gift shop purveying "chocolate-covered nuts", fresh nuggets "to crack when you get home" and plenty of "aloha" spirit courtesy of the "very colorful" owner and his stories about organic growing; the grove, situated two miles west of Kualapuu, was planted in 1929 and is on Hawaiian homestead land.

Lanai & Molokai Dining

Blue Ginger Café ⌦ *American/Pan-Asian* | 20 | 14 | 18 | $19 |

Lanai City | 409 Seventh St. (Lanai Ave.) | Lanai | 808-565-6363
"If you want a true Lanai" morning or midday meal, this "inexpensive" "plate-lunch" spot serving "tasty local" American and Pan-Asian fare like mahi mahi burgers, fried rice and saimin in an "unpretentious" setting is a "respite from the swanky, super-expensive resorts"; locals who "flock" here admit it's "not the healthiest" eating, but you've "gotta love" it all the same.

Café 565 ⌦ *American/Mediterranean* | - | - | - | I |

Lanai City | 408 Eighth St. (Kele St.) | Lanai | 808-565-6622
"One of the more reasonably priced restaurants on Lanai", this BYO American cafe with Mediterranean and local influences serves pizza, "good sandwiches" and salads, "huge calzones" and "plate lunches" in a casual setting.

Canoes Lanai ⌦ *American/Hawaiian* | ▽ 17 | 18 | 17 | $34 |

Lanai City | 419 Seventh St. (Lanai Ave.) | Lanai | 808-565-6537
Formerly known as Tanigawa's, this veteran Lanai City hole-in-the-wall – around since the 1920s – is a favorite among residents for its local-style, budget-friendly breakfasts (short stacks, fried rice, Spam bento, loco moco), simple plate lunches, hearty American and Hawaiian selections and "good" service.

Challenge at Manele Clubhouse *Pacific Rim* | 24 | 25 | 25 | $36 |

Manele | Four Seasons Resort Lanai at Manele Bay | 1 Manele Bay Rd. (Manele Rd.) | Lanai City | Lanai | 808-565-2290 | www.fourseasons.com
For the most "memorable" experience at this "relaxing" Pacific Rim clubhouse eatery on Lanai, "pick a spot on the patio" and enjoy the "breathtaking views" of "dolphins jumping" in Manele Bay and golfers finishing at the 18th; though the "amazing" setting is "the real draw", the "excellent", if "limited", fare – "ono shrimp pitas", "fresh fish tacos", "delicious Kobe beef strips" – is "worth the price."

Experience at Koele Clubhouse *Sandwiches* | 22 | 23 | 24 | $38 |

Koele | Four Seasons Lanai, The Lodge at Koele | 1 Keomoku Hwy. (Laniola Rd.) | Lanai City | Lanai | 808-565-4605 | www.fourseasons.com
"After a round" on the "spectacular" Koele golf course at the Four Seasons, you can "enjoy lunch" in "complete relaxation" at this clubhouse eatery where the "attentive" staff provides "wonderful" service in a "gorgeous" setting "overlooking the lush green fairway"; "amazing" cheeseburgers and a "venison pastrami" highlight the menu of "pricey" sandwiches "prepared with fresh ingredients from the islands", but others say it's "worth it for the view" alone.

Hula Shores *American/Pacific Rim* | - | - | - | M |

Kaunakakai | Hotel Molokai | Kamehameha Hwy. | Molokai | 808-553-5347 | www.hotelmolokai.com
"Vintage Hawaii" describes this casual American–Pacific Rim respite at Hotel Molokai, set outside Kaunakakai in a "breezy" (i.e. "comfortable" except when a real wind kicks up) oceanfront setting lit by tiki torches after dark; the "fresh fish" is accompanied by "nightly enter-

"tainment" and "beautiful views of Lanai"; N.B. the restaurant and the hotel are undergoing substantial renovations.

Hulopo'e Court *Pacific Rim*
▽ 23 | 24 | 25 | $63

Manele | Four Seasons Resort Lanai at Manele Bay | 1 Manele Bay Rd. (Manele Rd.) | Lanai City | Lanai | 808-565-2290 | www.fourseasons.com
"Top-notch service" sets the mood at this "classy-yet-casual" Pacific Rim restaurant at the Four Seasons Manele Bay; the "delightful breakfast buffet" and "limited" dinner menu – spotlighting "excellent fresh fish" – are enhanced by a "spectacular" "open terrace" setting with ocean views.

☑ Ihilani Restaurant *Italian*
24 | 24 | 26 | $63

Manele | Four Seasons Resort Lanai at Manele Bay | 1 Manele Bay Rd. (Manele Rd.) | Lanai City | Lanai | 808-565-2296 | www.fourseasons.com
For the "best special-occasion dinner you can imagine", this "memorable" Italian with "impeccable service" in the Four Seasons Manele Bay may be worth the trip to Lanai alone; with an "excellent tasting menu" and a formal space overlooking the ocean with its "soft breezes and sounds of distant waves", it's a "romantic", "opulent" "splurge."

Kanemitsu's Bakery & Restaurant *Bakery*
– | – | – | I

Kaunakakai | 79 Ala Malama St. (bet. Hotel & Manako Lns.) | Molokai | 808-553-5855
"Known throughout the islands" for its baked goods and local-style breakfasts, this legendary Kaunakakai bakery founded in 1922 exudes an "at-home feeling" in its bare-bones dining room; carbaholics confide "you don't leave Molokai without a loaf or two" of its famous bread.

NEW Lanai City Grille Ⓜ *Pacific Rim*
▽ 22 | 17 | 22 | $39

Lanai City | Hotel Lanai | 828 Lanai Ave. (9th Ave.) | Lanai | 808-565-7211 | www.hotellanai.com
With a menu created by Hawaii Regional cuisine pioneer Beverly Gannon that "runs the gamut from diner favorites to sophisticated" Pacific Rim entrees, everyone should find "something to love" at this Hotel Lanai "charmer" staffed by "friendly, engaging" servers; though some say the "homey" "plantation-style" digs leave "room for improvement", most toast an overall "lovely experience" that, thankfully, is "not overpriced."

☑ Lodge at Koele Dining Room *Pacific Rim*
26 | 27 | 27 | $79

Koele | Four Seasons Lanai, The Lodge at Koele | 1 Keomoku Hwy. (Laniola Rd.) | Lanai City | Lanai | 808-565-4580 | www.fourseasons.com
"A unique experience" awaits in this Four Seasons Koele venue voted No. 1 for Food on Lanai, which, in keeping with the "swanky" "grand lodge" concept, offers "robust meats, including game", plus Pacific Rim-accented seafood, all ferried by "precise" servers; though it's "a tad formal for Hawaii" (gents need long pants and collared shirts), if you come "prepared to spend" lots of money, "you won't be disappointed."

Mana'e Goods & Grindz *American*
– | – | – | I

Manae | off Kamehameha V Hwy. | Molokai | 808-558-8498
The only dining option "on the east end of Molokai", this inexpensive Manae grocery store across from a "beautiful" beach has a walk-up counter serving "good" American breakfasts, local-style plate lunches and "daily specials" for takeout.

	FOOD	DECOR	SERVICE	COST

Molokai Drive-Inn *American* | - | - | - | I |

Kaunakakai | 15 Kamoi St. (Kamehameha V Hwy.) | Molokai | 808-553-5655

Given there are "not too many options" for dining on Molokai, many find themselves at this "greasy spoon" in Kaunakakai with reasonably priced American plates and "local-style fast-food staples"; come as you are, as it's a strictly counter-serve, seat-yourself (inside or out) kind of place.

Molokai Pizza Café *Pizza* | ▽ 19 | 12 | 18 | $17 |

Kaunakakai | Kahua Ctr. | 15 Kaunakakai Pl. (Kamehameha V Hwy.) | Molokai | 808-553-3288

"The only game in town for pizza", this "friendly" Kaunakakai parlor "also serves sandwiches and other items" in addition to its "great" pies; video games keep the kids busy while the 'rents pay the bill with "cash only."

Ocean Grill *Pan-Asian/Seafood* | 23 | 25 | 25 | $58 |

Manele | Four Seasons Resort Lanai at Manele Bay | 1 Manele Bay Rd. (Manele Rd.) | Lanai City | Lanai | 808-565-2092 | www.fourseasons.com

With "food worthy" of its "divine" open-air setting with "gorgeous ocean views" at the Four Seasons Manele Bay, this seafooder boasts "expertly prepared", "innovative" Pan-Asian dishes using "local fish", as well as "stellar service"; still, a portion of penny-pinchers pout about "expense."

Oviedo's *Filipino* | - | - | - | I |

Kaunakakai | 145 Ala Malama Ave. (bet. Illo Rd. & Kokio St.) | Molokai | 808-553-5014

Occupying an unassuming space in Downtown Kaunakakai for over 30 years, this lunch counter is famous for its "great local" food, signature roast pork and limited menu of Filipino-style plate lunches like chicken papaya and pork adobo; the "good-value" pricing is a further draw.

Paddlers' Inn *American/Pacific Rim* | - | - | - | I |

Kaunakakai | 10 Mohala St. (Maluolu Pl.) | Molokai | 808-553-5256

"Paddle over to Molokai" for this "fun", "comfortable" eat-and-drinkery in central Kaunakakai serving "huge portions" of American and Pacific Rim fare (like cheap "burgers and fish sandwiches"); decor that's "what you'd expect for a laid-back island bar" is a plus, as are the "live entertainment" some evenings and happy-hour specials.

Pele's Other Garden *American/Italian* | ▽ 19 | 14 | 19 | $26 |

Lanai City | 811 Houston St. (8th St.) | Lanai | 808-565-9628 | www.pelesothergarden.com

If you need a "break from elaborate" resort dining, plant yourself at a table in this Lanai City "hole-in-the-wall", an American lunchtime deli that "turns into an Italian bistro at night"; the menu of "good but not extraordinary" fare "isn't extensive", but "economical" tabs and an owner who makes guests "feel welcome" add up to overall "enjoyment."

Terrace, The *American* | ▽ 23 | 24 | 25 | $56 |

Koele | Four Seasons Lanai, The Lodge at Koele | 1 Keomoku Hwy. (Laniola Rd.) | Lanai City | Lanai | 808-565-7300 | www.fourseasons.com

"In the massive, high-ceiling lodge" of the Four Seasons Koele, this casual New American offers a "breakfast you won't forget" with signature dishes like "huevos rancheros paniolo" and "French toast and waffles with a touch of tropical fruit flavors"; evening diners also rave about the "pleasant" space, "lovely garden" view and "attentive staff."

Lanai Golf

Symbols

Yardage, USGA Rating and Slope are listed after each address.

🏌 caddies/forecaddies   🛒 guests only
🛺 carts only   🕐 restricted tee times (call ahead)

🅩 Challenge at Manele 🛺

| 28 | 28 | 27 | 23 | $225 |

Manele | 1 Challenge Dr. | Lanai | 808-565-2222 | www.golfonlanai.com | 7039/5024; 73.7/68.8; 135/119

"A must-play on the secluded island of Lanai", this "spectacular" Jack Nicklaus design is "a challenge" indeed, with "punishing winds" making it "a monster" for "even experienced golfers" thanks to a seaside setting boasting "stunning" "ocean views from all 18 holes", including a "pictur-esque" par-3 12th that "plays over a cove" – so "if you're having a tough day, at least you can watch the whales"; yes, it's "an expensive round", but most agree it's "worth the investment for a golf game of a lifetime."

Experience at Koele 🛺

| 27 | 25 | 26 | 22 | $225 |

Koele | 1 Keomuku Hwy. | Lanai | 808-565-4653 | www.golfonlanai.com | 7000/5414; 75.3/68.1; 141/123

Fans aver it "can't get much better" than this "absolutely gorgeous" Greg Norman design in Lanai that's "unlike anything else in Hawaii", offering mountainous play through Cook pines, koa and eucalyptus trees, culminating in a "dramatic 200-plus-ft. drop" on the 17th; given a swift pace of play, "you can get 36 in before lunch" at the clubhouse, and the resort guest day rate allows unlimited play here or at the nearby Challenge at Manele.

Lanai & Molokai Hotels

Symbols

👪 children's programs   👀 views
✕ exceptional restaurant   ⌐ 18-hole golf course
Ⓗ historic interest   Ⓢ notable spa facilities
🍳 kitchens   🏊 swimming pool
🐾 allows pets   🎾 tennis

🅉 Four Seasons Lanai, | 27 | 28 | 25 | 27 | $375
The Lodge at Koele Ⓗ🐾⌐Ⓢ🏊🎾

Koele | 1 Keomoku Hwy. | Lanai | 808-565-4000 | fax 808-565-4561 | 800-321-4666 | www.fourseasons.com | 91 rooms, 11 suites

For a "totally different Hawaiian experience", consider this "sanctuary of relaxation", a "hunting lodge"-like resort perched "high on a hillside" amid "vast gardens" in "quiet" Lanai's Central Highlands; the "rooms and service are everything you'd expect from the Four Seasons", while the "dining alone is worth the visit"; guests can golf on the "amazing" Greg Norman–designed course, take afternoon tea or try "skeet shooting", "lawn bowling, croquet and horseback riding"; N.B. a shuttle runs to its sister property at Manele Bay.

🅉 Four Seasons Resort Lanai at | 27 | 26 | 24 | 27 | $445
Manele Bay 👪✕🐾👀⌐Ⓢ🏊🎾

Manele | 1 Manele Bay Rd. | Lanai City | Lanai | 808-565-7700 | fax 808-565-2483 | 800-321-4666 | www.fourseasons.com | 215 rooms, 21 suites

"If you want luxury in a quiet location" with "ocean views from almost everywhere", this "sprawling" "little piece of heaven" on Lanai's south shore – where you can snorkel, swim or watch "whales breaching right outside your windows" – is "paradise for the whole family"; the "opulent" rooms and service "make you feel you've arrived", and given its "wonderful" restaurants, "beautiful" Jack Nicklaus–designed golf course and "excellent" kids' club, there's "no need to leave the premises", unless it's to hop the free shuttle to sister property Lodge at Koele.

Lanai, Hotel Ⓗ | - | - | - | - | $139

Lanai City | 828 Lanai Ave. | Lanai | 808-565-7211 | fax 808-565-6450 | 800-795-7211 | www.hotellanai.com | 10 rooms, 1 cottage

A "small" 1920s-era country inn for "cost-conscious" folks who still "want to visit Lanai", this historic landmark stands in stark contrast to the only two major hotels (both Four Seasons) on this tiny island; the simple, "cozy" plantation-style rooms have Hawaiian quilts, local artwork, hardwood floors and ceiling fans, while an on-site restaurant has a menu designed by Hawaii Regional chef Beverly Gannon.

Molokai, Hotel 🏊 | - | - | - | - | $159

Kaunakakai | Kamehameha V Hwy. | Molokai | 808-553-5347 | fax 808-553-5047 | www.hotelmolokai.com | 39 rooms, 1 suite

Set on Kamilola Beach, adjacent to Hawaii's only barrier reef, this simple oceanfront resort on a sleepy island with just a handful of lodging options offers an "incredibly friendly staff that's eager to please" and wonderful Friday night live entertainment when the "elders of Molokai meet here and play music"; the local flavor and "cute", landscaped "bungalow" look make up for "poorly lit" rooms with tiny baths that have seen better days.

Molokai Shores 🏖️🏊

-	-	-	-	$210

Kaunakakai | 1000 Kamehameha V Hwy. | Molokai | 808-553-5954 | fax 808-553-3241 | 800-535-0085 | www.marcresorts.com | 35 condos

Located on Molokai beach, this all-suite condominium resort a mile from the ferry to Maui features an outdoor pool, barbecue grills and units with full kitchens, separate living areas and complimentary daily newspapers; N.B. no restaurant on-site.

HAWAII'S BEST SHOPPING

Shopping

A renaissance in Hawaii's shopping scene in recent years has brought retailers of every stripe to the islands. From the world's top designers such as Chanel, Dior and Hermès to home-grown talents like Tori Richard and Sig Zane, Hawaii's boutiques offer an incredible range of merchandise. On the following pages, we feature our voters' favorites throughout Hawaii, as well as Notable Mentions worth discovering. Most of our Survey's top-rated stores are in Oahu's recently expanded **Ala Moana Center,** the largest open-air mall in the country, with close to 300 stores. But label-lovers should also head to Waikiki for the **Royal Hawaiian Center** and the new **Beach Walk** district. Downtown Honolulu's tourist-heavy **Aloha Tower Marketplace, Ward Centre** and **Ward Warehouse** malls, the funky North Shore shops of Haleiwa, and, for thrifty sorts, the **Waikele Premium Outlets** in Waipahu offer further opportunities. Meanwhile, the neighbor islands have a fair share of high-end establishments – particularly in Maui's **Shops at Wailea** and **Whalers Village** in Kaanapali, and in the Big Island's **Kings' Shops at Waikoloa.** For a shot at more local designers, head to Maui's Front Street in Lahaina and its arty town of Paia, as well as the Big Island's Hilo, and Kauai's Hanalei and **Poipu Shopping Village.**

Most Popular

1. ABC Stores
2. Hilo Hattie
3. Macy's
4. Crazy Shirts
5. Nordstrom
6. Neiman Marcus
7. Tommy Bahama
8. Na Hoku
9. Cinnamon Girl
10. Banana Republic
11. Coach
12. Reyn's
13. Honolua Surf Co.*
14. Louis Vuitton
15. Blue Ginger
16. Tiffany & Co.
17. Hawaiian Island Creations
18. Tori Richard
19. Martin & MacArthur
20. Maui Divers Jewelry

Top Quality Ratings

29	Chanel
	Hermès
	Martin & MacArthur
28	Tiffany & Co.
	Academy Gift

Bulgari*
Sig Zane Designs*
Bottega Veneta
Louis Vuitton
Neiman Marcus

Top Display Ratings

28	Hermès
	Bulgari
27	Tiffany & Co.
	Sig Zane Designs
	Louis Vuitton

Chanel
26 Dior
Dolphin Galleries
Tommy Bahama
Martin & MacArthur

* Indicates a tie with store above

Top Service Ratings

28] Sig Zane Designs

26] Bulgari
Tiffany & Co.
Gucci

25] Nordstrom

Dior

24] Bottega Veneta
Island Soap & Candleworks*
Royal Hawaiian Jewelers*
Hermès

GOOD VALUES

Academy Gift
Betsey Johnson
Bulgari
Cinnamon Girl
Crazy Shirts
Dolphin Galleries
Hawaiian Island Creations
Island Soap & Candleworks
J. Crew
LeSportsac

Martin & MacArthur
Na Hoku
Nohea Galleries
Nordstrom
Red Pineapple
Reyn's
Sig Zane Designs
Tiffany & Co.
Tommy Bahama
Tori Richard

Shopping

☒ ABC Stores ◑ | 18 | 18 | 17 | I |

Ala Moana | Ala Moana Ctr. | 1450 Ala Moana Blvd. (bet. Atkinson Dr. & Piikoi St.) | Honolulu | Oahu | 808-941-3374 | 888-703-4222 |
www.abcstores.com
Additional locations throughout Hawaii

"What would a trip to Hawaii be?" without several stops at this "ubiquitous" "catch-all" chain ("the islands' 7-Eleven, but much better") with branches seemingly "on every corner" selling "anything you need" from "mac nuts" and "muu muus for Aunty Sue" to "staple items" like T-shirts, suntan location, liquor and "tourist trinkets"; further elevating it to Most Popular in our Survey are the "motivated" staffers and the "reasonable" prices.

Academy Gift Shop Ⓜ | 28 | 25 | 24 | M |

Ala Moana | Honolulu Academy of Arts | 900 S. Beretania St. (Ward Ave.) | Honolulu | Oahu | 808-532-8701 | 800-829-5211 |
www.honoluluacademy.org

With "wonderful Hawaiiana items" – prints, books, notecards, pottery – and "the best offering of unique jewelry" from throughout the world, this airy, 1,500-sq.-ft. museum gift shop in the Honolulu Academy of Arts just outside of Downtown provides "unique" merchandise "not found in other stores" (and much of it "associated with exhibits"); the "helpful, volunteer" staff directs you through the "attractive displays", making it that much easier to "max out your credit card" on "beautiful things."

A/X Armani Exchange ◑ | 22 | 21 | 20 | E |

Ala Moana | Ala Moana Ctr. | 1450 Ala Moana Blvd. (bet. Atkinson Dr. & Piikoi St.) | Honolulu | Oahu | 808-942-8147
Waikiki | 2270 Kalakaua Ave. (Seaside Ave.) | Honolulu | Oahu | 808-923-1663
Waipahu | Waikele Premium Outlets | 94-790 Lumiaina St. (Paiwa St.) | Oahu | 808-677-6901
www.armaniexchange.com

"Anything by Armani is worth buying" say fans of the "ritzy" Italian clothier's lower-priced mens- and womenswear line for "the young of age or at heart"; the "lovely" Ala Moana Center location gets extra props for its "beautiful", open-air setting, but it's "usually packed full of tourists" with "deep pockets" who don't mind a little attitude; N.B. head to the Waikele outlet for better deals.

Bag 'n Baggage ◑ | 25 | 21 | 21 | E |

Ala Moana | Ala Moana Ctr. | 1450 Ala Moana Blvd. (bet. Atkinson Dr. & Piikoi St.) | Honolulu | Oahu | 808-942-4998 | www.coloradobaggage.com
"If you need another bag to take home", roll into this "chic" Ala Moana Center store with a "huge selection of name-brand luggage" by labels like "Kipling, Lacoste", Tumi and Samsonite; sure, there's "a lot of high-end" merch, but some of the travel accessories (money belts, cosmetic containers) "aren't too expensive" and the staff is "helpful."

Banana Republic ◑ | 22 | 22 | 19 | M |

Wailea | Shops at Wailea | 3750 Wailea Alanui Dr. (Wailea Ike Dr.) | Maui | 808-875-9984

(continued)

Banana Republic

Ala Moana | Ala Moana Ctr. | 1450 Ala Moana Blvd. (bet. Atkinson Dr. & Piikoi St.) | Honolulu | Oahu | 808-955-2602
Kahala | Kahala Mall | 4211 Waialae Ave. (Hunakai St.) | Honolulu | Oahu | 808-737-4747
Waikiki | King Kalakaua Plaza | 2080 Kalakaua Ave. (bet. Kalaimoku & Olohana Sts.) | Honolulu | Oahu | 808-952-3130
Waipahu | Waikele Premium Outlets | 94-798 Lumiaina St. (Paiwa St.) | Oahu | 808-676-8689
www.bananarepublic.com

"You can only wear so many Aloha shirts" say Banana Republicans who come to island branches of this mainland chain for "wardrobe staples" like jeans, sweaters and other "timeless pieces"; there's generally "good quality" and service "for the price", and fans particularly admire the "beautiful multilevel" outpost in the Ala Moana Center.

BCBG Max Azria ●   24 | 22 | 22 | E

Wailea | Shops at Wailea | 3750 Wailea Alanui Dr. (Wailea Ike Dr.) | Maui | 808-875-2711
Ala Moana | Ala Moana Ctr. | 1450 Ala Moana Blvd. (bet. Atkinson Dr. & Piikoi St.) | Honolulu | Oahu | 808-946-9794
Waipahu | Waikele Premium Outlets | 94-790 Lumiaina St. (Paiwa St.) | Oahu | 808-671-4455
www.bcbg.com

BCBG may be French slang for preppy, but at the two Hawaii boutique outposts (plus a Waikele Outlet store) of this womenswear stalwart, it translates to "amazingly beautiful", "trendy dresses", timeless accessories, "cute shoes" and other "quality" partywear by the hip Gallic designer; even though it "takes a bite out of your wallet" and the service is only "great if you look like you're buying", some would "sell their first born" to shop here.

Betsey Johnson ●   24 | 25 | 24 | E

NEW **Wailea** | Shops at Wailea | 3750 Wailea Alanui Dr. (Wailea Ike Dr.) | Maui | 808-891-1135
Ala Moana | Ala Moana Ctr. | 1450 Ala Moana Blvd. (Atkinson Dr.) | Honolulu | Oahu | 808-949-3500
www.betseyjohnson.com

"Young, eclectic gals who don't mind spending money" frequent the Ala Moana Center and Wailea outposts of this quirky Manhattan designer, where there's "hot pink" on the walls (and quite a bit on the clothes) along with a "helpful, fun" staff; all the "cute" flirty dresses, embellished necklaces and "exquisite" accessories create a "funky, colorful" look.

Black Pearl Gallery ●   ∇ 23 | 23 | 22 | E

Wailea | Shops at Wailea | 3750 Wailea Alanui Dr. (Wailea Ike Dr.) | Maui | 808-875-1977
Downtown | Aloha Tower Mktpl. | 1 Aloha Tower Dr. (Fort St.) | Honolulu | Oahu | 808-524-5552
Ward | Ward Ctr. | 1200 Ala Moana Blvd. (bet. Kamakee & Queen Sts.) | Honolulu | Oahu | 808-597-1477
www.e-blackpearl.com

A "huge selection of Tahitian black pearls" set in 14- and 18-karat gold, including "things you don't see everywhere", earn the "love" of jewelry-seekers who find "beautiful" displays of bracelets, necklaces, earrings and rings as well as "charming" service at these three stores; sure, they're "expensive", but if you want "one-of-a-kind pieces" – some with a Hawaiian twist (like a maile leaf ring) – you'll find them here.

Blue Ginger ◐   24 | 23 | 22 | E

Waikoloa | Kings' Shops | 250 Waikoloa Beach Dr. (Queen Kaahumanu Hwy.) | Big Island | 808-886-2020

Kahului | Queen Kaahumanu Ctr. | 275 W. Kaahumanu Ave. (S. Kane St.) | Maui | 808-871-7002

Lahaina | Lahaina Cannery Mall | 1221 Honoapiilani Hwy. (Keawe St.) | Maui | 808-667-5433

Kaanapali | Whalers Vill. | 2435 Kaanapali Pkwy. (Kekaa Dr.) | Maui | 808-667-5793

Waikiki | 227 Lewers St. (Kalakaua Ave.) | Honolulu | Oahu | 808-924-7900

Blue Ginger/Blue Ginger Kids ◐

Wailea | Shops at Wailea | 3750 Wailea Alanui Dr. (Wailea Ike Dr.) | Maui | 808-891-0772

Blue Ginger Kids ◐

Kaanapali | Whalers Vill. | 2435 Kaanapali Pkwy. (Kekaa Dr.) | Maui | 808-661-1666

www.blueginger.com

Aloha comes in "so many shades" at this "low-key" islandwide chain filled with "tropical clothing that doesn't scream Hawaii" (and "doesn't look out of place when you go back home"); the "nicely displayed" "wonderful batik dresses" in "comfortable fabrics", shirts for dad with whimsical patterns ("blue and yellow fishies") and "adorable skirts" for your "little misses" are "just a little different than what's found at major stores", plus the "excellent quality" means they'll "last for years."

Bottega Veneta ◐   28 | 25 | 24 | VE

Wailea | Shops at Wailea | 3750 Wailea Alanui Dr. (Wailea Ike Dr.) | Maui | 808-891-7300

Ala Moana | Ala Moana Ctr. | 1450 Ala Moana Blvd. (bet. Atkinson Dr. & Piikoi St.) | Honolulu | Oahu | 808-946-0100

Waikiki | 2122 Kalakaua Ave. (Saratoga Rd.) | Honolulu | Oahu | 808-923-0800

877-362-1715 | www.bottegaveneta.com

"Bring lots of money" to one of the three outposts of this luxury Italian label, where "beautiful leather" accessories set in museumlike displays – signature "butter-soft purses in unusual colors", "classic" shoes, luggage, wallets – are the "ultimate in understated elegance"; "serious shoppers" also swear the "impeccable" service is truly "welcoming."

Bulgari ◐   28 | 28 | 26 | VE

Ala Moana | Ala Moana Ctr. | 1450 Ala Moana Blvd. (bet. Atkinson Dr. & Piikoi St.) | Honolulu | Oahu | 808-941-8338

Waikiki | Royal Hawaiian Ctr. | 2233 Kalakaua Ave. (Royal Hawaiian Ave.) | Honolulu | Oahu | 808-923-2600

www.bulgari.com

"An inviting storefront" "right on" Waikiki's bustling Kalakaua Avenue (where "close neighbors include Christian Dior"), as well as a sparkling outpost in the Ala Moana Center, give prominence to this Italian luxury purveyor of jewelry, watches, "fine glassware", "art items" and leather accessories; "go in and browse", since "it's rarely full of customers" and "you'll get lots of help and attention" from the "excellent staff."

	QUALITY	DISPLAY	SERVICE	COST

☑ Chanel ☻ | 29 | 27 | 24 | VE

Ala Moana | Ala Moana Ctr. | 1450 Ala Moana Blvd. (bet. Atkinson Dr. & Piikoi St.) | Honolulu | Oahu | 808-942-5555
Waikiki | 2116 Kalakaua Ave. (Saratoga Rd.) | Honolulu | Oahu | 808-923-0255
www.chanel.com

"To-die-for" tweed jackets, quilted bags, signature shoes and "high-quality" womenswear via designer Karl Lagerfeld converge at the two Honolulu locations of this "top-priced" French couture house, voted our Survey's No. 1 for Quality of merchandise in Hawaii; the Ala Moana Center outpost, with its crisp displays and "lovely service", is "so popular with Asian tourists" that it often "gets new things before New York", but if you can't afford them, don't despair, the staff "never gets annoyed when you don't buy."

Cinnamon Girl ☻ | 24 | 24 | 23 | M

Waikoloa | Kings' Shops | 250 Waikoloa Beach Dr. (Queen Kaahumanu Hwy.) | Big Island | 808-886-0241
Kaanapali | Whalers Vill. | 2435 Kaanapali Pkwy. (Kekaa Dr.) | Maui | 808-661-0441
Aiea | Pearlridge Ctr. Uptown | 98-1005 Moanalua Rd. (Kaonohi St.) | Oahu | 808-484-1613
Ala Moana | Ala Moana Ctr. | 1450 Ala Moana Blvd. (bet. Atkinson Dr. & Piikoi St.) | Honolulu | Oahu | 808-947-4332
Kahala | Kahala Mall | 4211 Waialae Ave. (Hunakai St.) | Honolulu | Oahu | 808-737-9425
Kaneohe | Windward Mall | 46-056 Kamehameha Hwy. (Haiku Rd.) | Oahu | 808-235-2500
Waikiki | Moana Surfrider | 2365 Kalakaua Ave. (Kaiulani Ave.) | Honolulu | Oahu | 808-922-5536
Ward | Ward Warehouse | 1050 Ala Moana Blvd. (bet. Kamakee St. & Ward Ave.) | Honolulu | Oahu | 808-591-6532
www.cinnamongirl.com

"If you want to feel like a girl, this is the place", a spicy, moderately priced trove of "feminine dresses and outfits" for "mothers, daughters, teens and bridesmaids"; the "well-kept", beachy boutiques "never look out of order", meaning they're great spots to rack up "special-occasion" clothes, "flirty summer" frocks and "one-of-a-kind tops"; P.S. "they have cute gifts and accessories too", like "flower slippers" hand-embellished by the owner's mom.

Coach ☻ | 26 | 23 | 23 | E

Waikoloa | Kings' Shops | 250 Waikoloa Beach Dr. (Queen Kaahumanu Hwy.) | Big Island | 808-886-4201 | 888-262-6224
Lahaina | Whalers Vill. | 2435 Kaanapali Pkwy. (Kekaa Dr.) | Maui | 808-667-0399
Wailea | Shops at Wailea | 3750 Wailea Alanui Dr. (Wailea Ike Dr.) | Maui | 808-891-8851
Ala Moana | Ala Moana Ctr. | 1450 Ala Moana Blvd. (bet. Atkinson Dr. & Piikoi St.) | Honolulu | Oahu | 808-947-4550
Waikiki | Honu Group | 2110 Kalakaua Ave. (Saratoga Rd.) | Honolulu | Oahu | 808-924-1677
Waikiki | Outrigger Waikiki | 2335 Kalakaua Ave. (bet. Kaiulani & Seaside Aves.) | Honolulu | Oahu | 808-923-0549

(continued)

(continued)

Coach

Waipahu | Waikele Premium Outlets | 94-790 Lumiaina St. (Paiwa St.) | Oahu | 808-678-6991
www.coach.com

"If you can't afford Chanel and Louis Vuitton", this "upscale handbag and accessories" label with multiple island branches offers "luxe for the masses" with a "bit more emphasis on tropical styles and patterns" than at mainland outlets; still, some coach potatoes say "all stores have essentially the same setup", so "if you've visited one" anywhere, you'll know what to expect; P.S. the "Waikele outlet has the best values."

◪ Crazy Shirts ● | 24 | 23 | 22 | M |

Waikoloa | Kings' Shops | 250 Waikoloa Beach Dr. (Queen Kaahumanu Hwy.) | Big Island | 808-886-9303
Poipu | Poipu Shopping Vill. | 2360 Kiahuna Plantation Dr. (Poipu Rd.) | Koloa | Kauai | 808-742-9000
Kaanapali | Whalers Vill. | 2435 Kaanapali Pkwy. (Kekaa Dr.) | Lahaina | Maui | 808-661-0117
Lahaina | 658 Front St. (Wharf St.) | Maui | 808-661-4712
Wailea | Shops at Wailea | 3750 Wailea Alanui Dr. (Wailea Ike Dr.) | Maui | 808-875-6435
Ala Moana | Ala Moana Ctr. | 1450 Ala Moana Blvd. (bet. Atkinson Dr. & Piikoi St.) | Honolulu | Oahu | 808-973-4000
Waikiki | Royal Hawaiian Ctr. | 2233 Kalakaua Ave. (Royal Hawaiian Ave.) | Honolulu | Oahu | 808-971-6024
Waikiki | Waikiki Beach Walk | 226 Lewers St. (Kalakaua Ave.) | Honolulu | Oahu | 808-971-6016
Waipahu | Waikele Premium Outlets | 94-798 Lumiaina St. (Paiwa St.) | Oahu | 808-671-6898
Ward | Ward Ctr. | 1220 Ala Moana Blvd. (Auahi St.) | Honolulu | Oahu | 808-592-5510
800-771-2720 | www.crazyshirts.com
Additional locations throughout Hawaii

You "can't beat the witty designs" at this statewide T-shirt chain where "notable items" include "chocolate-, wine-, coffee- and beer-dyed" tops with the "best quality fabric" that'll "last for years"; the stores "always look wonderful" and "each island has different offerings", but crazy critics cry "$20 is expensive for a tee" "to bring home for a souvenir"; P.S. check out the board shorts and caps with "local flavor."

Dior ● | 27 | 26 | 25 | VE |

Ala Moana | Ala Moana Ctr. | 1450 Ala Moana Blvd. (bet. Atkinson Dr. & Piikoi St.) | Honolulu | Oahu | 808-943-6900
Waikiki | 2222 Kalakaua Ave. (Lewers St.) | Honolulu | Oahu | 808-926-1947
www.dior.com

"Just like the French, wonderful and snooty" say status-seekers of this "high-end" atelier in Ala Moana Center and Waikiki that stocks the Paris design house's plush bags, "great lipsticks" and perfumes, and a "large selection" of women's apparel; the "bright and airy" layout allows John Galliano's designs to stand out, but true loyalists lament "they don't carry the full line."

Dolphin Galleries | 26 | 26 | 24 | E |

Waikoloa | Kings' Shops | 250 Waikoloa Beach Dr. (Queen Kaahumanu Hwy.) | Big Island | 808-886-5000 ⊠

(continued)

Dolphin Galleries

Kaanapali | Whalers Vill. | 2435 Kaanapali Pkwy. (Kekaa Dr.) | Maui | 808-661-5115 ●

Wailea | Shops at Wailea | 3750 Wailea Alanui Dr. (Wailea Ike Dr.) | Maui | 808-891-6000 ●

Waikiki | Hilton Hawaiian Vill. | 2005 Kalia Rd. (Ala Moana Blvd.) | Honolulu | Oahu | 808-951-5000 ●
800-669-5051 | www.dolphingalleries.com

It's "definitely worth a walk through" this gallery-cum-gift store statewide chain to see the "local and So-Cal" fine art including "unique jewelry pieces", "exclusives" by local artists and a "large selection of prints and originals" by international names like Alexandra Nechita and Jia Lu; even if "it's pricey", you "can't find these things at home" and the "helpful" staffers will "gladly ship to the mainland."

Elephant Walk ●

20 | 19 | 18 | M

Ala Moana | Ala Moana Ctr. | 1450 Ala Moana Blvd. (bet. Atkinson Dr. & Piikoi St.) | Honolulu | Oahu | 808-949-4011

Elephant Walk, A Gallery of Life ⓢ Ⓜ

Wailea | Shops at Wailea | 3750 Wailea Alanui Dr. (Wailea Ike Dr.) | Maui | 808-891-8684

Elephant Walk Gift Gallery ⓢ Ⓜ

Lahaina | 855 Front St. (bet. Lahainaluna Rd. & Papalaua St.) | Maui | 808-661-6129

"Take home a bit of the islands – carved koa wood boxes, traditional quilts, marine-life sculptures, paintings – from this "island-themed" gift store with branches on Maui and Oahu; though a few find a "nice collection of items for the home" and other "unique merchandise", others complain of "touristy", "pedestrian" products and wonder how much is "actually made in Hawaii" since the staff often "has no idea."

Fendi ●

25 | 23 | 23 | VE

Wailea | Shops at Wailea | 3750 Wailea Alanui Dr. (Wailea Ike Dr.) | Maui | 808-875-6505

Ala Moana | Ala Moana Ctr. | 1450 Ala Moana Blvd. (bet. Atkinson Dr. & Piikoi St.) | Honolulu | Oahu | 808-973-3311

Waikiki | Royal Hawaiian Ctr. | 2201 Kalakaua Ave. (Lewers St.) | Honolulu | Oahu | 808-971-5611
www.fendi.com

Fans who favor Karl Lagerfeld's styles – status purses, femme sunglasses, blingy watches and "the latest from Italy" – head to one of the three Hawaii outposts of this venerable Italian label where "attentive service" and jewel-box like spaces make shopping a dream for those "who don't have to ask 'how much'"; but working stiffs sigh, it's "just another fabulous", and fabulously expensive, store.

Gucci ●

28 | 26 | 26 | VE

Wailea | Shops at Wailea | 3750 Wailea Alanui Dr. (Wailea Ike Dr.) | Maui | 808-879-1060

Ala Moana | Ala Moana Ctr. | 1450 Ala Moana Blvd. (bet. Atkinson Dr. & Piikoi St.) | Honolulu | Oahu | 808-942-1148
www.gucci.com

Label-loyalists head to this "beautiful", "modernist" flagship at the Ala Moana Center (there's also one in Wailea, Maui), where a dramatic white stone facade gives way to subtly lit shelves stocked with a "wide selection of bags not available on the mainland", movie-star-worthy sunglasses, glamorous timepieces and chic clothing, all stamped with the ubiquitous logo; "polite", "attentive" service and a "big allocation of hard-to-find items" (many "geared to the Japanese customer") earn points.

Hanalei Surf Company ⏺
23 | 20 | 20 | M

Hanalei | Hanalei Ctr. | 5-5161 Kuhio Hwy. (Aku Rd.) | Kauai | 866-426-2534 | www.hanaleisurf.com

Hang ten to "the North Shore's best surf shop", located in a 1911 Hanalei school building decorated with posters of waves and vintage gear, where you can buy or rent a boogie board, score "a great T-shirt" in a "nice design" or pick up some sandals before hitting the Kauai waters; P.S. the funky style and moderate prices make it popular among "teens and young adults."

Hawaiian Island Creations
24 | 22 | 21 | M

NEW **Lahaina** | Lahaina Cannery Mall | 1221 Honoapiilani Hwy. (Keawe St.) | Maui | 808-667-6111 ⏺
Ala Moana | Ala Moana Ctr. | 1450 Ala Moana Blvd. (bet. Atkinson Dr. & Piikoi St.) | Honolulu | Oahu | 808-973-6780 ⏺
Haleiwa | 66-224 Kamehameha Hwy. (bet. Amara Rd. & Kilioe Pl.) | Oahu | 808-637-0991
Kailua | 348 Hahani St. (Hekili St.) | Oahu | 808-266-6730
Kakaako | 310 Kamakee St. (bet. Auahi & Queen Sts.) | Honolulu | Oahu | 808-593-7873 ⏺
Kapolei | Kapolei Shopping Ctr. | 590 Farrington Hwy. (Makakilo Dr.) | Oahu | 808-674-4001
Mililani | Mililani Town Ctr. | 95-1249 Meheula Blvd. (Kaonohi St.) | Oahu | 808-627-7100 ⏺
Pearl City | Pearlridge Ctr. Downtown | 98-1005 Moanalua Rd. (Kaonhoi St.) | Oahu | 808-483-6700 ⏺
www.hicsurf.com

"Locals stock up on the latest" wave-riding equipment from "Eric Arakawa and other legends", while tourists "make their own slippahs (flip-flops)" "in multiple colors" and grab "distinctive T-shirts" and "teen souvenirs" at this "all-encompassing, hip surf shop" with outlets scattered throughout Oahu; loyalists love the "quality" and "styles", and "if you're a brash" visitor, you can "ask for the kamaaina [local] price on staples" like board wax; N.B. a new branch opened post-Survey in Lahaina, Maui.

Hawaiian Moon ⏺
▽ 23 | 21 | 20 | M

Waikiki | Waikiki Beach Walk | 226 Lewers St. (Kalakaua Ave.) | Honolulu | Oahu | 808-922-1118
Ward | Ward Warehouse | 1050 Ala Moana Blvd. (bet. Kamakee St. & Ward Ave.) | Honolulu | Oahu | 808-596-2294
866-810-5584 | www.hawaiianmoon.com

You'll find locally made traditional Hawaiian clothing and Aloha wear in "lovely prints" (with "matching ensembles for the whole family"), along with "wonderful accessories" and "high-quality" items to "decorate your home" (quilted place mats, pillows, potholders) at these Oahu stores in Waikiki and Ward; they often "beat department-store prices" with "great sale items" and "unique gifts" (doggy islandwear, banana patch clocks), so go in and "feel like a kamaaina" coming out.

	QUALITY	DISPLAY	SERVICE	COST

☑ Hermès ◐ | 29 | 28 | 24 | VE

Ala Moana | Ala Moana Ctr. | 1450 Ala Moana Blvd. (bet. Atkinson Dr. & Piikoi St.) | Honolulu | Oahu | 808-947-3789
Waikiki | Royal Hawaiian Ctr. | 2201 Kalakaua Ave. (Lewers St.) | Honolulu | Oahu | 808-922-5780
Waikiki | DFS Galleria Waikiki | 330 Royal Hawaiian Ave. (Lauula St.) | Honolulu | Oahu | 808-931-2700
www.hermes.com

Status-seekers find the "holy grail of accessories", along with "gorgeous", "high-quality" apparel, at these three Oahu outposts of the luxury Parisian label, where the staff is "friendly", the merchandising "beautiful" (it ranks No. 1 for Display in this Survey) and the atmosphere "cool and quiet"; although some say these spots attract too "many tourists", "addicted" regulars "buy at least one new scarf per year" and claim "it's possible to find that rare Birkin bag."

☑ Hilo Hattie | 19 | 20 | 20 | I

Hilo | Prince Kuhio Plaza | 111 E. Puainako St., Bldg. G (Hawaii Belt Rd.) | Big Island | 808-961-3077 ◐
Kailua-Kona | 75-5597 Palani Rd. (Hawaii Belt Rd.) | Big Island | 808-329-7200 ◐
Lihue | 3-3252 Kuhio Hwy. (Ehiku St.) | Kauai | 808-245-3404
Lahaina | Lahaina Ctr. | 900 Front St. (Papalaua St.) | Maui | 808-667-7911 ◐
Ala Moana | Ala Moana Ctr. | 1450 Ala Moana Blvd. (bet. Atkinson Dr. & Piikoi St.) | Honolulu | Oahu | 808-973-3266 ◐
Iwilei | 700 N. Nimitz Hwy. (Pacific St.) | Honolulu | Oahu | 808-535-6500
888-526-0299 | www.hilohattie.com

"Outfit your entire family in matching Aloha gear" or "find just about anything" from Kona coffee to "muu muus galore" at this statewide Hawaiian "institution" that's "nirvana for souvenir"-hunters; even though some find it a "hokey", "mass-market" superstore with "pretty touristy stuff", the "friendly" staff "greets you with a shell lei" and gives you "juice or coffee", there are always "free promos" and the wide "selection at various price levels" means it's often the "best bargain" in town; N.B. a Waikiki outpost opens soon in the Royal Hawaiian Center.

Honolua Surf Company ◐ | 22 | 19 | 19 | M

Waikoloa | Kings' Shops | 250 Waikoloa Beach Dr. (Queen Kaahumanu Hwy.) | Big Island | 808-886-6422
Lihue | Anchor Cove Shopping Ctr. | 3416 Rice St. (Lala Rd.) | Kauai | 808-246-3636
Kaanapali | Whalers Vill. | 2435 Kaanapali Pkwy. (Kekaa Dr.) | Maui | 808-661-5455
Wailea | Shops at Wailea | 3750 Wailea Alanui Dr. (Wailea Ike Dr.) | Maui | 808-891-8229
Downtown | Aloha Tower Mktpl. | 1 Aloha Tower Dr. (Fort St.) | Honolulu | Oahu | 808-524-2277
Waikiki | Hilton Hawaiian Vill. | 2005 Kalia Rd. (Ala Moana Blvd.) | Honolulu | Oahu | 808-941-8684
Waikiki | Waikiki Beach Walk | 226 Lewers St. (Kalakaua Ave.) | Honolulu | Oahu | 808-923-4146
www.honoluasurf.com

"If you surf" or just want "trendy clothing" that makes you feel like you do, head to this statewide beachwear chain with "cute" men's and women's apparel ranging from "unique" board shorts and swimsuits to "great sunglasses" and "comfortable sweat shirts"; the slick dis-

plays "lure you in", but be sure to paddle over to the "marked-down
section" since the "sales racks are the way to go."

Island Soap & Candleworks — 25 | 23 | 24 | I

Koloa | Old Koloa Town Shopping Ctr. | 5356 Koloa Rd. (Kaumualii Hwy.) |
Kauai | 808-742-1945 | www.islandsoap.com ●

Maalaea | 300 Maalaea Rd. (Honoapiilani Hwy.) | Maui | 808-986-8383 |
www.mauisoapworks.com

Waikiki | Royal Hawaiian Ctr. | 2233 Kalakaua Ave. (Royal Hawaiian Ave.) |
Honolulu | Oahu | 808-922-7887 | www.honolulusoap.com ●

Ward | Ward Warehouse | 1050 Ala Moana Blvd. (bet. Kamakee St. &
Ward Ave.) | Honolulu | Oahu | 808-591-0533 | www.honolulusoap.com ●

"You can watch them make soaps and candles" with the "soothing
scents of Hawaii" at this "wonderful" mini-chain infused with "local"
aromas like "pikake, plumeria, tuberose", passion fruit and coconut;
though the "scent can be overwhelming" in the beach shack–like
spaces, they make "excellent" "souvenirs to bring back home."

NEW J. Crew On-the-Island ● — 23 | 24 | 21 | M

Ala Moana | Ala Moana Ctr. | 1450 Ala Moana Blvd. (bet. Atkinson Dr. &
Piikoi St.) | Honolulu | Oahu | 808-955-9517 | www.jcrew.com

"Not your typical J. Crew" boutique, this Ala Moana Center outpost of
the national chain carries "products only sold in Hawaii" including lots
of "island attire"; the "bright and lively" East-Coast-beach-house decor and the "sooo helpful" staff are pluses, but some are put off by the
"unexpected", "weirdly tropical", "preppy" clothing that seems best
suited for "vacationing in Nantucket."

LeSportsac ● — 25 | 23 | 21 | M

Ala Moana | Ala Moana Ctr. | 1450 Ala Moana Blvd. (bet. Atkinson Dr. &
Piikoi St.) | Honolulu | Oahu | 808-973-6306

NEW Waikiki | Royal Hawaiian Ctr. | 2301 Kalakaua Ave. (Dukes Ln.) |
Honolulu | Oahu | 808-971-2920
www.lesportsac.com

The "crushable bags" made of "lightweight, durable" "nylon fabric",
along with the "no-pressure" staff, draw lots of tourists to the two Oahu
outposts of this American label; there are "more prints than you can
shake a stick at", limited-edition tokidoki, Stella McCartney designs
and pieces with "island logos" that "you can't get anywhere else."

Louis Vuitton ● — 28 | 27 | 23 | VE

Waikoloa | Kings' Shops | 250 Waikoloa Beach Dr. (Queen Kaahumanu Hwy.) |
Big Island | 808-886-0262

Kaanapali | Whalers Vill. | 2435 Kaanapali Pkwy. (Kekaa Dr.) | Maui |
808-667-6114

Wailea | Shops at Wailea | 3750 Wailea Alanui Dr. (Wailea Ike Dr.) |
Maui | 808-875-6980

Ala Moana | Ala Moana Ctr. | 1450 Ala Moana Blvd. (bet. Atkinson Dr. &
Piikoi St.) | Honolulu | Oahu | 808-973-0580

Waikiki | Hilton Hawaiian Vill. | 2005 Kalia Rd. (Ala Moana Blvd.) |
Honolulu | Oahu | 808-973-3388

Waikiki | Gump Bldg. | 2200 Kalakaua Ave. (Lewers St.) | Honolulu |
Oahu | 808-971-6880
www.louisvuitton.com

A "mecca" for label-lovers, this French brand's "fabulous" Hawaii stores
boast "elegant" collections of logoed leather goods, luggage and cloth-

ing, along with "Pacific Rim items" you might not see on the mainland; there's "service with a smile", and, though the displays are "similar" to other cities', "surprisingly", the merch is "a bit less expensive."

Z Macy's
21 | 19 | 18 | M

Kailua-Kona | Makalapua Ctr. | 74-5475 Kamakaeha Ave. (Palani Rd.) | Big Island | 808-329-6300 🅾

Waikoloa | Kings' Shops | 250 Waikoloa Beach Dr. (Queen Kaahumanu Hwy.) | Big Island | 808-886-5385 🅾

Lihue | Kukui Grove Ctr. | 3-2600 Kaumualii Hwy. (Nawiliwili Rd.) | Kauai | 808-245-7751

Kahului | Queen Kaahumanu Ctr. | 275 W. Kaahumanu Ave. (off S. Kane St.) | Maui | 808-877-3361 🅾

Ala Moana | Ala Moana Ctr. | 1450 Ala Moana Blvd. (bet. Atkinson Dr. & Piikoi St.) | Honolulu | Oahu | 808-941-2345 🅾

Downtown | 1032 Fort St. (King St.) | Honolulu | Oahu | 808-521-5147 🅸

Kahala | Kahala Mall | 4211 Waialae Ave. (Hunakai St.) | Honolulu | Oahu | 808-737-5429 🅾

Kailua | 573 Kailua Rd. (Kuulei Rd.) | Oahu | 808-262-5395 🅾

Kaneohe | Windward Mall | 46-056 Kamehameha Hwy. (Haiku Rd.) | Oahu | 808-235-6612 🅾

Waikiki | 2314 Kalakaua Ave. (Dukes Ln.) | Honolulu | Oahu | 808-926-5217 🅾

www.macys.com

Although "Macy's is Macy's wherever you are" – with "everything you need" from "makeup to cookware to clothing" – the Hawaii branches carry some "unique island merchandise" such as "jewelry from local artists" like Nina Kuna, designs by Anne Namba, Tori Richard and Local Motion, and plenty of "high-end resortwear" and coverups; since "they run sales continuously" there are plenty of bargains, but those who "totally miss Liberty House" (the local chain that was acquired by Macy's parent eight years ago) say the "quality of the store depends on location" and the "Ala Moana branch is the only one worth going to."

NEW Marciano 🅾
- | - | - | E

Waikiki | Royal Hawaiian Ctr. | 2233 Kalakaua Ave. (Dukes Ln.) | Honolulu | Oahu | 808-931-6116 | www.marciano.com

The entry of Marciano in Hawaii comes via this new, two-level Royal Hawaiian Center boutique in Waikiki where the Guess-owned brand's trendsetting womens' styles – slinky tops, sexy cocktail dresses, shoes, handbags and accessories – are displayed amid loungey modern furnishings; the hip decor features animal prints, mirror collages and suspended chandeliers that create a feminine, sleek look.

Z Martin & MacArthur 🅾
29 | 26 | 22 | E

Wailea | Shops at Wailea | 3750 Wailea Alanui Dr. (Wailea Ike Dr.) | Maui | 808-891-8844

Ala Moana | Ala Moana Ctr. | 1450 Ala Moana Blvd. (bet. Atkinson Dr. & Piikoi St.) | Honolulu | Oahu | 808-941-0074

Waikiki | Hyatt Regency Waikiki | 2424 Kalakaua Ave. (Kaiulani Ave.) | Honolulu | Oahu | 808-923-5333

www.martinandmacarthur.com

"Beautifuly crafted furniture", much of it made from indigenous rare koa wood, draws devotees to these showrooms filled with "excellent quality art", crafts, housewares and other "unique" pieces "worth what you pay for them" (and they're "not cheap"); the arty displays bring you back to a "more gracious time", and many of the custom chairs, beds and other "posh" products become "cherished heirlooms"; N.B. there's a range of inexpensive island-themed gifts as well.

Maui Divers Jewelry
24 | 24 | 23 | E

Kaanapali | Whalers Vill. | 2435 Kaanapali Pkwy. (Kekaa Dr.) | Lahaina | Maui | 808-661-1097 ✆

Kahului | Queen Kaahumanu Ctr. | 275 W. Kaahumanu Ave. (S. Kane St.) | Maui | 808-871-7305 ✆

Ala Moana | Ala Moana Ctr. | 1450 Ala Moana Blvd. (bet. Atkinson Dr. & Piikoi St.) | Honolulu | Oahu | 808-949-0411 ✆

Ala Moana | Design Ctr. | 1520 Liona St. (Keeaumoku St.) | Honolulu | Oahu | 808-946-7979

Waikiki | Waikiki Beach Walk | 227 Lewers St. (bet. Kalakaua Ave. & Kalia Rd.) | Honolulu | Oahu | 808-922-1468 ✆

800-462-4454 | www.mauidivers.com

For "island-inspired jewelry" from "necklaces" and "Aloha heart" charms to "black coral" rings, dive into one of the "numerous" locations of this nearly 50-year-old chain, including "pick a pearl" kiosks where you can "try your luck opening an oyster shell"; sure, "the staff can be aggressive", but most agree the "selection of Hawaiian-themed" items is "great", even if "a bit overpriced."

Na Hoku ✆
26 | 25 | 24 | E

Kailua-Kona | Kona Mktpl. | 75-5719 Alii Dr. (Sarona Rd.) | Big Island | 808-329-5080

Waikoloa | Kings' Shops | 69-250 Waikoloa Beach Dr. (Queen Kaahumanu Hwy.) | Big Island | 808-886-7599

Poipu | Poipu Shopping Vill. | 2360 Kiahuna Plantation Dr. (Poipu Rd.) | Koloa | Kauai | 808-742-7025

Kahului | Queen Kaahumanu Ctr. | 275 W. Kaahumanu Ave. (Wakea Ave.) | Maui | 808-893-2110

Lahaina | Lahaina Cannery Mall | 1221 Honoapiilani Hwy. (Keawe St.) | Maui | 808-661-1731

Lahaina | 744 Front St. (Lahainaluna Rd.) | Maui | 808-661-5965

Wailea | Shops at Wailea | 3750 Wailea Alanui Dr. (Wailea Ike Dr.) | Maui | 808-891-8040

Ala Moana | Ala Moana Ctr. | 1450 Ala Moana Blvd. (bet. Atkinson Dr. & Piikoi St.) | Honolulu | Oahu | 808-946-2100

Waikiki | Hilton Hawaiian Vill. | 2005 Kalia Rd. (Ala Moana Blvd.) | Honolulu | Oahu | 808-942-4858

Waikiki | Waikiki Beach Walk | 226 Lewers St. (Kalakaua Ave.) | Honolulu | Oahu | 808-926-7700

800-260-3912 | www.nahoku.com

Additional locations throughout Hawaii

"The place to buy your 'slippah' [flip-flop] necklace" or other bling "with a Hawaii touch", this statewide chain presents a "beautiful selection" of "quality" jewelry; the "friendly and knowledgeable" staff can help you choose a "unique" gift, but it'll cost you, since detractors deem some of the "basic" pieces "pricey for what you get."

Na Mea Native Books ✆
- | - | - | M

Ward | Ward Warehouse | 1050 Ala Moana Blvd. (bet. Kamakee St. & Ward Ave.) | Honolulu | Oahu | 808-596-8885

Na Mea ✆

Waikiki | Hilton Hawaiian Vill. | 2005 Kalia Rd. (Ala Moana Blvd.) | Honolulu | Oahu | 808-949-3989

	QUALITY	DISPLAY	SERVICE	COST

(continued)

MANA Hawaii ❶

Waikiki | Waikiki Beach Walk | 226 Lewers St. (Kalakaua Ave.) |
Honolulu | Oahu | 808-923-2220
800-887-7751 | www.nativebooks.com

If you want to be sure you're getting "products that are really Hawaiian",
find the "perfect memento" at one of these three "wonderful" stores on
Beach Walk, in Ward Warehouse and in the Hilton Hawaiian Village,
where "each unique piece is locally made" and attractively displayed –
whether it's Niihau shell jewelry, fine furniture, paintings, books, food
products or Aloha wear; the stores also host live music, hula workshops and Hawaiian language classes, among other activities.

Neiman Marcus ❶

28 | 26 | 23 | VE

Ala Moana | Ala Moana Ctr. | 1450 Ala Moana Blvd. (bet. Atkinson Dr. &
Piikoi St.) | Honolulu | Oahu | 808-951-8887 | 877-951-8887 |
www.neimanmarcus.com

If you're up for "dropping the big bucks", grab the credit cards and
head to the "beautifully" merchandised Ala Moana Center branch of
the "Dallas-based giant", where the "floating gold butterflies above
the escalators", the "quality" "designer selections" – from "Armani to
Prada to Diane von Furstenberg" – and the elegant Mariposa restaurant with a "great view" of the ocean "don't disappoint"; even if a few
say they "hate begging to buy something" from the "snobbish" staff,
more maintain it's worth a "walk through" if nothing else.

Niketown ❶

22 | 20 | 19 | M

Waikiki | King Kalakaua Plaza | 2080 Kalakaua Ave. (bet. Kalaimoku &
Olohana Sts.) | Honolulu | Oahu | 808-943-6453 | www.nike.com

Runners, basketballers, "bored boys" and other sporty sorts swoop
into this sleek, three-level Waikiki megastore with the label's "best selection" of "current styles" in shoes, shorts, bags and more; a "great
place to prepare for the Honolulu Marathon" or just get "inspired to
start exercising", it "always has a sale going on" and you'll be "well
looked after"; N.B. check out the display of signed sneakers.

Nohea Galleries

27 | 24 | 23 | E

Kailua | Kailua Rd. & Hamakua Dr. (Oneawa St.) | Oahu | 808-262-2787
Waikiki | Moana Surfrider | 2365 Kalakaua Ave. (Kaiulani Ave.) | Honolulu |
Oahu | 808-923-6644 ❶
Ward | Ward Warehouse | 1050 Ala Moana Blvd. (bet. Kamakee St. &
Ward Ave.) | Honolulu | Oahu | 808-596-0074 ❶
www.noheagallery.com

For "island items that are classic, not chintzy", this trio of "local arts
and crafts" galleries boasts an "outstanding selection of Hawaiian
merch", including "glass objects with tropical themes", "koa bowls
and platters", silver jewelry and "striking scarves"; the cash-strapped
find them a "little pricey", but "fun" for "browsing."

NEW Nordstrom ❶

26 | 25 | 25 | E

Ala Moana | Ala Moana Ctr. | 1590 Kapiolani Blvd. (Kaheka St.) |
Honolulu | Oahu | 808-953-6100 | www.nordstrom.com

"The shoe section" makes this "elegant" Ala Moana Center "addition"
a "worthwhile stop for any Carrie Bradshaw wannabe", but the Hawaii
link of this Seattle-based chain also wins kudos for its "wide-open" de-

sign, "beautiful dressing areas" (the 'Girlfriend Room' has a flat-screen TV, couches and fashion 'zines), a "huge variety" of "quality" apparel and "excellent service" that includes a "fantastic return-and-exchange policy"; even if "way too many name brands" create "overkill" for the label-weary, the stock of "strictly local" goods helps; N.B. try the on-site Marketplace Cafe for a casual bite.

Parker Ranch Store
21 | 19 | 20 | M

Kamuela | Parker Sq. | 67-1185 Mamalahoa Hwy. (Hawaii Belt Rd.) | Big Island | 808-885-5669 | 800-262-7290 | www.parkerranch.com

Lasso up some "cowboy wear" and ranch-related souvenirs for your "l'il wranglers" (both old and young) along with a "surprising variety" of "real Hawaiian" goods at this Kamuela gift shop on the grounds of the 19th-century historic Parker Ranch, where *paniolos* once rounded up cattle for King Kamehameha; those who want to "support local artists", however, should "ask where" items are made.

Philip Rickard ❶
- | - | - | VE

NEW **Ala Moana** | Ala Moana Ctr. | 1450 Ala Moana Blvd. (bet. Atkinson Dr. & Piikoi St.) | Honolulu | Oahu | 808-949-2141

NEW **Waikiki** | Royal Hawaiian Ctr. | 2201 Kalakaua Ave. (Lewers St.) | Honolulu | Oahu | 808-924-7972

Waikiki | Hyatt Regency Waikiki | 2424 Kalakaua Ave. (Kaiulani Ave.) | Honolulu | Oahu | 808-922-9200

800-948-2616 | www.philiprickard.com

For "custom-made" Hawaiian heirloom jewelry "personalized with your name in Hawaiian" (an island tradition), many head to one of this expensive designer's Oahu boutiques or kiosks in Waikiki and Ala Moana, where the "beautiful" merchandise is attractively displayed; bling buyers may also be swayed by the island-themed pieces (petroglyph and plumeria pendants) and engagement/wedding ring collections.

Prada ❶
27 | 24 | 24 | VE

Ala Moana | Ala Moana Ctr. | 1450 Ala Moana Blvd. (bet. Atkinson Dr. & Piikoi St.) | Honolulu | Oahu | 808-955-5226

Waikiki | 2174 Kalakaua Ave. (Lewers St.) | Honolulu | Oahu | 808-921-0200

Prada Sport ❶

Waikiki | 2174 Kalakaua Ave. (Lewers St.) | Honolulu | Oahu | 808-921-0200
www.prada.com

Throngs of "tourists" "queue up to throw their money at the solicitous staff" in these Ala Moana Center and Waikiki "marquees" for Miuccia Prada's "chic" and forward-thinking bags, accessories and "quality leather goods" (they're "relatively lean on clothing" compared to other outposts); even if it all "makes your wallet bleed", it's "cheaper than flying to Italy."

Red Pineapple ❶
26 | 22 | 22 | M

Ward | Ward Ctr. | 1200 Ala Moana Blvd. (bet. Kamakee & Queen Sts.) | Honolulu | Oahu | 808-593-2733 | www.redpineapple.net

Shoppers "love to browse for a long time" at this "small store" in Ward Centre that's "packed full" of "stylish, modern" accessories, "whimsical" trinkets "you never knew you needed" and a "wide variety" of "hip choices" for that "unusual present"; even if the "eclectic mix" can be "pricey" and "you'll have to wait your turn" for service, regulars are rewarded with "items you don't see every day."

	QUALITY	DISPLAY	SERVICE	COST

Reyn's
27 | 23 | 24 | E

Kamuela | Parker Ranch Ctr. | 67-1185 Mamalahoa Hwy. (Hawaii Belt Rd.) | Big Island | 808-885-4493

Kohala Coast | Fairmont Orchid | 1 N. Kaniku Dr. (Hoohana St.) | Waikoloa | Big Island | 808-885-0035

Waikoloa | Queens' Mktpl. | 69-201 Waikoloa Beach Dr. (Queen Kaahumanu Hwy.) | Big Island | 808-886-1162 ◐

Poipu | Grand Hyatt | 1571 Poipu Rd. (Ainako St.) | Koloa | Kauai | 808-742-7279 ◐

Kaanapali | Whalers Vill. | 2435 Kaanapali Pkwy. (Kekaa Dr.) | Maui | 808-661-9032 ◐

Ala Moana | Ala Moana Ctr. | 1450 Ala Moana Blvd. (bet. Atkinson Dr. & Piikoi St.) | Honolulu | Oahu | 808-949-5929 ◐

Kahala | Kahala Mall | 4211 Waialae Ave. (Hunakai St.) | Honolulu | Oahu | 808-737-8313 ◐

Waikiki | Sheraton | 2255 Kalakaua Ave. (bet. Royal Hawaiian & Seaside Aves.) | Honolulu | Oahu | 808-923-0331 ◐

888-289-7396 | www.reyns.com

For the "classic" "Aloha shirts that local residents wear", as well as "women's dresses", accessories, childrenswear and "beautiful" tropical Christmas shirts, visit one of the many island locations of this 52-year-old chain founded by Reyn Spooner; although you can expect "knowledgeable" staffers and "classic designs" that "never go out of style", some cutting-edgers yawn they "still sell the same" "boring" stuff as "when I was a toddler"; N.B. the family business sold a majority stake in 2008 to an LA group, and plans a global expansion.

Royal Hawaiian Heritage Jewelers
24 | 23 | 24 | E

Kailua-Kona | Lanihau Shopping Ctr. | 75-5595 Palani Rd. (Hawaii Belt Rd.) | Big Island | 808-326-7599

Kahului | Maui Mall | 70 E. Kaahumanu Ave. (bet. Hana Hwy. & S. Puunene Ave.) | Maui | 808-871-6446

Aiea | Pearlridge Ctr. Downtown | 98-1005 Moanalua Rd. (Kaonohi St.) | Oahu | 808-487-0808 ◐

Downtown | 1130 Bishop St. (S. Hotel St.) | Honolulu | Oahu | 808-524-4313 ⓢ

800-843-2533 | www.rhhj.com

For a traditional Victorian-style gold bangle engraved with your name in Hawaiian – a custom in the islands since the 19th century – or another "great keepsake of your trip", head to one of the four branches of this jeweler specializing in unusual designs and "customized" pieces; but even if you must have those earrings in the shape of a plumeria or that black pearl necklace right away, "look for weekly sales" because it can be "outrageously expensive."

Sandal Tree ◐
23 | 20 | 19 | M

Waikoloa | Kings' Shops | 250 Waikoloa Beach Dr. (Queen Kaahumanu Hwy.) | Big Island | 808-886-2600

Waikoloa | Hilton Waikoloa Vill. | 425 Waikoloa Beach Dr. (Queen Kaahumanu Hwy.) | Big Island | 808-886-7884

Poipu | Grand Hyatt | 1571 Poipu Rd. (Pee Rd.) | Koloa | Kauai | 808-742-2009

Kaanapali | Hyatt Regency | 200 Nohea Kai Dr. (Kaanapali Pkwy.) | Maui | 808-661-3495

Kaanapali | Whalers Vill. | 2435 Kaanapali Pkwy. (Kekaa Dr.) | Lahaina | Maui | 808-667-5330

(continued)

SHOPPING

(continued)
Sandal Tree
Ala Moana | Ala Moana Ctr. | 1450 Ala Moana Blvd. (bet. Atkinson Dr. & Piikoi St.) | Honolulu | Oahu | 808-957-6300
Waikiki | Hyatt Regency Waikiki | 2424 Kalakaua Ave. (Kaiulani Ave.) | Honolulu | Oahu | 808-921-9936
www.sandaltree.com
For "shoes and bags perfectly chosen for the tropical climate", slip into these local his-and-hers footwear temples, where the "variety" of "expensive- to midpriced" offerings are hard "to resist" – "whether you need" a slipper, casual sandal, "dressy" heel or locally made, tropical-print fabric wedge; though some say the "store name" and display don't seem as upscale as the products, they usually "buy several pairs" once inside.

☒ Sig Zane Designs ☒   28 | 27 | 28 | E
Hilo | 122 Kamehameha Ave. (Walanuenue Ave.) | Big Island | 808-935-7077 | www.sigzane.com
"If you want to pass for a sophisticated local", snag some of the "tasteful", "top-of-the-line" Hawaiian wear for men and women at this Hilo shop, rated No. 1 for Service, where the namesake creator offers his "elegant" clothing in a newly renovated setting of shoji screens, gleaming wood floors and island art; "you can't go wrong" with any one of the "stunning" pieces, so it's no wonder Honolulu loyalists "wish he would open a store on Oahu."

T & C Surf Designs ●   22 | 20 | 20 | M
(fka Town & Country Surf)
Aiea | Pearlridge Ctr. Uptown | 98-1810 Kamehameha Hwy. (Pali Momi St.) | Oahu | 808-483-5499
Ala Moana | Ala Moana Ctr. | 1450 Ala Moana Blvd. (bet. Atkinson Dr. & Piikoi St.) | Honolulu | Oahu | 808-973-5199
Kahala | Kahala Mall | 4211 Waialae Ave. (Hunakai St.) | Honolulu | Oahu | 808-733-5699
Kaneohe | Windward Mall | 46-056 Kamehameha Hwy. (Haiku Rd.) | Oahu | 808-233-5799
Waikiki | Waikiki Trade Ctr. | 2255 Kuhio Ave. (Seaside Ave.) | Honolulu | Oahu | 808-971-5599
Waikiki | International Mktpl. | 2332 Kalakaua Ave. (Kaiulani Ave.) | Honolulu | Oahu | 808-971-7100
Ward | Ward Warehouse | 1050 Ala Moana Blvd. (bet. Kamakee St. & Ward Ave.) | Honolulu | Oahu | 808-973-5199
www.tcsurf.com
Wave-riders claim that this Oahu surf shop chain that's "been popular among a young crowd for nearly 30 years" "makes the best boards" ("smooth enough to ride on naked"), as well as "great local T-shirts", beach apparel and "skate clothing"; sure, some say the "setup is a little scattered" and the staff "just stands around talking", but that doesn't stop "local bruddas" from "hitting up" the place for some "casual" duds.

☒ Tiffany & Co. ●   28 | 27 | 26 | VE
Waikoloa | Kings' Shops | 250 Waikoloa Beach Dr. (Queen Kaahumanu Hwy.) | Big Island | 808-883-1467
Wailea | Shops at Wailea | 3750 Wailea Alanui Dr. (Wailea Ike Dr.) | Maui | 808-891-9226

(continued)

Tiffany & Co.

Ala Moana | Ala Moana Ctr. | 1450 Ala Moana Blvd. (bet. Atkinson Dr. & Piikoi St.) | Honolulu | Oahu | 808-943-6677
Waikiki | 2100 Kalakaua Ave. (Saratoga Rd.) | Honolulu | Oahu | 808-926-2600
800-843-3269 | www.tiffany.com

With branches in Waikiki, Ala Moana, Wailea and Waikoloa, this venerable jeweler known for "that little blue box" and "very expensive pieces" offers "subtle" designs that appeal to many and make "impressive" gifts; the "impeccable" service and "elegant" settings "have you channeling your inner Audrey Hepburn in no time", but spoilsports snap that they're "overpriced, overhyped" and "full of tourists."

Tommy Bahama ●   27 | 26 | 23 | E

Kamuela | 68-1330 Mauna Lani Dr. (Queen Kaahumanu Hwy.) | Big Island | 808-881-8688
Waikoloa | Kings' Shops | 250 Waikoloa Beach Dr. (Queen Kaahumanu Hwy.) | Big Island | 808-886-8865
Kaanapali | Whalers Vill. | 2435 Kaanapali Pkwy. (Kekaa Dr.) | Lahaina | Maui | 808-661-8823
Wailea | Shops at Wailea | 3750 Wailea Alanui Dr. (Wailea Ike Dr.) | Maui | 808-879-7828
Ala Moana | Ala Moana Ctr. | 1450 Ala Moana Blvd. (bet. Atkinson Dr. & Piikoi St.) | Honolulu | Oahu | 808-955-8869
866-986-8282 | www.tommybahama.com

"You'll feel like you're in a tropical rainforest" due to the "wonderful hues" and "enchanting patterns" decking the men's Aloha shirts, women's sundresses and home accessories at this Seattle-based purveyor of tropical casual "chic"; although the "great selection", "bright and attractive staff", "beautiful displays" and on-site bars win some over, others are turned off by "overpriced", "not-true-Hawaiian wear."

Tori Richard ●   26 | 25 | 24 | E

Wailea | Shops at Wailea | 3750 Wailea Alanui Dr. (Wailea Ike Dr.) | Maui | 808-891-8633
Ala Moana | Ala Moana Ctr. | 1450 Ala Moana Blvd. (bet. Atkinson Dr. & Piikoi St.) | Honolulu | Oahu | 808-749-5858
Waikiki | Hilton Hawaiian Vill. | 2005 Kalia Rd. (Ala Moana Blvd.) | Honolulu | Oahu | 808-943-9472
Waikiki | Hyatt Regency Waikiki | 2424 Kalakaua Ave. (Kaiulani Ave.) | Honolulu | Oahu | 808-924-1811
www.toririchard.com

For "funky designs" that are "part country-club, part island wear", head to one of this local designer's elegant stores for "unique" "Aloha shirts made of silk", hot-hued women's sundresses and other "seasonal styles" that "capture different aspects" of the area's "natural beauty"; yes, these "fine" duds are "expensive", but they're "hard to find on the mainland" and the "timeless" tropical look "never goes out of fashion."

NEW Tourneau ●   – | – | – | VE

Waikiki | Royal Hawaiian Ctr. | 2301 Kalakaua Ave. (Dukes Ln.) | Honolulu | Oahu | 808-922-4111 | www.tourneau.com

The world's largest watch retailer finally opened an outpost in Hawaii, with its first location at the newly revamped Royal Hawaiian Center, where a 2,000-sq.-ft. space fronts Kalakaua Avenue; expect an "excellent assortment" (some 8,000 styles) of "extremely expensive time-pieces" from brands such as Franck Muller, TAG Heuer and the store's own line, plus a huge selection of pre-owned watches and a repair center.

Under the Koa Tree ●

–	–	–	E

Waikoloa | Kings' Shops | 250 Waikoloa Beach Dr. (Queen Kaahumanu Hwy.) | Big Island | 808-886-7444
Waikiki | Waikiki Beach Walk | 226 Lewers St. (Kalia Rd.) | Honolulu | Oahu | 808-926-8733
www.koatree.com

The "unreal local woodwork" is so "beautiful" in these Waikoloa and Waikiki stores that "you can't walk out without a purchase" – whether it's a "koa frame", a kukui bowl or a milo canoe paddle – say astonished admirers of the expensive offerings; the walls are filled with paintings, photography, art glass, clocks and other crafts, while some of the jewelry and small gift items are less expensive "souvenir" options.

Volcano Art Center

25	23	20	E

Volcano | off Hwy. 11, bet. m.m. 28 & 29 (Hawaii Belt Rd.) | Big Island | 808-967-7565 | 866-967-7565 | www.volcanoartcenter.org

Visitors to Hawaii Volcanoes National Park flow into this "unique gallery" in "a beautiful little cottage" dating to 1877 where the "helpful" staff guides you through the "authentic" and "high-quality" Hawaiian jewelry, crafts, clothing and "glass pieces" inspired by the molten surroundings; if you come on the right day, you may meet one of the artists, but it's "a downer" to "have to pay" park entrance fees "to access" this shop.

Waimea General Store

18	15	15	M

Waimea | Parker Sq. | 65-1279 Kawaihae Rd. (Opelo Rd.) | Big Island | 808-885-4479

Find "drinks, trinkets", "travel items" and "lots of little knickknacks" (think "hand-painted Aloha shirt Christmas ornaments" and CDs of island music) at this store "in a small square in Waimea" that fans "look forward to going back" to; there's "not a lot of elbow room", so "be careful not to knock over the displays" on your way to the "large" kitchen-related area where there's "a gadget for anything you can think of."

Notable Mentions

Aloha Rag ● Mens/Womenswear
Ala Moana | Blackfield Bldg. | 1221 Kapiolani Blvd. (Pensacola St.) | Honolulu | Oahu | 808-589-1352 | www.aloharag.com

A Touch of Molokai Gifts/Novelties
Maunaloa | Kaluakoi Hotel & Golf Club | Kapuhi Bch. | Molokai | 808-552-0133

Big Wind Kite Factory Gifts/Novelties
Maunaloa | 120 Maunaloa Hwy. (Waieli St.) | Molokai | 808-552-2364 | www.bigwindkites.com

NEW Blue Buddha ●⊠ Mens/Womenswear
Ala Moana | Blackfield Bldg. | 1221 Kapiolani Blvd. (Pensacola St.) | Honolulu | Oahu | 808-591-1648

Catherine's Closet ⊠Ⓜ Vintage
Manoa | 2733 E. Manoa Rd. (bet. Keaunu St. & Oahu Ave.) | Honolulu | Oahu | 808-386-2746

Dis 'N Dat ☒ *Gifts/Novelties*
Lanai City | 418 Eighth St. (Fraser Ave.) | Lanai | 808-565-9170

Ehukai Original Authentic Niihau Shell Leis & Gifts ☒ *Jewelry*
Lihue | 9652 Kaumualii Hwy. (Kahill Rd.) | Kauai | 808-645-0267

88 Tees ◗ *Mens/Womenswear*
Waikiki | 2168 Kalakaua Ave. (Lewers St.) | Honolulu | Oahu |
808-922-8832
Waikiki | 2310 Kuhio Ave. (bet. Nahua & Nohonani Sts.) | Honolulu |
Oahu | 808-922-8822
www.88tees.com

Global Village *Accessories/Jewelry*
Kailua | 539 Kailua Rd. (Kuulei Rd.) | Oahu | 808-262-8183 |
www.globalvillagehawaii.com

Hawaiian Accessories ◗ *Jewelry*
Ala Moana | Ala Moana Ctr. | 1450 Ala Moana Blvd. (bet. Atkinson Dr. &
Piikoi St.) | Honolulu | Oahu | 808-944-9928
Waikiki | Outrigger Waikiki | 2335 Kalakaua Ave. (bet. Kaiulani &
Seaside Aves.) | Honolulu | Oahu | 808-921-3400
Waikiki | Waikiki Beach Marriott Resort & Spa | 2552 Kalakaua Ave.
(bet. Ohua & Paoakalani Aves.) | Honolulu | Oahu | 808-922-8957
888-747-9663 | www.hawaiianaccessories.com

Hui No'eau ☒ *Art*
Makawao | 2841 Baldwin Ave. (Kaluanui Rd.) | Maui | 808-572-6560 |
www.huinoeau.com

INTO ☒ *Gifts/Novelties*
Chinatown | 40 N. Hotel St. (Nuuanu Ave.) | Honolulu | Oahu |
808-536-2211 | www.intohonolulu.com

NEW **Juicy Couture** ◗ *Womenswear*
Ala Moana | Ala Moana Ctr. | 1450 Ala Moana Blvd. (Atkinson Dr.) |
Honolulu | Oahu | 808-942-7700
Waikiki | Royal Hawaiian Ctr. | 2301 Kalakaua Ave. (Dukes Ln.) |
Honolulu | Oahu | 808-922-9790
www.juicycouture.com

NEW **Kahala** ◗ *Aloha Wear*
Ala Moana | Ala Moana Ctr. | 1450 Ala Moana Blvd. (bet. Atkinson Dr. &
Piikoi St.) | Honolulu | Oahu | 808-941-2444 | www.kahala.com

Kahi Gallery *Art*
Waikiki | Alana Waikiki Business Ctr. | 460 Ena Rd. (bet. Ala Moana Blvd. &
Kalakaua Ave.) | Honolulu | Oahu | 808-941-0524

Maggie Coulombe ◗ *Womenswear*
Lahaina | 505 Front St. (Shaw St.) | Maui | 808-662-0696 |
www.maggiecoulombe.com

Mamo ◗ *Aloha Wear*
Ward | Ward Warehouse | 1050 Ala Moana Blvd. (bet. Kamakee St. &
Ward Ave.) | Honolulu | Oahu | 808-591-2002 | 877-825-8789 |
www.mamohowell.com

Manuhealii Fashions *Aloha Wear*
Kailua | Kailua Shopping Ctr. | 600 Kailua Rd. (bet. Hahani St. & Kuulei Rd.) |
Oahu | 808-261-9865
Makiki | 930 Punahou St. (King St.) | Honolulu | Oahu |
808-942-9868
www.manuhealii.com

Muumuu Heaven *Aloha Wear*
Kailua | 767 Kailua Rd. (Kuulei Rd.) | Oahu | 808-263-3366 |
www.muumuuheaven.com

Nui Mono 🆂🅼 *Womenswear*
Moiliili | 2745 King St. (Waialae Ave.) | Honolulu | Oahu | 808-946-7407

Shop Pacifica *Gifts/Novelties*
Kalihi | Bishop Museum | 1525 Bernice St. (Kapalama Ave.) | Honolulu |
Oahu | 808-847-3511 | www.bishopmuseum.org

Silver Moon Emporium *Jewelry/Womenswear*
Haleiwa | North Shore Mktpl. | 66-250 Kamehameha Hwy. (Achiu Ln.) |
Oahu | 808-637-7710

Tamara Catz *Womenswear*
Paia | 83 Hana Hwy. (Nalu Pl.) | Maui | 808-579-9184 | www.tamaracatz.com

Under a Hula Moon *Gifts/Novelties*
Kailua | Kailua Shopping Ctr. | 600 Kailua Rd. (bet. Hahani St. & Kuulei Rd.) |
Oahu | 808-261-4252
Ward | Ward Ctr. | 1200 Ala Moana Blvd. (bet. Kamakee & Queen Sts.) |
Honolulu | Oahu | 808-596-4442 ◐

NEW Valerie Joseph ◐ *Womenswear*
Waikiki | Ala Moana Ctr. | 1450 Ala Moana Blvd. (bet. Atkinson Dr. &
Piikoi St.) | Honolulu | Oahu | 808-942-5258 | www.valeriejoseph.com

Yellow Fish Trading Company ◐ *Gifts/Novelties*
Hanalei | Hanalei Ctr. | 5-5161 Kuhio Hwy. (Aku Rd.) | Kauai | 808-826-1227

INDEXES

Attractions Types

Includes attraction names, locations and Appeal ratings.

AQUARIUMS

Maui Ocean Ctr.	**Maalaea/Ma**	26
Sea Life Pk.	**Waimanalo/O**	22
Waikiki Aqua.	**Waikiki/O**	22

BEACHES

Ala Moana Bch.	**Ala Moana/O**	22
Anaeho'omalu Bch.	**Waikoloa/BI**	23
Banzai Pipeline	**Waimea/O**	27
Black Rock Bch.	**Kaanapali/Ma**	26
Haleiwa Bch.	**Haleiwa/O**	25
Hanalei Bay Bch.	**Hanalei/K**	27
Hanauma Bay	**Hanauma/O**	27
Hapuna Bch.	**Kohala/BI**	27
Ho'okipa Bch.	**Paia/Ma**	26
Kailua Bch.	**Kailua/O**	27
Kapalua Bch.	**Kapalua/Ma**	27
Kealakekua	**Kailua-Kona/BI**	27
🅩 Ke'e Bch.	**Hanalei/K**	28
Kuhio Bch.	**Waikiki/O**	23
🅩 Lanikai Bch.	**Kailua/O**	28
Lumahai Bch.	**Hanalei/K**	28
Makapu'u Bch.	**Waimanalo/O**	27
Makena Bch.	**Makena/Ma**	27
🅩 Manele Bay	**Manele/L**	28
Poipu Bch.	**Poipu/K**	25
🅩 Punalu'u Bch.	**Pahala/BI**	28
Sandy Bch.	**Hawaii Kai/O**	25
Sunset Bch.	**Waimea/O**	28
Turtle Bay	**Kahuku/O**	25
🅩 Waikiki Bch.	**Waikiki/O**	23
Wailea Bch.	**Wailea/Ma**	28
Waimanalo Pk.	**Waimanalo/O**	24
🅩 Waimea Bay	**Haleiwa/O**	28

FARMS/RANCHES

Kilohana Plant.	**Lihue/K**	23
Maui Plant.	**Wailuku/Ma**	21
Purdy's Nut	**Hoolehua/Mo**	22

GARDENS/ORCHARDS

Allerton Gdn.	**Koloa/K**	-
Fern Grotto	**Wailua/K**	22
Hawaii Trop. Gdn.	**Papaikou/BI**	27
Kilohana Plant.	**Lihue/K**	23
McBryde Gdn.	**Koloa/K**	-
Smith's	**Kapaa/K**	21

HISTORIC LANDMARKS

Iolani	**Downtown/O**	26
Punchbowl	**Makiki Hts/O**	25

HISTORICAL HOUSES

Baldwin Home	**Lahaina/Ma**	21
Queen Emma	**Nuuanu/O**	23

LUAUS

Drums/Pacif.	**Kaanapali/Ma**	23
Feast/Lele	**Lahaina/Ma**	27
Germaine's Luau	**Kapolei/O**	22
Grand Hyatt Luau	**Poipu/K**	23
Hilton Luau	**Waikoloa/BI**	21
Kona Luau	**Kailua-Kona/BI**	25
🅩 Old Lahaina Luau	**Lahaina/Ma**	28
Paradise Luau	**Kapolei/O**	26
Polynesian Luau	**Laie/O**	23
Royal Kona Luau	**Kailua-Kona/BI**	26
Marriott Luau	**Wailea/Ma**	23

MUSEUMS

Alexander/Sugar	**Puunene/Ma**	20
Bishop Mus.	**Kalihi/O**	25
Contemp. Mus.	**multi.**	22
Hawaii Art Mus.	**Downtown/O**	22
Honolulu Acad./Arts	**Ala Moana/O**	26
Kauai Mus.	**Lihue/K**	23
Molokai Mus.	**Kualapuu/Mo**	-
Polynesian Ctr.	**Laie/O**	26
Whalers Mus.	**Lahaina/Ma**	19

NATIONAL MONUMENTS/MEMORIALS

Battleship Miss.	**Pearl Harbor/O**	28
Punchbowl	**Makiki Hts/O**	25
🅩 USS Arizona	**Pearl Harbor/O**	29

NEIGHBORHOODS

Chinatown	**Chinatown/O**	20
Makawao	**Makawao/Ma**	22
Paia	**Paia/Ma**	23

PARKS

Akaka Falls	**Honomu/BI**	26
Ala Moana Bch.	**Ala Moana/O**	22

Diamond Head | **Kahala/O** 26

Ft. DeRussy | **Waikiki/O** 21

Haena Tunnels | **Hanalei/K** 25

Z Haleakala Pk. | **Makawao/Ma** 28

Z Hawaii Volcanoes Pk. | 29
   Hawaii Nat'l Pk/BI

Kaloko-Honokohau | 27
   Honokohau/BI

Kapiolani Pk. | **Waikiki/O** 23

Lydgate Bch. | **Koloa/K** 22

Manoa Falls | **Manoa/O** 26

Polihale Pk. | **Lihue/K** 28

Pools at O'heo | **Hana/Ma** 26

Z Waimea Canyon | **Waimea/K** 28

Wainapanapa Pk. | **Hana/Ma** 28

SHOPPING CENTERS/ STORES/MALLS

Aloha Swap | **Aiea/O** 22

Aloha Mktpl. | **Downtown/O** 20

THEME PARKS

Hawaiian Waters | **Kapolei/O** 23

Polynesian Ctr. | **Laie/O** 26

TOURS

Atlantis Sub | **multi.** 24

Kauai Coffee | **Kalaheo/K** 22

Lahaina-Kaanapall Train | 17
   Kaanapali/Ma

Molokai Mule | **Kalaupapa/Mo** 25

Purdy's Nut | **Hoolehua/Mo** 22

ZOOS/ ANIMAL PARKS

Honolulu Zoo | **Waikiki/O** 21

Kilauea Point | **Kilauea/K** 26

ATTRACTIONS

TYPES

Dining Cuisines

Includes restaurant names, locations and Food ratings.

AMERICAN (NEW)

NEW Beachhse. | **Waikiki**/O	21
Colleen's | **Haiku**/Ma	–
NEW Downtown | **Downtown**/O	–
Joe's B&G | **Wailea**/Ma	22
Lahaina Grill | **Lahaina**/Ma	26
Lahaina Store | **Lahaina**/Ma	18
NEW MAC 24/7 | **Waikiki**/O	19
Mariposa | **Ala Moana**/O	22
Prince Ct. | **multi.**	23
NEW Stage | **Ala Moana**/O	–
NEW Tangö | **Downtown**/O	–
Terrace | **Koele**/L	23
town | **Kaimuki**/O	23
12th Ave. | **Kaimuki**/O	23

AMERICAN (TRADITIONAL)

AK's | **Wailuku**/Ma	20
Alexander's | **Kihei**/Ma	22
Barefoot Burger | **Waimea**/K	18
Big City Diner | **multi.**	18
Big Island Grill | **Kailua-Kona**/BI	21
Blue Ginger | **Lanai City**/L	20
Brennecke's | **Poipu**/K	18
Bubba Burger | **multi.**	21
Bubba Gump | **multi.**	15
Buzz's | **Pearl City**/O	19
Café 565 | **Lanai City**/L	–
Café 100 | **Hilo**/BI	19
Canoes Lanai | **Lanai City**/L	17
Charley's | **Paia**/Ma	19
Cheeseburger/Paradise | **multi.**	17
Cheesecake Fac. | **Waikiki**/O	21
Chowder Hse. | **Ward**/O	16
CJ's Deli | **Kaanapali**/Ma	18
Contemp. Café | **Makiki Hts**/O	19
Dani's | **Lihue**/K	20
Dollie's Pub | **Lahaina**/Ma	16
Duane's Ono | **Anahola**/K	23
Z Duke's | **multi.**	19
Eggbert's | **Kapaa**/K	18
Eggs 'n Things | **Waikiki**/O	23
Gazebo | **Napili**/Ma	24
Grandma's | **Kula**/Ma	20
Hanalei Gourmet | **Hanalei**/K	21
Hana Ranch | **Hana**/Ma	22
Harbor Hse. | **Kailua-Kona**/BI	19

Hard Rock | **multi.**	14
Hula Shores | **Kaunakakai**/Mo	–
Ige's/19th Puka | **Aiea**/O	19
I Love Country | **Ala Moana**/O	17
Island Burger | **Ala Moana**/O	18
Jameson's | **multi.**	19
JJ's Broiler | **Nawiliwili**/K	17
Ken's/Pancakes | **Hilo**/BI	19
Kihei Caffe | **Kihei**/Ma	23
Kimo's | **Lahaina**/Ma	20
Koho | **Kahului**/Ma	18
Kona Brewing | **multi.**	18
Kula Lodge | **Kula**/Ma	20
Lihue BBQ | **Lihue**/K	20
Mama's Ribs | **Napili**/Ma	21
Mana'e Goods | **Manae**/Mo	–
Manago | **Captain Cook**/BI	21
Mermaid Bar | **Ala Moana**/O	21
Molokai Dr. | **Kaunakakai**/Mo	–
Oceanarium | **Waikiki**/O	17
OnO B&G | **Kaanapali**/Ma	21
Ono Family | **Kapaa**/K	19
Original Pancake | **multi.**	21
Paddlers' Inn | **Kaunakakai**/Mo	–
Pele's Gdn. | **Lanai City**/L	19
Pioneer Inn | **Lahaina**/Ma	15
Plantation Café | **Ala Moana**/O	17
Poipu Broiler | **Poipu**/K	19
Ruby's | **Kahului**/Ma	17
Ruby Tues. | **multi.**	15
NEW Sammy's | **Kahului**/Ma	–
Shore Bird | **Waikiki**/O	19
Side St. Inn | **Ala Moana**/O	25
Stella Blues | **Kihei**/Ma	19
Tasty Crust | **Wailuku**/Ma	19
Therapy Sports | **Hawaii Kai**/O	17
TomKat's | **Koloa**/K	18
NEW Uncle's Fish | **Iwilei**/O	18
Volcano Golf | **Volcano**/BI	15
Wailana Coffee | **Waikiki**/O	17
Willows | **Moiliili**/O	18
Zippy's | **multi.**	16

ASIAN FUSION

Indigo | **Chinatown**/O	22
NEW Kenichi | **multi.**	24
Tommy Bahama | **multi.**	20

BAKERIES

Hanapepe Café | **Hanapepe/K**	22
Kanemitsu's | **Kaunakakai/Mo**	–
Oki Diner | **Lihue/K**	15
T. Komoda | **Makawao/Ma**	24

BARBECUE

Dixie Grill | **Aiea/O**	16
Garden Is. | **Lihue/K**	19
L&L Drive-Inn | **multi.**	16
Mama's Ribs | **Napili/Ma**	21
Scotty's BBQ | **Kapaa/K**	22
Tony Roma | **multi.**	19

BURGERS

Barefoot Burger | **Waimea/K**	18
Bubba Burger | **multi.**	21
NEW Burgers/Edge | **Kapahulu/O**	–
Cheeseburger/Paradise | **multi.**	17
Duane's Ono | **Anahola/K**	23
Hana Ranch | **Hana/Ma**	22
Hard Rock | **multi.**	14
Island Burger | **Ala Moana/O**	18
Kalapaki Hut | **Kalapaki Bch/K**	22
Koho | **Kahului/Ma**	18
Kua 'Aina | **multi.**	22
Peggy Sue's | **Kihei/Ma**	17

CALIFORNIAN

Beach Tree | **Kaupulehu-Kona/BI**	23
Planet Hollywood | **Waikiki/O**	12
Ⓩ Spago | **Wailea/Ma**	26

CARIBBEAN

Tommy Bahama | **multi.**	20

CHINESE

(* dim sum specialist)

China Boat/Bowl | **multi.**	16
Ciao Mein | **Waikiki/O**	21
Dragon Dragon | **Kahului/Ma**	20
Fook Yuen | **Moiliili/O**	20
Garden Is. | **Lihue/K**	19
Hee Hing* | **Kapahulu/O**	20
Kirin* | **Ala Moana/O**	24
Legend Sea.* | **Chinatown/O**	23
Little Village | **Chinatown/O**	23
Mei Sum* | **Chinatown/O**	21
Pah Ke's | **Kaneohe/O**	23
P.F. Chang's | **multi.**	19

COFFEEHOUSES

Anthony's Coffee | **Paia/Ma**	20
Dani's | **Lihue/K**	20
Grandma's | **Kula/Ma**	20
Kalaheo Café | **Kalaheo/K**	23

COFFEE SHOPS/DINERS

Highway Inn | **Waipahu/O**	23
Ken's/Pancakes | **Hilo/BI**	19
NEW Market St. | **Lihue/K**	–
Original Pancake | **multi.**	21
Peggy Sue's | **Kihei/Ma**	17
Ruby's | **Kahului/Ma**	17
Wailana Coffee | **Waikiki/O**	17

CONTINENTAL

Aaron's | **Ala Moana/O**	20
Castaway | **Kaanapali/Ma**	22

CRAB HOUSES

Dixie Grill | **Aiea/O**	16

DELIS

CJ's Deli | **Kaanapali/Ma**	18
Pele's Gdn. | **Lanai City/L**	19

DESSERT

BJ's | **Lahaina/Ma**	19
Cheesecake Fac. | **Waikiki/O**	21
Kincaid's | **Ward/O**	20
Matsumoto's | **Haleiwa/O**	24
U-Top-It | **Kailua-Kona/BI**	23

ECLECTIC

Banyan Tree | **Kapalua/Ma**	24
Café Mambo | **Paia/Ma**	23
Café Pesto | **multi.**	23
Casa di Amici | **Poipu/K**	23
Diamond Head | **Waikiki/O**	22
Hanalei Gourmet | **Hanalei/K**	21
I Love Country | **Ala Moana/O**	17
Jackie Rey's | **Kailua-Kona/BI**	21
Ke'ei Café | **Honaunau/BI**	24
Kilauea Lodge | **Volcano/BI**	23
Lahaina Coolers | **Lahaina/Ma**	18
Lucy's Grill | **Kailua/O**	18
Maui Brewing | **Kahana/Ma**	19
Pagoda | **Ala Moana/O**	16
Paniolo | **Kamuela/BI**	16
Polynesia Café | **Hanalei/K**	18

Postcards Café | **Hanalei/K** 24
NEW Waimea Brew | **Waimea/K** 19

EURASIAN

Z Hiroshi | **Restaurant Row/O** 26

EUROPEAN FUSION

Lighthouse | **Kilauea/K** 21

FILIPINO

Oviedo | **Kaunakakai/Mo** -

FRENCH

Z Chef Mavro | **Moiliili/O** 26
Chez Paul | **Olowalu/Ma** 26
Duc's Bistro | **Chinatown/O** 24
NEW 'Elua | **Ala Moana/O** 24
Formaggio | **multi.** 22
Z Gerard's | **Lahaina/Ma** 28
Hale Samoa | **Kailua-Kona/BI** 26
La Bourgogne | **Kailua-Kona/BI** 25
Z La Mer | **Waikiki/O** 27
Z Le Bistro | **Niu Valley/O** 27
Z Michel's | **Waikiki/O** 25
NEW Panya | **Ala Moana/O** 17
Peaberry/Galette | **Keauhou/BI** 21
U-Top-It | **Kailua-Kona/BI** 23

FRENCH (BRASSERIE)

Brasserie/Vin | **Chinatown/O** 20

GREEK

NEW Fat Greek | **Kaimuki/O** 19
Olive Tree | **Kahala/O** 24

HAWAIIAN

Aloha Mix Plate | **Lahaina/Ma** 21
Blane's | **Hilo/BI** 15
Café 100 | **Hilo/BI** 19
Canoes Lanai | **Lanai City/L** 17
Da Kitchen | **multi.** 22
Dani's | **Lihue/K** 20
Z Helena's | **Kalihi/O** 26
Highway Inn | **Waipahu/O** 23
Kaka'ako | **Ward/O** 21
Z Koloa Fish | **Koloa/K** 25
Kona Mix | **Kailua-Kona/BI** 21
Kuhio Grille | **Hilo/BI** 21
Lahaina Store | **Lahaina/Ma** 18
L&L Drive-Inn | **multi.** 16
Manago | **Captain Cook/BI** 21

Nori's | **Hilo/BI** 20
Oki Diner | **Lihue/K** 15
OnO B&G | **Kaanapali/Ma** 21
Ono Family | **Kapaa/K** 19
Ono Hawaii | **Kapahulu/O** 25
People's Café | **Downtown/O** 21
Tasty Crust | **Wailuku/Ma** 19
U-Top-It | **Kailua-Kona/BI** 23
Willows | **Moiliili/O** 18
You Hungry? | **Ala Moana/O** 18
Young's Fish | **Kapalama/O** 24

HAWAII REGIONAL

Z Alan Wong's | **McCully/O** 28
Z Chef Mavro | **Moiliili/O** 26
Daniel's | **Waimea/BI** 23
Z Hali'imaile Gen. | **Makawao/Ma** 27
Z Hualalai Grille | **Kaupulehu-Kona/BI** 28
Hukilau | **Kapaa/K** 25
NEW Lanai City | **Lanai City/L** 22
Mala | **multi.** 25
Z Merriman's | **multi.** 27
Ola | **Kahuku/O** 21
Z Pahu | **Kaupulehu-Kona/BI** 26
Pineapple Rm. | **Ala Moana/O** 25
Z Roy's | **multi.** 26
Sam Choy's | **Iwilei/O** 20
Tiki Terr. | **Kaanapali/Ma** 19

HEALTH FOOD

(See also Vegetarian)
AK's | **Wailuku/Ma** 20
Caffe Coco | **Kapaa/K** 23

INDIAN

India Café | **Kapahulu/O** 19

ITALIAN

(N=Northern; S=Southern)
Arancino | **Waikiki/O** 22
Aroma D'Italia | S | **Kihei/Ma** 18
Assaggio | **multi.** 21
Auntie Pasto | **multi.** 17
Baci Bistro | **Kailua/O** 24
Beach Tree | **Kaupulehu-Kona/BI** 23
Brick Oven | **Kalaheo/K** 24
Cafe Portofino | N | **Kalapaki Bch/K** 21
Cafe Sistina | N | **Makiki/O** 21
Capische? | N | **Wailea/Ma** 25

Casa di Amici	**Poipu/K**	23
Casanova	N	**Makawao/Ma**	20
Ciao Mein	**Waikiki/O**	21
Donatoni's	**Kohala/BI**	22
Dondero's	N	**Poipu/K**	23
NEW 'Elua	**Ala Moana/O**	24
Z Ferraro's	**Wailea/Ma**	25
Z Ihilani	**Manele/L**	24
Kauai Pasta	**multi.**	21
Longhi's	**multi.**	20
Marco's Grill	**Kahului/Ma**	17
Matteo's	**Wailea/Ma**	19
Mediterraneo	**Makiki/O**	21
Paesano	**multi.**	21
Pele's Gdn.	**Lanai City/L**	19
Penne	**Lahaina/Ma**	20
Pizza Paradiso	**Lahaina/Ma**	20
Pomodoro	**Poipu/K**	23
Romano	**Ala Moana/O**	18
Sarento's Top	**Waikiki/O**	22
Sergio's	**multi.**	17
Tavola	**Diamond Head/O**	19
Town	**Kaimuki/O**	23
Verbano	S	**multi.**	18
Vino	**Restaurant Row/O**	23

JAPANESE

(* sushi specialist)

Akasaka*	**Ala Moana/O**	25
Benihana	**Waikiki/O**	18
Café O Lei*	**Kihei/Ma**	24
California Bch.*	**Ward/O**	23
Cascades*	**Kaanapali/Ma**	23
Curry Hse.	**multi.**	20
Ezogiku	**multi.**	19
Genki Sushi*	**multi.**	17
Goma Tei	**Ward/O**	21
Gyotaku	**multi.**	19
NEW Hakkei	**Makiki/O**	25
Hakone*	**multi.**	25
Hanama'ulu*	**Hanamaulu/K**	20
Ichiriki	**Ala Moana/O**	24
Imari*	**Kohala/BI**	21
NEW Kenichi*	**multi.**	24
Kintaro*	**Kapaa/K**	25
Kobe/Oku's*	**multi.**	22
Kochi	**Moiliili/O**	18
Kozo Sushi*	**multi.**	17
Kyoto Ohsho	**Ala Moana/O**	18
Makino Chaya*	**multi.**	14
Miyo's	**Hilo/BI**	22

Mr. Ojisan	**Kapahulu/O**	22
Nihon*	**Hilo/BI**	19
NEW Z Nobu*	**Waikiki/O**	26
Norio's*	**Kohala/BI**	27
Okonomiyaki	**Waikiki/O**	21
NEW Panya	**Ala Moana/O**	17
Rokkaku	**Ala Moana/O**	24
Z Sansei*	**multi.**	26
Shirokiya	**Ala Moana/O**	20
Shokudo	**Ala Moana/O**	20
Suntory	**Waikiki/O**	22
NEW Sushi Doraku*	**Waikiki/O**	-
Sushi King*	**Moiliili/O**	19
Z Sushi Sasabune*	**Makiki/O**	28
Tanaka	**multi.**	21
Tanioka's	**Waipahu/O**	24
Teshima	**Kealakekua/BI**	22
Therapy Sports*	**Hawaii Kai/O**	17
Tokyo Tei	**Wailuku/Ma**	21
Tsukuneya	**University/O**	20
NEW Wasabi	**Kapahulu/O**	22
Yanagi*	**Kakaako/O**	23
Yohei*	**Kapalama/O**	26

KOREAN

(* barbecue specialist)

Camellia*	**Moiliili/O**	20
Isana*	**Kihei/Ma**	-
Sorabol*	**Ala Moana/O**	22
Yakiniku Seoul*	**McCully/O**	22

MALAYSIAN

Green Door	**Kahala/O**	22

MEDITERRANEAN

Bar Acuda	**Hanalei/K**	23
Café 565	**Lanai City/L**	-
Casablanca	**Poipu/K**	19
Formaggio	**Kailua/O**	22
Kiawe Kitchen	**Volcano/BI**	23
Merriman's Café	**Waikoloa/BI**	20
Pavilion Café	**Ala Moana/O**	21
Plantation Hse.	**Kapalua/Ma**	24
Saffron	**Princeville/K**	20
Sarento's/Bch.	**Kihei/Ma**	23
Sergio's	**multi.**	17

MEXICAN

Cholo's	**Haleiwa/O**	18
Cilantro Grill	**Lahaina/Ma**	22
Maui Tacos	**multi.**	19
Milagros	**Paia/Ma**	21

Norberto's | **Kapaa/K**	–
Pancho/Lefty | **Kailua-Kona/BI**	15
Polli's | **Makawao/Ma**	21
NEW Taqueria Cruz | **Kihei/Ma**	–
Tropical Taco | **Hanalei/K**	21
Wahoo's Fish | **Ward/O**	17

MIDDLE EASTERN

Da Spot | **Moiliili/O**	20

NOODLE SHOPS

Ezogiku | **multi.**	19
Goma Tei | **Ward/O**	21
Hamura Saimin | **Lihue/K**	24
House/Noodles | **Kapaa/K**	22

NORTH AFRICAN

Casablanca | **Poipu/K**	19

PACIFIC RIM

Z Bali/Sea | **Waikiki/O**	24
Bamboo | **Hawi/BI**	23
Z Beach Hse. | **Poipu/K**	25
Caffe Coco | **Kapaa/K**	23
CanoeHouse | **Kohala/BI**	24
Cascades | **Kaanapali/Ma**	23
Chai's Is. | **Downtown/O**	23
Challenge/Manele | **Manele/L**	24
Coast Grille | **Kohala/BI**	20
Don/Beachcomber | **Kailua-Kona/BI**	19
Five Palms | **Kihei/Ma**	20
Gaylord's | **Lihue/K**	22
Hale Samoa | **Kailua-Kona/BI**	26
Z Hau Tree | **Waikiki/O**	21
Hilo Bay Café | **Hilo/BI**	25
Hoku's | **Kahala/O**	25
Huggos | **Kailua-Kona/BI**	19
Z Hula Grill | **multi.**	21
Hula Shores | **Kaunakakai/Mo**	–
Hulopo'e Ct. | **Manele/L**	23
Humu's | **Wailea/Ma**	22
Kamuela Provision | **Kohala/BI**	21
Kauai Hula Girl | **Kapaa/K**	19
Kawaihae Grill | **Kawaihae/BI**	20
Keoki's Paradise | **Poipu/K**	20
Kiawe Kitchen | **Volcano/BI**	23
Kukui's | **Kalapaki Bch/K**	19
Lahaina Fish | **Lahaina/Ma**	21
NEW Lanai City | **Lanai City/L**	22
Lei Lei's | **Kahuku/O**	22

Lighthouse | **Kilauea/K**	21
Z Lodge/Koele | **Koele/L**	26
Ma'alaea Grill | **Maalaea/Ma**	22
Z Mama's Fish | **Paia/Ma**	27
Naupaka Terr. | **Lihue/K**	19
Nori's | **Hilo/BI**	20
Ocean Hse. | **Waikiki/O**	23
Z Orchids | **Waikiki/O**	26
NEW Pacific Is. | **Kapaa/K**	24
Pacific'O | **Lahaina/Ma**	25
Paddlers' Inn | **Kaunakakai/Mo**	–
Pineapple Grill | **Kapalua/Ma**	23
Plantation Gdns. | **Poipu/K**	23
Prince Ct. | **multi.**	23
Z Roy's | **Kahana/Ma**	26
Z Sansei | **multi.**	26
Sea House | **Napili/Ma**	22
Z Spago | **Wailea/Ma**	26
Z 3660/Rise | **Kaimuki/O**	25
Tidepools | **Poipu/K**	24
Tiki's Grill | **Waikiki/O**	19
Wahoo | **Kapaa/K**	19

PAN-ASIAN

Blue Ginger | **Lanai City/L**	20
Daniel's | **Waimea/BI**	23
I'O Rest. | **Lahaina/Ma**	24
Lemongrass | **Kapaa/K**	17
Lihue BBQ | **Lihue/K**	20
Ocean Grill | **Manele/L**	23
NEW Pacific Is. | **Kapaa/K**	24
Spices | **Moiliili/O**	20
NEW Stage | **Ala Moana/O**	–
NEW Wild Ginger | **Kaimuki/O**	17

PIZZA

Antonio's | **multi.**	21
BJ's | **Lahaina/Ma**	19
Brick Oven | **Kalaheo/K**	24
California Pizza | **multi.**	20
Dollie's Pub | **Lahaina/Ma**	16
NEW Flatbread | **Paia/Ma**	23
Kula Lodge | **Kula/Ma**	20
Maui Brewing | **Kahana/Ma**	19
Molokai Pizza | **Kaunakakai/Mo**	19
Pizza Paradiso | **Lahaina/Ma**	20
Round Table | **multi.**	18

PUB FOOD

Dollie's Pub | **Lahaina/Ma**	16
Kona Brewing | **Kailua-Kona/BI**	18
NEW Waimea Brew | **Waimea/K**	19

SANDWICHES

Ba-Le | multi.	20
Experience/Koele | Koele/L	22
Kalapaki Hut | Kalapaki Bch/K	22
Kua 'Aina | multi.	22
Marco's Grill | Kahului/Ma	17
Molokai Pizza | Kaunakakai/Mo	19
Kippy's | multi.	16

SEAFOOD

Alexander's | Kihei/Ma	22
Blane's | Hilo/BI	15
Brennecke's | Poipu/K	18
Brown's Bch. | Kohala/BI	25
Bubba Gump | multi.	15
Buzz's Wharf | Maalaea/Ma	19
Café O Lei | Kihei/Ma	24
CJ's Steak | Princeville/K	17
🆕 DUO | Wailea/Ma	24
Five Palms | Kihei/Ma	20
Hanalei Dolphin | Hanalei/K	22
🎇 Hau Tree | Waikiki/O	21
Huggos | Kailua-Kona/BI	19
Jameson's | multi.	19
Kalypso Island | Hanalei/K	16
Kamuela Provision | Kohala/BI	21
Kawaihae Grill | Kawaihae/BI	20
Kimo's | Lahaina/Ma	20
Kincaid's | Ward/O	20
🎇 Koloa Fish | Koloa/K	25
Lahaina Fish | Lahaina/Ma	21
Leilani's | Kaanapali/Ma	21
Lei Lei's | Kahuku/O	22
Lemongrass | Kapaa/K	17
Longhi's | multi.	20
Makino Chaya | multi.	14
Mala | multi.	25
🎇 Mama's Fish | Paia/Ma	27
Nick's Fishmkt. | Waikiki/O	22
Nick's Fishmkt. | Wailea/Ma	25
Nico's/Pier 38 | Iwilei/O	23
Nori's | Hilo/BI	20
Oceanarium | Waikiki/O	17
Ocean Grill | Manele/L	23
Ocean Hse. | Waikiki/O	23
Pacific'O | Lahaina/Ma	25
🎇 Pahu | Kaupulehu-Kona/BI	26
Paia Fish | Paia/Ma	24
Postcards Café | Hanalei/K	24
Quinn's | Kailua-Kona/BI	18

🎇 Roy's | Poipu/K	26
🎇 Sansei | multi.	26
Seaside Rest. | Hilo/BI	23
SeaWatch | Wailea/Ma	22
Shells | Poipu/K	20
Shrimp Sta. | Waimea/K	24
🎇 Son'z | Kaanapali/Ma	24
🆕 Stage | Ala Moana/O	-
Tanioka's | Waipahu/O	24
Tidepools | Poipu/K	24
🆕 Uncle's Fish | Iwilei/O	18
Wahoo | Kapaa/K	19
Waterfront | Maalaea/Ma	25

SINGAPOREAN

Green Door | Kahala/O	22

SMALL PLATES

Bar Acuda | Med. | Hanalei/K	23
Brasserie/Vin | French | Chinatown/O	20
E&O | SE Asian | Ward/O	20
Formaggio | Med. | Kaimuki/O	22
🎇 Hiroshi | Eurasian | Restaurant Row/O	26
Mr. Ojisan | Japanese | Kapahulu/O	22
Vino | Italian | Restaurant Row/O	23

SOUTHEAST ASIAN

E&O | Ward/O	20
Spices | Moiliili/O	20

STEAKHOUSES

🆕 Beachhse. | Waikiki/O	21
Bull Shed | Kapaa/K	17
Buzz's | Lanikai/O	19
Buzz's Wharf | Maalaea/Ma	19
Café O Lei | Kihei/Ma	24
CJ's Steak | Princeville/K	17
d.k Steak | Waikiki/O	22
🆕 DUO | Wailea/Ma	24
Hy's Steak | Waikiki/O	25
Jameson's | multi.	19
Kamuela Provision | Kohala/BI	21
Kincaid's | Ward/O	20
Kobe/Oku's | multi.	22
Leilani's | Kaanapali/Ma	21
Lei Lei's | Kahuku/O	22
Makawao Steak | Makawao/Ma	22
Morton's | Ala Moana/O	25
Outback | multi.	16

Poipu Broiler | **Poipu/K**	19	Singha Thai | **Waikiki/O**	21
NEW RB Black Angus | **Kahana/Ma**	_	Sweet Basil | **Downtown/O**	19
		Thai Cuisine | **Kihei/Ma**	23
🅱 Ruth's Chris | **multi.**	25	Thai Thai | **Volcano/BI**	24
Shells | **Poipu/K**	20		
🅱 Son'z | **Kaanapali/Ma**	24		

VEGETARIAN

(* vegan)

TEAROOMS

Pacific Place | **Ala Moana/O**	_	Blossoming Lotus* | **Kapaa/K**	24
		Hanapepe Café | **Hanapepe/K**	22
		Postcards Café | **Hanalei/K**	24

THAI

Bangkok Hse. | **Kailua-Kona/BI**	22	Stella Blues* | **Kihei/Ma**	19

Chiang Mai Thai | **Moiliili/O**	22
Haleiwa Eats Thai | **Haleiwa/O**	26

VIETNAMESE

Keo's | **Waikiki/O**	21	A Saigon Café | **Wailuku/Ma**	23
Mekong Thai | **multi.**	25	Asian Star | **Wailuku/Ma**	20
Orchid Thai | **Kailua-Kona/BI**	24	Bac Nam | **Downtown/O**	24
Phuket Thai | **multi.**	25	Ba-Le | **multi.**	20
Saeng's Thai | **Wailuku/Ma**	20	Duc's Bistro | **Chinatown/O**	24
		Hale Vietnam | **Kaimuki/O**	23
		Vietnam/Pho | **Chinatown/O**	19

Dining Locations

Includes restaurant names, cuisines and Food ratings.

Big Island

CAPTAIN COOK

Manago | *Amer./Hawaiian* — 21

HAWI

Bamboo | *Pac. Rim* — 23

HILO

Blane's | *Hawaiian* — 15
Café 100 | *Amer./Hawaiian* — 19
Café Pesto | *Eclectic* — 23
Hilo Bay Café | *Pac. Rim* — 25
Ken's/Pancakes | *Amer./Diner* — 19
Kuhio Grille | *Hawaiian* — 21
L&L Drive-Inn | *BBQ/Hawaiian* — 16
Maui Tacos | *Mexican* — 19
Miyo's | *Japanese* — 22
Nihon | *Japanese* — 19
Nori's | *Hawaiian/Pac.Rim* — 20
Seaside Rest. | *Seafood* — 23

HONAUNAU

Ke'ei Café | *Eclectic* — 24

KAILUA-KONA

Ba-Le | *Viet.* — 20
Bangkok Hse. | *Thai* — 22
Big Island Grill | *Amer.* — 21
Bubba Gump | *Amer./Seafood* — 15
Don/Beachcomber | *Pac. Rim* — 19
Hale Samoa | *French/Pac. Rim* — 26
Harbor Hse. | *Amer.* — 19
Huggos | *Pac. Rim/Seafood* — 19
Jackie Rey's | *Eclectic* — 21
Jameson's | *Seafood/Steak* — 19
Kona Brewing | *Amer.* — 18
Kona Mix | *Hawaiian* — 21
La Bourgogne | *French* — 25
L&L Drive-Inn | *BBQ/Hawaiian* — 16
Orchid Thai | *Thai* — 24
Outback | *Steak* — 16
Pancho/Lefty | *Mex.* — 15
Quinn's | *Seafood* — 18
U-Top-It | *Hawaiian* — 23

KAMUELA

L&L Drive-Inn | *BBQ/Hawaiian* — 16
Paniolo | *Eclectic* — 16

KAUPULEHU-KONA

Beach Tree | *Cal./Italian* — 23
🅩 Hualalai Grille | *Hawaii Reg.* — 28
🅩 Pahu | *Hawaii Reg./Seafood* — 26

KAWAIHAE HARBOR

Café Pesto | *Eclectic* — 23
Kawaihae Grill | *Pac. Rim/Seafood* — 20

KEAAU

L&L Drive-Inn | *BBQ/Hawaiian* — 16

KEALAKEKUA

Teshima | *Japanese* — 22

KEAUHOU

NEW Kenichi | — 24
   Asian Fusion/Japanese
Peaberry/Galette | *French* — 21

KOHALA COAST

Brown's Bch. | *Seafood* — 25
CanoeHouse | *Pac. Rim* — 24
Coast Grille | *Pac. Rim* — 20
Donatoni's | *Italian* — 22
Imari | *Japanese* — 21
Kamuela Provision | *Pac. Rim* — 21
NEW Kenichi | — 24
   Asian Fusion/Japanese
Norio's | *Japanese* — 27
🅩 Roy's | *Hawaii Reg.* — 26
🅩 Ruth's Chris | *Steak* — 25
🅩 Sansei | *Japanese/Pac. Rim* — 26
Tommy Bahama | — 20
   Asian Fusion/Carib.

PAHOA

L&L Drive-Inn | *BBQ/Hawaiian* — 16

VOLCANO

Kiawe Kitchen | *Med./Pac. Rim* — 23
Kilauea Lodge | *Eclectic* — 23
Thai Thai | *Thai* — 24
Volcano Golf | *Amer.* — 15

WAIKOLOA

Merriman's Café | *Med.* — 20

WAIMEA

Daniel's | *Hawaii Reg./Pan-Asian* — 23
🅩 Merriman's | *Hawaii Reg.* — 27

Kauai

ANAHOLA

Duane's Ono | Burgers — 23

HANALEI

Bar Acuda | Med. — 23
Bubba Burger | Burgers — 21
Hanalei Dolphin | Seafood — 22
Hanalei Gourmet | Amer./Eclectic — 21
Kalypso Island | Seafood — 16
Polynesia Café | Eclectic — 18
Postcards Café | Eclectic — 24
Tropical Taco | Mex. — 21

HANAMAULU

Hanama'ulu | Japanese/Tea — 20

HANAPEPE

Hanapepe Café | Bakery/Veg. — 22

KALAHEO

Brick Oven | Italian/Pizza — 24
Kalaheo Café | Coffee — 23

KALAPAKI BEACH

Cafe Portofino | Italian — 21
🅩 Duke's | Amer. — 19
Kalapaki Hut | Burgers/Sandwiches — 22
Kukui's | Pac. Rim — 19

KAPAA

Blossoming Lotus | Vegan — 24
Bubba Burger | Burgers — 21
Bull Shed | Steak — 17
Caffe Coco | Health/Pac. Rim — 23
Eggbert's | Amer. — 18
House/Noodles | Noodle Shop — 22
Hukilau | Hawaii Reg. — 25
Kauai Hula Girl | Pac. Rim — 19
Kauai Pasta | Italian — 21
Kintaro | Japanese — 25
L&L Drive-Inn | BBQ/Hawaiian — 16
Lemongrass | Pan-Asian/Seafood — 17
Norberto's | Mex. — -
Ono Family | Amer./Hawaiian — 19
NEW Pacific Is. | — 24
   Pac. Rim/Pan-Asian
Scotty's BBQ | BBQ — 22
Wahoo | Pac. Rim/Seafood — 19

KILAUEA

Lighthouse | Pac. Rim — 21

KOLOA

🅩 Koloa Fish | Hawaiian/Seafood — 25
TomKat's | Amer. — 18

LIHUE

Dani's | Hawaiian — 20
Garden Is. | BBQ/Chinese — 19
Gaylord's | Pac. Rim — 22
Genki Sushi | Japanese — 17
Hamura Saimin | Noodle Shop — 24
Kauai Pasta | Italian — 21
L&L Drive-Inn | BBQ/Hawaiian — 16
Lihue BBQ | Amer./Pan-Asian — 20
NEW Market St. | Diner — -
Naupaka Terr. | Pac. Rim — 19
Oki Diner | Bakery/Hawaiian — 15

NAWILIWILI

JJ's Broiler | Amer. — 17

POIPU

🅩 Beach Hse. | Pac. Rim — 25
Brennecke's | Amer./Seafood — 18
Casablanca | African/Med. — 19
Casa di Amici | Eclectic/Italian — 23
Dondero's | Italian — 23
Keoki's Paradise | Pac. Rim — 20
Plantation Gdns. | Pac. Rim — 23
Poipu Broiler | Amer./Steak — 19
Pomodoro | Italian — 23
🅩 Roy's | Hawaii Reg. — 26
Shells | Seafood/Steak — 20
Tidepools | Pac. Rim/Seafood — 24

PRINCEVILLE

CJ's Steak | Seafood/Steak — 17
Saffron | Med. — 20

WAIMEA

Barefoot Burger | Burgers — 18
Shrimp Sta. | Seafood — 24
NEW Waimea Brew | Eclectic/Pub — 19

Lanai

KOELE

Experience/Koele | Sandwiches — 22
🅩 Lodge/Koele | Pac. Rim — 26
Terrace | Amer. — 23

LANAI CITY

Blue Ginger | Amer./Pan-Asian — 20
Café 565 | Amer./Med. — -

Canoes Lanai | Amer./Hawaiian 17
NEW Lanai City | Pac. Rim 22
Pele's Gdn. | Amer./Italian 19

MANELE

Challenge/Manele | Pac. Rim 24
Hulopo'e Ct. | Pac. Rim 23
☑ Ihilani | Italian 24
Ocean Grill | Pan-Asian/Seafood 23

Maui

HAIKU

Colleen's | Amer. -

HANA

Hana Ranch | Amer./Burgers 22

KAANAPALI

Cascades | Japanese/Pac. Rim 23
Castaway | Continental 22
China Boat/Bowl | Chinese 16
CJ's Deli | Amer. 18
☑ Hula Grill | Pac. Rim 21
Leilani's | Seafood/Steak 21
OnO B&G | Amer./Hawaiian 21
Round Table | Pizza 18
☑ Son'z | Seafood/Steak 24
Tiki Terr. | Hawaii Reg. 19

KAHANA

Maui Brewing | Eclectic/Pizza 19
NEW RB Black Angus | Steak -
☑ Roy's | Hawaii Reg. 26

KAHULUI

Ba-Le | Viet. 20
Da Kitchen | Hawaiian 22
Dragon Dragon | Chinese 20
Koho | Amer. 18
L&L Drive-Inn | BBQ/Hawaiian 16
Marco's Grill | Italian 17
Maui Tacos | Mexican 19
Ruby's | Diner 17
NEW Sammy's | Amer. -
Zippy's | Amer. 16

KAPALUA

Banyan Tree | Eclectic 24
☑ Merriman's | Hawaii Reg. 27
Pineapple Grill | Pac. Rim 23
Plantation Hse. | Med. 24
☑ Sansei | Japanese/Pac. Rim 26

KIHEI

Alexander's | Amer. 22
Aroma D'Italia | Italian 18
Café O Lei | Seafood/Steak 24
Da Kitchen | Hawaiian 22
Five Palms | Pac. Rim/Seafood 20
Isana | Korean -
Kihei Caffe | Amer. 23
L&L Drive-Inn | BBQ/Hawaiian 16
Maui Tacos | Mexican 19
Outback | Steak 16
Peggy Sue's | Diner 17
Round Table | Pizza 18
☑ Roy's | Hawaii Reg. 26
☑ Sansei | Japanese/Pac. Rim 26
Sarento's/Bch. | Med. 23
Stella Blues | Amer. 19
NEW Taqueria Cruz | Mex. -
Thai Cuisine | Thai 23

KULA

Grandma's | Coffee 20
Kula Lodge | Amer. 20

LAHAINA

Aloha Mix Plate | Hawaiin 21
Ba-Le | Viet. 20
BJ's | Pizza 19
Bubba Gump | Amer./Seafood 15
Cheeseburger/Paradise | Amer. 17
China Boat/Bowl | Chinese 16
Cilantro Grill | Mex. 22
Dollie's Pub | Amer. 16
Genki Sushi | Japanese 17
☑ Gerard's | French 28
Hard Rock | Amer. 14
I'O Rest. | Pan-Asian 24
Kimo's | Amer./Seafood 20
Kobe/Oku's | Japanese 22
Lahaina Coolers | Eclectic 18
Lahaina Fish | Pac. Rim/Seafood 21
Lahaina Grill | Amer. 26
Lahaina Store | Amer./Hawaiian 18
L&L Drive-Inn | BBQ/Hawaiian 16
Longhi's | Italian 20
Mala | Hawaii Reg./Seafood 25
Maui Tacos | Mexican 19
Outback | Steak 16
Pacific'O | Pac. Rim/Seafood 25
Penne | Italian 20
Pioneer Inn | Amer. 15

Pizza Paradiso | *Italian*	20
Z Ruth's Chris | *Steak*	25

MAALAEA

Buzz's Wharf | *Seafood/Steak*	19
Ma'alaea Grill | *Pac. Rim*	22
Waterfront | *Seafood*	25

MAKAWAO

Casanova | *Italian*	20
Z Hali'imaile Gen. | *Hawaii Reg.*	27
Makawao Steak | *Steak*	22
Polli's | *Mex.*	21
T. Komoda | *Bakery*	24

MAKENA

Hakone | *Japanese*	25
Prince Ct. | *Amer./Pac. Rim*	23

NAPILI

Gazebo | *Amer.*	24
Mama's Ribs | *BBQ*	21
Maui Tacos | *Mexican*	19
Sea House | *Pac. Rim*	22

OLOWALU

Chez Paul | *French*	26

PAIA

Anthony's Coffee | *Coffee*	20
Café Mambo | *Eclectic*	23
Charley's | *Amer.*	19
NEW Flatbread | *Pizza*	23
Z Mama's Fish | *Seafood*	27
Milagros | *Mex.*	21
Paia Fish | *Seafood*	24

WAILEA

Capische? | *Italian*	25
NEW DUO | *Seafood/Steak*	24
Z Ferraro's | *Italian*	25
Humu's | *Pac. Rim*	22
Joe's B&G | *Amer.*	22
Longhi's | *Italian*	20
Mala | *Hawaii Reg./Seafood*	25
Matteo's | *Italian*	19
Nick's Fishmkt. | *Seafood*	25
Z Ruth's Chris | *Steak*	25
SeaWatch | *Seafood*	22
Z Spago | *Cal./Pac. Rim*	26
Tommy Bahama | *Asian Fusion/Carib.*	20

WAILUKU

AK's | *Amer.*	20
A Saigon Café | *Viet.*	23
Asian Star | *Viet.*	20
Kozo Sushi | *Japanese*	17
L&L Drive-Inn | *BBQ/Hawaiian*	16
Saeng's Thai | *Thai*	20
Tasty Crust | *Amer./Hawaiian*	19
Tokyo Tei | *Japanese*	21

Molokai

KAUNAKAKAI

Hula Shores | *Amer./Pac. Rim*	–
Kanemitsu's | *Bakery*	–
Molokai Dr. | *Amer.*	–
Molokai Pizza | *Pizza*	19
Oviedo | *Filipino*	–
Paddlers' Inn | *Amer./Pac. Rim*	–

MANAE

Mana'e Goods | *Amer.*	–

Oahu

AIEA

Ba-Le | *Viet.*	20
Big City Diner | *Amer.*	18
California Pizza | *Pizza*	20
Curry Hse. | *Japanese*	20
Dixie Grill | *BBQ/Crab*	16
Ezogiku | *Japanese/Noodle Shop*	19
Ige's/19th Puka | *Amer.*	19
Kozo Sushi | *Japanese*	17
Makino Chaya | *Japanese*	14
Paesano | *Italian*	21
Tony Roma | *BBQ*	19
Verbano | *Italian*	18

ALA MOANA

Aaron's | *Continental*	20
Akasaka | *Japanese*	25
Assaggio | *Italian*	21
Ba-Le | *Viet.*	20
Bubba Gump | *Amer./Seafood*	15
California Pizza | *Pizza*	20
Curry Hse. | *Japanese*	20
NEW 'Elua | *French/Italian*	24
Genki Sushi | *Japanese*	17
Ichiriki | *Japanese*	24
I Love Country | *Amer.*	17

and Burger | *Burgers* — 18
rin | *Chinese* — 24
oto Ohsho | *Japanese* — 18
nghi's | *Italian* — 20
ariposa | *Amer.* — 22
ekong Thai | *Thai* — 25
ermaid Bar | *Amer.* — 21
orton's | *Steak* — 25
riginal Pancake | *Diner* — 21
cific Place | *Tea* — -
goda | *Eclectic* — 16
🆕 Panya | *French/Japanese* — 17
vilion Café | *Med.* — 21
neapple Rm. | *Hawaii Reg.* — 25
antation Café | *Amer.* — 17
kkaku | *Japanese* — 24
omano | *Italian* — 18
uby Tues. | *Amer.* — 15
irokiya | *Japanese* — 20
okudo | *Japanese* — 20
de St. Inn | *Amer.* — 25
rabol | *Korean* — 22
🆕 Stage | *Amer./Pan-Asian* — -
naka | *Japanese* — 21
ony Roma | *BBQ* — 19
u Hungry? | *Hawaiian* — 18
ppy's | *Amer.* — 16

HINATOWN

a-Le | *Viet.* — 20
asserie/Vin | *French* — 20
uc's Bistro | *French/Viet.* — 24
digo | *Asian Fusion* — 22
egend Sea. | *Chinese* — 23
ttle Village | *Chinese* — 23
akino Chaya | *Japanese* — 14
ei Sum | *Chinese* — 21
etnam/Pho | *Viet.* — 19

IAMOND HEAD

&L Drive-Inn | *BBQ/Hawaiian* — 16
avola | *Italian* — 19

OWNTOWN

untie Pasto | *Italian* — 17
ac Nam | *Viet.* — 24
a-Le | *Viet.* — 20
hai's Is. | *Pac. Rim* — 23
🆕 Downtown | *Amer.* — -
yotaku | *Japanese* — 19

L&L Drive-Inn | *BBQ/Hawaiian* — 16
People's Café | *Hawaiian* — 21
Sweet Basil | *Thai* — 19
🆕 Tangö | *Amer.* — -

HALEIWA

Cholo's | *Mex.* — 18
Haleiwa Eats Thai | *Thai* — 26
Jameson's | *Seafood/Steak* — 19
Kua 'Aina | *Burgers/Sandwiches* — 22
Matsumoto's | *Dessert* — 24

HAWAII KAI

Assaggio | *Italian* — 21
Ba-Le | *Viet.* — 20
Kona Brewing | *Amer.* — 18
Outback | *Steak* — 16
🇿 Roy's | *Hawaii Reg.* — 26
Therapy Sports | *Amer.* — 17
Zippy's | *Amer.* — 16

IWILEI

Nico's/Pier 38 | *Seafood* — 23
Sam Choy's | *Hawaii Reg.* — 20
🆕 Uncle's Fish | *Seafood* — 18

KAHALA

Antonio's | *Pizza* — 21
Ba-Le | *Viet.* — 20
California Pizza | *Pizza* — 20
Green Door | *Malaysian/Singaporean* — 22
Hoku's | *Pac. Rim* — 25
Kozo Sushi | *Japanese* — 17
L&L Drive-Inn | *BBQ/Hawaiian* — 16
Olive Tree | *Greek* — 24
Zippy's | *Amer.* — 16

KAHUKU

Lei Lei's | *Pac. Rim* — 22
Ola | *Hawaii Reg.* — 21

KAILUA

Assaggio | *Italian* — 21
Baci Bistro | *Italian* — 24
Ba-Le | *Viet.* — 20
Big City Diner | *Amer.* — 18
Formaggio | *Med.* — 22
Lucy's Grill | *Eclectic* — 18
Round Table | *Pizza* — 18
Zippy's | *Amer.* — 16

DINING

LOCATIONS

KAIMUKI

Big City Diner	*Amer.*	18
NEW Fat Greek	*Greek*	19
Formaggio	*Med.*	22
Hale Vietnam	*Viet.*	23
⚡ 3660/Rise	*Pac. Rim*	25
town	*Amer./Italian*	23
12th Ave.	*Amer.*	23
NEW Wild Ginger	*Pan-Asian*	17
Zippy's	*Amer.*	16

KAKAAKO

Yanagi	*Japanese*	23

KALIHI

⚡ Helena's	*Hawaiian*	26
Zippy's	*Amer.*	16

KANEOHE

Pah Ke's	*Chinese*	23
Zippy's	*Amer.*	16

KAPAHULU

NEW Burgers/Edge	*Burgers*	-
Hee Hing	*Chinese*	20
India Café	*Indian*	19
Kozo Sushi	*Japanese*	17
Mr. Ojisan	*Japanese*	22
Ono Hawaii	*Hawaiian*	25
Sergio's	*Italian/Med.*	17
NEW Wasabi	*Japanese*	22
Zippy's	*Amer.*	16

KAPALAMA

Original Pancake	*Diner*	21
Yohei	*Japanese*	26
Young's Fish	*Hawaiian*	24

KAPOLEI

Assaggio	*Italian*	21
Outback	*Steak*	16
⚡ Roy's	*Hawaii Reg.*	26

LANIKAI

Buzz's	*Steak*	19

MAKIKI

Cafe Sistina	*Italian*	21
NEW Hakkei	*Japanese*	25
Mediterraneo	*Italian*	21
⚡ Sushi Sasabune	*Japanese*	28

MAKIKI HEIGHTS

Contemp. Café	*Amer.*	1

MANOA

Ba-Le	*Viet.*	2
Paesano	*Italian*	2

MCCULLY

⚡ Alan Wong's	*Hawaii Reg.*	2
Curry Hse.	*Japanese*	2
Phuket Thai	*Thai*	2
Yakiniku Seoul	*Korean*	2

MILILANI

Assaggio	*Italian*	2
L&L Drive-Inn	*BBQ/Hawaiian*	1
Maui Tacos	*Mexican*	1
Phuket Thai	*Thai*	2
Ruby Tues.	*Amer.*	1
Zippy's	*Amer.*	1

MOANALUA

Ruby Tues.	*Amer.*	1

MOILIILI

Camellia	*Korean*	2
⚡ Chef Mavro	*French/Hawaii Reg.*	2
Chiang Mai Thai	*Thai*	2
Curry Hse.	*Japanese*	2
Da Spot	*Mideastern*	2
Fook Yuen	*Chinese*	2
Kochi	*Japanese*	1
Kozo Sushi	*Japanese*	1
Mekong Thai	*Thai*	2
Spices	*Pan-Asian*	2
Sushi King	*Japanese*	1
Willows	*Amer./Hawaiian*	1

NIU VALLEY

Gyotaku	*Japanese*	1
⚡ Le Bistro	*French*	2

PEARL CITY

Antonio's	*Pizza*	2
Ba-Le	*Viet.*	2
Buzz's	*Steak*	1
Ezogiku	*Japanese/Noodle Shop*	1
Gyotaku	*Japanese*	1
Kozo Sushi	*Japanese*	1

PEARL HARBOR

L&L Drive-Inn | *BBQ/Hawaiian* 16

RESTAURANT ROW

Z Hiroshi | *Eurasian* 26
Z Ruth's Chris | *Steak* 25
Vino | *Itallan* 23

UNIVERSITY

Ezogiku | *Japanese/Noodle Shop* 19
Tsukuneya | *Japanese* 20

WAIKIKI

Arancino | *Italian* 22
Z Bali/Sea | *Pac. Rim* 24
NEW Beachhse. | *Amer./Steak* 21
Benihana | *Japanese* 18
California Pizza | *Pizza* 20
Cheeseburger/Paradise | *Amer.* 17
Cheesecake Fac. | *Amer.* 21
Ciao Mein | *Chinese/Italian* 21
Diamond Head | *Eclectic* 22
d.k Steak | *Steak* 22
Z Duke's | *Amer.* 19
Eggs 'n Things | *Amer.* 23
Ezogiku | *Japanese/Noodle Shop* 19
Hakone | *Japanese* 25
Hard Rock | *Amer.* 14
Z Hau Tree | *Pac. Rim* 21
Z Hula Grill | *Pac. Rim* 21
Hy's Steak | *Steak* 25
Keo's | *Thai* 21
Kobe/Oku's | *Japanese* 22
Z La Mer | *French* 27
L&L Drive-Inn | *BBQ/Hawaiian* 16
NEW MAC 24/7 | *Amer.* 19
Maui Tacos | *Mexican* 19
Z Michel's | *French* 25
Nick's Fishmkt. | *Seafood/Steak* 22
NEW Z Nobu | *Japanese* 26
Oceanarium | *Amer./Seafood* 17
Ocean Hse. | *Pac. Rim/Seafood* 23
Okonomiyaki | *Japanese* 21
Z Orchids | *Pac. Rim* 26

Outback | *Steak* 16
P.F. Chang's | *Chinese* 19
Planet Hollywood | *Cal.* 12
Prince Ct. | *Amer./Pac. Rim* 23
Round Table | *Pizza* 18
Z Roy's | *Hawaii Reg.* 26
Z Ruth's Chris | *Steak* 25
Z Sansei | *Japanese/Pac. Rim* 26
Sarento's Top | *Italian* 22
Sergio's | *Italian/Med.* 17
Shore Bird | *Amer.* 19
Singha Thai | *Thai* 21
Suntory | *Japanese* 22
NEW Sushi Doraku | *Japanese* -
Tanaka | *Japanese* 21
Tiki's Grill | *Pac. Rim* 19
Tony Roma | *BBQ* 19
Verbano | *Italian* 18
Wailana Coffee | *Diner* 17

WAIPAHU

Auntie Pasto | *Italian* 17
Big City Diner | *Amer.* 18
Highway Inn | *Diner* 23
Outback | *Steak* 16
Tanioka's | *Japanese/Seafood* 24
Verbano | *Italian* 18
Zippy's | *Amer.* 16

WARD

Ba-Le | *Viet.* 20
Big City Diner | *Amer.* 18
California Bch. | *Japanese* 23
Chowder Hse. | *Seafood* 16
E&O | *SE Asian* 20
Genki Sushi | *Japanese* 17
Goma Tei | *Japanese/Noodle Shop* 21
Kaka'ako | *Hawaiian* 21
Kincaid's | *Seafood/Steak* 20
Kua 'Aina | *Burgers/Sandwiches* 22
L&L Drive-Inn | *BBQ/Hawaiian* 16
P.F. Chang's | *Chinese* 19
Phuket Thai | *Thai* 25
Wahoo's Fish | *Mex.* 17

DINING

LOCATIONS

Dining Special Features

Listings cover the best in each category and include names, locations and Food ratings. Multi-location restaurants' features may vary by branch.

BREAKFAST

(See also Hotel Dining)

Anthony's Coffee	**Paia/Ma**	20
Big City Diner	**multi.**	18
Blue Ginger	**Lanai City/L**	20
Café 100	**Hilo/BI**	19
CJ's Deli	**Kaanapali/Ma**	18
Dani's	**Lihue/K**	20
Eggbert's	**Kapaa/K**	18
Eggs 'n Things	**Waikiki/O**	23
Grandma's	**Kula/Ma**	20
Kihei Caffe	**Kihei/Ma**	23
Kimo's	**Lahaina/Ma**	20
Oki Diner	**Lihue/K**	15
Ono Family	**Kapaa/K**	19
Original Pancake	**multi.**	21
Paniolo	**Kamuela/BI**	16
Postcards Café	**Hanalei/K**	24
Ruby's	**Kahului/Ma**	17
Sam Choy's	**Iwilei/O**	20
Wailana Coffee	**Waikiki/O**	17

BRUNCH

Daniel's	**Waimea/BI**	23
Hoku's	**Kahala/O**	25
Kozo Sushi	**Kahala/O**	17
Mariposa	**Ala Moana/O**	22
☑ Michel's	**Waikiki/O**	25
☑ Orchids	**Waikiki/O**	26
☑ Pahu	**Kaupulehu-Kona/BI**	26
Sam Choy's	**Iwilei/O**	20

BUFFET

(Check availability)

Beach Tree	**Kaupulehu-Kona/BI**	23
Camellia	**Moiliili/O**	20
☑ Duke's	**Waikiki/O**	19
Fook Yuen	**Moiliili/O**	20
Hakone	**Waikiki/O**	25
Hoku's	**Kahala/O**	25
Indigo	**Chinatown/O**	22
Kona Brewing	**Kailua-Kona/BI**	18
Makino Chaya	**multi.**	14
Naupaka Terr.	**Lihue/K**	19
Oceanarium	**Waikiki/O**	17
☑ Orchids	**Waikiki/O**	26

Pagoda	**Ala Moana/O**	16
Prince Ct.	**Makena/Ma**	23
Shells	**Poipu/K**	20
Shirokiya	**Ala Moana/O**	20
Shore Bird	**Waikiki/O**	19

BUSINESS DINING

☑ Alan Wong's	**McCully/O**	28
☑ Bali/Sea	**Waikiki/O**	24
NEW Beachhse.	**Waikiki/O**	21
☑ Chef Mavro	**Moiliili/O**	26
Diamond Head	**Waikiki/O**	22
Dondero's	**Poipu/K**	23
Hoku's	**Kahala/O**	25
Hy's Steak	**Waikiki/O**	25
Indigo	**Chinatown/O**	22
Kincaid's	**Ward/O**	20
☑ La Mer	**Waikiki/O**	27
Morton's	**Ala Moana/O**	25
Nick's Fishmkt.	**Waikiki/O**	22
NEW ☑ Nobu	**Waikiki/O**	26
Ola	**Kahuku/O**	21
☑ Orchids	**Waikiki/O**	26
☑ Roy's	**Hawaii Kai/O**	26
☑ 3660/Rise	**Kaimuki/O**	25

BYO

Antonio's	**multi.**	21
Bac Nam	**Downtown/O**	24
Barefoot Burger	**Waimea/K**	18
Big Island Grill	**Kailua-Kona/BI**	21
Bubba Burger	**multi.**	21
Café 565	**Lanai City/L**	-
Caffe Coco	**Kapaa/K**	23
Canoes Lanai	**Lanai City/L**	17
Cilantro Grill	**Lahaina/Ma**	22
CJ's Deli	**Kaanapali/Ma**	18
Contemp. Café	**Makiki Hts/O**	19
Duane's Ono	**Anahola/K**	23
NEW Fat Greek	**Kaimuki/O**	19
Genki Sushi	**multi.**	17
NEW Hakkei	**Makiki/O**	25
Haleiwa Eats Thai	**Haleiwa/O**	26
Hanapepe Café	**Hanapepe/K**	22
☑ Helena's	**Kalihi/O**	26
Little Village	**Chinatown/O**	23

Mekong Thai | **Moiliili/O** 25
Miyo's | **Hilo/BI** 22
Oki Diner | **Lihue/K** 15
Olive Tree | **Kahala/O** 24
Ono Family | **Kapaa/K** 19
Orchid Thai | **Kailua-Kona/BI** 24
Pah Ke's | **Kaneohe/O** 23
Phuket Thai | **McCully/O** 25
Polynesia Café | **Hanalei/K** 18
NEW Taqueria Cruz | **Kihei/Ma** ─
Tropical Taco | **Hanalei/K** 21

CELEBRITY CHEFS

Z Alan Wong's | *Alan Wong* | **McCully/O** 28
Bar Acuda | *Jim Moffat* | **Hanalei/K** 23
Chai's Is. | *Chai Chaoawasaree* | **Downtown/O** 23
Z Chef Mavro | *George Mavrothalassitis* | **Moiliili/O** 26
d.k Steak | *D.K. Kodama* | **Waikiki/O** 22
NEW 'Elua | *Donato Loperfido & Philippe Padovani* | **Ala Moana/O** 24
Z Gerard's | *Gerard Reversade* | **Lahaina/Ma** 28
NEW Hakkei | *Seiya Masahara* | **Makiki/O** 25
Z Hali'imaile Gen. | *Beverly Gannon* | **Makawao/Ma** 27
Z Hiroshi | *Hiroshi Fukui* | **Restaurant Row/O** 26
Joe's B&G | *Beverly Gannon* | **Wailea/Ma** 22
Kalaheo Café | *John Ferguson* | **Kalaheo/K** 23
Z Lodge/Koele | *Oliver Beckert* | **Koele/L** 26
Mala | *Mark Ellman* | **Wailea/Ma** 25
Nico's/Pier 38 | *Nicolas Chaize* | **Iwilei/O** 23
NEW Z Nobu | *Nobu Matsuhisa* | **Waikiki/O** 26
Ola | *Fred DeAngelo* | **Kahuku/O** 21
Pineapple Rm. | *Alan Wong* | **Ala Moana/O** 25
Z Roy's | *Roy Yamaguchi* | **Hawaii Kai/O** 26
Sam Choy's | *Sam Choy* | **Iwilei/O** 20
Z Sansei | *D.K. Kodama* | **Waikiki/O** 26
town | *Ed Kenney* | **Kaimuki/O** 23

DANCING

Aaron's | **Ala Moana/O** 20
Auntie Pasto | **Waipahu/O** 17
Casanova | **Makawao/Ma** 20
Chai's Is. | **Downtown/O** 23
Diamond Head | **Waikiki/O** 22
E&O | **Ward/O** 20
NEW Flatbread | **Paia/Ma** 23
Hard Rock | **Waikiki/O** 14
Kobe/Oku's | **Lahaina/Ma** 22
Lahaina Store | **Lahaina/Ma** 18
NEW Lanai City | **Lanai City/L** 22
Longhi's | **Lahaina/Ma** 20
Z Sansei | **Waikiki/O** 26

DINING ALONE

(Other than hotels and places with counter service)
Barefoot Burger | **Waimea/K** 18
Big City Diner | **multi.** 18
Blue Ginger | **Lanai City/L** 20
Bubba Burger | **multi.** 21
Canoes Lanai | **Lanai City/L** 17
Curry Hse. | **Ala Moana/O** 20
Dani's | **Lihue/K** 20
Da Spot | **Moiliili/O** 20
Duane's Ono | **Anahola/K** 23
Eggs 'n Things | **Waikiki/O** 23
Ezogiku | **multi.** 19
NEW Fat Greek | **Kaimuki/O** 19
Genki Sushi | **multi.** 17
Goma Tei | **Ward/O** 21
Hale Vietnam | **Kaimuki/O** 23
Hamura Saimin | **Lihue/K** 24
Hanalei Gourmet | **Hanalei/K** 21
Hanapepe Café | **Hanapepe/K** 22
Z Helena's | **Kalihi/O** 26
House/Noodles | **Kapaa/K** 22
I Love Country | **Ala Moana/O** 17
Island Burger | **Ala Moana/O** 18
Kaka'ako | **Ward/O** 21
Kalapaki Hut | **Kalapaki Bch/K** 22
Z Koloa Fish | **Koloa/K** 25
Kozo Sushi | **multi.** 17
Kua 'Aina | **Ward/O** 22
L&L Drive-Inn | **Ward/O** 16
Mana'e Goods | **Manae/Mo** ─
Nico's/Pier 38 | **Iwilei/O** 23
Olive Tree | **Kahala/O** 24
Ono Hawaii | **Kapahulu/O** 25

DINING

SPECIAL FEATURES

Oviedo | **Kaunakakai/Mo**	-
Paddlers' Inn | **Kaunakakai/Mo**	-
People's Café | **Downtown/O**	21
Pineapple Rm. | **Ala Moana/O**	25
Shirokiya | **Ala Moana/O**	20
Side St. Inn | **Ala Moana/O**	25
Sweet Basil | **Downtown/O**	19
Tanioka's | **Waipahu/O**	24
NEW Uncle's Fish | **Iwilei/O**	18
Wailana Coffee | **Waikiki/O**	17
You Hungry? | **Ala Moana/O**	18
Young's Fish | **Kapalama/O**	24
Zippy's | **multi.**	16

DRAMATIC INTERIORS

Banyan Tree | **Kapalua/Ma**	24
Cafe Sistina | **Makiki/O**	21
Dondero's | **Poipu/K**	23
E&O | **Ward/O**	20
Gaylord's | **Lihue/K**	22
Hy's Steak | **Waikiki/O**	25
Indigo | **Chinatown/O**	22
Keo's | **Waikiki/O**	21
Lahaina Grill | **Lahaina/Ma**	26
Z Lodge/Koele | **Koele/L**	26
Z Orchids | **Waikiki/O**	26
Rokkaku | **Ala Moana/O**	24
Shokudo | **Ala Moana/O**	20
Tidepools | **Poipu/K**	24
Willows | **Moiliili/O**	18

EARLY-BIRD MENUS

Banyan Tree | **Kapalua/Ma**	24
Brown's Bch. | **Kohala/BI**	25
Buzz's | **Pearl City/O**	19
California Bch. | **Ward/O**	23
NEW 'Elua | **Ala Moana/O**	24
Gyotaku | **multi.**	19
Hukilau | **Kapaa/K**	25
Z Hula Grill | **Waikiki/O**	21
Kincaid's | **Ward/O**	20
Kochi | **Moiliili/O**	18
Longhi's | **multi.**	20
Oceanarium | **Waikiki/O**	17
Paddlers' Inn | **Kaunakakai/Mo**	-
Z Roy's | **multi.**	26
Z Ruth's Chris | **Lahaina/Ma**	25
Sea House | **Napili/Ma**	22
Willows | **Moiliili/O**	18

FAMILY-STYLE

Alexander's | **Kihei/Ma**	22
BJ's | **Lahaina/Ma**	19
Ciao Mein | **Waikiki/O**	21
d.k Steak | **Waikiki/O**	22
Formaggio | **Kailua/O**	22
Garden Is. | **Lihue/K**	19
Gazebo | **Napili/Ma**	24
Hale Vietnam | **Kaimuki/O**	23
Z Hiroshi | **Restaurant Row/O**	26
Hoku's | **Kahala/O**	25
Z Hula Grill | **Waikiki/O**	21
Isana | **Kihei/Ma**	-
Kaka'ako | **Ward/O**	21
Ken's/Pancakes | **Hilo/BI**	19
Kona Brewing | **Kailua-Kona/BI**	18
Kona Mix | **Kailua-Kona/BI**	21
Manago | **Captain Cook/BI**	21
Z Merriman's | **multi.**	27
Pah Ke's | **Kaneohe/O**	23
P.F. Chang's | **Waikiki/O**	19
Saffron | **Princeville/K**	20
Side St. Inn | **Ala Moana/O**	25
Singha Thai | **Waikiki/O**	21

HISTORIC PLACES

(Year opened; * building)

1901 | Beachhse.* | **Waikiki/O**	21
1901 | Pioneer Inn* | **Lahaina/Ma**	15
1913 | Bamboo* | **Hawi/BI**	23
1916 | Lahaina Store* | **Lahaina/Ma**	18
1916 | T. Komoda | **Makawao/Ma**	24
1917 | Manago | **Captain Cook/BI**	21
1918 | Grandma's | **Kula/Ma**	20
1920 | Hanama'ulu | **Hanamaulu/K**	20
1921 | Seaside Rest. | **Hilo/BI**	23
1923 | Lanai City* | **Lanai City/L**	22
1926 | Kanemitsu's | **Kaunakakai/Mo**	-
1930 | Plantation Gdns.* | **Poipu/K**	23
1932 | Hanapepe Café* | **Hanapepe/K**	22
1935 | Gaylord's* | **Lihue/K**	22
1935 | Tokyo Tei | **Wailuku/Ma**	21
1937 | Kilauea Lodge* | **Volcano/BI**	23
1937 | Lahaina Grill* | **Lahaina/Ma**	26

1940 | Jameson's* | **Haleiwa/O** 19
1940 | Kihei Caffe* | **Kihei/Ma** 23
1940 | Lihue BBQ | **Lihue/K** 20
1940 | Tasty Crust | **Wailuku/Ma** 19
1941 | Teshima | **Kealakekua/BI** 22
1942 | Kula Lodge | **Kula/Ma** 20
1946 | Café 100 | **Hilo/BI** 19
1946 | Helena's | **Kalihi/O** 26
1947 | Highway Inn | **Waipahu/O** 23
1948 | Kiawe Kitchen* | **Volcano/BI** 23
1948 | Ono Hawaii | **Kapahulu/O** 25
1950 | Ocean Hse.* | **Waikiki/O** 23
1951 | Matsumoto's | **Haleiwa/O** 24
1951 | Young's Fish | **Kapalama/O** 24
1958 | Hamura Saimin | **Lihue/K** 24
1958 | Pagoda | **Ala Moana/O** 16
1958 | People's Café | **Downtown/O** 21

HOTEL DINING

Ala Moana Hotel
Aaron's | **Ala Moana/O** 20
Plantation Café | **Ala Moana/O** 17
Best Western Pioneer Inn
Pioneer Inn | **Lahaina/Ma** 15
Colony Surf Hotel
☑ Michel's | **Waikiki/O** 25
Diamond Resort
Capische? | **Wailea/Ma** 25
Fairmont Kea Lani
Nick's Fishmkt. | **Wailea/Ma** 25
Fairmont Orchid
Brown's Bch. | **Kohala/BI** 25
Norio's | **Kohala/BI** 27
Four Seasons Lanai
Experience/Koele | **Koele/L** 22
☑ Lodge/Koele | **Koele/L** 26
Terrace | **Koele/L** 23
Four Seasons Resort Hualalai
Beach Tree | **Kaupulehu-Kona/BI** 23
☑ Hualalai Grille | **Kaupulehu-Kona/BI** 28
☑ Pahu | **Kaupulehu-Kona/BI** 26
Four Seasons Resort Lanai
Challenge/Manele | **Manele/L** 24
☑ Ihilani | **Manele/L** 24
Ocean Grill | **Manele/L** 23
Hulopo'e Ct. | **Manele/L** 23

Four Seasons Resort Maui
🆕 DUO | **Wailea/Ma** 24
☑ Ferraro's | **Wailea/Ma** 25
☑ Spago | **Wailea/Ma** 26
Grand Hyatt
Dondero's | **Poipu/K** 23
Tidepools | **Poipu/K** 24
Grand Wailea Resort
Humu's | **Wailea/Ma** 22
Halekulani
☑ La Mer | **Waikiki/O** 27
☑ Orchids | **Waikiki/O** 26
Hana-Maui, Hotel
Hana Ranch | **Hana/Ma** 22
Hapuna Beach Prince Hotel
Coast Grille | **Kohala/BI** 20
Hawaii Prince Hotel Waikiki
Hakone | **Waikiki/O** 25
Prince Ct. | **Waikiki/O** 23
Hilton Hawaiian Vill.
☑ Bali/Sea | **Waikiki/O** 24
Benihana | **Waikiki/O** 18
Round Table | **Waikiki/O** 18
Sergio's | **Waikiki/O** 17
Hilton Kauai Beach Resort
Naupaka Terr. | **Lihue/K** 19
Hilton Waikiki Prince Kuhio
🆕 MAC 24/7 | **Waikiki/O** 19
Hilton Waikoloa Vill.
Donatoni's | **Kohala/BI** 22
Imari | **Kohala/BI** 21
Kamuela Provision | **Kohala/BI** 21
Hyatt Regency Maui
Cascades | **Kaanapali/Ma** 23
☑ Son'z | **Kaanapali/Ma** 24
Hyatt Regency Waikiki
Ciao Mein | **Waikiki/O** 21
Ilikai
Sarento's Top | **Waikiki/O** 22
Kaanapali Beach Hotel
Tiki Terr. | **Kaanapali/Ma** 19
Kahala Hotel & Resort
Hoku's | **Kahala/O** 25
Kapalua Resort
Pineapple Grill | **Kapalua/Ma** 23
☑ Sansei | **Kapalua/Ma** 26
Kauai Coast Resort
Hukilau | **Kapaa/K** 25
Kauai Marriott Resort
Cafe Portofino | **Kalapaki Bch/K** 21

🅩 Duke's | **Kalapaki Bch/K**	19	
Kukui's | **Kalapaki Bch/K**	19	
Kona Village Resort		
Hale Samoa | **Kailua-Kona/BI**	26	
Ko Olina Resort & Marina		
🅩 Roy's | **Kapolei/O**	26	
Lanai, Hotel		
NEW Lanai City | **Lanai City/L**	22	
Maui Prince Hotel		
Hakone | **Makena/Ma**	25	
Prince Ct. | **Makena/Ma**	23	
Mauna Lani Resort		
CanoeHouse | **Kohala/BI**	24	
Moana Surfrider		
NEW Beachhse. | **Waikiki/O**	21	
Molokai, Hotel		
Hula Shores | **Kaunakakai/Mo**	-	
Napili Kai Beach Resort		
Sea House | **Napili/Ma**	22	
New Otani Kaimana		
🅩 Hau Tree | **Waikiki/O**	21	
Ohana East Hotel		
Round Table | **Waikiki/O**	18	
Outrigger Reef on the Beach		
Shore Bird | **Waikiki/O**	19	
Outrigger Waikiki		
🅩 Duke's | **Waikiki/O**	19	
🅩 Hula Grill | **Waikiki/O**	21	
Pacific Beach Hotel		
Oceanarium | **Waikiki/O**	17	
Pagoda Hotel		
Pagoda | **Ala Moana/O**	16	
Plantation Inn		
🅩 Gerard's | **Lahaina/Ma**	28	
ResortQuest Maui		
Castaway | **Kaanapali/Ma**	22	
ResortQuest Waikiki Beach		
Tiki's Grill | **Waikiki/O**	19	
Ritz-Carlton Kapalua		
Banyan Tree | **Kapalua/Ma**	24	
Royal Kona Resort		
Don/Beachcomber |	19	
Kailua-Kona/BI		
Sheraton		
Shells | **Poipu/K**	20	
Turtle Bay Resort		
Lei Lei's | **Kahuku/O**	22	
Ola | **Kahuku/O**	21	
Waiakea Villas Hotel		
Miyo's | **Hilo/BI**	22	

Waikiki Beach Marriott Resort	
Arancino | **Waikiki/O**	22
d.k Steak | **Waikiki/O**	22
🅩 Sansei | **Waikiki/O**	26
Waikiki Gateway Hotel	
Nick's Fishmkt. | **Waikiki/O**	22
Waikiki Parc Hotel	
NEW 🅩 Nobu | **Waikiki/O**	26
Waikoloa Beach Resort	
🅩 Sansei | **Kohala/BI**	26
Wailea Beach Marriott	
Mala | **Wailea/Ma**	25
Westin Maui Resort & Spa	
OnO B&G | **Kaanapali/Ma**	21
W Honolulu	
Diamond Head | **Waikiki/O**	22

LATE DINING

(Weekday closing hour)	
Akasaka | 2 AM | **Ala Moana/O**	25
Big City Diner | varies | **Aiea/O**	18
Bubba Gump | 12 AM | **Ala Moana/O**	15
Fook Yuen | 3 AM | **Moiliili/O**	20
Ken's/Pancakes | 24 hrs. | **Hilo/BI**	19
Kimo's | 12 AM | **Lahaina/Ma**	20
Kincaid's | 12 AM | **Ward/O**	20
Kochi | 2 AM | **Moiliili/O**	18
Lahaina Coolers | 12 AM | **Lahaina/Ma**	18
L&L Drive-Inn | varies | **Waikiki/O**	16
NEW MAC 24/7 | 24 hrs. | **Waikiki/O**	19
Maui Brewing | 12:30 AM | **Kahana/Ma**	19
Oki Diner | 12 AM | **Lihue/K**	15
Paddlers' Inn | 1 AM | **Kaunakakai/Mo**	-
Round Table | varies | **Waikiki/O**	18
Sarento's Top | 12 AM | **Waikiki/O**	22
Shokudo | 12 AM | **Ala Moana/O**	20
Sorabol | 24 hrs. | **Ala Moana/O**	22
NEW Sushi Doraku | varies | **Waikiki/O**	-
Therapy Sports | 2 AM | **Hawaii Kai/O**	17
Tsukuneya | 12 AM | **University/O**	20
Wailana Coffee | 24 hrs. | **Waikiki/O**	17
Yanagi | 2 AM | **Kakaako/O**	23
Zippy's | varies | **multi.**	16

LOCAL FAVORITES

Aloha Mix Plate | Lahaina/Ma	21
Anthony's Coffee | Paia/Ma	20
Bamboo | Hawi/BI	23
Beach Tree | Kaupulehu-Kona/BI	23
Big City Diner | multi.	18
Blue Ginger | Lanai City/L	20
Brown's Bch. | Kohala/BI	25
Bull Shed | Kapaa/K	17
Buzz's | Lanikai/O	19
Café Pesto | multi.	23
Camellia | Moiliili/O	20
Canoes Lanai | Lanai City/L	17
Charley's | Paia/Ma	19
CJ's Steak | Princeville/K	17
Da Kitchen | multi.	22
Dani's | Lihue/K	20
Duane's Ono | Anahola/K	23
Eggbert's | Kapaa/K	18
NEW Flatbread | Paia/Ma	23
Fook Yuen | Moiliili/O	20
Grandma's | Kula/Ma	20
Green Door | Kahala/O	22
Gyotaku | multi.	19
Z Hali'imaile Gen. | Makawao/Ma	27
Hamura Saimin | Lihue/K	24
Hanalei Dolphin | Hanalei/K	22
Z Helena's | Kalihi/O	26
Highway Inn | Waipahu/O	23
Z Hualalai Grille | Kaupulehu-Kona/BI	28
Huggos | Kailua-Kona/BI	19
I Love Country | Ala Moana/O	17
Kaka'ako | Ward/O	21
Kanemitsu's | Kaunakakai/Mo	–
Kauai Pasta | Kapaa/K	21
NEW Kenichi | Keauhou/BI	24
Kihei Caffe | Kihei/Ma	23
Kintaro | Kapaa/K	25
Z Koloa Fish | Koloa/K	25
Kua 'Aina | Ward/O	22
L&L Drive-Inn | Ward/O	16
Lighthouse | Kilauea/K	21
Little Village | Chinatown/O	23
Manago | Captain Cook/BI	21
Matsumoto's | Haleiwa/O	24
Mei Sum | Chinatown/O	21
Ono Family | Kapaa/K	19
Ono Hawaii | Kapahulu/O	25
Pah Ke's | Kaneohe/O	23
Paia Fish | Paia/Ma	24
People's Café | Downtown/O	21
Phuket Thai | McCully/O	25
Quinn's | Kailua-Kona/BI	18
Sam Choy's | Iwilei/O	20
Side St. Inn | Ala Moana/O	25
Tanioka's | Waipahu/O	24
T. Komoda | Makawao/Ma	24
Tropical Taco | Hanalei/K	21
Yanagi | Kakaako/O	23
Young's Fish | Kapalama/O	24
Zippy's | multi.	16

MEET FOR A DRINK

Aaron's | Ala Moana/O	20
Z Beach Hse. | Poipu/K	25
Brasserie/Vin | Chinatown/O	20
Brennecke's | Poipu/K	18
Diamond Head | Waikiki/O	22
d.k Steak | Waikiki/O	22
Z Duke's | multi.	19
E&O | Ward/O	20
Formaggio | multi.	22
Hula Shores | Kaunakakai/Mo	–
Indigo | Chinatown/O	22
JJ's Broiler | Nawiliwili/K	17
Joe's B&G | Wailea/Ma	22
Kalypso Island | Hanalei/K	16
Keoki's Paradise | Poipu/K	20
Lucy's Grill | Kailua/O	18
Maui Brewing | Kahana/Ma	19
Nick's Fishmkt. | Waikiki/O	22
NEW Z Nobu | Waikiki/O	26
Paddlers' Inn | Kaunakakai/Mo	–
Z Roy's | Hawaii Kai/O	26
Sarento's/Bch. | Kihei/Ma	23
Side St. Inn | Ala Moana/O	25
Therapy Sports | Hawaii Kai/O	17
Tiki's Grill | Waikiki/O	19
town | Kaimuki/O	23
Vino | Restaurant Row/O	23

MICROBREWERIES

Kona Brewing | multi.	18
Maui Brewing | Kahana/Ma	19
Nick's Fishmkt. | Waikiki/O	22
Sam Choy's | Iwilei/O	20
TomKat's | Koloa/K	18
NEW Waimea Brew | Waimea/K	19

NOTEWORTHY NEWCOMERS

Beachhse. | **Waikiki/O**	21
Burgers/Edge | **Kapahulu/O**	–
Downtown | **Downtown/O**	–
DUO | **Wailea/Ma**	24
'Elua | **Ala Moana/O**	24
Fat Greek | **Kaimuki/O**	19
Flatbread | **Paia/Ma**	23
Hakkei | **Makiki/O**	25
Lanai City | **Lanai City/L**	22
MAC 24/7 | **Waikiki/O**	19
Market St. | **Lihue/K**	–
Z Nobu | **Waikiki/O**	26
Panya | **Ala Moana/O**	17
RB Black Angus | **Kahana/Ma**	–
Sammy's | **Kahului/Ma**	–
Sergio's | **Kapahulu/O**	17
Stage | **Ala Moana/O**	–
Sushi Doraku | **Waikiki/O**	–
Tangö | **Downtown/O**	–
Taqueria Cruz | **Kihei/Ma**	–
Uncle's Fish | **Iwilei/O**	18
Waimea Brew | **Waimea/K**	19
Wasabi | **Kapahulu/O**	22
Wild Ginger | **Kaimuki/O**	17

OFFBEAT

Akasaka | **Ala Moana/O**	25
Bac Nam | **Downtown/O**	24
Blue Ginger | **Lanai City/L**	20
Café 565 | **Lanai City/L**	–
Caffe Coco | **Kapaa/K**	23
Canoes Lanai | **Lanai City/L**	17
Casablanca | **Poipu/K**	19
Casa di Amici | **Poipu/K**	23
Da Spot | **Moiliili/O**	20
Duane's Ono | **Anahola/K**	23
Duc's Bistro | **Chinatown/O**	24
NEW Flatbread | **Paia/Ma**	23
Green Door | **Kahala/O**	22
Z Hali'imaile Gen. | **Makawao/Ma**	27
Hamura Saimin | **Lihue/K**	24
Hanalei Gourmet | **Hanalei/K**	21
Hanapepe Café | **Hanapepe/K**	22
Z Helena's | **Kalihi/O**	26
Mana'e Goods | **Manae/Mo**	–
Nico's/Pier 38 | **Iwilei/O**	23
Ono Hawaii | **Kapahulu/O**	25
Oviedo | **Kaunakakai/Mo**	–
Peggy Sue's | **Kihei/Ma**	17
People's Café | **Downtown/O**	21
Side St. Inn | **Ala Moana/O**	25
Stella Blues | **Kihei/Ma**	19
NEW Uncle's Fish | **Iwilei/O**	18
Young's Fish | **Kapalama/O**	24

PARKING

(V=valet, *=validated)

Aaron's | V* | **Ala Moana/O**	20
Z Alan Wong's | V | **McCully/O**	28
Arancino | V* | **Waikiki/O**	22
A Saigon Café* | **Wailuku/Ma**	23
Z Bali/Sea | V* | **Waikiki/O**	24
Banyan Tree | V | **Kapalua/Ma**	24
Z Beach Hse. | V | **Poipu/K**	25
NEW Beachhse. | V* | **Waikiki/O**	21
Benihana | V* | **Waikiki/O**	18
Big City Diner | V | **Ward/O**	18
Brown's Bch. | V* | **Kohala/BI**	25
California Pizza* | **multi.**	20
Capische? | V | **Wailea/Ma**	25
Cascades | V | **Kaanapali/Ma**	23
Chai's Is. | V* | **Downtown/O**	23
Cheesecake Fac.* | **Waikiki/O**	21
Z Chef Mavro | V | **Moiliili/O**	26
Ciao Mein | V* | **Waikiki/O**	21
Cilantro Grill* | **Lahaina/Ma**	22
Coast Grille | V | **Kohala/BI**	20
Diamond Head | V | **Waikiki/O**	22
d.k Steak | V* | **Waikiki/O**	22
Donatoni's | V* | **Kohala/BI**	22
Dondero's* | **Poipu/K**	23
Don/Beachcomber* | **Kailua-Kona/BI**	19
Duc's Bistro | V | **Chinatown/O**	24
Z Duke's | V* | **multi.**	19
NEW DUO | V | **Wailea/Ma**	24
E&O | V | **Ward/O**	20
Z Ferraro's | V | **Wailea/Ma**	25
Five Palms | V | **Kihei/Ma**	20
Genki Sushi | V | **multi.**	17
Hakone | V | **multi.**	25
Hard Rock* | **Lahaina/Ma**	14
Z Hau Tree | V | **Waikiki/O**	21
Hee Hing | V | **Kapahulu/O**	20
Z Hiroshi | V* | **Restaurant Row/O**	26
Hoku's | V | **Kahala/O**	25
Z Hualalai Grille | V | **Kaupulehu-Kona/BI**	28

PEOPLE-WATCHING

POWER SCENES

🔡 Alan Wong's | **McCully/O**	28
Bar Acuda | **Hanalei/K**	23
🆕 Beachhse. | **Waikiki/O**	21
🔡 Chef Mavro | **Moiliili/O**	26
Diamond Head | **Waikiki/O**	22
Dondero's | **Poipu/K**	23
🔡 Ferraro's | **Wailea/Ma**	25
Hoku's | **Kahala/O**	25
Indigo | **Chinatown/O**	22
🔡 La Mer | **Waikiki/O**	27
Mariposa | **Ala Moana/O**	22
Morton's | **Ala Moana/O**	25
🆕🔡 Nobu | **Waikiki/O**	26
🔡 Sansei | **Waikiki/O**	26
🔡 3660/Rise | **Kaimuki/O**	25

QUICK BITES

AK's | **Wailuku/Ma**	20
Anthony's Coffee | **Paia/Ma**	20
Antonio's | **multi.**	21
Barefoot Burger | **Waimea/K**	18
Big City Diner | **multi.**	18
BJ's | **Lahaina/Ma**	19
Blue Ginger | **Lanai City/L**	20
Bubba Burger | **multi.**	21
Café 565 | **Lanai City/L**	-
California Pizza | **multi.**	20
Canoes Lanai | **Lanai City/L**	17
Cheeseburger/Paradise | **multi.**	17
Chowder Hse. | **Ward/O**	16
Curry Hse. | **Ala Moana/O**	20
Da Spot | **Moiliili/O**	20
Duane's Ono | **Anahola/K**	23
🔡 Duke's | **multi.**	19
Eggs 'n Things | **Waikiki/O**	23
Experience/Koele | **Koele/L**	22
Ezogiku | **multi.**	19
🆕 Fat Greek | **Kaimuki/O**	19
Goma Tei | **Ward/O**	21
Grandma's | **Kula/Ma**	20
Hale Vietnam | **Kaimuki/O**	23
Hamura Saimin | **Lihue/K**	24
Hanapepe Café | **Hanapepe/K**	22
🔡 Helena's | **Kalihi/O**	26
House/Noodles | **Kapaa/K**	22
I Love Country | **Ala Moana/O**	17
Island Burger | **Ala Moana/O**	18
Kaka'ako | **Ward/O**	21
Kalaheo Café | **Kalaheo/K**	23

Kalapaki Hut | **Kalapaki Bch/K**	2
Kanemitsu's | **Kaunakakai/Mo**	-
Kihei Caffe | **Kihei/Ma**	2
🔡 Koloa Fish | **Koloa/K**	2
Kua 'Aina | **Ward/O**	2
L&L Drive-Inn | **Ward/O**	1
Mana'e Goods | **Manae/Mo**	-
Mermaid Bar | **Ala Moana/O**	2
Molokai Dr. | **Kaunakakai/Mo**	-
Nico's/Pier 38 | **Iwilei/O**	2
Pacific Place | **Ala Moana/O**	-
Pizza Paradiso | **Lahaina/Ma**	2
Sweet Basil | **Downtown/O**	1
Tanioka's | **Waipahu/O**	2
Tropical Taco | **Hanalei/K**	2
🆕 Uncle's Fish | **Iwilei/O**	1
Vietnam/Pho | **Chinatown/O**	1
Wahoo's Fish | **Ward/O**	1
You Hungry? | **Ala Moana/O**	1
Zippy's | **multi.**	1

QUIET CONVERSATION

🔡 Bali/Sea | **Waikiki/O**	2
🆕 Beachhse. | **Waikiki/O**	2
Cafe Portofino | **Kalapaki Bch/K**	2
🔡 Chef Mavro | **Moiliili/O**	2
Dondero's | **Poipu/K**	2
Gaylord's | **Lihue/K**	2
🆕 Hakkei | **Makiki/O**	2
Hana Ranch | **Hana/Ma**	2
Hukilau | **Kapaa/K**	2
🔡 Ihilani | **Manele/L**	2
🔡 La Mer | **Waikiki/O**	2
Lighthouse | **Kilauea/K**	2
🔡 Lodge/Koele | **Koele/L**	2
Ola | **Kahuku/O**	2
🔡 Orchids | **Waikiki/O**	2
Sarento's Top | **Waikiki/O**	2

RESERVE AHEAD

🔡 Alan Wong's | **McCully/O**	28
A Saigon Café | **Wailuku/Ma**	23
🔡 Bali/Sea | **Waikiki/O**	24
CJ's Steak | **Princeville/K**	1
🆕 'Elua | **Ala Moana/O**	24
Genki Sushi | **Lihue/K**	1
Hakone | **Waikiki/O**	25
Hanapepe Café | **Hanapepe/K**	2
Hoku's | **Kahala/O**	25

Hy's Steak | **Waikiki/O** 25
☑ Koloa Fish | **Koloa/K** 25
Pineapple Grill | **Kapalua/Ma** 23
own | **Kaimuki/O** 23

ROMANTIC PLACES

Aaron's | **Ala Moana/O** 20
☑ Alan Wong's | **McCully/O** 28
Baci Bistro | **Kailua/O** 24
☑ Bali/Sea | **Waikiki/O** 24
Banyan Tree | **Kapalua/Ma** 24
☑ Beach Hse. | **Poipu/K** 25
NEW Beachhse. | **Waikiki/O** 21
Cafe Portofino | **Kalapaki Bch/K** 21
Casa di Amici | **Poipu/K** 23
Dondero's | **Poipu/K** 23
NEW 'Elua | **Ala Moana/O** 24
Gaylord's | **Lihue/K** 22
☑ Gerard's | **Lahaina/Ma** 28
☑ Hau Tree | **Waikiki/O** 21
Hoku's | **Kahala/O** 25
Hukilau | **Kapaa/K** 25
Humu's | **Wailea/Ma** 22
Kimo's | **Lahaina/Ma** 20
☑ La Mer | **Waikiki/O** 27
Lighthouse | **Kilauea/K** 21
☑ Lodge/Koele | **Koele/L** 26
☑ Michel's | **Waikiki/O** 25
Nick's Fishmkt. | **Wailea/Ma** 25
NEW ☑ Nobu | **Waikiki/O** 26
Ola | **Kahuku/O** 21
☑ Orchids | **Waikiki/O** 26
Pacific'O | **Lahaina/Ma** 25
Plantation Gdns. | **Poipu/K** 23
Sarento's/Bch. | **Kihei/Ma** 23
Sarento's Top | **Waikiki/O** 22
☑ Son'z | **Kaanapali/Ma** 24
☑ 3660/Rise | **Kaimuki/O** 25
Tidepools | **Poipu/K** 24

SENIOR APPEAL

Assaggio | **Ala Moana/O** 21
NEW Beachhse. | **Waikiki/O** 21
Big City Diner | **multi.** 18
Bull Shed | **Kapaa/K** 17
Buzz's | **Lanikai/O** 19
Cafe Portofino | **Kalapaki Bch/K** 21
Chowder Hse. | **Ward/O** 16
CJ's Steak | **Princeville/K** 17
Contemp. Café | **Makiki Hts/O** 19

Dani's | **Lihue/K** 20
Eggbert's | **Kapaa/K** 18
Gaylord's | **Lihue/K** 22
Hanalei Dolphin | **Hanalei/K** 22
☑ Hau Tree | **Waikiki/O** 21
Hy's Steak | **Waikiki/O** 25
JJ's Broiler | **Nawiliwili/K** 17
Kauai Hula Girl | **Kapaa/K** 19
Keoki's Paradise | **Poipu/K** 20
Keo's | **Waikiki/O** 21
Legend Sea. | **Chinatown/O** 23
Ocean Hse. | **Waikiki/O** 23
☑ Orchids | **Waikiki/O** 26
Original Pancake | **Kapalama/O** 21
Pagoda | **Ala Moana/O** 16
Pavilion Café | **Ala Moana/O** 21
Plantation Café | **Ala Moana/O** 17
Ruby Tues. | **multi.** 15
Wailana Coffee | **Waikiki/O** 17
Willows | **Moiliili/O** 18

SINGLES SCENES

Brasserie/Vin | **Chinatown/O** 20
Brennecke's | **Poipu/K** 18
Diamond Head | **Waikiki/O** 22
☑ Duke's | **multi.** 19
E&O | **Ward/O** 20
Formaggio | **multi.** 22
Hard Rock | **Lahaina/Ma** 14
Indigo | **Chinatown/O** 22
Kalypso Island | **Hanalei/K** 16
Keoki's Paradise | **Poipu/K** 20
NEW ☑ Nobu | **Waikiki/O** 26
Therapy Sports | **Hawaii Kai/O** 17
Tiki's Grill | **Waikiki/O** 19
town | **Kaimuki/O** 23

SLEEPERS

(Good to excellent food, but little known)

Bangkok Hse. | **Kailua-Kona/BI** 22
Café Mambo | **Paia/Ma** 23
Caffe Coco | **Kapaa/K** 23
NEW Hakkei | **Makiki/O** 25
Haleiwa Eats Thai | **Haleiwa/O** 26
Hale Samoa | **Kailua-Kona/BI** 26
House/Noodles | **Kapaa/K** 22
Hukilau | **Kapaa/K** 25
Hulopo'e Ct. | **Manele/L** 23
Kalapaki Hut | **Kalapaki Bch/K** 22
Kiawe Kitchen | **Volcano/BI** 23
NEW Lanai City | **Lanai City/L** 22

Lei Lei's | **Kahuku/O**	22	
Miyo's | **Hilo/BI**	22	
Norio's | **Kohala/BI**	27	
Orchid Thai | **Kailua-Kona/BI**	24	
NEW Pacific Is. | **Kapaa/K**	24	
Rokkaku | **Ala Moana/O**	24	
Seaside Rest. | **Hilo/BI**	23	
Terrace | **Koele/L**	23	
Thai Cuisine | **Kihei/Ma**	23	
Thai Thai | **Volcano/BI**	24	
U-Top-It | **Kailua-Kona/BI**	23	
NEW Wasabi | **Kapahulu/O**	22	
Yakiniku Seoul | **McCully/O**	22	

SPECIAL OCCASIONS

Aaron's | **Ala Moana/O**	20
Z Alan Wong's | **McCully/O**	28
Z Bali/Sea | **Waikiki/O**	24
Z Beach Hse. | **Poipu/K**	25
NEW Beachhse. | **Waikiki/O**	21
Z Chef Mavro | **Moiliili/O**	26
Chez Paul | **Olowalu/Ma**	26
Diamond Head | **Waikiki/O**	22
Dondero's | **Poipu/K**	23
NEW 'Elua | **Ala Moana/O**	24
Gaylord's | **Lihue/K**	22
Z Gerard's | **Lahaina/Ma**	28
Z Hau Tree | **Waikiki/O**	21
Hoku's | **Kahala/O**	25
Hukilau | **Kapaa/K**	25
Hy's Steak | **Waikiki/O**	25
Z La Mer | **Waikiki/O**	27
Z Lodge/Koele | **Koele/L**	26
Mariposa | **Ala Moana/O**	22
Z Michel's | **Waikiki/O**	25
Nick's Fishmkt. | **Waikiki/O**	22
NEW Z Nobu | **Waikiki/O**	26
Ola | **Kahuku/O**	21
Z Orchids | **Waikiki/O**	26
Z Roy's | **Hawaii Kai/O**	26
Sarento's Top | **Waikiki/O**	22
NEW Stage | **Ala Moana/O**	-
Z 3660/Rise | **Kaimuki/O**	25
Tidepools | **Poipu/K**	24

TAKEOUT

Alexander's | **Kihei/Ma**	22
Antonio's | **multi.**	21
Asian Star | **Wailuku/Ma**	20
Ba-Le | **multi.**	20
Blane's | **Hilo/BI**	15

Brick Oven | **Kalaheo/K**	24
Bubba Burger | **multi.**	21
NEW Burgers/Edge | **Kapahulu/O**	-
Café O Lei | **Kihei/Ma**	24
Café 100 | **Hilo/BI**	19
CJ's Deli | **Kaanapali/Ma**	18
Da Kitchen | **multi.**	22
Da Spot | **Moiliili/O**	20
Duane's Ono | **Anahola/K**	23
Hamura Saimin | **Lihue/K**	24
Hanapepe Café | **Hanapepe/K**	22
Z Helena's | **Kalihi/O**	26
I Love Country | **Ala Moana/O**	17
India Café | **Kapahulu/O**	19
Kaka'ako | **Ward/O**	21
Kalaheo Café | **Kalaheo/K**	23
Kalapaki Hut | **Kalapaki Bch/K**	22
Kanemitsu's | **Kaunakakai/Mo**	-
Kihei Caffe | **Kihei/Ma**	23
Z Koloa Fish | **Koloa/K**	25
Kua 'Aina | **Ward/O**	22
L&L Drive-Inn | **multi.**	16
Mana'e Goods | **Manae/Mo**	-
Marco's Grill | **Kahului/Ma**	17
Matsumoto's | **Haleiwa/O**	24
Maui Tacos | **multi.**	19
Molokai Dr. | **Kaunakakai/Mo**	-
Nico's/Pier 38 | **Iwilei/O**	23
Pizza Paradiso | **Lahaina/Ma**	20
Shrimp Sta. | **Waimea/K**	24
NEW Taqueria Cruz | **Kihei/Ma**	-
Tropical Taco | **Hanalei/K**	21
Wahoo's Fish | **Ward/O**	17
Young's Fish | **Kapalama/O**	24

TASTING MENUS

Z Alan Wong's | **McCully/O**	28
Z Bali/Sea | **Waikiki/O**	24
Brown's Bch. | **Kohala/BI**	25
Chai's Is. | **Downtown/O**	23
Z Chef Mavro | **Moiliili/O**	26
Hoku's | **Kahala/O**	25
Lahaina Grill | **Lahaina/Ma**	26
Z Lodge/Koele | **Koele/L**	26
Longhi's | **Wailea/Ma**	20
Pacific'O | **Lahaina/Ma**	25
Z Roy's | **Hawaii Kai/O**	26
Z Sansei | **Kihei/Ma**	26
Z Spago | **Wailea/Ma**	26
NEW Stage | **Ala Moana/O**	-

40,000 places to eat, drink, stay & play - free at ZAGAT.com

TEEN APPEAL

Antonio's | **multi.**	21
Auntie Pasto | **multi.**	17
Barefoot Burger | **Waimea/K**	18
Benihana | **Waikiki/O**	18
Big City Diner | **multi.**	18
Brennecke's | **Poipu/K**	18
Bubba Burger | **multi.**	21
Café 565 | **Lanai City/L**	-
California Bch. | **Ward/O**	23
California Pizza | **multi.**	20
Cheeseburger/Paradise | **multi.**	17
Cheesecake Fac. | **Waikiki/O**	21
CJ's Steak | **Princeville/K**	17
Duane's Ono | **Anahola/K**	23
☑ Duke's | **multi.**	19
Genki Sushi | **multi.**	17
Hard Rock | **Lahaina/Ma**	14
☑ Hula Grill | **Waikiki/O**	21
Island Burger | **Ala Moana/O**	18
Kalapaki Hut | **Kalapaki Bch/K**	22
Kalypso Island | **Hanalei/K**	16
Kua 'Aina | **Ward/O**	22
NEW MAC 24/7 | **Waikiki/O**	19
Matsumoto's | **Haleiwa/O**	24
Molokai Pizza | **Kaunakakai/Mo**	19
P.F. Chang's | **Ward/O**	19
Planet Hollywood | **Waikiki/O**	12
Romano | **Ala Moana/O**	18
Ruby Tues. | **multi.**	15
Sam Choy's | **Iwilei/O**	20
Shokudo | **Ala Moana/O**	20
Shore Bird | **Waikiki/O**	19
Tanaka | **multi.**	21
Tiki's Grill | **Waikiki/O**	19
Wahoo's Fish | **Ward/O**	17
Zippy's | **multi.**	16

THEME RESTAURANTS

Benihana | **Waikiki/O**	18
Cheeseburger/Paradise | **multi.**	17
Hard Rock | **Lahaina/Ma**	14
Kauai Hula Girl | **Kapaa/K**	19
Keoki's Paradise | **Poipu/K**	20
Planet Hollywood | **Waikiki/O**	12

TRENDY

Bar Acuda | **Hanalei/K**	23
Brasserie/Vin | **Chinatown/O**	20
Diamond Head | **Waikiki/O**	22

E&O | **Ward/O**	20
Formaggio | **multi.**	22
Hanalei Gourmet | **Hanalei/K**	21
☑ Hiroshi | **Restaurant Row/O**	26
Hoku's | **Kahala/O**	25
Ichiriki | **Ala Moana/O**	24
NEW ☑ Nobu | **Waikiki/O**	26
Ola | **Kahuku/O**	21
Shokudo | **Ala Moana/O**	20
Tiki's Grill | **Waikiki/O**	19
town | **Kaimuki/O**	23
12th Ave. | **Kaimuki/O**	23

TWENTYSOMETHINGS

Bar Acuda | **Hanalei/K**	23
Brasserie/Vin | **Chinatown/O**	20
Brennecke's | **Poipu/K**	18
Caffe Coco | **Kapaa/K**	23
California Bch. | **Ward/O**	23
Casablanca | **Poipu/K**	19
Casa di Amici | **Poipu/K**	23
Diamond Head | **Waikiki/O**	22
☑ Duke's | **multi.**	19
E&O | **Ward/O**	20
Formaggio | **multi.**	22
Hanalei Gourmet | **Hanalei/K**	21
Hanapepe Café | **Hanapepe/K**	22
Hard Rock | **Lahaina/Ma**	14
Ichiriki | **Ala Moana/O**	24
Indigo | **Chinatown/O**	22
Kalypso Island | **Hanalei/K**	16
Keoki's Paradise | **Poipu/K**	20
Little Village | **Chinatown/O**	23
Longhi's | **Ala Moana/O**	20
Lucy's Grill | **Kailua/O**	18
NEW MAC 24/7 | **Waikiki/O**	19
NEW ☑ Nobu | **Waikiki/O**	26
Ola | **Kahuku/O**	21
☑ Sansei | **Waikiki/O**	26
Shokudo | **Ala Moana/O**	20
Sorabol | **Ala Moana/O**	22
Therapy Sports | **Hawaii Kai/O**	17
Tiki's Grill | **Waikiki/O**	19
town | **Kaimuki/O**	23
12th Ave. | **Kaimuki/O**	23

VIEWS

Aaron's | **Ala Moana/O**	20
Alexander's | **Kihei/Ma**	22
☑ Bali/Sea | **Waikiki/O**	24
Banyan Tree | **Kapalua/Ma**	24

☑ Beach Hse. | **Poipu/K**	25
NEW Beachhse. | **Waikiki/O**	21
Beach Tree | **Kaupulehu-Kona/BI**	23
Brennecke's | **Poipu/K**	18
Brown's Bch. | **Kohala/BI**	25
Bull Shed | **Kapaa/K**	17
Cafe Portofino | **Kalapaki Bch/K**	21
Capische? | **Wailea/Ma**	25
Casablanca | **Poipu/K**	19
Cascades | **Kaanapali/Ma**	23
Castaway | **Kaanapali/Ma**	22
Challenge/Manele | **Manele/L**	24
d.k Steak | **Waikiki/O**	22
Donatoni's | **Kohala/BI**	22
Dondero's | **Poipu/K**	23
Don/Beachcomber | **Kailua-Kona/BI**	19
Duane's Ono | **Anahola/K**	23
☑ Duke's | **multi.**	19
NEW DUO | **Wailea/Ma**	24
Experience/Koele | **Koele/L**	22
☑ Ferraro's | **Wailea/Ma**	25
Five Palms | **Kihei/Ma**	20
Formaggio | **Kailua/O**	22
Grandma's | **Kula/Ma**	20
Hakone | **Waikiki/O**	25
Hanalei Dolphin | **Hanalei/K**	22
Hanalei Gourmet | **Hanalei/K**	21
Hana Ranch | **Hana/Ma**	22
Hard Rock | **Lahaina/Ma**	14
☑ Hau Tree | **Waikiki/O**	21
Hoku's | **Kahala/O**	25
Huggos | **Kailua-Kona/BI**	19
Hukilau | **Kapaa/K**	25
☑ Hula Grill | **multi.**	21
Hula Shores | **Kaunakakai/Mo**	–
Hulopo'e Ct. | **Manele/L**	23
Humu's | **Wailea/Ma**	22
I'O Rest. | **Lahaina/Ma**	24
Isana | **Kihei/Ma**	–
Jameson's | **multi.**	19
JJ's Broiler | **Nawiliwili/K**	17
Joe's B&G | **Wailea/Ma**	22
Kamuela Provision | **Kohala/BI**	21
Kiawe Kitchen | **Volcano/BI**	23
Kihei Caffe | **Kihei/Ma**	23
Kincaid's | **Ward/O**	20
Kona Brewing | **Kailua-Kona/BI**	18
Kuhio Grille | **Hilo/BI**	21

Kula Lodge | **Kula/Ma**	20
La Bourgogne | **Kailua-Kona/BI**	25
Lahaina Fish | **Lahaina/Ma**	21
Lahaina Store | **Lahaina/Ma**	18
☑ La Mer | **Waikiki/O**	27
Leilani's | **Kaanapali/Ma**	21
Lei Lei's | **Kahuku/O**	22
☑ Lodge/Koele | **Koele/L**	26
Mala | **multi.**	25
☑ Mama's Fish | **Paia/Ma**	27
Mariposa | **Ala Moana/O**	22
Matteo's | **Wailea/Ma**	19
☑ Michel's | **Waikiki/O**	25
Naupaka Terr. | **Lihue/K**	19
Nick's Fishmkt. | **Wailea/Ma**	25
Nihon | **Hilo/BI**	19
Ocean Grill | **Manele/L**	23
Ocean Hse. | **Waikiki/O**	23
Ola | **Kahuku/O**	21
OnO B&G | **Kaanapali/Ma**	21
☑ Orchids | **Waikiki/O**	26
Pacific'O | **Lahaina/Ma**	25
☑ Pahu | **Kaupulehu-Kona/BI**	26
Pineapple Grill | **Kapalua/Ma**	23
Pioneer Inn | **Lahaina/Ma**	15
Plantation Gdns. | **Poipu/K**	23
Plantation Hse. | **Kapalua/Ma**	24
Postcards Café | **Hanalei/K**	24
Prince Ct. | **multi.**	23
☑ Ruth's Chris | **Lahaina/Ma**	25
Saffron | **Princeville/K**	20
☑ Sansei | **Kohala/BI**	26
Sarento's/Bch. | **Kihei/Ma**	23
Sea House | **Napili/Ma**	22
Seaside Rest. | **Hilo/BI**	23
SeaWatch | **Wailea/Ma**	22
Shore Bird | **Waikiki/O**	19
☑ Son'z | **Kaanapali/Ma**	24
☑ Spago | **Wailea/Ma**	26
Tiki's Grill | **Waikiki/O**	19
Tiki Terr. | **Kaanapali/Ma**	19
Tommy Bahama | **Kohala/BI**	20
Volcano Golf | **Volcano/BI**	15
Waterfront | **Maalaea/Ma**	25

WATERSIDE

☑ Bali/Sea | **Waikiki/O**	24
☑ Beach Hse. | **Poipu/K**	25
Beach Tree | **Kaupulehu-Kona/BI**	23
Brennecke's | **Poipu/K**	18

Brown's Bch. | **Kohala/BI** — 25
Bubba Gump | **multi.** — 15
Bull Shed | **Kapaa/K** — 17
Cafe Portofino |
  Kalapaki Bch/K — 21
CanoeHouse | **Kohala/BI** — 24
Cascades | **Kaanapali/Ma** — 23
Castaway | **Kaanapall/Ma** — 22
Challenge/Manele | **Manele/L** — 24
Donatoni's | **Kohala/BI** — 22
Don/Beachcomber |
  Kailua-Kona/BI — 19
🔏 Duke's | **Kalapaki Bch/K** — 19
🆕 DUO | **Wailea/Ma** — 24
Experience/Koele | **Koele/L** — 22
🔏 Ferraro's | **Wailea/Ma** — 25
Hanalei Dolphin | **Hanalei/K** — 22
Hana Ranch | **Hana/Ma** — 22
Harbor Hse. | **Kailua-Kona/BI** — 19
Hard Rock | **Lahaina/Ma** — 14
🔏 Hau Tree | **Waikiki/O** — 21
Hukilau | **Kapaa/K** — 25
🔏 Hula Grill | **multi.** — 21
Hula Shores | **Kaunakakai/Mo** — -
Hulopo'e Ct. | **Manele/L** — 23
Humu's | **Wailea/Ma** — 22
I'O Rest. | **Lahaina/Ma** — 24
Kimo's | **Lahaina/Ma** — 20
Kona Brewing | **Hawaii Kai/O** — 18
Lahaina Fish | **Lahaina/Ma** — 21
Leilani's | **Kaanapali/Ma** — 21
Ma'alaea Grill | **Maalaea/Ma** — 22
Mala | **multi.** — 25
🔏 Mama's Fish | **Paia/Ma** — 27
🔏 Michel's | **Waikiki/O** — 25
Nihon | **Hilo/BI** — 19
Norio's | **Kohala/BI** — 27
Ocean Grill | **Manele/L** — 23
Ola | **Kahuku/O** — 21
OnO B&G | **Kaanapali/Ma** — 21
🔏 Orchids | **Waikiki/O** — 26
Pacific'O | **Lahaina/Ma** — 25
Pineapple Grill | **Kapalua/Ma** — 23
Pioneer Inn | **Lahaina/Ma** — 15
Sarento's/Bch. | **Kihei/Ma** — 23
Sea House | **Napili/Ma** — 22
Shells | **Poipu/K** — 20
🔏 Spago | **Wailea/Ma** — 26
Tidepools | **Poipu/K** — 24
Waterfront | **Maalaea/Ma** — 25

WINE BARS

Brasserie/Vin | **Chinatown/O** — 20
Formaggio | **multi.** — 22
Matteo's | **Wailea/Ma** — 19
Vino | **Restaurant Row/O** — 23

WINNING WINE LISTS

Aaron's | **Ala Moana/O** — 20
🔏 Alan Wong's | **McCully/O** — 28
🔏 Bali/Sea | **Waikiki/O** — 24
Bar Acuda | **Hanalei/K** — 23
🆕 Beachhse. | **Waikiki/O** — 21
Brasserie/Vin | **Chinatown/O** — 20
Cafe Portofino |
  Kalapaki Bch/K — 21
Casablanca | **Poipu/K** — 19
Casa di Amici | **Poipu/K** — 23
🔏 Chef Mavro | **Moiliili/O** — 26
Diamond Head | **Waikiki/O** — 22
d.k Steak | **Waikiki/O** — 22
Dondero's | **Poipu/K** — 23
🆕 'Elua | **Ala Moana/O** — 24
🔏 Ferraro's | **Wailea/Ma** — 25
Formaggio | **multi.** — 22
Gaylord's | **Lihue/K** — 22
🔏 Gerard's | **Lahaina/Ma** — 28
🔏 Hiroshi | **Restaurant Row/O** — 26
Hoku's | **Kahala/O** — 25
Hukilau | **Kapaa/K** — 25
Hy's Steak | **Waikiki/O** — 25
🔏 Ihilani | **Manele/L** — 24
Lahaina Grill | **Lahaina/Ma** — 26
🔏 La Mer | **Waikiki/O** — 27
🔏 Lodge/Koele | **Koele/L** — 26
🔏 Michel's | **Waikiki/O** — 25
Nick's Fishmkt. | **Wailea/Ma** — 25
🔏 Orchids | **Waikiki/O** — 26
Pineapple Grill | **Kapalua/Ma** — 23
Plantation Hse. | **Kapalua/Ma** — 24
🔏 Roy's | **Hawaii Kai/O** — 26
🔏 Son'z | **Kaanapali/Ma** — 24
🔏 Spago | **Wailea/Ma** — 26
Tidepools | **Poipu/K** — 24
Vino | **Restaurant Row/O** — 23

WORTH A TRIP

Anahola/Kauai
  Duane's Ono — 23
Hanalei/Kauai
  Bar Acuda — 23

Kahala/Oahu		
Hoku's	25	
Kahuku/Oahu		
Ola	21	
Kaimuki/Oahu		
☑ 3660/Rise	25	
town	23	
Kalihi/Oahu		
☑ Helena's	26	
Kapaa/Kauai		
Hukilau	25	
Lahaina/Maui		
☑ Gerard's	28	
Lihue/Kauai		
Hamura Saimin	24	
Makawao/Maui		
☑ Hali'imaile Gen.	27	
Makiki/Oahu		
☑ Sushi Sasabune	28	
McCully/Oahu		
☑ Alan Wong's	28	
Moiliili/Oahu		
☑ Chef Mavro	26	
Olowalu/Maui		
Chez Paul	26	
Paia/Maui		
☑ Mama's Fish	27	
Poipu/Kauai		
Dondero's	23	
Waikiki/Oahu		
Diamond Head	22	
☑ Michel's	25	
Wailea/Maui		
Mala	25	

Golf Features

stings cover the best in each category and include names, locations
nd course ratings.

UDGET

la Wai | **Waikiki/O**	14
Vailua | **Kapaa/K**	20

UNKERING

Kapalua, Plantation | **Kapalua/Ma**	29
oyal Kunia | **Waipahu/O**	22

ELEBRITY DESIGNS

ARNOLD PALMER

lawaii Prince | **Ewa Beach/O**	22
apalua, Bay | **Kapalua/Ma**	25
Mauna Kea | **Kohala Coast/BI**	24
Turtle Bay, Palmer | **Kahuku/O**	26

EN CRENSHAW/BILL COORE

Kapalua, Plantation | **Kapalua/Ma**	29

ACK NICKLAUS

Challenge | **Manele/L**	28
lualalai | **Kaupulehu-Kona/BI**	26
auai Lagoons, Kiele | **Lihue/K**	26

ETE DYE

ig Island | **Kailua-Kona/BI**	20
uana Hills | **Kailua/O**	25

ROBERT TRENT JONES JR.

Kiahuna | **Poipu/K**	19
Makena, North | **Makena/Ma**	25
oipu Bay | **Poipu/K**	27
Princeville | **Princeville/K**	28
Vaikoloa, Beach | **Kohala Coast/BI**	23
Vaikoloa Vill. | **Kohala Coast/BI**	22
Vailea, Emerald | **Wailea/Ma**	26
Vailea, Gold | **Wailea/Ma**	26

ROBERT TRENT JONES SR.

Kaanapali, Royal | **Kaanapali/Ma**	22

TOM WEISKOPF/JAY MORRISH

Vaikoloa, Kings' | **Kohala Coast/BI**	23

CONDITIONING

Challenge | **Manele/L**	28
lualalai | **Kaupulehu-Kona/BI**	26
auai Lagoons, Kiele | **Lihue/K**	26

Mauna Lani, North | **Kohala Coast/BI**	26
Mauna Lani, South | **Kohala Coast/BI**	26
Wailea, Gold | **Wailea/Ma**	26

EASIEST

(Courses with the lowest slope
ratings from the back tees)

Ala Wai | **Waikiki/O**	14
Hawaii Kai, Championship | **Hawaii Kai/O**	19
Wailea, Emerald | **Wailea/Ma**	26

EXPENSE ACCOUNT

($200 and over)

Challenge | **Manele/L**	28
Experience | **Koele/L**	27
Hualalai | **Kaupulehu-Kona/BI**	26
Kaanapali, Royal | **Kaanapali/Ma**	22
Kapalua, Bay | **Kapalua/Ma**	25
Kapalua, Plantation | **Kapalua/Ma**	29
Makena, North | **Makena/Ma**	25
Mauna Lani, North | **Kohala Coast/BI**	26
Mauna Lani, South | **Kohala Coast/BI**	26
Poipu Bay | **Poipu/K**	27
Princeville | **Princeville/K**	28

FINISHING HOLES

Kapalua, Plantation | **Kapalua/Ma**	29
Kauai Lagoons, Kiele | **Lihue/K**	26
Ko'olau | **Kaneohe/O**	25

JUNIOR-FRIENDLY

Hawaii Prince | **Ewa Beach/O**	22
Poipu Bay | **Poipu/K**	27

LINKS-STYLE

Kapalua, Plantation | **Kapalua/Ma**	29
Wailua | **Kapaa/K**	20

OPENING HOLES

Kapalua, Plantation | **Kapalua/Ma**	29
Poipu Bay | **Poipu/K**	27
Princeville | **Princeville/K**	28

PACE OF PLAY

- ☑ Challenge | **Manele/L** — 28
- Experience | **Koele/L** — 27
- Hualalai | **Kaupulehu-Kona/BI** — 26
- ☑ Mauna Lani, North | **Kohala Coast/BI** — 26
- Mauna Lani, South | **Kohala Coast/BI** — 26
- Wailea, Gold | **Wailea/Ma** — 26

PAR-3 HOLES

- ☑ Challenge | **Manele/L** — 28
- Kapalua, Bay | **Kapalua/Ma** — 25
- ☑ Mauna Lani, North | **Kohala Coast/BI** — 26
- Mauna Lani, South | **Kohala Coast/BI** — 26
- ☑ Princeville | **Princeville/K** — 28

PAR-4 HOLES

- ☑ Challenge | **Manele/L** — 28
- ☑ Kapalua, Plantation | **Kapalua/Ma** — 29
- Kauai Lagoons, Kiele | **Lihue/K** — 26
- Poipu Bay | **Poipu/K** — 27
- ☑ Princeville | **Princeville/K** — 28

PAR-5 HOLES

- ☑ Kapalua, Plantation | **Kapalua/Ma** — 29
- ☑ Princeville | **Princeville/K** — 28

PRO-EVENT HOSTS

- Hualalai | **Kaupulehu-Kona/BI** — 26
- Kaanapali, Royal | **Kaanapali/Ma** — 22
- Kapalua, Bay | **Kapalua/Ma** — 25
- ☑ Kapalua, Plantation | **Kapalua/Ma** — 29
- Ko Olina | **Kapolei/O** — 23
- ☑ Turtle Bay, Palmer | **Kahuku/O** — 26
- Wailea, Gold | **Wailea/Ma** — 26

SCENIC

- ☑ Challenge | **Manele/L** — 2
- Experience | **Koele/L** — 2
- Hualalai | **Kaupulehu-Kona/BI** — 2
- ☑ Kapalua, Plantation | **Kapalua/Ma** — 2
- Kauai Lagoons, Kiele | **Lihue/K** — 2
- Ko'olau | **Kaneohe/O** — 2
- Makena, North | **Makena/Ma** — 2
- ☑ Mauna Lani, North | **Kohala Coast/BI** — 2
- Mauna Lani, South | **Kohala Coast/BI** — 2
- Pearl | **Aiea/O** — 1
- Poipu Bay | **Poipu/K** — 2
- ☑ Princeville | **Princeville/K** — 28
- Puakea | **Lihue/K** — 2
- Wailea, Emerald | **Wailea/Ma** — 2
- Wailua | **Kapaa/K** — 2

STORIED

- Kaanapali, Royal | **Kaanapali/Ma** — 22
- ☑ Kapalua, Plantation | **Kapalua/Ma** — 29
- Poipu Bay | **Poipu/K** — 27
- Puakea | **Lihue/K** — 2
- ☑ Turtle Bay, Palmer | **Kahuku/O** — 26

TOUGHEST

(Courses with the highest slope ratings from the back tees)
- Dunes | **Kahului/Ma** — 23
- Experience | **Koele/L** — 27
- Ko'olau | **Kaneohe/O** — 25
- ☑ Turtle Bay, Palmer | **Kahuku/O** — 26

WOMEN-FRIENDLY

- ☑ Challenge | **Manele/L** — 28
- Hualalai | **Kaupulehu-Kona/BI** — 26
- Mauna Lani, South | **Kohala Coast/BI** — 26
- Wailea, Emerald | **Wailea/Ma** — 26

Nightlife Special Appeals

Listings cover the best in each category and include venue names, locations and Appeal ratings. Multi-location nightspots' features may vary by branch.

AFTER WORK

Aku Bone	Kakaako	21
Bar 35	Chinatown	22
8 Bar	Maikiki	20
Murphy's	Downtown	21
O'Toole's	Downtown	-
Ryan's	Ward	18
thirtyninehotel	Chinatown	25
Uncle Bo's	Kapahulu	23

BEAUTIFUL PEOPLE

Amuse	Ala Moana	20
Angles	Waikiki	19
8 Bar	Maikiki	20
☑ House Without	Waikiki	29
☑ Indigo	Chinatown	23
☑ Lewers	Waikiki	27
Pearl Ultra	Ala Moana	20
RumFire	Waikiki	22
Twist	Waikiki	25

BOTTLE SERVICE

(Bottle purchase sometimes required to secure a table)

Bar 35	Chinatown	22
Pearl Ultra	Ala Moana	20
Twist	Waikiki	25

CELEB-SIGHTINGS

Aaron's	Waikiki	21
Amuse	Ala Moana	20
☑ Duke's	Waikiki	24
Pearl Ultra	Ala Moana	20
Twist	Waikiki	25
Zanzabar	Waikiki	17

CHEAP DRINKS

Chiko's	McCully	-
8 Bar	Maikiki	20
Mai Tai	Ala Moana	23
Mercury	Downtown	-
Moose McGill.	Waikiki	17
Pipeline	Kakaako	16
Shack	multi.	20

CIGAR-FRIENDLY

Anna Bannana's	Moiliili	15
Mai Tai	Ala Moana	23

DANCING

Aaron's	Waikiki	21
Angles	Waikiki	19
Anna Bannana's	Moiliili	15
Bar 35	Chinatown	22
Dave/Buster's	Ward	20
Don Ho's	Downtown	19
☑ Indigo	Chinatown	23
Mariana Club	Sand Is	24
thirtyninehotel	Chinatown	25
Twist	Waikiki	25

DIVES

Anna Bannana's	Moiliili	15
Chiko's	McCully	-
8 Bar	Maikiki	20
Mercury	Downtown	-

DJs

Angles	Waikiki	19
Brew Moon	Ward	20
Mercury	Downtown	-
Moose McGill.	Waikiki	17
Pearl Ultra	Ala Moana	20
thirtyninehotel	Chinatown	25
Zanzabar	Waikiki	17

DRINK SPECIALISTS

BEER
(* Microbrewery)

Bar 35	Chinatown	22
Brew Moon*	Ward	20
Gordon Biersch*	Downtown	21
Kona Brew*	Hawaii Kai	23
Shack	multi.	20
Yard Hse.	Waikiki	23

CHAMPAGNE

Aaron's	Waikiki	21
Amuse	Ala Moana	20
☑ Lewers	Waikiki	27
Pearl Ultra	Ala Moana	20
RumFire	Waikiki	22
Twist	Waikiki	25
Zanzabar	Waikiki	17

COCKTAILS

Bar 35	Chinatown	22
Dragon	Chinatown	25

Z House Without | **Waikiki**	29
Z Lewers | **Waikiki**	27
Mai Tai | **Ala Moana**	23
RumFire | **Waikiki**	22
thirtyninehotel | **Chinatown**	25
Twist | **Waikiki**	25

MARTINIS

Aaron's | **Waikiki**	21
Z Indigo | **Chinatown**	23
Mercury | **Downtown**	-
Pearl Ultra | **Ala Moana**	20
thirtyninehotel | **Chinatown**	25
Twist | **Waikiki**	25
Uncle Bo's | **Kapahulu**	23

SCOTCH/SINGLE MALTS

| Sansei \| **Waikiki** | 22 |

VODKA

| Z Lewers \| **Waikiki** | 27 |

WINE BARS

| Amuse \| **Ala Moana** | 20 |

WINE BY THE GLASS
(See also Wine Bars, above)

| Z Indigo \| **Chinatown** | 23 |

EXPENSE-ACCOUNTERS

Aaron's | **Waikiki**	21
Amuse | **Ala Moana**	20
Brew Moon | **Ward**	20
Z House Without | **Waikiki**	29
Z Lewers | **Waikiki**	27
Mariana Club | **Sand Is**	24
Pearl Ultra | **Ala Moana**	20
Ryan's | **Ward**	18
Sansei | **Waikiki**	22
Twist | **Waikiki**	25
Uncle Bo's | **Kapahulu**	23

FINE FOOD TOO

Aaron's | **Waikiki**	21
Aku Bone | **Kakaako**	21
Brew Moon | **Ward**	20
8 Bar | **Maikiki**	20
Z Indigo | **Chinatown**	23
Z Lewers | **Waikiki**	27
Pipeline | **Kakaako**	16
Sansei | **Waikiki**	22
Tiki's | **Waikiki**	21
Twist | **Waikiki**	25

GAMES

BOARD GAMES

Moose McGill. | **Waikiki**	17
Pipeline | **Kakaako**	16
Shack | **Hawaii Kai**	20

DARTS

Anna Bannana's | **Moiliili**	15
Chiko's | **McCully**	-
Señor Frog | **Waikiki**	16
Shack | **multi.**	20

FOOSBALL

| Moose McGill. \| **Waikiki** | 17 |

POOL TABLES

Angles | **Waikiki**	19
Dave/Buster's | **Ward**	20
Hula's | **Waikiki**	23
Pipeline | **Kakaako**	16
Shack | **multi.**	20

SKEE-BALL

| Dave/Buster's \| **Ward** | 20 |

VIDEO GAMES

Aku Bone | **Kakaako**	21
Angles | **Waikiki**	19
Dave/Buster's | **Ward**	20
Hula's | **Waikiki**	23
LuLu's | **Waikiki**	21
Señor Frog | **Waikiki**	16
Shack | **multi.**	20

HAWAII STATE OF MIND

Aku Bone | **Kakaako**	21
8 Bar | **Maikiki**	20
Z House Without | **Waikiki**	29
Mai Tai | **Ala Moana**	23
Mariana Club | **Sand Is**	24
Shack | **Hawaii Kai**	20

HOTEL BARS

Ala Moana Hotel
| Aaron's \| **Waikiki** | 21 |
Halekulani
| Z House Without \| **Waikiki** | 29 |
| Z Lewers \| **Waikiki** | 27 |
Moana Surfrider
| Beach Bar \| **Waikiki** | 23 |
Outrigger Waikiki
| Z Duke's \| **Waikiki** | 24 |
Park Shore Hotel
| LuLu's \| **Waikiki** | 21 |

ResortQuest Waikiki Beach
  Tiki's | **Waikiki** 21

Sheraton Waikiki
  RumFire | **Waikiki** 22
  Twist | **Waikiki** 25

Waikiki Beach Marriott
  Sansei | **Waikiki** 22

Waikiki Beach Walk
  Yard Hse. | **Waikiki** 23

Waikiki Grand Hotel
  Hula's | **Waikiki** 23

JAZZ CLUBS

Dragon | **Chinatown** 25

KARAOKE BARS

(Call to check nights, times and
prices)

Chiko's | **McCully** -

LIVE ENTERTAINMENT

(See also Jazz Clubs, Karaoke Bars,
Music Clubs)

Brew Moon | varies | **Ward** 20
🅉 Duke's | varies | **Waikiki** 24
Gordon Biersch | varies | 21
  Downtown
🅉 Indigo | varies | **Chinatown** 23
Kona Brew | Hawaiian | **Hawaii Kai** 23
🅉 Lewers | varies | **Waikiki** 27
Mai Tai | Hawaiian | **Ala Moana** 23
Tiki's | Hawaiian | **Waikiki** 21
Twist | rock | **Waikiki** 25

LOUNGES

Aaron's | **Waikiki** 21
Aku Bone | **Kakaako** 21
Bar 35 | **Chinatown** 22
3 Bar | **Maikiki** 20
🅉 Lewers | **Waikiki** 27
Pearl Ultra | **Ala Moana** 20
RumFire | **Waikiki** 22
thirtyninehotel | **Chinatown** 25
Twist | **Waikiki** 25
Zanzabar | **Waikiki** 17

MATURE CROWDS

Aaron's | **Waikiki** 21
Aku Bone | **Kakaako** 21
Amuse | **Ala Moana** 20
Dragon | **Chinatown** 25

🅉 Duke's | **Waikiki** 24
🅉 House Without | **Waikiki** 29
🅉 Lewers | **Waikiki** 27
Mariana Club | **Sand Is** 24
Sansei | **Waikiki** 22
Tiki's | **Waikiki** 21

MEAT MARKETS

Angles | **Waikiki** 19
Brew Moon | **Ward** 20
🅉 Duke's | **Waikiki** 24
🅉 Indigo | **Chinatown** 23
LuLu's | **Waikiki** 21
Mai Tai | **Ala Moana** 23
Moose McGill. | **Waikiki** 17
Pearl Ultra | **Ala Moana** 20
Pipeline | **Kakaako** 16
Ryan's | **Ward** 18
Señor Frog | **Waikiki** 16

MUSIC CLUBS

(See also Jazz Clubs)

O'Toole's | **Downtown** -
Pipeline | **Kakaako** 16

OUTDOOR SPACES

GARDEN DINING

Bar 35 | **Chinatown** 22
Beach Bar | **Waikiki** 23
Haleiwa Joe's | **Haleiwa** 24
🅉 Indigo | **Chinatown** 23
🅉 Lewers | **Waikiki** 27
RumFire | **Waikiki** 22
Shack | **Kailua** 20

PATIO/TERRACE

Brew Moon | **Ward** 20
Don Ho's | **Downtown** 19
🅉 Duke's | **Waikiki** 24
Gordon Biersch | **Downtown** 21
🅉 House Without | **Waikiki** 29
Kona Brew | **Hawaii Kai** 23
RumFire | **Waikiki** 22
Ryan's | **Ward** 18
Sansei | **Waikiki** 22
Señor Frog | **Waikiki** 16
Shack | **multi.** 20
Tiki's | **Waikiki** 21

ROOFTOP

Dave/Buster's | **Ward** 20
thirtyninehotel | **Chinatown** 25

WATERSIDE

Beach Bar	**Waikiki**	23
Don Ho's	**Downtown**	19
☑ Duke's	**Waikiki**	24
Gordon Biersch	**Downtown**	21
Haleiwa Joe's	**Haleiwa**	24
☑ House Without	**Waikiki**	29
Kona Brew	**Hawaii Kai**	23
Mariana Club	**Sand Is**	24
Sansei	**Waikiki**	22
Shack	**Hawaii Kai**	20

PEOPLE-WATCHING

Angles	**Waikiki**	19
Hula's	**Waikiki**	23
☑ Indigo	**Chinatown**	23
Pearl Ultra	**Ala Moana**	20
Pipeline	**Kakaako**	16
Shack	**Hawaii Kai**	20
Twist	**Waikiki**	25
Zanzabar	**Waikiki**	17

PUNK BARS

Anna Bannana's	**Moiliili**	15

QUIET CONVERSATION

Aaron's	**Waikiki**	21
Aku Bone	**Kakaako**	21
Brew Moon	**Ward**	20
Dragon	**Chinatown**	25
☑ House Without	**Waikiki**	29
☑ Lewers	**Waikiki**	27
Mariana Club	**Sand Is**	24
Mercury	**Downtown**	-
thirtyninehotel	**Chinatown**	25

ROMANTIC

Aaron's	**Waikiki**	21
Dragon	**Chinatown**	25
☑ Indigo	**Chinatown**	23
☑ Lewers	**Waikiki**	27
RumFire	**Waikiki**	22
Sansei	**Waikiki**	22
Twist	**Waikiki**	25

SMOKING PERMITTED

Anna Bannana's	**Moiliili**	15
Mai Tai	**Ala Moana**	23

SPORTS BARS

Pipeline	**Kakaako**	16
Shack	**multi.**	20

SUITS

Aaron's	**Waikiki**	21
☑ Lewers	**Waikiki**	27
Twist	**Waikiki**	25

TRENDY

Aaron's	**Waikiki**	21
☑ Indigo	**Chinatown**	23
LuLu's	**Waikiki**	21
Mai Tai	**Ala Moana**	23
Pearl Ultra	**Ala Moana**	20
Pipeline	**Kakaako**	16
RumFire	**Waikiki**	22
thirtyninehotel	**Chinatown**	25
Twist	**Waikiki**	25
Uncle Bo's	**Kapahulu**	23
Yard Hse.	**Waikiki**	23
Zanzabar	**Waikiki**	17

VIEWS

Beach Bar	**Waikiki**	23
Dave/Buster's	**Ward**	20
Don Ho's	**Downtown**	19
☑ Duke's	**Waikiki**	24
Haleiwa Joe's	**Haleiwa**	24
☑ House Without	**Waikiki**	29
Hula's	**Waikiki**	23
☑ Indigo	**Chinatown**	23
Kona Brew	**Hawaii Kai**	23
LuLu's	**Waikiki**	21
Mariana Club	**Sand Is**	24
RumFire	**Waikiki**	22
Sansei	**Waikiki**	22
Shack	**Hawaii Kai**	20
Tiki's	**Waikiki**	21
Twist	**Waikiki**	25

Shopping Merchandise

Includes store names, locations and Quality ratings. Property names in italics
are in the Notable Mentions category. All other listings have full reviews.

ACCESSORIES

BCBG Max Azria	**multi.**	24
Betsey Johnson	**multi.**	24
Bottega Veneta	**multi.**	28
Bulgari	**multi.**	28
Chanel	**multi.**	29
Cinnamon Girl	**Waikoloa/BI**	24
Dior	**Ala Moana/O**	27
Fendi	**multi.**	25
Gucci	**multi.**	28
Hawaiian Accessories	**multi.**	–
Hermès	**multi.**	29
Hilo Hattie	**Lihue/K**	19
Honolua Surf Co.	**multi.**	22
🆕 *Juicy Couture*	**Ala Moana/O**	–
Prada	**multi.**	27
Reyn's	**multi.**	27

ACTIVEWEAR

A Touch/Molokai	**Maunaloa/Mo**	–
Crazy Shirts	**multi.**	24
Hanalei Surf Co.	**Hanalei/K**	23
Honolua Surf Co.	**multi.**	22
Loketown	**Waikiki/O**	22
Reyn's	**multi.**	27
T & C Surf	**multi.**	22

ALOHA WEAR

ABC Stores	**Ala Moana/O**	18
Blue Ginger	**multi.**	24
Hawaiian Accessories	**multi.**	–
Hawaiian Moon	**multi.**	23
Hilo Hattie	**multi.**	19
🆕 *Kahala*	**Ala Moana/O**	–
Macy's	**multi.**	21
Manuhealii Fashions	**multi.**	–
Muumuu Heaven	**Kailua/O**	–
Na Mea/MANA	**Waikiki/O**	–
Neiman Marcus	**Ala Moana/O**	28
🆕 Nordstrom	**Ala Moana/O**	26
Reyn's	**multi.**	27
Sig Zane Designs	**Hilo/BI**	28
Tori Richard	**multi.**	26

CLOTHING: CHILDREN'S

Blue Ginger	**multi.**	24
Crazy Shirts	**multi.**	24
Hawaiian Moon	**multi.**	23
🆕 Hilo Hattie	**multi.**	19
Reyn's	**multi.**	27

CLOTHING: MEN'S/WOMEN'S

(Stores carrying both)

A Touch/Molokai	**Maunaloa/Mo**	–
A/X Armani	**multi.**	22
Banana Republic	**Wailea/Ma**	22
Blue Ginger	**multi.**	24
🆕 Crazy Shirts	**multi.**	24
Hawaiian Island	**multi.**	24
Hawaiian Moon	**multi.**	23
🆕 Hermès	**multi.**	29
🆕 Hilo Hattie	**multi.**	19
Honolua Surf Co.	**Wailea/Ma**	22
Prada	**Waikiki/O**	27
Reyn's	**multi.**	27
🆕 Sig Zane Designs	**Hilo/BI**	28
Tommy Bahama	**multi.**	27
Tori Richard	**Wailea/Ma**	26

CLOTHING: WOMEN'S

BCBG Max Azria	**multi.**	24
Betsey Johnson	**Wailea/Ma**	24
Catherine's Closet	**Manoa/O**	–
🆕 Chanel	**multi.**	29
Cinnamon Girl	**multi.**	24
Dior	**Ala Moana/O**	27
Fendi	**Wailea/Ma**	25
Gucci	**multi.**	28
🆕 *Juicy Couture*	**Ala Moana/O**	–
Maggie Coulombe	**Lahaina/Ma**	–
🆕 Marciano	**Waikiki/O**	–
Tori Richard	**multi.**	26

DEPARTMENT STORES

🆕 Macy's	**multi.**	21
Neiman Marcus	**Ala Moana/O**	28
🆕 Nordstrom	**Ala Moana/O**	26
Reyn's	**multi.**	27

FURNITURE/HOME FURNISHINGS

Elephant Walk	**multi.**	20
🆕 Martin/MacArthur	**Wailea/Ma**	29

Under/Koa Tree | **multi.**	⏛
Yellow Fish | **Hanalei/K**	⏛

GIFTS/NOVELTIES

Big Wind | **Maunaloa/Mo**	⏛
Dis 'N Dat | **Lanai City/L**	⏛
Dolphin Galleries | **Waikoloa/BI**	26
Elephant Walk | **multi.**	20
⚡ Hilo Hattie | **multi.**	19
Island Soap | **multi.**	25
Na Mea/MANA | **Ward/O**	⏛
Nohea Galleries | **multi.**	27
Parker Ranch | **Kamuela/BI**	21
Red Pineapple | **Ward/O**	26
Under/Koa Tree | **multi.**	⏛
Yellow Fish | **Hanalei/K**	⏛

HANDBAGS

Bottega Veneta | **Wailea/Ma**	28
⚡ Chanel | **multi.**	29
Coach | **multi.**	26
Fendi | **multi.**	25
NEW *Juicy Couture* | **Ala Moana/O**	⏛
LeSportsac | **multi.**	25
Louis Vuitton | **multi.**	28
Prada | **multi.**	27

JEWELRY

COSTUME/SEMIPRECIOUS

Academy Gift | **Ala Moana/O**	28
Blue Ginger | **multi.**	24
Cinnamon Girl | **multi.**	24
NEW *Juicy Couture* | **multi.**	⏛

⚡ Macy's | **multi.**	2
⚡ Martin/MacArthur | **multi.**	2
Nohea Galleries | **multi.**	2

FINE

Black Pearl Gallery | **Wailea/Ma**	2
Dolphin Galleries | **Waikoloa/BI**	2
Maui Divers | **multi.**	2
Na Hoku | **multi.**	2
Philip Rickard | **multi.**	⏛
Royal Hawaii | **Kailua-Kona/BI**	2
⚡ Tiffany & Co. | **multi.**	2

LUGGAGE

Bag 'n Baggage | **Ala Moana/O**	2
Louis Vuitton | **Waikoloa/BI**	2

SURF SHOPS

Hanalei Surf Co. | **Hanalei/K**	2
Hawaiian Island | **multi.**	2
Honolua Surf Co. | **multi.**	2
T & C Surf | **multi.**	2

SWIMWEAR

A Touch/Molokai | **Maunaloa/Mo**	⏛
Hanalei Surf Co. | **Hanalei/K**	2
Hawaiian Island | **multi.**	2
⚡ Hilo Hattie | **Lihue/K**	1
Honolua Surf Co. | **multi.**	2
T & C Surf | **multi.**	2

WATCHES

Royal Hawaii | **Kailua-Kona/BI**	2
⚡ Tiffany & Co. | **multi.**	2
NEW Tourneau | **Waikiki/O**	⏛

Shopping Special Features

Listings cover the best in each category and include store names, locations and Quality ratings. Property names in italics are in the Notable Mentions category. All other listings have full reviews.

CUSTOM/ HANDMADE GOODS

Academy Gift | **Ala Moana/O**	28
Black Pearl Gallery | **multi.**	23
Blue Ginger | **Lahaina/Ma**	24
Bottega Veneta | **multi.**	28
Dis 'N Dat | **Lanai City/L**	–
Dolphin Galleries | **multi.**	26
Elephant Walk | **Ala Moana/O**	20
Fendi | **multi.**	25
Global Vill. | **Kailua/O**	–
Hawaiian Accessories | **multi.**	–
Hawaiian Island | **multi.**	24
Hui No'eau | **Makawao/Ma**	–
Island Soap | **multi.**	25
NEW *Kahala* | **Ala Moana/O**	–
Louis Vuitton | **multi.**	28
Maggie Coulombe | **Lahaina/Ma**	–
Maui Divers | **multi.**	24
Muumuu Heaven | **Kailua/O**	–
Na Hoku | **multi.**	26
Na Mea/MANA | **multi.**	–
Nui Mono | **Moiliili/O**	–
Philip Rickard | **multi.**	–
Prada | **multi.**	27
Red Pineapple | **Ward/O**	26
Royal Hawaii | **multi.**	24
T & C Surf | **multi.**	22
Z Tiffany & Co. | **multi.**	28
Under/Koa Tree | **Waikoloa/BI**	–
Volcano Art Ctr. | **Volcano/BI**	25

HIP/HOT PLACES

Aloha Rag | **Ala Moana/O**	–
A/X Armani | **Ala Moana/O**	22
BCBG Max Azria | **multi.**	24
Betsey Johnson | **Wailea/Ma**	24
Hawaiian Island | **Mililani/O**	24
NEW J. Crew | **Ala Moana/O**	23
NEW Nordstrom | **Ala Moana/O**	26
Red Pineapple | **Ward/O**	26
T & C Surf | **multi.**	22

INSIDER SECRETS

Academy Gift | **Ala Moana/O**	28
Elephant Walk | **Ala Moana/O**	20
Hawaiian Island | **multi.**	24
Parker Ranch | **Kamuela/BI**	21
Z Sig Zane Designs | **Hilo/BI**	28

LEGENDARY

(Date company founded)

1837 | Tiffany & Co. | **Waikoloa/BI**	28
1854 | Louis Vuitton | **multi.**	28
1858 | Macy's | **multi.**	21
1884 | Bulgari | **Waikiki/O**	28
1900 | Tourneau | **Waikiki/O**	–
1901 | Nordstrom | **Ala Moana/O**	26
1907 | Neiman Marcus | **Ala Moana/O**	28
1914 | Chanel | **multi.**	29
1924 | Na Hoku | **multi.**	26
1925 | Fendi | **multi.**	25
1928 | *Dis 'N Dat* | **Lanai City/L**	–
1934 | *Hui No'eau* | **Makawao/Ma**	–
1936 | *Kahala* | **Ala Moana/O**	–
1940 | Coach | **Waikoloa/BI**	26
1956 | Tori Richard | **multi.**	26

NOTEWORTHY NEWCOMERS

Blue Buddha | **Ala Moana/O**	–
Hawaiian Island | **Lahaina/Ma**	24
J. Crew | **Ala Moana/O**	23
Juicy Couture | **multi.**	–
Kahala | **Ala Moana/O**	–
Marciano | **Waikiki/O**	–
Nordstrom | **Ala Moana/O**	26
Tourneau | **Waikiki/O**	–
Valerie Joseph | **Waikiki/O**	–

STATUS GOODS

Bottega Veneta | **multi.**	28
Bulgari | **multi.**	28
Z Chanel | **Ala Moana/O**	29
Dior | **Ala Moana/O**	27
Fendi | **multi.**	25

Gucci	**multi.**	28
Z Hermès	**multi.**	29
Louis Vuitton	**multi.**	28
NEW Marciano	**Waikiki/O**	–
Neiman Marcus	**Ala Moana/O**	28
NEW Nordstrom	**Ala Moana/O**	26
Prada	**Ala Moana/O**	27
NEW Tourneau	**Waikiki/O**	–

TWEEN/TEEN APPEAL

Betsey Johnson	**multi.**	24
Blue Ginger	**Wailea/Ma**	24
Cinnamon Girl	**multi.**	24
Coach	**multi.**	26
LeSportsac	**multi.**	25
Niketown	**Waikiki/O**	22
Parker Ranch	**Kamuela/BI**	21

ALPHABETICAL
PAGE INDEX

et your voice be heard – visit ZAGAT.com/vote

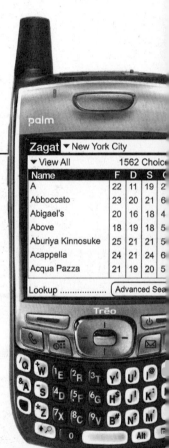